Wars and Soldiers in the Early Reign of Louis XIV

Volume 2: The Imperial Army 1657–1687

Text and Illustrations by Bruno Mugnai

Helion & Company

Helion & Company Limited
Unit 8 Amherst Business Centre
Budbrooke Road
Warwick
CV34 5WE
England
Tel. 01926 499 619
Email: info@helion.co.uk
Website: www.helion.co.uk
Twitter: @helionbooks

Published by Helion & Company 2019
Designed and typeset by Mach 3 Solutions Ltd (www.mach3solutions.co.uk)
Cover designed by Paul Hewitt, Battlefield Design (www.battlefield-design.co.uk)

Text © Bruno Mugnai 2019
Colour artwork by Bruno Mugnai © Helion & Company 2019
Maps drawn by George Anderson © Helion & Company 2019

Every reasonable effort has been made to trace copyright holders and
to obtain their permission for the use of copyright material.
The author and publisher apologise for any errors or omissions in this work and would be grateful
if notified of any corrections that should be incorporated in future reprints or editions of this book.

ISBN 978-1-912866-55-7

British Library Cataloguing-in-Publication Data.
A catalogue record for this book is available from the British Library.
All rights reserved. No part of this publication may be reproduced, stored in a retrieval
system, or transmitted, in any form, or by any means, electronic, mechanical, photocopying,
recording or otherwise, without the express written consent of Helion & Company Limited.

For details of other military history titles published by Helion & Company Limited,
contact the above address, or visit our website: http://www.helion.co.uk

We always welcome receiving book proposals from prospective authors.

In memory of Raimondo Luraghi (1921–2012), whose books on Raimondo Montecuccoli revealed to me how much fascinating past lies behind our eerie present. (BM)

Contents

Foreword		viii
Acknowledgements		ix
Imperial Chronology		x
1.	The Age of Limited Warfare?	15
2.	*Austria Erit In Orbe Ultima*	21
	The House of Austria	22
	Habsburg Geostrategy	28
	The *Reich*	38
3.	The Army of the Emperor	50
	Military Administration	57
	The High Command	66
	The *Obrist-Inhaber*	73
	Logistics and Quartering	78
	Infantry Organisation	82
	Cavalry Organisation	87
	Artillery Organisation	94
	The Royal Hungarian Army and the *Militärgrenze*	**97**
	The Provincial Militia	103
4.	The *Reichsarmee*	108
	The *Reichsmatricel*	109
	The *Reich* in War	115
	The 'Laxenburg Alliance'	121
5.	The Imperial Army on Campaign	124
	Poland, Jutland and Pomerania, 1657–60	126
	The Ottoman War of 1663–64 and the Miracle of Szentgotthárd	141
	Insurgencies and Rebellions, 1671–1681	160
	Duel on the Rhine, 1673–78	170
	Prelude to Vienna, 1682–1683	193

6.	Uniforms, Equipment and Ensigns	201
	Infantry	209
	Cavalry	222
	Artillery	234
	Ensigns	235

Appendices
I	*Reichsmatricel of 1663 (in simplum)*	240
II	Orders of Battle and Army Lists	248
III	List of Regiments	263

Colour Plate Commentaries	289
Bibliography	298

Note on Imperial and Austrian Currency

The Imperial *Goldgulden* was divided in 75 *kreutzer*; the official currency was represented by *Reichstaler*, *Halb-Reichstaler* and *Viertel-Reichstaler*, respectively, 60, 34 and 17 *kreutzer*. In the Habsburgs' domains the ordinary currency was the *Florin* divided in 60 *groschen* of 4 *pfenninge*.

Foreword

I felt very honoured when asked by Bruno to write the foreword to the second volume of his works on the armies of the later part of the 17th century.

When we launched 'Century of the Soldier 1618–1721' in the early spring of 2015, it was envisioned as a book series that would see perhaps three publications a year. We were soon proven wrong. In May 2015 we had our first inkling that this would not be the case when over 250 people came to the series launch event in Shrewsbury. In no time at all, we published our tenth book in the series and found ourselves to be in the fortunate position of working with a growing number of authors, artists and like-minded organisations. As of late 2019, 'Century of the Soldier 1618–1721' will soon be publishing its 50th book and has two companion series, 'Reason to Revolution 1721–1815' examining the 18th and early 19th centuries and 'From Retinue to Regiment 1453–1618' that covers the period from the fall of Constantinople and the Battle of Castillon, the last major battle of the Hundred Years War to the eve of the Thirty Years War. 'COS' as the series is called at Helion is supported by annual events and has a truly global readership.

Bruno Mugnai's artwork has played a significant contribution to the success of the series. Bruno's work has a crispness and clarity of detail that makes for a distinctive style that can be easily identified as the work of the artist. His brush strokes are backed up with a considerable amount of research and a fantastic 'can-do' attitude when it comes to the demands of author and Series Editor. I am proud to count him as a friend.

Charles Singleton
Series Editor Century of the Soldier 1618–1721

Acknowledgements

Someone said that life is a circle and that, at a certain point, one goes back to doing the same things done in youth. In the 80s, I left model soldiers to start the adventure of historical research and illustration. The first subject I addressed was the Imperial Army in the age of the wars against the Ottoman Empire in the 17th century. To the many who have encouraged me to continue on this path, my most sincere thanks.

Naturally, also my thanks go to Serena Jones, who this time not only has patiently edited my manuscript, but she has even faced my inveterate use of the ancient German terminology.

Florence, 11 June 2019.
BM

Imperial Chronology

1657

2 April: death of Emperor Ferdinand III of Habsburg.
6 June: first Imperial campaign in Poland.
July–August: Tatar incursion in Transylvania.
1st August: coronation of Leopold of Habsburg as Emperor.
24 August: the Imperial–Polish army seizes Cracow.

1658

16 May: the Imperialists besiege Torun; the Swedish garrison surrenders on 21 December.
June: Ottomans invade Transylvania.
9 September: the Imperial army enters Holstein-Gottorp.

1659

9 February: the Swedes besiege Copenhagen.
6 May: Montecuccoli begins the campaign in Jutland.
27 May: Imperialists and allies seize Fredriksodde.
12 June: the allies occupy Fænø Island
30 June: Imperial campaign in Pomerania under Souches.
3 July: Montecuccoli leads the successful landing on Funen Island
18 September: Imperial and Brandenburg troops besiege Stettin.
14 November: Swedes are defeated in the battle of Nyborg on Funen Island.

1660

March–April: Imperial troops under Montecuccoli conquer Wismar, Darss and Warnemünde in West Pomerania.

May: Transylvanian delegates offer *Partium* and some western Transylvanian forts to the Emperor in exchange for his support against the Ottomans.
2 May. Treaty of Oliva, Sweden signs peace with the Emperor.
22 May: Prince of Transylvania György II Rákóczi is defeated by the Ottomans at Szászfenes.
30 May: the Emperor sends a corps under Souches into Transylvania.

1661

June: Ottoman raids in Habsburg Hungary.

1662

22 January: Ottomans defeat the besieging Transylvanian corps at Nagyszöllös; the Imperial pretender Prince Janos Kemény is mortally wounded.
Spring: Habsburg–Ottoman negotiations to avoid the war in Hungary.
Summer–autumn: Prince Mihály I Apafy, supported by the Porte, takes control of the whole of Transylvania, except the Imperial-held fortress in *Partium*.

1663

12 April: the Porte declares war on the Emperor.
7 August: the Ottomans defeat the Imperialists at Párkány.
August–September: Tatar raids in Moravia.
16 August: Grand Vizier Köprülü Ahmed lays siege to Érsekúivár, defended by 3,500 men under Ádám Forgách; the Imperial garrison surrenders on 8 September.
11 October: Miklós Zrínyi defeats the Ottomans at Karolyváros.
18 October: the Ottomans seize the fortress of Niytra in Upper Hungary.

1664

29 January: Imperialists under Miklós Zrínyi besiege Pécs.
2 February: Zrínyi destroys the Ottoman bridges on the Drava River near Eszék (Osijek) with a successful surprise action.
7 May: Souches re-takes Niytra.
16 May: Imperialists defeat the Ottomans at Szent-Benedek in Upper Hungary.
7 July: Ottomans seizes the fortress of Zrínyivár.
9 July: Souches defeats the Ottomans at Léva.

1st August: after successfully crossing the Rába River, the Ottomans are defeated at Szentgotthárd after a seven-hour battle,
10 August: a 20-year truce between the Emperor and the Sultan is signed in Vasvár,

1670

March: the Hungarian and Croatian magnates' conspiracy is discovered by the Imperial court.
12 April: the Hungarian insurgents besiege Tokay.
June: Imperial troops under Sporck take quarters in Upper Hungary.

1671

30 April: the Hungarian and Croatian conspirators are sentenced to death.

1672

12 June: French troops invade the Dutch Republic; start of the Franco-Dutch War.
20 August: Hungarian rebels launch a massive incursion into Habsburg Hungary.
13 September: Hungarian rebels defeat the Imperialists at Enyiczko.
26 September: Imperial and Brandenburg armies join near Hildesheim.
10 October: the Imperial garrison of Eperies surrenders to the rebels.
Autumn-winter: the rebellion against the Emperor spreads in Upper-Hungary.

1673

1 July: Leopold I enters into an alliance with Spain, Lorraine and the Dutch Republic against France.
6 September: the French occupy the city of Trier.
11 November: Imperialists and Dutch-Spaniards seize Bonn.

1674

31 March: the Imperial Diet declares *Reichskrieg* (Imperial War) against France.
June–July: Hungarian incursions in Moravia, Silesia and Western Hungary.
June–July: French devastation in the Palatinate.
16 June: the French at Sinsheim defeat an Imperial corps under Caprara.

11 August: battle of Seneffe; the Imperial corps under Souches is partially involved in the fighting.
16 September: Imperialists and Dutch-Spaniards besiege Oudenarde, but Souches leaves the camp two days later.
4 October: Imperialists and allies under Bournonville are defeated at Entzheim.
29 December: Turenne defeats the Imperialists at Mulhouse.

1675

5 January: the Imperial–Brandenburg army is defeated at Türckheim.
February: Transylvanian and Ottoman troops join the Hungarian rebels.
July–August: Hungarian offensive against the Imperial fortresses in Upper Hungary.
27 July: encounter at Salsbach, Turenne's death.
1 August: battle of Altenheim between Imperialists and French.
11 August: Imperial and allied victory at Konzer Brücke.
4 September: Trier surrenders to the Imperial army.
6 December: Imperial troops under Strassoldo occupy Debrecen in Transylvanian and Ottoman territory.

1676

9 June: encounter of Saverne between Imperialists and French.
12 August: Imperial troops in Upper Hungary are defeated at Kálló by the *Kuruc* army.
9 September: the Imperial army under Charles V of Lorraine seizes Philippsburg after 76 days of siege.

1677

February–March: the Imperialists under Cob deport en masse the Upper-Hungary villagers who had provided aid to the *Kuruc* troops.
15 June: encounter of Pont-à-Mousson between Imperialists and French.
7 September: Imperial corps under Saxe-Eisenach is defeated by Créquy at Gengenheim.
10 October: Imperial defeat of Szatmár; the fortress surrenders to the rebels on 22 November but is abandoned months later.
16 November: Freiburg in Breisgau surrenders to the French.

1678

13 April: the Imperialists cross the Rhine at Strasbourg and destroy the French magazines at Bitche and Saarbrucken.

3 May: as retaliation, the French destroy the Imperial facilities at Bad Säckingen.
6 July: French defeat an Imperial corps under Starhemberg at Rheinfelden.
23 July: cavalry encounter at Ortenbach won by the Imperialists.
27 July–8 August: the French destroy the bridges on the Rhine at Kehl and Strasbourg.

1679

26 January: peace is signed at Nijmegen between France and the Empire; Leopold I follows on 2 February.
Summer: *Kuruc* offensive in central Hungary
Autumn: the plague epidemic extends from Hungary to Austria.
3 November: Imperialists are defeated at Uifalu.

1680

May: peasant uprising in Bohemia.
15 November: a truce is signed at Jolsva between the Emperor and the *Kuruc* leaders.

1681

3 May: Interruption of negotiations of Sopron between the Emperor and the *Kuruc* league.
12 September: *Kuruc* supported by Transylvanian and Ottoman troops capture Böszörmény.
25 September: the Imperial garrison of Kálló surrenders to the *Kuruc* army after seven days of siege.
11 November: new talks for an agreement between Vienna and the Hungarian rebels open at Szoboszló.

1682

20 June: peace negotiation fails.
7 July: the *Kuruc* army conquers Kassa.
6 August: the Sultan declares war on the House of Austria.

1683

12 June: the Imperial army under Lorraine besieges Érsekújvár, but leaves after 10 days.
7 July: Ottomans and Tatars defeat the Imperialists at Petronell – the Habsburg court leaves Vienna.

1

The Age of Limited Warfare?

'Do not be carried away by boldness, because a war easily starts but hardly ends'
(Raimondo Montecuccoli, *Treaty of War*)

The most decisive phenomenon in the warfare of the second half of the 17th century was the significant growth of manpower in the armies. This period witnessed a series of epic struggles of which the most dramatic were the wars between the Austrian Habsburgs and the Ottoman Empire and the ones derived from French expansionism, which involved the first actual modern armies. During these conflicts, the armed forces of the major European states experimented with important tactical developments, although it would be mistaken to imply by any periodisation that all forces were developing in a uniform and consistent fashion. As rightly outlined by authoritative historians, it would not only be inappropriate to present the period in 'progressive' or teleological terms, as if greater ability in pursuing war is clearly a benefit, but also inaccurate, for the period began across most of Europe with an extensive slackening of tension and accordingly with a disbanding of much military strength after 1648, not least in England, Habsburg Austria and the United Provinces of the Netherlands.[1]

The lengthy and bitter struggle between France and Spain had been continuous since 1628, with formal hostilities continual since 1635, and ended with the Peace of the Pyrenees of 1659. Further conflicts continued to engage Sweden against Poland, Denmark, Austria, Brandenburg until the peace treaties of Oliva and Copenhagen signed in 1660. The Treaty of Kardis of 1661 marked Sweden's continued success in preventing Russia from gaining a Baltic coastline. War over control of the Ukraine engaged Russia and Poland until 1667, and it was only in 1668 that Spain conceded independence to Portugal. Despite this scenario, the years between the treaties of Westphalia and the Grand Alliance have been considered very superficially as a period of small wars and relative peace. Instead, even ignoring the colonial conflicts in Asia and South America, 43 different wars, occupations, uprisings and crises occurred in Europe in less than 50 years. Even from the point of view

---

1   J. Black, 'Warfare in 1660–1721', in *European Warfare 1660–1815* (London: UCL Press), p. 87.

of the countries involved, this figure does not seem irrelevant: as many as 20 different states, with England, France, the Dutch Republic, Sweden and Poland which were belligerent each for more than eight years and often in more than one conflict; while for Austria the war involvement lasted 29 years, 36 for Venice, and 46 for the Ottoman Empire.

Wars and Conflicts after Westphalia and Countries involved:

French–Spanish War: (1635)–1659, France, Spain, England.
Portuguese Restoration War: (1640)–1668, Portugal, Spain, England, France.
Cretan War: (1645)–1671, Venice, Italian States, France, Ottoman Empire.
Naples Revolt: 1647–1648, Spain.
Cossack Rebellion in Ukraine: 1648–1654, Poland–Lithuania, Cossack Hetmanate, Russia, Tatar Khanate of Crimea.
Cromwell's Campaign in Ireland: 1649–1653, England, Ireland.
Anglo-Scottish War: 1650–1651, England, Scotland.
1st Anglo-Dutch War: 1652–1654, England, Dutch Republic.
Swiss Peasant Revolt: 1653, Swiss.
1st Sweden's Bremen War: 1653–1654, Sweden, Free City of Bremen.
Russo-Polish War: 1654–1667, Poland-Lithuania, Russia, Cossack Hetmanate.
Valdese Repression in Savoy and Piedmont: 1655, Savoy–Piedmont.
2nd Northern War: 1655–1660, Sweden, Poland–Lithuania, Transylvania, Denmark, Habsburg-Austria, Brandenburg, Dutch Republic, Ottoman Empire, Russia.
First War of Villmergen: 1656, Swiss.
Münster's Submission: 1661, city of Münster, Prince-bishopric of Münster, Dutch Republic.
French conquest of Marsal: 1663, France, Lorraine.
Münster–East Frisia Border Conflict: 1663–1664, Prince-bishopric of Münster, Duchy of East-Frisia, Dutch Republic.
Austrian–Ottoman War: 1663–1664, Habsburg-Austria, German Empire, France, Ottoman Empire.
Polish Civil War or Lubomirski's Rebellion: 1665–66, Poland.
Erfurt's Submission: 1664, city of Erfurt, Electorate of Mainz.
2nd Anglo-Dutch War: 1665–1667, Dutch Republic, England, Prince-bishopric of Münster, France.
2nd Sweden–Bremen War: 1666, Sweden, Free City of Bremen.
Polish–Cossack–Tatar War: 1666–1671, Poland, Tatar Khanate of Crimea, Cossack Hetmanate.
Magdeburg's submission: 1666, city of Magdeburg, Brandenburg.
War of Devolution: 1667–1668, France, Spain.
Cologne's submission: 1668, city of Cologne, Electorate of Cologne, Dutch Republic.
French Occupation of Lorraine: 1670, France, Lorraine.
Siege of Braunschweig: 1671, city of Braunschweig, Braunschweig-Wolfenbüttel.

First Hungarian *Kuruc* Rebellion: 1671–1679, Habsburg-Austria, Transylvania, Poland.
Polish–Ottoman War: 1672–1676, Poland–Lithuania, Ottoman Empire.
Dutch War: 1672–1678, France, Dutch Republic, Prince-bishopric of Münster, Electorate of Cologne, England, Spain, Habsburg-Austria, German Empire, Sweden, Brandenburg.
Genoese–Savoyard War: 1672–1673, Savoy-Piedmont, Republic of Genoa.
Scanian War: 1675–1679, Sweden, Denmark.
Russian–Ottoman War, 1676–1681, Russia, Ottoman Empire, Tatar Khanate of Crimea.
Second Hungarian *Kuruc* Rebellion: 1681–1697, Habsburg-Austria.
Peasant Rebellion in Bohemia: 1680, Habsburg-Austria.
French Occupation of Strasbourg: 1680, France, German Empire.
French Dragonnades: 1681–1686, France.
Holy League War: 1683–1699, Habsburg-Austria, Ottoman Empire, Poland-Lithuania, German Empire, Republic of Venice, Italian States, Russia.
Landing of Genoa: 1684, France, Republic of Genoa, Spain.
French Occupation of Luxembourg: 1684, France, Spain.
Danish Siege of Hamburg: 1686, Denmark, Free city of Hamburg, Brandenburg, Hannover.
War against the Valdese in Piedmont: 1686–1689, Savoy-Piedmont

These conflicts involved just the European continent, but we have to consider that the Portuguese faced the Dutch in Brazil from 1630 to 1654; England conquered Spanish Jamaica in 1655, while in 1662–84 maintained a garrison in Tangiers, and French, English and Dutch fleets launched several actions against Algerian privateers from 1667 to 1686.

In early 18th century, most of the European states had been left exhausted and indebted, and their armed forces were the focus of expenditure and debt. As the wars continued, the extent of money owed depressed the credibility of the entire military 'system'. To modern eyes, such a system appears anachronistic and primitive; but in fact, it was both a fundamental aspect of a range of governmental activities and a sensible and necessary response to the limitations of state power and capability. Recruiting, supplying and supporting military units were crucial aspects of financial administration, and private individuals and consortia were important in this matter. Probably the judgement so hastily formulated to qualify these conflicts as episodes of limited warfare comes from a superficial knowledge of the episodes and from the conditionings derived from the 19th century vision of war, as formulated by Clausewitz and Jomini. In their work, and despite the growth of permanent forces, both these authors focused on the total forces involved in a single campaign, which rarely exceeded 90,000 soldiers overall. However, the campaign of Louis XIV against the Dutch Republic in 1672, and those of the Ottomans in 1663 and 1683 against the Habsburgs, would represent significant exceptions, but it is effectively rare to find armies under the orders of a single commanders that number over 40,000

Louis XIV, portrayed by Charles Lebrun in 1661. The Sun King was the central figure of this age. According to most authoritative historians, his government action marks the actual turning point in the formation of permanent armies and their use as political instruments. (Author's collection)

men.[2] The number of troops is a fundamental discriminating and important factor to better understand the dynamics of war campaigns in this period. When 19th century military historians dismissed the campaigns as numerically insignificant examples, they neglected a fundamental factor, namely the relationship between the military force and the civil population.[3]

In the 1660s, armies began to increase in size, but this took place at a time when the growth of Europe's population was not rapid at all. In France, for instance, the population even decreased by the end of the century. Except for country like England and the Dutch Republic, there was no change in the level of agricultural production, nor in that of transportation facilities. So it happened that, given substantially unchanged population numbers and no agricultural progress, food had to be provided for armies in campaign larger than in the previous decades. The problems involved in the provisioning of great armies had a decisive influence on strategy. France inaugurated the 'magazines system' and portable ovens, introduced by Le Tellier father and son, but all this resulted in command difficulties never experimented before.[4] What actually happened therefore was that, owing to the aggressive intentions of the European foreign policy, the numerical growth of the armies far exceeded progress in the means of production, and surpassed the limits at which armies still could have been provisioned and led properly considering the existing potentialities of supply, transport and technical devices, such as the mountable ovens introduced by Louvois in 1672.

Some regions of Europe were self-supporting, namely they grew their bread-grain themselves; granting further that crop rotation was employed in the 17th century just as in the early 19th century, one must also consider, that in the 17th century it took 35 inhabitants per square kilometre to provision an army of 40–45,000 men without magazines. Relying on the demographic research, the trends of population in various European countries, would indicate that density over 35 people per square kilometre existed only in France, the Low Countries, the Rhineland, Westphalia and the Po Valley.[5] The relation between population density, resources and a large army is therefore an assumption that puts into question the term 'low intensity warfare' applied to the war of this age when armies operated in war theatres like Hungary, Poland or the Balkans. The effort to maintain these forces on campaign in

---

2   The great *maréchal* Turenne declared that he preferred to lead an army of 20–25,000 men in order to maintain mobility: 'with a small army is possible to distinguish the troops and perform the marches without losing the control of the deployment or the soldiers. While large armies generate confusion and consume a great deal of resources, without considering that it is always difficult to find places that can support them.' Turenne to Venetian ambassador Primo Visconti, January 1674, in J. Bérenger, *Turenne* (Paris: Fayard, 1987), p. 394.

3   About this criticism, see also R. Luraghi, *Le Opere di Raimondo Montecuccoli* (Rome: USSME, 1988), vol. I, pp. 90–95.

4   G. Perjés, 'Army Provisioning, Logistics and Strategy in the Second Half of the 17th Century' in *Acta Historica Academiae Scientiarum Hungaricae* (Budapest: Institute of History, Research Centre for the Humanities, Hungarian Academy of Sciences), Vol. 16, No.1/2 (1970), p. 4.

5   *Ibidem*, p. 5.

THE AGE OF LIMITED WARFARE?

Detail from a battle scene of the 1670s by an anonymous engraver and artist. After the Thirty Years' War, conflicts remained costly in terms of financial resources and human lives, but the authors of the 19th century imposed their vision about the wars of this age, considered as low-impact conflicts. Probably the judgment, so hastily formulated, to qualify these wars as episodes of limited warfare comes from a superficial knowledge of the facts and from the conditioning derived from their vision of war, as formulated by Clausewitz and Jomini. (Author's collection)

such regions, almost deprived of sufficient resources, was considerable, and has very little consistency with the term 'low intensity warfare'.

Another aspect often eluded to by the historiography regarding the wars of the second half of the 17th century is that relating to winter campaigns. The possibility of conducting a campaign even in the absence of fundamental resources, such as forage for horses, was closely linked to the level of supply through an efficient network of magazines. This aspect became more important as the armies increased their size and very often, the war campaigns closed with the arrival of the cold season more or less all over Europe. This was a constant feature of the Ottoman armies, which normally included a large number of horsemen, however little emphasis has been given to the winter campaigns fought between the 1650s and 1670s. Apart from the famous winter campaigns of 1672–73 and 1674–75 in the Franco-Dutch war, military historiography rarely deals with military operations continued until December or even January, such as the ones that occurred during the Northern War of 1655–60. It is indeed surprising to note that the Imperial cavalry forded the Baltic Sea at Als in December 1658, or that in the same year sieges of Torun ended on 21 December, and that the battle of Nyborg, on Funen Island, was fought on 14 November 1659. This is another reason to advance further doubts regarding the 'low intensity warfare' concept.

Another aspect opposing this vision has often been marginalised by the historians, namely cruelty against the civilian population. In October 1659, the militiamen of the besieged Stettin captured by the Imperialists were put to the sword without mercy, alongside their officers.[6] Some might argue that the beleaguered militiamen were combatants, however this conflict, often related as a relatively bloody war, had its corollary of destruction and misery. Peasants in Mecklenburg and Holstein-Gottorp fled the regions in terror

---

6   G. Gualdo-Priorato, *Historia di Leopoldo Cesare, contenente le cose più memorabili successe in Europa dal 1656 al 1670* (Vienna, 1670), vol. I, p. 580.

German peasant mistreated by soldiers, from a painting of the late 17th century. The conflicts of the second half of the 17th century had their corollary of destruction and misery. In 1658, peasants in Mecklenburg and Holstein-Gottorp fled the regions in terror as conditions returned to those experienced during the Thirty Years' War. Even more frightening were the excesses that occurred in the wars against the Ottomans, where operations were characterised by a level of brutality unknown in the west. (Author's collection)

as conditions returned to those experienced during the Thirty Years' War.[7] Even the devastation of the Palatinate, which took place for the first time in the summer of 1674, is rarely taken into account by historians, perhaps only because the one that occurred in 1688 caused more sensation. Even more frightening excesses occurred in the wars against the Ottomans, where the operations had been characterised by a level of brutality unknown in the west. Unlike those elsewhere, after 1683 Ottoman commanders of major fortresses had rarely surrendered once the walls were breached, compelling their opponents to fight their way in. Officers quickly lost control of their soldiers, who were enraged by the inevitable heavy losses and intoxicated by xenophobia and religious hatred. Several eyewitnesses was amazed by what was done in Esztergom and Buda, and to see that mankind shows itself far crueller to its own than the beasts.'[8]

The ingenuous and Romantic idea of a 'limited war' without cruelty became a myth useful only to justify 'total war'.

---

7 H. Klaje, *Der Feldzug der Kaiserlichen unter Souches nach Pommern im Jahre 1659* (Gotha, 1906), p. 9.
8 Johann Dietz's eyewitness description of the scenes following the capture of Buda in 1686 surpasses anything conjured up in Grimmelshausen's fictional account of atrocities during the Thirty Years' War: 'Not even the child in the mother's body was spared ... naked children of one or two years of age were spitted and flung over the city walls!', in P. Wilson, *War and German Politics, 1648–1806* (London: UCL Press, 1998), p. 84.

2

Austria Erit In Orbe Ultima[1]

Austria, the House of Habsburg, Vienna: names evoking in each one the splendour of the waltz era, or the atmosphere of perpetual 'felix' existing under the Empress Maria Theresa. An idyllic scenario utterly different from the aftermath of the Peace of Westphalia, when the House of Austria was going through one of its darkest moments. Huge resources had been consumed in the disastrous war that had involved the Habsburg domains for 30 years against internal and external enemies. The devastation of that conflict had strongly reduced the population of the provinces; the economy of the Habsburg domains seemed incapable of recovering from the crisis, while in the east the expansionism of the Ottoman sultans was once again threatening the borders. It is possible to obtain an impression of the gloomy atmosphere of these years, observing the monument erected in Vienna by Emperor Leopold I in 1679: the column of the plague at the Graben, where the monarch is represented in the act of prayer. His words are carved in the stone: *Ego Leopoldus humilis servus tuus* (I am Leopold, Thy humble servant). Penance, expiation, religious belief – which transfigured events – increased the sense of agony in which the destiny of the House of Austria seemed to be collapsed.

Historians often represent this portrait of Imperial monarchy in the second half of the 17th century, especially because this gloomy vision has received an impulse from the literature of the Romantic era. Friedrich Schiller, Franz Grillparzer, Rainer Maria Rilke and others passed on this age as the darkest of Austrian history and after them, Joseph Roth and Stefan Zweig resumed some characters to evoke the incoming *finis Austriae*. Today historians look at this age also as a period of transformation and evolution for Imperial policy. The Habsburg domains suffered greatly in the Thirty Years' War, but territorial losses were few in all, considering that the major sacrifice, Lusatia, was ceded to the elector of Saxony in exchange for breaking the alliance with Sweden. Although the Treaty of Westphalia had been a blow

---

[1] 'Austria will be the last (to survive) in the world'. A.E.I.O.U. was the symbolic device personally used by Habsburg Emperor Frederick III (1415–1493), who had a fondness for mystical formulae. He habitually signed buildings such as the Burg Wiener Neustadt or the Graz Cathedral, as well as his tableware and other objects with the vowel graphemes.

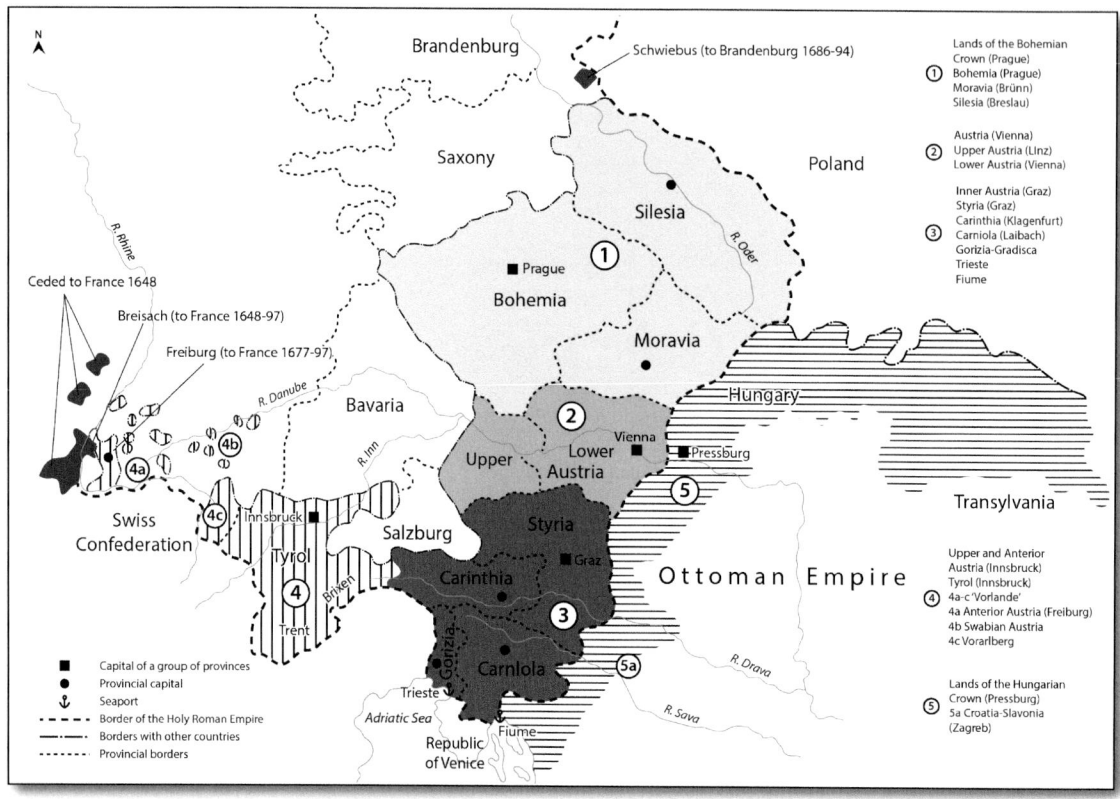

The Austrian Habsburgs' domains.

to Habsburg ambitions, the agreement was substantially a compromise. The Holy Roman-German Empire maintained its unity and the title of Emperor remained in Habsburg hands until the male line was extinct. Ultimately, the defeat of the Protestants in Bohemia and the introduction of the Counter-Reformation in hereditary domains strengthened the power of the Habsburgs in their lands. This was surely the major success for the Austrian monarchy, and even their attempt to create an Imperial monarchy strongly centralised and the submission of the reformed princes had been frustrated, the Peace of Westphalia had rejected the opposite plan to transform the Empire into an aristocratic republic.[2]

The House of Austria

According to the German historian Bernhard Kroener,[3] the Thirty Years' War had been a laboratory of state formation, and this sentence is especially true for the Austrian Habsburg domains. The years following 1648 opened a completely new phase for the House of Austria. The Habsburgs maintained

---

2 *New Cambridge Modern History*, 'The Ascendancy of France, 1648–1688' (Cambridge University Press, 1968), vol. V, p. 551.

3 B. Kroener, 'Kriegswesen, Herrschaft und Gesellschaft, 1300–1800', in *Enzyklopädie der deutscher Geschichte*, B. 92 (Munich: Oldenbourg 2013).

their Imperial status notwithstanding the failure to restore the hegemony over Germany, and after 1648, the dual nature of the monarchy began to assume its modern meaning. The age of Habsburg absolutism began in these years and became concrete with the administrative unification of the ancient Habsburg provinces through a gradual reform of the local institutions to transform the composite domains into a unitary state. The Emperor ruled his own domains, but contemporarily he was the *Kaiser*, sovereign of a great federation of states taking the title of *Reichsoberhaupt*, an updated version of a role that identifies him as the political centre of the *Reich* (empire) from which a new reputation derives.[4]

This phase of the history of the Habsburgs is well represented by Emperor Leopold I (1640–1705). His destiny arrived in June 1653, following the premature death of his firstborn brother Ferdinand, who had obtained the election as Emperor and, according to tradition, had already received the crowns of Bohemia and Hungary. Leopold was then removed from his theological studies in Spain and presented as the new heir to the House of Austria. Few dynasties have given a series of sovereigns so faithful to a single model. Historians have outlined his figure by returning the image of a monarch with an ambivalent personality. Like his predecessors, Leopold reigned by presenting all the virtues but also the typical weaknesses of his house. He was a devoted Catholic and protector of the arts, but without the necessary qualities to govern, probably he looked on with envy at the unlimited power held by some of the sovereigns who were his contemporaries. However, Leopold was profoundly aware of the rights and duties that entailed the Imperial dignity. For twice he faced the risk of an Ottoman assault in the heart of Austria, but he constantly watched over every square metre of the Empire; and in 1674 did not hesitate to dismiss and arrest the prime minister and his personal friend Wenzel Eusebius von Lobkowicz, who supported an acquiescent policy with France, for engaging a war with an uncertain outcome against Louis XIV.[5] Moreover, Leopold proved to be able to choose good collaborators in the state's affairs, among all Giovanni Ferdinando Portia and Franz von Lisola, but above all skilled

Emperor Leopold I von Habsburg (1640–1705), portrayed in a dancer costume during his youth. Leopold became emperor in 1658, but initially he had been destined for an ecclesiastical career. Faith and strong religious zeal always conditioned his actions throughout his long reign. He cared about military matters, but unlike his archenemy Louis XIV, Leopold did not command his army on campaign. (Author's collection)

---

4   'For Austria, this scenario set a development, which is called "outward development from the Reich", or – from another perspective – as becoming German Empire.', H.D. Heimann, *Die Habsurger, Dynastie und Keiserreiche* (Munich: C. H. Beck, 2001), p. 69.

5   The fall of the three most powerful court figures in the 1670s, Auersperg, Lobkowicz, and Sinzendorff, is a clear proof of the attitude to the rigor of Leopold I.

commanders for his army, such as Raimondo Montecuccoli, Charles V of Lorraine and Eugene of Savoy. Throughout his life, Leopold I preferred to entrust the government to men coming from the great aristocratic families of Bohemia and Moravia with a long tradition of service. Feelings of friendship were present in his choices, as was the case with some ministers, such as the court chamberlain and *Hofmeister* Johann Maximilian Lamberg. In 1682, Ferdinand Joseph von Dietrichstein succeeded in this charge, while another of Leopold's friends, Ferdinand von Harrach, became a member of the government in 1679. In the same year, Albert von Zinzendorf was appointed court marshal. None of them was distinguished by political quality, but they were personally linked to the sovereign and other personalities of the court. The character of Leopold I was also reflected in the composition of the court apparatus. As there was in Vienna an Imperial chancellery, an Imperial treasury and an Imperial tribunal, each hereditary province had its own government offices; as a result, in Vienna there was a bewildering mixture of Imperial and Habsburg institutions. Normally the Emperor solicited the council of chancellors or presidents of most of these offices. This confusing jumble of administrative and court offices contributed to making the government action slow and complicated, and it is not always easy to distinguish between internal and external influences.[6]

The central government office of the state was the *Hofkanzlei* (Aulic Chancellery) separated from that of the Empire in 1620. The chancellor acted also as ambassador in the Imperial Diet, as happened in 1665 with the skilled and diligent Johann Paul Hocher, who held the position until 1683. The third major office, in charge of the finances and the economic affairs, was the *Hofkammer* (Aulic Chamber, the treasury), which controlled the treasury and the balance of expenditure for all the matters, army included. This office managed a part of the state administration, of which the Aulic Chamber occupied the place of main financial authority for Upper and Lower Austria, Bohemia, Moravia and Silesia and after 1686 also Hungary and Croatia. The Aulic Chamber controlled the activity of the Provincial Chambers, which in this period had lost their decisional power and they could express their opinion only to suggest deductions and forms of payment. Finally, the military affairs of the Habsburg domains were dealt with by the *Hofkriegsrat* (Aulic War Council). The importance of this office was considerable, because the distribution of the Imperial troops in campaign depended on the opinion of its president.

As occurred in other contemporary monarchies, the Habsburgs tried to attract nobles to their service in order to connect them closely to their interests. Consequently, the essential problem became to contain within the tolerable limits the influence of the nobles within the court or the army and that autonomous decision-making areas were not formed. To achieve this goal Leopold, and after him also his sons, assured that the mutual sphere of competence among the government offices remained undefined. Leopold established the practice, which was then increasingly frequent, to appoint ad

---

6   J. Stoye, *The Siege of Vienna* (Edinburgh: Birlinn, second edition, 2006), p. 47.

hoc commissions, within which he put people of his choice, and weakened the strength of the office that had been his traditional governing instrument, the *Geheimrat* (Secret Council). It was the most important governing advisory office, as it was customary that any decision of the monarch would take place only after he had listened to his councillors. The president of the council, the *Hofhochmeister*, was the person closest to the sovereign and he could be considered like a Prime Minister. The secret council included all the major position-holders of the court, including the Marshall of court, the vice-chancellor, and a variable number or intimate counsellors.[7] In 1670, Leopold I created another council to counterbalance the previous one, called the *Geheim Konferenz* (Secret Conference), convened only on the monarch's order. Inside it Leopold I involved only a few trusted people for the resolution of the most confidential issues. In this period, five senior personalities constituted the core of this council: General Raimondo Montecuccoli, Count Georg Ludwig von Zinzendorff, the great butler Count Johann Maximilian von Lamberg, Prince Ferdinand Wilhelm von Schwarzenberg and the chancellor Johann Paul Hocher. A second generation of ministers was included among the private councillors after the 1680s, with Christoph von Abele and Johann Jörger as president and vice-president of the Aulic Chamber, Leopold Wilhelm von Königsegg, Imperial vice chancellor and Ferdinand Wilhelm Eusebius von Schwarzenberg, president of the Imperial council. During the years following the fall of Prince Johann Weikhard von Auersperg in 1670, and the even more sensational fall of Lobkowicz four years later, there were no more personalities capable of dominating the court and the state, and in 1680, after the removal of the president of the *Aulic Chamber* Georg Ludwig von Sinzendorf, any minister in Austria could succeed in obtaining a position of strength comparable to that of the aforementioned personalities.[8] In the following years, Leopold turned often his trust to external councillors, such as the Capuchin monk Marco d'Aviano (alias Carlo Domenico Cristofori, 1631–1699), who in 1683 supported the Habsburg policy against the Porte with his tireless propaganda.

Even though he was not an actual minister, Raimondo Montecuccoli represents the most considerable exception of court personality capable of effective ascendancy on the Emperor. Appointed as *General-Lieutenant* in 1660 and President of the Aulic War Council in 1668, Montecuccoli held both these high offices until his death in 1680. Although he remained a stranger to matters of civil government, after 1664 he was the soul of Habsburg policy and the true reformer and creator of the modern Imperial army. Montecuccoli certainly owed his astonishing career not only to his exceptional talent and skill, but also to an element of luck. Given the traditions and standards of the time, as well as his social background, he was destined to be an officer who would probably have reached the rank of colonel. His fortune came from

---

7 In 1678, the secret council was composed of 20 members, progressively increased to 114 at the end of the century, but only a few could attend the meeting. See also in H. Ehalt, *Ausdrucken Absolutischer Herrschaft. Der Wiener Hof im 17. Und 18, Jahrhundert* (Munich: Oldenbourg Verlag, 1980), pp. 44–45.

8 *Ibidem*, p. 46.

being the right man at the right time, whose talent was soon recognised also by Ferdinand III. His competence, honesty, huge knowledge and experience were successively recognised and rewarded by his contemporaries. The Montecuccoli family had supplied soldiers to the Emperor since the 16th century, and his cousin and brother were also soldiers too. Raimondo's career is highly exemplificative of the 17th century military scenario. In the summer of 1625, aged 16, Count Raimondo Montecuccoli left his native Modena for Austria, having obtained entry into the infantry regiment of General Rambaldo Collalto through the intercession of his cousin Ernesto, an Imperial officer who served in Germany. He had to accept the conditions imposed by the Colonel: no special privileges, no duty exemptions and no rapid promotions to officer level, despite his family credentials. Thus, he began his career as a soldier, but fairly quickly, he reached the rank of lieutenant, which could have been expected for someone carrying the title of count. Contemporaries describe him as thirsty for knowledge in every military field. In Germany and Bohemia, Montecuccoli dedicated himself to study during every period of truce, reading day and night. In 1632, he was promoted captain and then finally he gained the rank of colonel, taking full command of a cuirassier regiment. Captured by the Swedes at Lützen, he wrote the *Trattato della Guerra* (Treatise of War) and the *Quaderni*, but today only one chapter remains: *Delle Battaglie* (on the Battles). After the Thirty Years' War, he completed *I Viaggi* (Travels), the *Zibaldone* and the transformation of the 'Treatise of War' in the 'Treatise of the Art of War'. Coeval accounts testify to his audacity, gallantry and physical courage. Even when he became a senior officer, Montecuccoli took many risks, by commanding on the front line.

In his numerous writings Montecuccoli appears a curious and clever man, showing great interest in the world around him. He mastered German, French, Spanish, Latin and also the English language. His work is dominated throughout by rectitude, efficiency and rationalism. His actions seem to

Raimondo Montecuccoli (1609–1680). Commemorative stamp issued by the Austrian Post in 2009 for the 400-year anniversary of his birth. A military commander and theorist, Montecuccoli had an effective ascendency in the Imperial court, a considerable exception for a military officer after the experience with Wallenstein. Appointed as *General-Lieutenant* in 1660 and President of the Aulic War Council in 1668, Montecuccoli held both these high positions until his death in 1680. Although he remained a stranger to matters of civil government, after 1664 he was the main inspirer of Habsburg policy and the true reformer and creator of the modern Imperial army. The cult of the great Italian general and his scientific approach to modern warfare remained alive for a long time; however, his theoretical work and many of his memories were long equivocated or misunderstood, leaving open many questions about the decisions taken by him, especially during the war against the Porte in 1663–64. (Author's collection)

reveal a man of sympathy, who was proud and courageous yet charitable towards the less fortunate. As a military commander, he always tried to spare the blood of his soldiers and the lives of civilians. With his collaborators and subordinates, he was severe but at the same benevolent. He was not afraid to listen and adopt other people's ideas if they were good. One of his great strengths was to be able to choose good advisers. He was capable of using good judgement and quickly evolving decisive action. He was not reluctant to deal with secondary details but always kept the larger picture in mind, with a remarkable clearness of views in conception and execution.

After rescue from captivity he was called by his sovereign, the Duke of Modena, for the incoming conflict against the Holy See for the fief of Castro. Montecuccoli led the Modenese army at Nonantola, where he defeated Pope Barberini's force on 20 July 1643. Before the end of the summer, Montecuccoli came back to Austria where he was promoted to *Feldmarschall-Lieutenant*. In 1645–46, he served in Hungary against Prince György I Rákóczi of Transylvania, on the Neckar against the French, and in Silesia and Bohemia against the Swedes. The victory of Triebel in Silesia won him the rank of *General der Cavallerie*, and at the battle of Zusmarshausen in 1648 his stubborn rearguard fighting rescued the Imperialists from annihilation. For some years after the Peace of Westphalia, Montecuccoli was concerned with foreign affairs, travelling to Flanders and England, as the representative of the Emperor, and to Sweden as the envoy of the Pope to Queen Christina of Sweden. In 1658, he became *Generalfeldmarshall* of the imperial army, a seat in the *Hofkriegsrat*, and president of the same council in 1668.

Although his promotion was based on merit, and for a large part of his life he remained a modest, quiet and simple man, with age he become more ambitious, less patient, and more authoritarian. However, he never gave his opinion on subjects outside of his own field of competence. Historians have long debated about the bitter controversy between him and the talented Hungarian-Croatian commander Miklós Zrínyi. The contrast was the result of diametrically and intellectually conflicting opposition. Furthermore, Montecuccoli had little confidence in the Hungarian aristocracy, as he confessed in his writing:

> Hungarians are fierce, restless, fickle, never satisfied. They possess the spirit of the Scythians and Tatars, their predecessors. They yearn to an unbridled license, and, therefore they become, without realising it, the slaves of vices and the injustices of who is stronger […] Looking at their history, in less than two centuries of continuous external and civil wars, betrayal, revolutions, confusion and superficiality, nothing else appears in the minds of these people […] and in the many contradictions they involve themselves in.[9]

The Italian general accused the Hungarian aristocracy of fermenting insubordination amongst the Estates so that several times they refused winter quarters to the Imperial troops. Bluntly, and in direct contradiction

---

9   Montecuccoli, *L'Ungheria, l'anno MDCVXXIII*, p. 2.

with his own privileged background, he accused some of his own Hungarian peers of even divulging intelligence to the Ottomans, in attempts to preserve their own autonomy.[10]

After his celebrated victory at the battle of Szentgotthárd in 1664, Montecuccoli wrote his major work, *Della Guerra contro il Turco in Ungheria* (The War Against the Turks in Hungary) and the famous 'Aphorisms'. He also devoted much time to compiling his various works on military history and science. As a prince of the Empire and high commander of the Imperial army, he conducted his last campaigns on the Rhine against the French, in the Dutch War of 1672–78. His legacy in the army remained fundamental and he was able to form several talented commanders, such as Charles V of Lorraine and Ludwig of Baden, who later proved to be valuable in the crucial years of the war against the Ottomans.

It has often been pointed out that in these years there were numerous foreigners at the court of Vienna, especially Italians, with senior positions in the government and in the army. Their presence was not only due to the ascendancy of the Italian culture on Leopold I, but also to his conviction that foreigners, being strangers to the relations of the Habsburgs domains, were the most suitable to manage the state's affairs with impartiality.[11]

Habsburg Geostrategy

The presence of foreigners also meant an enrichment of experiences and, certainly, it was necessary to have a preparation and a knowledge out of the ordinary to keep the House of Austria's rank among the European powers in such unfavourable geostrategic context. In the third quarter of the 17th century the Habsburgs' *Erbländer* (hereditary domains) extended inside a large square running from the Alps to Poland and from Swabia to Hungary for 340,000 square kilometres overall. This area represented the most extended state of the Empire, even without Hungary and Croatia, which formerly did not belong to the *Reich*. Nevertheless, Habsburg domains were sparsely inhabited, with a population of no more than 8,500,000 inhabitants mostly employed in agriculture and breeding. Vast areas were wooded and mountainous, and almost devoid of the necessary resources to support large manufactutere. The most urbanised areas of Austria and Bohemia were in strong contrast to the southern and eastern regions, and especially to Hungary, where the largest cities under the Habsburgs' rule rarely exceeded 10,000 people, and only the capital Bratislava (Pressburg in German and

---

10 A. Testa, *Le Opere di Raimondo Montecuccoli*, vol. III, 'Giudizio congetturale sopra le intenzioni e consigli degli Ungheri' (Rome, USSME, 2000), pp. 126–127.
11 One of the considerations that encouraged Vienna to accept foreigners graciously, especially Italians, can be guessed from the words of the philosopher and historian Giambattista Vico: '... to be Italian and therefore free from any suspicion ... the captain from Italy proves to be suitable for governing with harshness people with whom he was not familiar.' See in Gueze, 'La Liberazione dell'Ungheria dal Turco La Liberazione dell'Ungheria dal Turco (1683–1699) nelle fonti conservate in alcuni fra i principali Archivi di Stato Italiani', in *OSZK – Rivista di Studi Ungheresi* (Rome-Budapest, 1986), p. 45.

Pozsony in Hungarian) had more than 20,000.[12] Overall, the Habsburg's Hungarian domains represented one-fourth of the original kingdom. The Ottoman sultans ruled the main part of the country and regarding the border there were large sectors under double sovereignty. However, the Habsburgs held the richest area, included the mining provinces in Slovakia and the larger part of the population, estimated at about 2,500,000.

In the 17th century the Habsburgs' policy, like that of other ruling princes in Germany, was aimed at eliminating or at least reducing the rights still held by the provincial *Stände* (Estates).[13] Their functions included several matters of government; in particular they were called upon to approve the plans for financing and organising military endeavours. Within the Austrian lands themselves, the suppression of Protestantism also reduced the influence of the provincial Estates, whose nobles had once spearheaded the advance of the new faith. The defeat of the Protestants in Bohemia and Moravia provided the Habsburgs with ideal terrain for carrying out a historical experiment to impose an autocratic and absolute system of government.[14] Ferdinand III was the instigator of the plan and his son Leopold I continued it with the same rigour, but the experiment could be carried out thanks to the support of the local aristocracy.

Protestantism and noble particularism had been brutally suppressed in Austria, Bohemia and Moravia, following the Habsburg victory on the White Mountain in 1620. The property of rebel noblemen had been redistributed to Catholic loyalists to extend the basis of Habsburg support.[15] After 1648, the Estates of Bohemia and Moravia continued to meet but only with the permission of the sovereign. Soon both Estates lost many of their powers and privileges as well, though they retained residual rights to negotiate financial arrangements with their Habsburg rulers. Under the control of the nobles and clergy loyal to the Habsburgs, the Estates could still discuss the fiscal measures demanded by Vienna, but rarely succeeded in opposing them. Progressively

---

12 According to H. Langer and J. Dudás, in 'Die Kämpfe in Ungarn 1684 bis 1686 und die Rückeroberung Budas im Spiegel des *Theatrum Europaeum*', in *Acta Historica Academiae Scientiarum Hungaricae*, Vol. 34, No. 1 (Budapest: Institute of History, Research Centre for the Humanities, Hungarian Academy of Sciences, 1988), pp. 17–25. The urban population in 1650s Hungary did not exceed 60,000 inhabitants.
13 Estates were the civil authorities representing the people, exercising local administration, judiciary and tax collection.
14 The Emperor had subdued the Protestants in his domains, but the offensive against the Reformed churches had been not an exclusive Habsburg affair: 'Crucial in this development was the re-emergence of an aggressive form of "state-dominated Catholicism", a phrase coined by Peter Rietbergen to describe the emergence of this phenomenon [...] The term seems very useful; after Westphalia, religious differences as such would no longer form a cause for conflict. But this aggressive form of Catholicism was an entirely different matter. In France Louis XIV persecuted hundreds of thousands of Huguenots, whereas in England, and especially Ireland, James II rapidly Catholicised the military and tried to gain control of Parliament. These two monarchs made the bolstering of Catholicism with the means of the state central to their policy. And, in all appearance, it influenced their foreign policy as well, and rumours spread about a secret mutual alliance.' D. Onnekink 'The Last War of Religion? The Dutch and the Nine Years' War', in *War and Religion after Westphalia, 1648–1713* (Ashgate, Burlington VT, 2009), p. 72.
15 However, there were limits to the consolidation of the emperor's executive power, and Bohemia and Moravia only received 'renewed constitutions' rather than outright abolition. See in P. Wilson, *German Armies*, p. 38.

the power of the Estates diminished throughout the whole state. The last vestiges of autonomy from which the Estates had benefited in the past had almost disappeared in 1648. As early as 1632 Moravia was governed without even a semblance of respect for the rights of the Estates, and only Silesia, due to the fact that it had not participated in the 1618–20 rebellion, was able to preserve the Diets and did not undergo any constitutional change. Together with Bohemia, Moravia was governed by Vienna through the Bohemian Chancellery, made up of aristocrats appointed by the sovereign. The situation remained unchanged also in Hungary, due to the political privileges held by the kingdom. The Hungarian nobility, who included several Lutherans and Calvinists, had held tenaciously to many features of their medieval constitution, including the right of armed resistance to any ruler who violated their privileges. The Hungarian Estate elected the *nádor* (Palatine Count), in charge of the direction of the army, and enacted continuous laws on social, economic, juridical and religious matters. Although the Hungarian chancellery was in Vienna, the Hungarian *Kammer* (chamber, namely the finances), and the parliament resided in Bratislava. The only Imperial offices that could somehow exert authority over Hungary were those relating to the army and the fiscal policy. Over time, the struggle around Hungarian autonomy triggered revolts of the native aristocracy that would subside only in the following century.

Menaced from the north by Sweden, from the west by French and from the south-east by the Porte, the Habsburgs could not hope to maintain their autonomy in the absence of a foreign policy strongly supported by arms. Among all the major powers of Europe, the House of Austria was among those who knew almost no peace at the borders. The Austrian monarchy at the time of Leopold I was marked by an almost uninterrupted series of disputes, both in domestic policy or actual military confrontation with enemy powers. Except for the period of non-belligerence between 1665 and 1672, the Habsburg domains were involved without interruption in more than one conflict at a time from 1673 to 1699. Even when there was no real conflict with an opposing power, there were internal disputes to occupy the scene, as happened with the bitter rebellion of the Hungarian magnates that started in 1670.

Whenever peace was reached, another crisis opened more or less connected to the previous one. This does not necessarily mean that Austrian diplomacy had moved like an elephant into glassware and effectively, it was impossible to remain neutral in such a context. The first major engagement occurred in the war between Sweden and Poland in 1655. Charles X of Sweden was determined to resolve the dynastic differences with the Polish Republic and to extend Swedish influence in eastern Europe. In Vienna it was feared that after the Polish defeat, the presence of a powerful and hostile Protestant state close to the Moravian border represented a nightmare for Vienna. This fear was not entirely unfounded, considering that fewer than 40 years had passed since the revolt of 1618, and just five since the departure of the Swedish Army from the Austrian domains. The danger became even more concrete when the son of an old Habsburg enemy, the bold and ambitious prince of Transylvania, György II Rákóczi, joined an alliance with the Swedes and invaded Poland from the south. The partition of Poland between the two allies, both Protestant, could trigger an irreversible crisis in the Hungarian domains too, where Calvinists and Lutherans were numerous and openly hostile to the Habsburgs. On 11 April 1657, when the victorious allies joined their army at Sandomierz, Ferdinand III of Habsburg had died nine days earlier. The heir Leopold was then only 16 years old and found himself facing an equally critical situation to the one experienced by his grandfather in 1618. Just a month after the coronation, Leopold I was at war with Sweden and the Transylvanians, and allied to Poland. Fortune favoured the young monarch, because at the same time Denmark and Brandenburg also entered the war against Charles X and after a short time Rákóczi was forced to suspend the campaign in Poland due to the threats coming from the Porte, which did not tolerate its own tributary state being aggressive against a state that each year paid a tribute to the sultan. The strategic situation had changed and this facilitated the task for Vienna, which could calmly prepare the army, and enter into the first of a series of agreements with Poland in December 1656, which resulted in a promise of active intervention one year later. In July 1657, Imperial troops marched into Poland under *Feldmarschall-General* Melchior von Hatzfeld. Here the Imperialists joined the Polish and Brandenburg armies, gaining final victory after three years of campaign under Montecuccoli, who had replaced Hatzfeld after he died in 1658.

The involvement in Poland had been resolved favourably, paying a low cost, but it triggered in Transylvania a series of events perhaps more dangerous than the previous ones.

During its centuries-old history, the House of Austria clashed with the Ottoman Empire in eight separate conflicts, but before 1660 the Emperor had faced the *Erbfeind* (hereditary enemy) only in the Long War of 1593–1606. All the clashes were fought on the same territory of Hungary, Croatia and Transylvania. On several occasions the Ottomans threatened Vienna. In 1529 they laid siege to the capital for the first time as well as menacing the provinces, with devastating raids in Austria, Styria, Krain and Moravia. Although the aim to take the Austrian capital failed, the Porte had historically always militarily prevailed: three-quarters of Hungary was ruled by a Turkish *paşa* sent from Constantinople. As a result, the Habsburgs maintained only a narrow strip of territory in the northern area of the Drina and Raab rivers, leaving them dangerously exposed to enemy attacks. Even when modest territorial gains had been achieved, the Sultan had always managed to impose his political conditions on the Emperor. Though the absence of an active Ottoman threat after 1606 had given the Emperor a freer hand during the Thirty Years' War, it also undermined German support for him. The renewed Ottoman advance after 1657 reawakened German fears and permitted Leopold to don the traditional Imperial mantle as defender of Christendom, a task that he not only took seriously, through personal conviction, but one which re-emphasised the pan-European pretensions of his title. However, it seemed that even with divine blessing, victory would prove hard to achieve.

In 1658, the Ottoman army under Grand Vizier Köprülü Mehmed had invaded the princedom, and in July 1660 definitively defeated Rákóczi. The presence of Ottoman troops near the eastern border opened a new dramatic threat. Upper Hungary was dangerously exposed to an easy invasion due to the lack of strong defences after the loss of *Partium*, annexed to Transylvania in 1604 after István Bocskay's rebellion against the Habsburgs.[16] The princedom had gained the important fortresses of Tokay, Kálló and Szatmár (today Satu Mare in Romania). This latter, a newly modernised border fortress, was a crucial hub for the Transtisza region, and had played a special role in the defence system by impeding attacks from the east. Therefore, the risk of these fortresses being occupied by the Ottomans was another reason for Austria's obsessive interest in Transylvania. Due to its geographical position, control of the princedom not only made secure Upper Hungary, but also ensured a military outpost in Moldavia and Wallachia, two states that openly showed their lack of allegiance to the Sultan. Moreover, creating a platform for the Imperial eagle in both provinces provided an opportunity to reaffirm primacy of the House of Austria over the turbulent Reformed Hungarian nobility, and showed the large majority of the population a renewed respect for Catholicism. The consolidation of power through political centralisation and Catholic confessionalisation continued, after Bohemia and Moravia, in Hungary, as Leopold intensified Ferdinand III's efforts to subordinate the still largely Calvinist Hungarian nobility. Moreover the presence of the 'hereditary enemy of Christianity', in such close proximity to Vienna, provided a major reason for the existence of the Hungarian Kingdom and the Habsburg authority within it. From Luther onwards, Protestant and Catholic clerics had propagandised against the Ottomans, reinforcing the stereotypical cliché of them as bloodthirsty infidels who murdered children and enslaved entire populations. In an age where Christian rulers could seriously consider liberating Jerusalem, the Turkish Wars took on the identity of Europe's final crusade.

Although after 1606 Vienna and the Porte maintained peace in Hungary, incursions and looting conducted by fewer than 5,000 men without artillery was not considered a breach of the truce. Reciprocal demonstrative actions and provocations of various kinds took place in 1648, while in 1652 the Hungarian fortresses of Léva (Levice in Slovakia) and Győr had been seriously threatened by the Ottomans. An encounter of considerable proportions had taken place at Nagyverekés, ending with the victory of the Hungarian frontiersmen under Ádám Forgách, against 5,000 Ottomans. Further skirmishing and looting had occurred along the border, without any retaliation from Vienna.[17]

---

16 *Partium* is a term identifying a historical and geographical region in the Kingdom of Hungary during the early modern period. It consisted of the eastern and northern parts of Hungary proper. At times, it included Miskolc, and Kassa (today Košice, Slovakia). When in 1570 János II Zsigmond abdicated as king of Hungary, a new duchy was invented for him: 'Joannes, serenissimi olim Joannis regis Hungariae, Dalmatiae, Croatiae etc. filius, Dei gratia princeps Transsylvaniae ac partium regni Hungarie', from which derives the name *Partium*. Initially, *Partium* consisted of the Transylvanian counties of Máramaros, Közép-Szolnok, Kraszna, and Bihar, as well as the Kővárvidék. In 1604 further Royal Hungarian counties were added, including Szatmár, Kassa, Kálló and Tokay. These territories were ruled by Transylvania, but were not formally part of the princedom.

17 Another violent incursion performed by the Hungarian border commanders occurred on 23–26 January 1657. The raid was conducted by Ferenc Nádasdy and Ádám Batthyány from the county

In 1658, the Ottoman campaign in Transylvania could reopen the duel and therefore it was necessary to hurry to obtain the greatest gains from the new situation. Before being definitively defeated, Rákóczi had asked for help from the Emperor by offering the restitution of *Partium*. In May 1660 Leopold and his councillors evaluated an intervention in Transylvania, but the small Imperial expeditionary corps, after occupying the major strongholds, avoided facing the Ottomans, abandoning Prince Rákóczi to his fate.[18] A new armed confrontation against the Porte had been avoided, despite the president of the Secret Council, Johann Adolph von Schwarzenberg, declaring himself in favour of the war. However, it was unthinkable to leave Transylvania without trying to turn the situation in Austria's own favour. Therefore, new troops marched into Transylvania to support the election of a prince on whom it could rely.

The other influential councillors, Giovanni Ferdinando Portia and Franz Paul von Lisola, recommended prudence or at least facing the Ottomans through those Transylvanians willing to ally with the House of Austria. To have any chance of success against the Ottomans there was an urgent need for a rapid conclusion to the war, an event that the Austrian court considered likely, because since 1645 the sultan was already fighting a war in Crete against Venice. Further east, on the border of the Persian Empire, the risk of a resumption of hostilities with the Safavids could discourage the Ottomans from stepping up the struggle in Transylvania. However, the Porte did not appear intimidated and, unfortunately for Vienna, the sultan opened the conflict with renewed energy. Austrian policy encountered several problems, for as soon as Leopold began his interference in Transylvania, with the intention of curbing Ottoman influence in this strategic principality on his north-eastern frontier, the Emperor sent 15,000 men to support his own candidate as prince in May 1660.

Transylvania turned out to be a more insidious terrain than expected and finally, in 1663, became – with Hungary – the battlefield of the conflict with the Porte. The Ottoman danger, however, was a powerful propaganda argument, which served to regain a position of prestige in the Empire, where the Habsburgs could introduce themselves as the traditional defenders of Christianity. The Ottoman emergence and the news of the Tatar raids in Moravia gained the support of the Diet in the call for a new *Türkenkrieg*. The

---

of Somogy. According to the *Chronicles of Ortelius*, the Hungarian horsemen set out 'to make a try and to make a turn towards Kaposvár castle, then they headed for Mozsgó, 100 kilometres south to Lake Balaton. During the raid they took 150 Serbs into captivity, slaughtered more than 100, burned seven villages and herded away 400 cows, losing only four soldiers...' The Croatian *banus* described in verse the courage of his compatriots, deploring the indifference and immobility of the Austrian ministers, about which he wrote: 'The princes cannot oppose the opinion of 100 advisers more than the gusts of wind they can placate the fury of the sea.' P. Lendvai, *The Hungarians, a Thousand Years of Victory in Defeat* (Princeton NJ: Princeton University Press, 2003), p. 120.

18 In July 1660 the Transylvanian fortress of Várad, defended by the town militia and just 850 mercenaries under György II Rákóczi, held out for 45 days against an enemy force of 50,000 men. The Ottoman siege took place in relative safety, however the Imperial corps, camped a few miles away, made no attempt to relieve the besieged garrison.

alliance was also extended to Louis XIV, who contributed a corps of 6,000 infantrymen and horsemen.[19]

The victory at Szentgotthárd in September 1664 brought peace to the borders, but the terms of Vasvár's armistice, signed in the aftermath of the battle, deeply disappointed the Hungarians. The controversy, fuelled by French diplomacy, did not subside until it resulted in open rebellion in the years following, when the Hungarian magnates, alongside the Palatine of the kingdom Ferenc Wesselényi, orchestrated a secession from Habsburg rule. According to their position, the Hungarians had determined the appointment of Leopold I as King of Hungary and not the dynastic right, excluded by the Hungarian law. The Emperor, according to Wesselényi and his followers, having granted unfavourable conditions of peace for the kingdom, moreover accompanied by a donation of 200,000 florins, had broken the pact with the nation and therefore was deposed from the Royal charge. The Vasvár Treaty had a devastating effect on the morale of the Hungarian elite. There can be no doubt about their disillusionment with the Habsburgs and the role this disillusionment played in convincing many Hungarian nobles to join the rebels' side.[20]

The conspirators tried to obtain external political support, and the Porte was the first option. They demanded the sultan assume the role of protector of Hungarian religious freedom. Contacts between Hungarian Protestants and Ottoman emissaries had not gone unnoticed in Vienna.[21] This was a

---

19 Louis XIV participated in the war in Hungary as a member of the *Deutsche Allianz* rather than as a full belligerent, allowing him to honour his credentials as 'Most Christian King', but without formally breaking his good relations with the Porte. In doing so, he publicly humiliated Leopold I, who was seen as dependent on French help. See in J. Wolf, *Louis XIV* (New York: W.W. Norton & Company, 1974), p. 187.

20 One interesting and fascinating historical document was discovered in the 1890s by Gyula Pauler in the Hungarian National Archives but has not yet received a careful historical analysis. This document provides an important key to understanding why so many members of the Hungarian elite were willing to secede from the Habsburg to the Ottoman Empire. Signed by the Palatine Count Ferenc Wesselényi, the document is dated 27 August 1666, almost exactly two years after the signing of the Vasvár Treaty. It contains detailed instructions to an emissary who was to negotiate the secession of all of Royal Hungary to the Ottoman Empire. It bears the title *Instructio, mely szerént kell procedálni az portán levő követnek* (Instruction according to which the emissary has to proceed at the Porte). Unfortunately, we know almost nothing about the actual negotiations, but later testimonies by participants suggest that the meetings were dominated by Hungary's most important Protestant leaders. However, religion does not seem the only explanation for the conspiracy, because the Palatine Wesselényi was a Roman Catholic. The *Instructio* has survived in the archive of Mihály Teleki, one of Transylvania's principal Calvinist leaders, in a collection of letters by Hungarian Protestant exiles who fled to Transylvania and Ottoman-held territory after the Habsburg court's discovery of Wesselényi's conspiracy. See in G.B. Michels, 'Ready to Secede to the Ottoman Empire: Habsburg Hungary after the Vasvár Peace Treaty (1664–1674)', in *AHEA: E-Journal of the American Hungarian Educators Association*, volume 5 (2012).

21 *Ibidem*. On January 1670, Count Petar Zrínyi met the Ottoman emissaries promising an annual tribute of 60,000 *goldthalers* in exchange for the Porte's military aid in Hungary. Vienna had informants inside the group of nobles, and had heard from several sources of their wide-ranging and almost desperate attempts to gain foreign and domestic aid. However, no action was taken because the conspirators had attracted liittle support and were bound by inaction. At first, Emperor Leopold I seems to have considered the rebels' actions as only half-hearted schemes that were never truly serious.

AUSTRIA ERIT IN ORBE ULTIMA

matter of urgency for the Emperor's most intolerant counsellors, who were convinced that there would be no order in Hungary until Imperial soldiers were placed in the Hungarian towns.

As a result of these aggressive policy, the rebels' party had grown in Upper Hungary. The conspirators planned a number of plots that they never followed through, including the kidnapping of Emperor Leopold. Though the prospect of actual success seemed low, new rumours and evidences revealed the existence of a wide net of conspiracy, forcing the Habsburg court to arrest the leading rebel nobles. Soon the spiral of events became a battle without mercy, marked by fierce repressions that hit the confessional freedoms of the kingdom with extreme harshness. Thousands of people were arrested or deported. Many of the lesser nobles and the Protestant clergy had had no part in the events, but Leopold aimed to prevent similar revolts in the future. Protestant churches were burned to the ground in a show of force against any uprisings. Persecution was also inflicted on Hungarian and Croatian commoners, as Habsburg soldiers moved in and secured the region. News regarding Protestant clergymen convicted and sent to the oars on the Maltese galleys spread through the European courts, causing indignant reaction and request for clarification from William III of Orange, Leopold's ally in the war against France.[22] Leopold I ordered all Hungarian laws suspended, in retaliation for the conspiracy: the gesture caused an end to the self-government which Royal Hungary had nominally been granted, a situation which remained unchanged for the following 10 years. In 1673, the Hungarian council of vice-regency was disbanded and the Palatine's power strongly diminished, while in Croatia, where Petar Zrínyi had participated in the conspiracy, there would not be any new *banus* of Croatian origin for the next 60 years.

The execution of the Hungarian magnates in 1671, in a contemporary print. The picture shows interesting details concerning the dress and equipment of the Imperial infantry in this age. Note on the left, the NCO wearing a coat with plain cuffs and pockets without flaps. (Author's collection).

The most important means for imposing these changes were the army, the huge state tax obligations, and the unbridled Reformation. The court's steps were, however, so fully characterised by sheer vengeance that it could not counterbalance its unpopular measures with any constructive programme or internal reform. The crude steps taken by Habsburg absolutism created a revival of the Hungarian Estates even after the unsuccessful 1670 uprising. As early as 1672, armed resistance re-emerged, starting in Transylvania and the frontier regions of the Ottoman-occupied territories. In the next decade, Hungary would become the centre of gravity of Viennese policy, consuming

---

22 Great indignation spread through northern Europe, when Dutch admiral Michiel de Ruyter noticed hundreds of Hungarian Reformed clergymen convicted on the Spanish galleys in Naples. On 11 February 1676 the Dutch Admiral secured the release of the convicted men, sending his marines on to the galleys and freeing them, and they were taken back to Amsterdam. See in A. Wheatcroft, *The Enemy at the Gate. Habsburgs, Ottomans and the Battle for Europe* (Basic Books: New York NY, 2009), p. 108.

considerable resources and men, and even conditioning the Habsburgs' effort in the war against France of 1673–79. Although there were councillors who tried to agree a truce and opening negotiations, Leopold's uncompromising attitude towards Hungary continued, without realising the depth of the ditch excavated between the monarchy and his subjects.[23]

The Hungarian question remained one of the most delicate political arguments even in the 1680s, when the Ottoman threat came back strongly in current affairs, involving factions at court for a solution in the crucial months before 1683. These 'parties' had already assumed a distinct profile in the previous decade. The 'Spanish party' opposed the so-called 'German party', in which the exponents of a policy of agreement with France also militated, although they did not state their position openly. The first party appeared as the most hostile to France and eager to keep the Austrian Habsburgs close to Spanish interests in the Low Countries. The 'German party', on the contrary, was most favourable to an agreement with France in order to have a free hand in Hungary. In a waiting position and subordinated to events, there was also a 'Papal' faction that supported alternatively one or other of the parties. The official position of this latter can be summarised in two points: the re-Catholicisation of Hungary and the war against the Porte. Regarding the first point there was the unconditional support of the powerful Jesuitical order and the primate of Hungary, the resolute Cardinal Leopold Carl von Kollonics.[24] The rise to the papal throne of Innocent XI in 1676 made any possibility of compromise much more difficult. This Pope believed in the absolute priority of the Eastern question over the Western one. For him the treaties of Nijmegen were only the instrument to reach this end, and in his view it represented the stubborn refusal of the Habsburgs to accept the further territorial demands of Louis XIV after 1679.

Definitively, it was a very complicated game. Most of the Emperor's advisers and collaborators avoided as much as possible to expose themselves openly, preferring each time to choose to support one position at a time, avoiding siding with one of the parties present at court. Moreover the 'parties', rather than embodying themselves in a personality or in a sector of the court, were the fluid and changeable result of a multiplicity of tendencies. Leopold I was always sensitive to the reasoning of the Spanish party, also because he wished to reaffirm his inheritance rights to Madrid's throne and was also

---

23 F. Cardini, *Il Turco a Vienna. Storia del grande assedio del 1683* (Bari: Laterza, 2011), p.191: 'It would be simplistic to think of this movement as intended solely for the defence and recovery of religious freedoms. In reality, at its base there was also the strong opposition to the Germanization of Hungary and its partisans, indicated with the term *labanc*, and the proud claim of traditional *libertates*, which expressed itself also in the fierce customs and the impatient attitude to the limits insubordination.'

24 Leopold Karl von Kollonics (1631–1707), was a cardinal of the Holy Roman Church, Archbishop of Kalocsa and later of Esztergom, and Primate of Hungary. Also a count of the Holy Roman Empire, he was a leading figure of the Hungarian counter-reformation. As an imperial minister, Kollonics was responsible for reorganising the new Hungarian territories conquered from the Ottoman Empire after the Treaty of Karlowitz. He was said to have gained over 100,000 converts to Rome.

convinced, as the adherents of that party claimed, that a de facto alliance existed between Constantinople and Versailles.[25]

Therefore, there was a fair diversity of opinion about the measures to be taken against the Hungarians. The supporters of the soft line, even if hesitating, justified themselves firstly with the fear that a contrary choice could weld even more the rebels to alliance with the Porte, and secondly with the prospect that a submissive but stable solution of the conflict with the Hungarian 'malcontents' would have allowed the transfer of soldiers and resources to face French expansionism. Moreover, the most determined exponents of the Spanish party supported, in good or bad faith, that there was an overestimation of the Ottoman threat. Although apparently there was an agreement on the severe judgement against France, many at court were sure that the Porte would renew the truce of Vasvár signed in 1664. The Spanish party was headed by Madrid's ambassador himself, Carlo Emanuele d'Este-Borgomanero, who arrived in Vienna in 1681, and enjoyed the authoritative support of the ousted Charles V of Lorraine, who was – not wrongly – feeling damaged by the politics of the French 'Chambers of Reunion' and that he had become the commander-in-chief of the Emperor's army after the death of Montecuccoli. Against Borgomanero acted Girolamo Buonvisi, cardinal and Papal nuncio in Vienna, who exhorted Leopold I to adopt a detente policy towards France, and the result was a bitter court struggle that lasted until 1683.[26]

Leopold had been caught at a disadvantage in the winter of 1678–79, as the peace settlement with France signed at Nijmegen coincided with an escalation of the Hungarian revolt and the outbreaks of both a serious peasant rising in Bohemia and plague in Vienna. The last war against France had demonstrated that he could expect little from Spain, while attempts to continue co-operation with the Dutch Republic broke down after the fruitless negotiations of 1680–81. Diplomatic isolation was paralleled by dwindling support in the Empire, where it was obvious that Leopold could neither protect his traditional supporters nor satisfy the growing demands of the major princes. Any solution to either the 'Réunion crisis'[27] or defence

---

25 The political convergences between France and the Ottoman Empire against the Habsburgs are evident, and it is equally evident that Louis XIV pursued this 'alliance' by considerations of convenience. 'French diplomacy pushed the Porte to the war against the Emperor to have free hand to the West. If an agreement favourable to him was found for the Rhine's area and the Spanish Low Countries, Louis XIV would certainly have stopped his support to the Hungarian insurgents and put an end to the accusations of who described him as a friend of the heretics and Muslims, reassumed in the epithet that identified the Sun King with the "Turk of Versailles".' Cardini, *Il Turco a Vienna*, p. 180.

26 It did not go unnoticed by contemporary Austrian commentators that the main actors of this political conflict were Italians. Cardinal Buonvisi and the Pope were also the weavers of the relationship with Poland and Jan III Sobiesky, and therefore opposed to Charles of Lorraine, who in 1674 had applied for election to the Polish throne. See in Stoye, *The Siege of Vienna*, pp. 52–53. It is worthy of mention that in 1686, Cardinal Buonvisi was appointed by Leopold I as a member of the Aulic War Council. See in R. Gueze, 'La Liberazione dell'Ungheria dal Turco', p. 46.

27 Between autumn 1679 and summer 1684, France used a mixture of real and invented claims, backed by the threat of renewed war, to extend its eastern and northern frontiers. Operating through the *Parlements* (regional supreme courts) of Metz and newly-acquired Besançon,

reform had to be linked to his attempts to rebuild Habsburg influence in Germany. As outlined by some scholars: 'for this reason it is necessary to reject the traditional interpretation of this period as a Habsburg sell-out of German interests, culminating in the Truce of Regensburg with France in August 1684, whereby Leopold recognised the validity of the French requests and pursued a war of conquest against the Ottomans instead.'[28] Far from abandoning the Empire, the Habsburg geostrategy was preoccupied with restoring and upholding its integrity, recognising the importance of this to Imperial recovery for Leopold I and turning eastwards only with reluctance, when this became unavoidable with the Ottoman attack on Vienna in 1683.

The *Reich*

As rightly mentioned by Peter Wilson, in the mid 17th century the Holy Roman-German Empire – the *Reich* – was considered a 'monstrosity'.[29] The difficulties of government action and the complexity of the political mechanisms that regulated the internal balance of the Empire aroused criticism from contemporary commentators who condemned it as an anachronistic institution.

After 1648, the Empire ceased to be a unitary organism. Although French politics had not prevailed to grant full sovereignty to the princes of Germany, the scenario had changed little. To the princes was granted the right to make alliances with each other and with foreign powers, but this was a right that they had been carrying out for a long time; and if they were forbidden to conclude alliances against the Emperor or against the Empire, the prohibition could be interpreted differently. Therefore, it is not surprising that the political writers of those years could not give a univocal definition of the *Reich*, and some jurists negated even the Emperor's authority over it.[30] However, for other commentators all this appeared as a prodigy. Prodigious was the fact that, despite the rivalries and tensions between the states, the frontiers established in 1648 did not undergo significant changes for more than a century.

The borders between the religions were even more stable, and rare were the cases in which the local authorities exercised the right to expel subjects who professed a religion different from their prince. After all, the war had deprived many lands of inhabitants, and the workforce was a not negligible resource. Most Germans lived in small communities governed by

---

as well as special *Chambres de Réunion*, French lawyers reinterpreted the peace treaties of 1648 and 1678–9 to 'reunite' additional areas as alleged dependencies of the recent gains. Simultaneously a diplomatic offensive was launched to secure German and international recognition of the additional areas as permanent acquisitions and to sound out the possible candidacy of the Dauphin as king of the Romans.

28 P. Wilson, *German Armies*, p. 60.
29 The quotation belongs to the German philosopher Samuel von Pufendorf, who in 1667 famously described the *Reich* as 'Irregulare aliquod corpus et monstro simile' (An irregular as well as a monstrous body). *Die Verfassung des deutschen Reiches* (1667), p. 12.
30 *The Cambridge Modern History*, vol. V, p. 552.

the heads of the richer well-established families, who normally controlled the election or appointment of the village council and law court, except in eastern Germany, where the nobility had greater influence over these affairs. Though territorial rulers were trying to bring these positions under their control by integrating them into their own administrative infrastructure, most communities retained considerable autonomy over their own affairs until well into the 19th century. Even where peasants were not tied directly to the nobles as serfs, like those in parts of northern and eastern Germany, they were usually still bound by other feudal obligations in varying degrees of dependency and servitude.

Several historians point out that despite such a critical situation, the institutions of the Empire continued to exist. Apart from the divisions fuelled by French diplomacy, the unity of the Empire was preserved and the *Reichstag* (the Imperial Diet) continued to operate as it did prior to the Thirty Years' War. Ultimately, the threat posed to the west by French expansionism and the resumption of the Ottoman offensive from the south helped to strengthen the cohesion between the states. Some historians rightly point out that it was not only the Rhenish states that coalesced against France – indeed, Louis XIV initially found among them many more or less sincere allies – and it was not only the states of south-eastern Germany who fought against the Ottomans. This should make us realise how miraculous the Habsburgs' political success was, in preserving unity despite many dividing factors.

Originally, the *Reich* was divided into two kingdoms: the German kingdom and the Italian or Lombard kingdom. This division represented a purely formal concept, since, at the end of the 17th century, Imperial authority in northern Italy was almost non-existent and the predominant influence in those regions came from the Habsburgs of Spain, who ruled the state of Milan. The 'Germanic Kingdom' included roughly the current borders of Germany and Austria, Bohemia and Moravia, Belgium with Luxembourg, Franche-Comte, Savoy, a part of Alsace and Lorraine. This territory had an area of 701,085.37 square kilometres and an estimated population of 17–18,000,000 inhabitants in 1650.

Each prince's power depended on his position within the *Reich* and it was determined by a combination of his formal status and material resources. The first distinction was between the princes relating to their territorial immediacy, namely those allowed the right to vote within the *Reichstag*, and those who lacked this quality. In other words, some princes and free cities were vassals subordinate directly to the Emperor, while others had an intermediate link with him and were considered as simple sub-vassals.[31]

All the 'immediate' states of the Empire were represented in the Diet, which met in Regensburg in 1663 and was divided into three separate colleges: that of the electors, that of the princes and that of the Imperial cities. The importance of the qualification of electoral princes resided in their specific qualification, namely the election of the emperors. For almost three

---

31 The two ranks were distinguished by the German terms *Unmittelbarkeit* (immediability) and *Mittelbarkeit* (mediability). For instance the Duke of Pfalz-Neuburg was a *Unmittelbar* prince, while Count Jörger zu Tollett was a simple *Mittelbar* lord.

centuries, the Habsburgs had always managed to confirm their candidates, but their re-election had not always been so obvious. The main office of the Imperial government was the Diet, composed of three chambers, or *collegium*. The first branch was the electoral one, which comprised the ruling princes in charge of the election of the Emperor. In 1648 there were eight, but the elector of Bohemia – the Habsburg prince – did not exercise his prerogative in the Emperor's election. The electors divided themselves into two branches: ecclesiasal and secular. The three religious electorates – Mainz, Cologne, Trier – were ruled by prince-archbishops elected by their cathedral chapter, which was dominated by aristocratic canons who controlled considerable wealth, within and outside the territory, as well as many of the chief offices of state.

The other group of electors consisted of the princes of Brandenburg, Saxony, the Palatinate and Bavaria. The secular electors were also the sovereigns of the major states of Germany, while the territorial extension of the prince-archbishops' domains was less, but their political importance remained considerable. The electors conducted the affairs of the Empire when the throne remained vacant: in this case, the Mainz elector held the office of arch-chancellor for Germany.[32] The elector of Cologne was the arch-chancellor for Italy, and Trier managed the same for 'Gallia and the kingdom of Arles', but these last two offices were purely symbolic. The elector of Mainz also held the office of president of the *Corpus Catholicorum*, in charge of all matters concerning religion, while the elector of Saxony was entitled to the presidency of the *Corpus Evangelicorum*.

The second *collegium* was the princes' chamber, the *Fürstentümer*, also divided into an ecclesial and secular branch. In 1660, this chamber comprised 63 ecclesial and 234 secular members or 'benches'. All princely estates enjoyed the privilege of independent status, but those of the *Reichsgrafen*, Counts of Empire and *Reichsprälaten* were slow to gain representation at national level. The counts and prelates failed to secure parity with their more illustrious neighbours and had to accept limited representation in six benches, each sharing a single collective vote in the *Fürstenrat*, or Council of Princes. About 21 of the princely territories were ruled by prince-bishops and prince-archbishops, similarly chosen by local chapters among the most important aristocratic families of Germany, while two of the collective votes were shared by 42 prelates who included a few abbesses, the only women to hold formal political power in the *Reich*. Among the ecclesial princes were also the Grand Masters of the Teutonic Order and of the Knights of Malta.

Together all these territories comprised the Imperial church – the *Reichskirche* – solidly Catholic with the exception, after 1648, of the prince-bishop of Osnabrück, and closely associated with the Emperor's traditional pan-European pretensions as the secular defender of Christendom. Rule over the secular electorates, principalities and counties was decided by hereditary succession and the prevailing laws of inheritance, which permitted their accumulation and partition subject to formal Imperial approval.

---

32 In this case, the Elector of Mainz had to call for the Diet and reunite the electors within three months of the emperor's death.

Consequently, it was possible for a ruler to exercise different forms of power depending on the combination of lands he had inherited.[33]

The third chamber was formed by the 51 Free Imperial cities, the *Reichsstädte*, 13 Catholic, 34 Reformed and four mixed. In comparison, the urban population – accounting for about a fifth in 1650[34] – was often comparatively privileged, as most major towns were entitled to send one or two members of their council to sit in the local assemblies alongside the clergy and nobility. However, this latter chamber carried a minor political weight, and eventually gained individual voting rights in 1648, but had to accept these within a third, subordinate college of their own. Apart from Hamburg, Frankfurt and Nurnberg, which continued to progress in economic and political status, the majority of the Free Imperial cities suffered greatly after 1648. After the cession of the Alsatian cities to France, the threat of losing independence became serious. Mostly these cities were small and unable to cope with the surrounding principalities. Even the largest, such as Augsburg, Ulm, Regensburg in the south, and Cologne, Aachen, Bremen and Lübeck to the north-west, were unable to adapt to the changed situation, and the decline in trade and the Dutch competition were severely undermining their economy. Unlike the principalities, the free Imperial cities continued to function as autonomous civic republics under their own magistrates, and also secured access to national politics after the Treaty of Westphalia. However, the loss of power continued, and in 1653 the Diet gave them the right to vote only after an agreement was reached by the first two chambers. Finally, the 350 or so families of Imperial knights – *Reichsritter* – along with a few others failed to gain any representation at all and remained under direct Imperial overlordship. The colleges of electors and princes were called *superiores*, to distinguish them from the college of the free cities, which in turn was divided into the Rhenish and Swabian branch. The deliberations of the Diet had to be approved by all three colleges.

The Thirty Years' War had been an actual turning point for the history of the Empire. To avoid reciprocal involvement in future crises, the potential union of the two Habsburg branches ruling the Austrian and Spanish monarchies was inhibited by the Westphalian peace settlement that divided them into two parts. The *Instrumentum pacis Osnabrugense*, or Treaty of Osnabrück, secured peace for the *Reich* east of the River Rhine, while the *Instrumentum pacis Monasteriense*, the Treaty of Münster, partially resolved the western European conflict, and included recognition of Dutch independence from Spain. Though their formal influences were limited, the presence of France and Sweden as external guarantors of the Osnabrück treaty marked the internationalisation of Imperial politics, which was to grow as the years

---

33 Princes, especially secular electors like Brandenburg, Bavaria and Saxony, often held several pieces of land qualifying for full votes along with shares in collective ones derived from possession of relevant counties, and they could also inherit or purchase property belonging to the Imperial knights or within the jurisdiction of other rulers. Feudal ties were an imperfect match for this complex web of rights and privileges so that while most territories constituted separate Imperial fiefs, held by their rulers as vassals of the emperor, others were dependencies of secular or ecclesiastical princes. See in Wilson, *German Armies*, p. 12.

34 *Ibidem*, p. 9.

progressed.[35] Already Denmark had substantial territory in Germany, entitling it to a formal presence in the Empire, while the Dutch retained garrisons in a number of Westphalian and Rhenish towns occupied during the war. The implementation of the peace treaty did secure the withdrawal of Swedish and French troops by 1650 but had serious repercussions for the Habsburg domains west of the Rhine, which had been excluded from the Münster's agreement on the grounds that it consisted nearly entirely of Spanish territory. The Austrian Habsburgs were forbidden to use their hold on the Imperial title to facilitate German assistance to Spain, which remained at war with France, reinforcing the general intention that the *Reich* was to remain non-aligned with regard to its great power relations. On the other hand, the main aim of the Westphalia Treaty was to avoid other devastating wars within the Empire's territory.

The internal structure of the *Reich* evolved to this end, with the emphasis being on peaceful, diplomatic resolutions and defensive cooperation. Collective security had emerged already as a major issue from the early 16th century. The mechanisms developed to mobilise territorial resources for internal peacekeeping, and peace-enforcement were adapted to provide defence against external threats, whilst denying the Emperor the opportunity to exploit them for his own offensive operations. Prohibitions to this effect were written into the electoral agreements – the *Wahlkapitulationen* – containing concessions wrung from each new Emperor by the electors, whilst the Treaty of Osnabrück imposed additional restrictions obliging him to seek *Reichstag* approval, before sanctioning a full Imperial war effort in the so-called *Reichskrieg*.

Historians underline that the need for money to defend the *Reich* against the Porte was the primary reason why the Habsburg emperors convened the *Reichstag* to back up their demands relating to *Reichstürkensteuer,* the Imperial Turkish tax. The subventions for the defences from the 'Ottoman scourge' were the subject of the usual haggling and wrangling in the Diets and in the *Kreise*: the Circles of the Empire. The *Kreise* had been established at the Cologne Diet of 1521 for military purpose, dividing the Empire's territories into initially six, and then into 10 regions, to maintain the public peace and resolve common problems. They were: Austria and Bohemia, Franconia, Swabia, Bourgogne, Bavaria, Lower Rhine-Westphalia, Upper Rhine, Rhine-Electoral, Lower Saxony, Upper Saxony.

After 1648, the Austrian Habsburgs enjoyed considerable advantages within this structure. Initially the circles had been established on condition that hereditary lands were grouped into their own distinct *Kreis*. The Habsburgs could later extend this repartition to include the enclaves in south-western Germany and the Breisgau region on the Rhine. The few other princes included within the Austrian *Kreis* had been reduced to the status of the lesser Habsburg territorial nobility by 1648, except for the bishops of

---

35 In addition to foreign interference in Imperial affairs, Habsburg and Hohenzollern (Brandenburg) possessions outside the formal *Reich* boundaries extended German interests into other parts of Europe; a factor that was to increase with the involvement of other dynasties in international affairs.

Trent and Brixen and the archdukes of Habsburg Tyrol, who maintained an independent institutional identity alone, the latter until 1668. Nonetheless, the formal existence of the Austrian *Kreis* was preserved as a useful construct to influence Imperial politics, without having to intervene directly in the role of Emperor. The Habsburgs also controlled the Burgundian *Kreis,* although this passed to the Spanish line when Charles V partitioned his possessions in 1556. Indirect rule from Madrid merely widened the separation of these areas from the rest of the *Reich,* already underway during Charles V's reign, and reflected in their exclusion from the jurisdiction of the Imperial courts, in favour of subordination to a separate institution.

The circles established the military geography of the Empire for the future. In fact, the circles had been formed to facilitate the setting up of the army, in accordance with the maintenance of internal peace. The circle structure reproduced, and thereby reinforced, the basic constitutional equilibrium, illuminating both the strengths and weaknesses of national politics.[36]

Given its complexity and the large number of representatives, the Imperial diet was conditioned to carry out its activity through a slow and complicated series of formal acts. In the mid 80s, the English diplomat Sir George Etherege wrote that diet deputies met only by formality and had no argument to discuss until the two major colleges had agreed.[37] The diplomat had little esteem of his German colleagues, especially when he complained of the coldness and privacy of German ladies, with whom it was impossible to enjoy an adventure, however he was not the only one to criticise the machinosity and the slowness of the diet. Every question, even those of minor importance, were the subject of long discussions and finally published in the form of a *Rezess* (agreement), and the meetings continued because the representatives of the sovereigns took no decision without having waited for their prince's opinion. Sir George again informed his readers with bitter sentences: 'Those who are not used to the work of this assembly [the Diet] will wonder why so many ministers are so lavishly paid by their lords, although so little work is done and that little so slowly.'[38]

If to foreign observers the work of the Diet appeared incomprehensible, others understood very well how these were managed by the princes to obtain an ever greater autonomy. The major dispute in this matter regarded the taxation. The tax was collected through a system that reflected the divided, corporate nature of the Holy Roman Empire. Though the local territorial powers recognised the need for a common purse to protect and preserve the Empire, they were simultaneously unwilling to surrender power to the Emperor. In 1653, the Diet approved the proposal of the Elector of Brandenburg with which it was established that the granting of any credit had to be approved unanimously. Emperor Ferdinand III was forced to renounce the project of making minorities also binding the decisions taken

---

36 Wilson, *German Armies*, p. 17.
37 'The deputies are forced to conform to this situation, since the principle that no college could be defeated by the joint vote of the other two.' Sybil Rosenfeld, *The Letterbook of Sir George Etherege* (London, 1928), pp. 61.
38 *Ibidem*, p. 328.

by the minority in tax matters. The aftermath was a further dilatation of the Diet's work with exhausting debate for an agreement.

One year later the electors preached another important point in their favour with the approval of paragraph 180 to the *Rezess* licensed at the end of the Diet of that year. The act established that the subjects of every state of the Empire were obliged to provide their sovereigns with the necessary means for the maintenance of fortresses and strongholds complete with garrisons. This measure modified the military policy of the *Reich*, which until then had been based on the cooperation of all immediate states to the financing of a common armed force through the payment of the *Römer-monat* (Roman month).[39] The provision affected the prerogative of the local estates, which in many states exercised the control of taxation, and a further step in the same direction was made after the death of Ferdinand III in April 1657.

In fact, at that time the election of the Habsburg candidate to the Imperial throne did not appear so obvious. The existence of a number of other candidates and the opposition of French cardinal Mazarin, Charles X of Sweden, and Cromwell to another Habsburg emperor, represented realistic threats for Leopold's election. Mazarin first pushed for the young prince-elector Ferdinand Maria of Bavaria, who declined immediately. Then he turned to the late Emperor's brother Archduke Leopold Wilhelm, until 1656 governor of the Spanish Low Countries, and Archduke Ferdinand of Tyrol: an older candidate would at least offer the prospect of a further election in the not too distant future, before which it might even be possible to prepare the way for the election of Louis XIV himself. The Elector of Bavaria realised that he did not have either the resources or the power to become emperor; Duke Philipp Wilhelm of Pfalz-Neuburg was even less qualified in those respects, and he was in any case unacceptable to Brandenburg owing to the dispute over the Jülich-Cleve inheritance. Almost from the outset, Johann Philipp von Schönborn, Archbishop and prince elector of Mainz, was convinced that Leopold was the inevitable choice. He soon also gained the Bavarian vote, but to convince the rest of the electors was necessary to grant some ample concessions. Frederick William of Brandenburg (The Great Elector) demanded the prohibition for the estates to meet without summoning the sovereign and to appeal against him to the Imperial courts. Initially the demands of the elector of Brandenburg did not find the support of all the electors. The Palatinate, Saxony and Trier declared that they wanted to maintain the status quo and Saxony in particular opposed the ban on appealing to the courts. The elector of Saxony was in fact the only one, together with Mainz, Palatinate and Bavaria, to have obtained the privilege that placed them outside the jurisdiction of the Imperial courts – the *privilegium de non appellando* – while among the Hohenzollern domains this right was in force only for Brandenburg. However, if he wanted to be

---

39 The *Römer-monat* was the basic unit of Imperial taxation in the *Reich*, initially worth around 128,000 Rhenish *guilder* when the underlying tax was created in 1521 by Emperor Charles V, equivalent to a month's wages for around 4,202 cavalry and 20,063 infantrymen. It gained this title due to its initial purpose of providing for one month's escort for the emperor's trip to Rome to be crowned by the Pope, though it was rarely, if ever, used for this purpose.

elected emperor, Leopold had to accept the conditions of the electors. It was therefore agreed that the estates did not have the right to refuse payment of contributions for military expenses relating to fortresses and garrisons, nor to meet without being summoned by the sovereign, nor even to independently use the revenue from local taxes. All the appeals in this sense would have been rejected and any privilege contrary to these resolutions would have been annulled, just as all the alliances or unions between the estates had to be abolished. After obtaining these concessions, the princes elected Leopold unanimously.

However, it is incorrect to think that the young Leopold I was at the mercy of the prince-electors. Since the early phase of his reign, he exploited some political results and even more significant was the early progress made in relation to the succession and the managing of the Reichstag. Leopold was helped by the conflict that resurfaced after the war between the electors and the princes. The former were bent on reasserting their pre-eminent position; many of the latter wanted 'parification', a cancellation of the electors' prerogatives that would have paved the way to a truly federal system in the Empire. The core of the opposition was a group of Protestant princes, such as Hessen-Kassel, the Brunswick dukes and Württemberg, with some Catholic support, especially from Pfalz-Neuburg. They objected to the pre-eminence of the electors, the majority of whom were Catholics, the elector of Mainz's position as director of the *Reichstag*, and to the fact that the directorate of the College of Princes at the Diet was held by Austria and Salzburg, all of which, they believed, reinforced the Catholics in the key places of the Empire.[40] The most radical opposition princes, encouraged by France, envisaged banning elections while the reigning emperor was still alive (elections *vivente imperatore*), which would have resulted in truly open contests without being influenced by a reigning emperor.[41] Furthermore, they argued that since the electoral capitulation was essentially a law of the Empire, it should be formulated and agreed by the Diet as a whole. The ultimate implication of their arguments was that all princes should participate in Imperial elections. Now, this scenario shifted the interests of the electors to the side of the emperor.

Equally significant was the resolution of the matter of debts incurred during the war. By 1648, almost all Imperial cities and many of the states were bankrupt. The case of the Palatinate, whose debts were catastrophic, was referred to the *Reichshofrat* (the council of finance for the Empire) and thus to the Emperor, who granted a moratorium of 10 years followed by a 50 percent reduction of interest payments for a further 10 years after that. These arrangements represented a principle, and in the following

---

40 'Not unreasonably, they argued that this bias was incompatible with the principle of confessional parity laid down by the peace treaties. Their aim, of course, was not just to extend the parity principle but also to enhance their own status and power in a reformed Reich that would become a true federation of equals. That fundamental tension promised disagreement on many of the most important constitutional issues that the peace treaties had referred to a forthcoming Reichstag.' J. Whaley, *Germany and the Holy Roman Empire. From the Peace of Westphalia to the Dissolution of the Reich, 1648–1806* (Oxford: Oxford University Press, 2012), p. 18.

41 *Ibidem*, p. 19.

year the states frequently manipulated and abused the matter. Like his father Ferdinand III, Leopold I successfully defended his own dynastic interests. He parried all efforts by Brandenburg and others princes to raise the question of the plight of the Protestants in his own hereditary lands. He thereby reaffirmed their exemption from the legislation of the *Reich* and hastened the process of re-Catholicisation there. He also retained all seigneurial and property rights in Upper and Lower Swabia, a significant vehicle of Habsburg influence in the region.

The election of Leopold as Holy Roman-German Emperor was countered by a political event unfavourable for the Habsburgs. The interests of Mazarin and the Rhenish electors were always well matched, and reached their most perfect expression in the formation in 1658 of the *Rheinbund*, or Rhenish Alliance, which was dedicated to collective security and Imperial reform. The immediate impulse for its formation was the interregnum after the death of Ferdinand III, and the main actor was the Mainz elector Prince-archbishop Johann Philipp von Schönborn. The league was formed by Mainz, Cologne, Pfalz-Neuburg, Hessen-Kassel, Brunswick-Lüneburg, and Sweden (in respect of Bremen and Verden); France was also invited to join the alliance as a 'protector'. By 1665, all the leading princes except the electors of Bavaria, Brandenburg, Saxony, and the Palatinate were members. Schönborn thus succeeded in combining both Catholics and Protestants in a union dedicated to upholding the Peace of Westphalia. To this end, members contributed money or troops to a peacekeeping force of 10,000, including 2,400 French soldiers, that was also intended to block any attempt to send Imperial troops to the Low Countries in support of Spain.

Despite the formation of leagues and the inclusion of northern princes in the Rhenish Alliance, the situation in the north of Germany became much less secure. This was largely because of the presence of Sweden as a new territorial power in the Empire. Neither Saxony nor Brandenburg evinced much enthusiasm for the Swedish presence in Verden and Bremen. The dynastic ambitions of the Guelf dukes of Brunswick with regard to the archbishopric of Bremen were also frustrated by Swedish possession. The Dukes of Mecklenburg resented the loss of Wismar and of their control of Warnemünde and its customs tolls, as well as the Swedes' efforts to take more than the Treaty of Westphalia had actually granted. In general, Sweden's possession of territory in each of the northern circles (the Lower Saxon, Upper Saxon, and Westphalian circle), with a share in the executive of the Lower Saxon *Kreistag*, gave her an influence that Stockholm exploited ruthlessly. The Swedes avoided open confrontation with any of the major territories. In 1653, however, they have launched an armed offensive against the Imperial City of Bremen in an attempt to revive the ancient rights of the archbishopric over the city. The crisis was resolved by December 1654 with a compromise, after the immediate support of the Brunswick dukes and the Emperor. Sweden's reputation in the *Reich* was badly dented, because thanks to the compromise the city could retain its immediate status in return for rendering a rather vague act of homage to the Swedish crown. A more dangerous situation soon developed as a consequence of the aggressive policies pursued by Charles X, the former *Pfalzgraf* of Pfalz-Zweibrücken-Kleeburg, who succeeded to the

Swedish crown on Queen Christina's abdication in July 1654. The Swedish decision to attack Poland in 1655 was prompted by the welcome crisis caused by the Muscovite invasion of Lithuania in 1654. The start of the Thirteen Years' War between Russia and Poland (1654–67) led directly to the outbreak of the Second Northern War between Sweden and Poland (1655–60), known also as 'the deluge'. Charles X ensured the alliance of the Prince of Transylvania, but he neglected several obvious consequences. The conflict inevitably would have threatened the Brandenburg Duchy of East Prussia, which the elector held as a fief of the Polish crown. After a series of extraordinary victories, the Swedes found themselves trapped in the 'Polish swamp'. In 1656, the war involved Denmark, while the Dutch Republic sent a war fleet to protect the semi-autonomous port of Danzig threatening to disrupt Sweden's maritime lines of communication. After the Austrian abandonment of the neutrality, Brandenburg too intervened against Sweden with army and diplomacy. Brandenburg and Austrian propaganda was primarily directed at the courts and chancelleries of the German princes and at educated and informed opinion in the German territories and their foreign neighbours. The crisis was compared with the 'national emergency' of the Thirty Years' War, in which Germany had been overrun by foreign armies.[42]

At the same time, Mazarin began to forge an alliance in support of Sweden. In May 1659, he secured Dutch and English support in favour of a mediated peace, in which cause he also mobilised the Rhenish Alliance, with the result that Schönborn offered to mediate between the Emperor and his formal vassal, the King of Sweden. Moreover, following the conclusion of the Peace of the Pyrenees between France and Spain in November 1659, Louis XIV threatened to send 30,000 troops to support a peace initiative in northern Germany. Vienna was unwilling to risk a confrontation on German soil with France and wary about supporting Brandenburg plans for the invasion and occupation of Swedish territory in the Reich, since that would contravene the peace of 1648. Furthermore, accepting, or being forced to accept, the elector of Mainz's offer of mediation risked diminishing the Emperor's position in the Reich. Since Poland and Denmark now also wanted peace, Leopold was obliged to acquiesce in the agreements brokered by France at the monastery of Oliva, near Danzig.

As a consequence, the Rhenish Alliance was losing its main purpose after the foundation. The league was renewed in 1661 and again in 1663; in 1665, Brandenburg also joined the league, but enthusiasm waned. However, following the peace treaties of the Pyrenees in 1659 and Oliva in 1660, the immediate fear of being dragged into a European war between the Habsburgs and their enemies receded, and it became increasingly clear that the Alliance was little more than an instrument of French policy in the Empire.

The Imperial Diet of 1657 was the last to be called. In 1663, the Ottoman threat and other circumstances led the Emperor to convene another assembly, which met again in Regensburg. From this date, the Diet became permanent, formed by representatives of the princes and all the other states

---

42 *Ibidem*, p. 21.

of the Empire.[43] The work of the Diet thus became a perpetual quarrel on every subject, both on matters of rank and procedure. The discussions regarding the promulgation of a new *Reichsmatricel* (the quote of troops for the *Reichsarmee*, the army of the Empire) were protracted throughout 1663 and only in the first days of the following year was authorised the formation of a contingent to be associated with the forces who fought in Hungary against the Ottomans. Four years later, at the outbreak of the Devolution War between France and Spain, the Diet had to decide whether to intervene or not with the weapons to defend the Spanish Low Countries, which were part of the Empire. French diplomacy used all means of exposure to divide the Diet and prevent an intervention in favour of the Spaniards. Thus a strong pro-French party was formed, and another inclined to help Spain, headed by the Prince-Archbishop of Salzburg, Guidobald von Thun (1616–68). Only in September 1667, after the French conquest of several Spanish fortresses, did the electors propose a mediation for an armistice, but neglecting the question of whether or not to include Spanish possessions as belonging to the Empire. This motion obtained the majority of votes, but in the following months, the parties continued to debate the question until the dispute broke off and the following year the war ended with the intervention of the triple alliance formed by England, Sweden and the Dutch Republic.

Further tensions arose in the 1660s. After the crisis between the city of Münster and Prince-bishop Bernhard von Galen in 1661, in 1664 a similar episode occurred between Erfurt and the archbishop-elector of Mainz, in 1668 between Cologne and the Prince-bishop Maximilian Heinrich von Wittelsbach, and in 1666 Magdeburg and Brandenburg; while larger scale crises emerged in 1664 with the Münster–East Frisia border conflict, and again in 1666 with the second Swedish siege of Bremen. Further concerns arose in 1665–67, when the Prince-bishop of Münster joined England in alliance against the Dutch Republic, and in 1672, when Cologne joined Münster in the French alliance against the United Provinces.

German historians of the 19th century complained at how the image offered of the German Empire in those years appeared so distressing. The western states were obviously the ones most interested in maintaining good relations with France, but there were also princes who considered a question only from the point of view of the political advantages they could obtain. Alongside the states that had formed the Rhenish Alliance were added Bavaria

---

43 When the Diet was not yet a permanent institution of the Empire, the assembly began with the reading of the 'Imperial Proposition', which was established by the emperor, and ended with the reading and promulgation of the decisions of the Diet: the *recessus imperii* or *Rezess*. Officially the last Diet before the establishment of the perpetual assembly was convened in Regensburg in 1657, to deal with topics that had not been considered by the Peace of Westphalia. There was any formal decision that made 'perpetual' the diet of 1663, but this was implicit in the provisions of the Peace of Westphalia. The Diet – according to the opinion of modern historiography – never became a real parliament, nor a permanent organ of representation of the people, but remained an institution that represented states and electors. It soon became a gathering of representatives, to whom the Imperial princes rarely took part. Not for this reason its importance can be considered marginal: even the act that, in fact, ended the Holy Roman Empire (*Reichsdeputationshauptschluss*) was deliberated by the Diet. See also in K.O. von Aretin, *Das Alte Reich 1648–1806*, (Stuttgart: Klett-Cotta, 1993–2000), vol. I, pp. 68–79.

and Saxony, and this block was able to paralyse any aggressive military policy of the Diet or at least to influence foreign affairs. This attitude to immobility did not change even when in 1672 Louis XIV declared war on the Dutch Republic. Only in 1674, with the increasingly aggressive conduct of France, did the attitude of some states change, above all Brandenburg, threatened in its domains in the Rhine area. On 31 March 1674, Leopold informed the assembly in Regensburg that France was now considered as an enemy of Germany, the Diet received this address and declared war on France. However, even once all the states joined the formation of the contingents and after the first military campaign, numerous problems and unending protests erupted for the expenses and damages caused by the passage of troops. After the peace of Nijmegen of 1678, no less than six electors – Bavaria, Brandenburg, Cologne, Mainz, Trier and Saxony – belonged to the pro-France party, some of them because they were forced by their geographical position to maintain good relations with Louis XIV, and others to achieve their political objectives through an alliance with the *Grand Roi*. After 1680, electors Johann Georg III of Saxony and Maximilian Emmanuel of Bavaria adopted a more friendly policy towards the Emperor and left the leadership of the pro-French party to the Great Elector of Brandenburg.

The German princes feared a strong emperor, but that did not mean that they would acclaim a weak one either. The ideal was an emperor who would defend the *Reich* against its enemies but abstain from exercising undue power in the *Reich* itself. Leopold was still some way from approaching that position, though the challenges of the next decade or so brought him much closer to it.

3

The Army of the Emperor

Though the Emperor had raised standing regiments since the second half of the 16th century, the Estates-based structure of the Habsburg domains had resisted the creation of a large permanent army under the exclusive control of the sovereign.[1] The military establishment was then slow and led to the critical situation of 1620 and the creation of Wallenstein's private force, which could easily be turned against the Emperor. The year 1649 has been considered as the official date of birth of the Imperial standing army, notwithstanding the House of Austria maintained already a permanent force, comprising infantry, cavalry and artillery. It was a relatively small but experienced force, which had been campaigning for many years under able commanders. Some regiments had already been in existence for many years and certain units continued to be part of the Habsburg army until its dissolution in 1918. From this core group of veterans, the modern Imperial army was about to be born. According to the Imperial decree of March 1649, the army war-strength was established at 37 cavalry regiments and 30 infantry regiments, totalling around 37,000 men. In peacetime, this force had to be decreased to 15–20,000 men, gathered in nine cuirassier, one dragoon and nine infantry regiments.[2] By now, the first Imperial standing armies had been formed, more or less made up of professional officers and soldiers, completing the process begun in the 16th century, and providing a permanent army with social prestige and relevance. In the opinion of many contemporary commentators, this process offered an opportunity to exploit strategic knowledge, to examine the effectiveness of military tactics and become aware of the increasing importance of the overall organisation of the army. It would allow the Imperial military classes to occupy a significant place alongside the military classes of the other major European powers.

In 1649–59, the Imperial troops were pulled back to the Habsburgs' hereditary provinces, waiting to be disbanded. They were a colossal financial burden on these territories, which were in any case exhausted at the end

---

1 'A Catholic sovereign imbued with the idea of absolutism and Counter-reformation confronted the predominant Protestant provincial Estates', Hochedlinger, *Austria's Wars of Emergence, 1683–1797* (Routledge: New York NY, 2013), p. 99.
2 *Ibidem*, p. 101.

THE ARMY OF THE EMPEROR

of a long and destructive war, but now the provinces had to bear the cost of quartering and provisioning until the final disbanding. In June 1650, the army still numbered some 30,000 soldiers but it declined in size thereafter. By the following September the strength had shrunk to 24,500 foot and horse, and in 1655 the standing army numbered just 13,732 soldiers.[3] In the years preceding the Second Northern War (1655–1660), the army grew in size, reaching a 'full strength' on paper of 64,000 foot and 27,000 horse in April 1660. The size of the army had been expanded already in 1655, with the formation of three infantry and two cuirassier regiments, followed one year later by a further six infantry and two cuirassier regiments. In 1657, when the Emperor was setting up his contingent for Poland, eight new cuirassier regiments, three dragoon regiments and 10 infantry regiments had been recruited. In 1659, as the emergency in Poland decreased, 21 infantry, 10 cuirassier and two dragoon regiments were licensed, but in the following years new regiments were raised or hired from other German states, when the news from Transylvania urged Vienna to rearm. Shortage of funds did not allow for adequate reinforcement. In August 1660, when the Ottomans were performing their final offensive against Transylvania, the Emperor managed a force of 10 infantry, 12 cuirassier, two dragoon and two Croat–Hussar regiments, which barely totalled 32,000 men.[4] In 1662, after new recruitments to face the Ottomans in Transylvania, the overall force of the Austrian Habsburg army was 30,345 foot, 10,180 cuirassiers, 2,754 dragoons and about 800 Croats.[5] When the war against the Porte seemed inevitable, the Imperial standing army increased its numbers again with four infantry and three cuirassier regiments in 1663 and a further seven infantry regiments in 1664. Most of these regiments were dissolved after the peace of Vasvár, or were ceded to the Spanish Habsburgs, as happened between 1663 and 1668 with six infantry and two cuirassier regiments.

Scene from Bartholomeus Kilian's series of engravings dated 1663, depicting a death sentence in the Imperial army. On campaign, military discipline was maintained with hard corporeal pain, such as the wheel punishment here illustrated. Note the convicted man with his military equipment abandoned in the centre, indicating that the crime had been considered as dishonourable, thus he is deprived of all the marks of a soldier, and the punishment is inflicted by the executioners.

As discussed before, the decrease of the armed forces did not occur with the reduction of the regimental strength, but with the dismissal of whole regiments. As early as the end of the previous century, the repeated disbanding and re-enlistment accompanied by the paying for engagement of new recruits was denounced as costly and

---
3   Ibidem, p. 104.
4   A. von Wrede, *Geschichte der K. und K. Wehrmacht* (Wien 1898–1901), vol. I, pp. 34–37.
5   Hochedlinger, *Austria's Wars of Emergence*, p. 101.

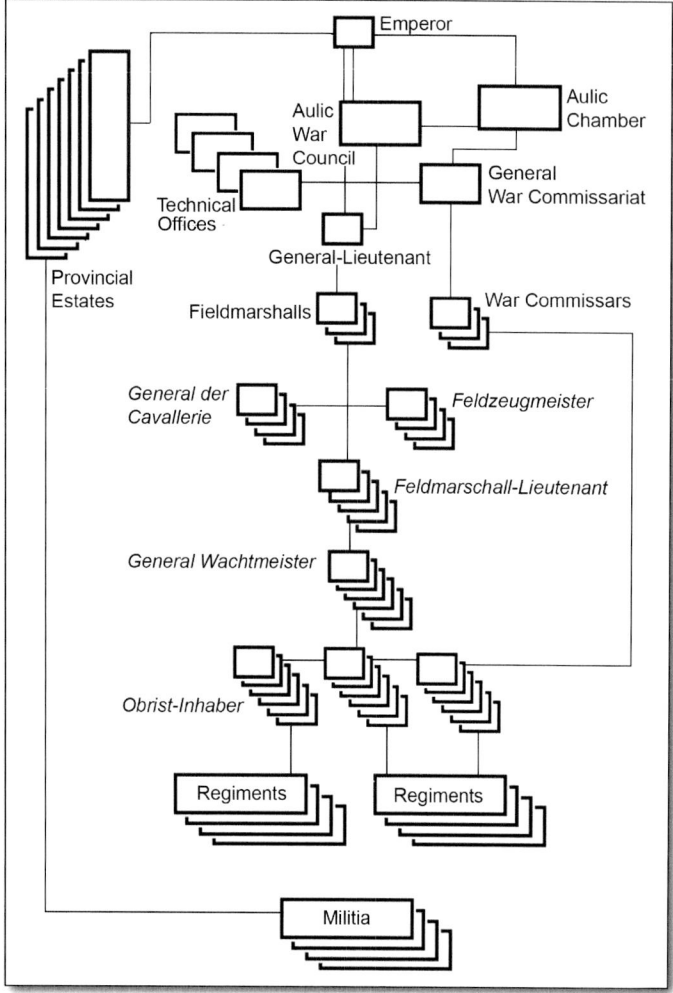

The Imperial army chain of command. (Author's illustration)

ineffective for the army, but was not possible to derogate from this rule.[6] Nevertheless, armies had been largely seasonal in the early modern era and the practice of disbanding regiments after a campaign seemed almost inevitable. A strong contribution to this policy came from the resistance of the veteran colonel proprietors, who did not appreciate the reduction of strength and the consequent decrease of the business. However, when it was then necessary to increase the strength of the army, to avoid the presence in the field of regiments completely formed by inexperienced soldiers, it became necessary to extract one or more companies from the veteran units to obtain a satisfactory level of preparation of the troops. However, the momentary economic relief obtained with the dismissal of the regiments turned into such a high loss of knowledge that the highest ranks of the army were harshly critical. In 1668, Raimondo Montecuccoli wrote on this subject, declaring that 'joining together new and unruly soldiers and officers, who do not know each other, and who have no confidence in each other, therefore what success will it have?'[7] Montecuccoli bitterly listed the different phases of rearmament and subsequent disarmament in the 1660s:

> When the army increased its strength with new recruits for the noises of war in Milan, to which were soon added those of Poland, which demanded reinforcements of greater armies. War lasted until 1660, and immediately a new dismissal of excellent soldiers was ordered, but one year later, it agreed to enlist new recruits to enter Transylvania. In 1663, troops were sent to Spain for Italy and Flanders, but then it was time to re-enlist them at great price, and to call also auxiliary soldiers, who cost much more than its own. Peace was then made in 1664: foreign troops returned to their countries and half of own soldiery were licensed […] If we now had need to recruit more soldiers, where to find them? In

---

6 Between 1618 and 1650, 246 regiments had been formed and then disbanded. See in Wrede, vols. II and III.
7 'In soggetto del disarmamento cesareo', dated 20 September 1668; in A. Testa, *Le Opere di Raimondo Montecuccoli*, part III, (Rome: USSME, 2000) p. 210.

THE ARMY OF THE EMPEROR

the Empire, the princes do not issue permissions. In our own provinces? […] And then, the veteran soldiers are licensed, the new ones are recruited, but the experts and the seasoned let themselves go, so we paid twice and the strength decreases. What an economy? What great military policies are these?[8]

The accordion trend of the overall strength of the Imperial army follows the succession of military crises that occurred during this period. In 1672, at the eve of the war against France, the army had 13 regiments of infantry, 14 of cuirassiers and three of dragoons. However, one year after, the size of the army began to grow with some regularity. The Austrian involvement in support of the United Provinces of the Netherlands acted as a detonator for a new rearmament. In July 1672, Leopold I had promised William III he would raise 16,000 soldiers in exchange for a subsidy of 30,000 rix-dollars a month,[9] for deploying them in conjunction with the Brandenburg army on the middle Rhine. From the 31,200 soldiers mustered in October 1672, the army strength doubled in 1673, with the definitive Habsburg engagement in the war. In the spring of 1673, a massive recruitment campaign was launched for mobilising 31,000 soldiers, quartered near Eger (today Cheb, in the Czech Republic) in western Bohemia. Five new infantry regiments were raised between 1674 and 1678, alongside eight cuirassier and two dragoon regiments,[10] increasing the overall force to 77,000 men on paper.[11] This was a considerable number, but it remained insufficient to face the commitments that awaited the army on the three fronts of war: Rhine and Flanders, Pomerania, and the no less important one represented by the rebelling Upper Hungary.

As happened in the previous decades, after the peace of Nijmegen, the total force had fallen to about 38,000 men, divided into 11 infantry regiments, became 12 in 1679, 10 cuirassier and five dragoon regiments.

As for other European armies in this age, the actual strength of the Imperial army is ambiguous and difficult to interpret. The absence of precise population figures, in what was on the whole a

Imperial artilleryman, 1658–60. Buff sleeveless *kollet* with red string; medium blue doublet on white shirt and white rabat collar; medium blue breeches; grey stockings over white, red ribbon; dark brown hat with red ribbon. (Author's reconstruction after Donath, Wilke and contemporary engravings)

---

8   *Ibidem*.
9   O. van Nimwegen, *The Dutch Army and the Military Revolution, 1588–1688* (Woodbridge: Boydell Press, 2010), p. 445.
10 A further seven independent dragoon companies were raised for Hungary in 1675 and two more in 1679. *Ibidem*, vol. III part two, pp. 900–903.
11 Hochedlinger, *Austria's Wars of Emergence*, p. 103.

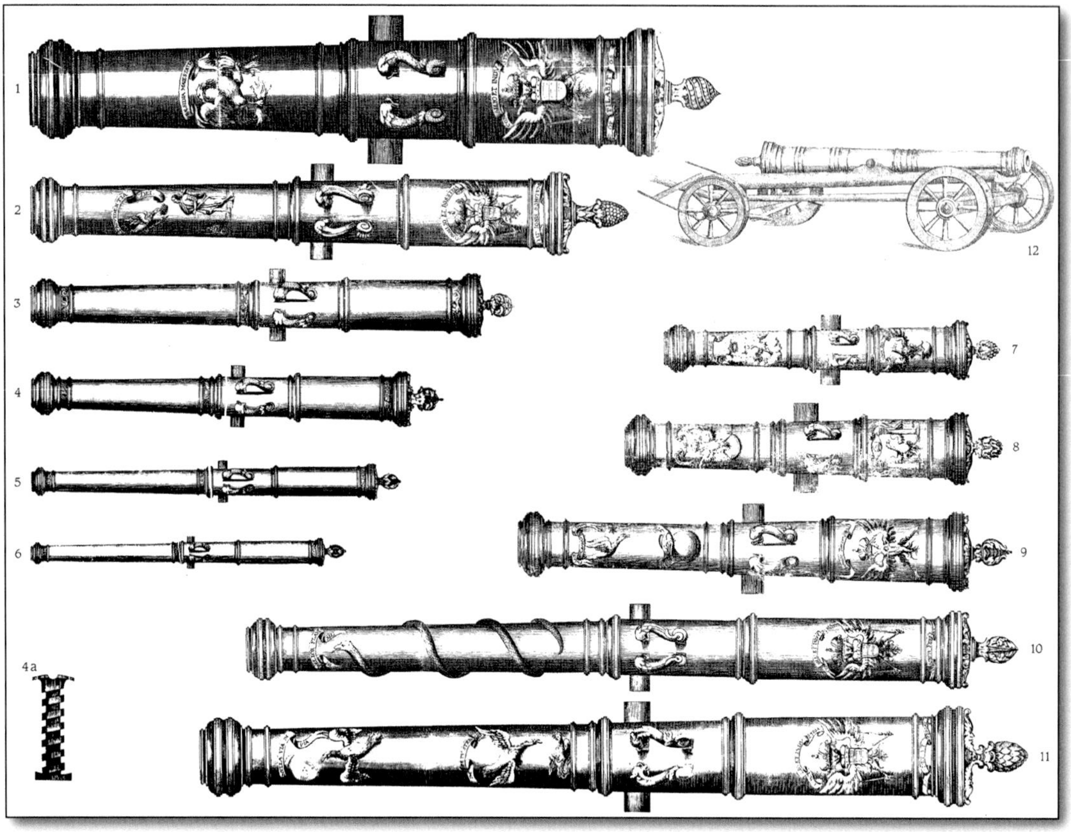

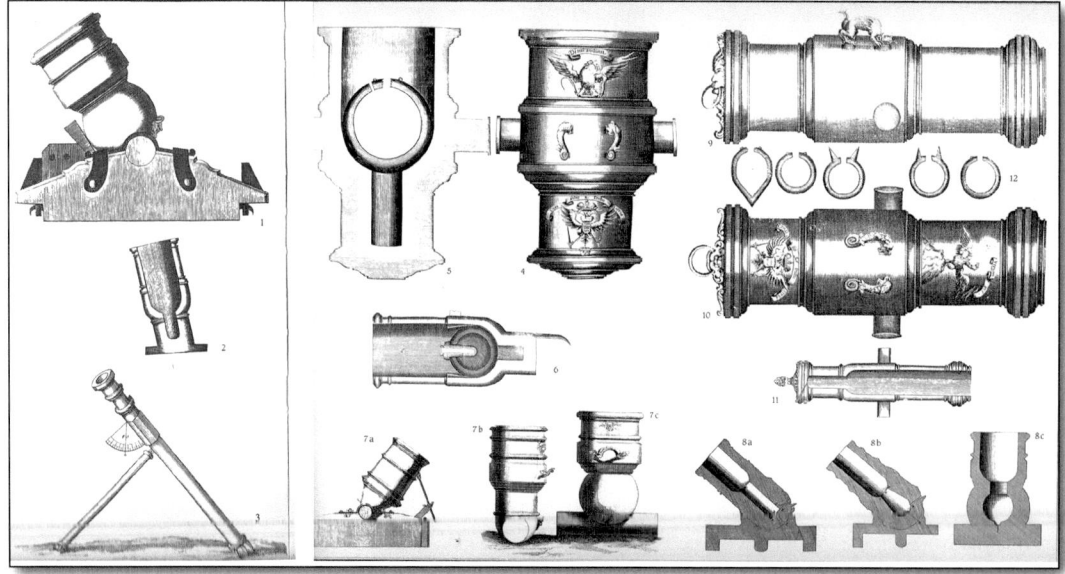

Imperial guns classified according their calibre, in a contemporary treaty. 1 – *Ganze Kartaune*, 48 lb; 2 – *Viertel-Kartaune*, 12 lb; 3 – *Falkaune*, 6 lb; 4 – *Regimentsstück*, 3 lb; 4a – adjusting screw; 5 – *Falconet*, 2 lb; 6 – *Serpentinel*; ½ lb; 7 – *Verjüngtes Regimentsstück*, 3 lb; 8 – *Kammerstück*, 6 lb; 9 – *Verjüngte Falkaune*, 6 lb; 10 – *Halbe Feldschlange*, 9 lb: 11 – *Ganze Feldschlange*, 18 lb; 12 – *Sattelwagen* for *Ganze Kartaune*. (Author's collection)

Imperial Mortars. 1 – *Stehenden Mörser*; 2 – *Fussmörser*; 3 – *Handmörser*; 4 – *Hängender Mörser*; 5 – section of the chamber; 6 – *Hackenmörser* with hand grenade; 7 – different mortar positions; 8 – different forms of the chamber; 9, 10 – howitzer; 11 – section of the howitzer; 12 – different section of howitzer's projectiles. (Author's collection)

THE ARMY OF THE EMPEROR

Austrian 3 lb cast-bronze cannon casted in 1655 in Vienna, and preserved for almost four centuries in Dubravica village in central Serbia. Recently acquired by the Military Museum in Belgrade. The heraldic symbols and inscriptions which decorate the barrel refer to the persons of the Emperor Ferdinand III, the Imperial Commander of Artillery Count Ernst of Abensperg and Traun, and the Imperial gunfounder Balthasar Herold, as well as to the Viennese gunfoundry as the place where the cannon was manufactured. Detail of the Imperial double-headed eagle and coat of arms of the high court and commander of the artillery, Count Ernst of Abensperg and Traun with the corresponding inscription. (Author's photograph)

pre-census age, ensures that it is impossible to form a precise percentage of the men under arms. Although governments sought to obtain precise figures, and paid wages and allowances accordingly, it was difficult (both then and now) to have much confidence in the figures available. Officers who wished to avoid problems, and to embezzle pay, overlooked death, disease and desertion in order to present their units as being up to strength. In addition, there were and are problems in assessing the figures, because sometimes the indicated strength is the theoretical one or it records only the number of companies. Therefore, there was always a considerable difference between paper strength and effective strength, and the latter could and can be assessed differently. It is often not even clear if figures refer only to the Emperor's own troops or include the *Reichstruppen* and foreign auxiliary forces, or whether all Imperial troops rather than those in a specific theatre of war are included in the total. Irregular units, border garrisons, as well as artillery and other specialists were usually excluded in the documents relating the available force. Prior to 1683, data are often incomplete and unreliable, and only from the last decades of the century information become more detailed. Obviously, the need to know exactly their own strength was an indispensable requisite on the eve of the new war against the Ottoman Empire. In the winter of 1682–83, the Aulic War Council estimated that a field army of 80,000 men would be needed to deal with adversaries with a reasonable expectation of success. In addition to these, at least 27–28,000 soldiers had to be added for the garrisons in defence of the strategically most important places[12]. In December 1682, the Emperor could deploy 26 regiment of infantry, 10 of cuirassiers, five of dragoons and three of hussars and *Croater*.[13] Patents for the raising of new regiments were released at the beginning of the following year, which would have increased the army with a further four regiments of infantry, five of cuirassiers and three of dragoons. The theoretical total of the army exceeded the figure of 85,000 men, but the musters executed in March 1683 showed a very different scenario. The new regiments were still

---

12 Hochedlinger, *Austria's Wars of Emergence*, p. 183.
13 Wrede, *Geschichte der K. und K. Wehrmacht*, vol. II, p. 152.

incomplete, and the already existing ones were far below the expected strength. Excluding the Hungarian forces and the *Frei-Compagnien*, the Emperor deployed just 32,000 men as field troops. This force could have ascended to 43,000 men before the summer with the completion of the new regiments, while 12,700 were already garrisoned in the border frontiers. Reducing by half the regular forces destined for the garrisons, and reinforcing these later with the call to arms of the militia and the irregulars, the field army would have totalled fewer than 65,000 men. Furthermore, the strategic plan did not take into account the need to reinforce Vienna or even all those factors that reduced the availability of troops for the field army. To keep this force in service with the certainty of paying salaries regularly, refunding arrears, organising the army train, and supplying food and ammunition, required 5.7 million florins. Instead, the amount collected up by the Aulic Chamber amounted to just 2.4 million florins.[14] In short, the field force available to Charles of Lorraine in May 1683 was 22,000 infantry and 11,000 cuirassiers and dragoons. By November 1683, some 75,000 regular soldiers may have been in the regiments, and the following year 90,000 were finally under arms, at least on paper.[15] Differences between the theoretical and effective strength continued to be physiological, and little improvement seems to have been achieved in the 1680s, when the difference between effective and official size was about 65–70 percent.[16]

Count Ernst of Abensperg and Traun (1608–1668). (Author's collection)

In wartime, the Imperial army was constantly obliged to hire auxiliary troops alongside its own forces but without ever reaching a proportion of foreign troops as high as that in France, Spain or in the Dutch Republic. Already in 1659–60, the Emperor had hired four infantry and one cuirassier regiments from Trier, Brandenburg and Münster for the war against Sweden and the Porte. Then, in 1674, 2,140 auxiliary troops arrived from Würzburg, increased to 6,000 in 1674 and was finally agreed at 5,000 until 1678. In 1674, one regiment of 1,000 foot was hired in Saxe-Eisenach and in 1676 a further 3,000 infantrymen arrived from this latter alongside Saxe-Gotha.[17] The incoming war against the Ottomans also forced the Emperor to search for soldiers outside Germany. In 1683, four cavalry regiments, 3,000 troopers, were hired after a private agreement with Prince Hieronim Augustyn Lubomirski.[18] Finally, further precious auxiliary

---

14   Cardini, *Il Turco a Vienna*, p. 257.
15   54,968 foot and 21,118 horse, Hochedlinger, *Austria's Wars of Emergence*, p. 103.
16   For more details, see the Appendix.
17   Wilson, *German Armies*, p. 53.
18   The Polish 'help' cost an unprecedented sum, but at the end of 1682, ignoring the objections of the Aulic Chamber, Leopold accepted the request of Sobieski. The main economic aid was 360,000 florins. This figure is to be added 70,000 to Polish councillors as regalia and another 150,000 paid to Lubomirski for the three cavalry regiments. The final total was 580,000 florins,

troops arrived from Saxony and Bavaria in 1683 and from Brandenburg in 1685. In 1683, a further 10,000 troops arrived from Hannover for the Upper Rhine, in order to leave available the Imperial regiments for the Hungarian front. All these agreements were accorded after negotiations that involved not only the financial aspect but, overall, the political one.

This military policy seems contradictory when compared with the simultaneous transfer of troops to the Spanish Habsburgs. Between 1663 and 1668, Leopold I ceded six infantry and two cuirassier regiments, and another infantry regiment was ceded in 1679. Except for the latter, no regiment came back to Austria.

Military Administration

In addition to having larger and more expensive regiments, the Habsburgs, like other European monarchies, gradually gained more centralised control over the army with the aid of a specific administrative office. As long as warfare had been based on a provincial defence system and on mercenary troops hired for limited periods, there had been little need for permanent administrative offices. However the never-ending struggle against the Porte eventually necessitated the creation of a central structure responsible for these matters, extending its authority to all parts of the monarchy.[19] Over the years, the military organisation grew considerably and by the middle of the 17th century, the Imperial army disposed of an imposing and assorted apparatus. This does not mean that this organisation was able to produce solutions to the problems and contingencies of the 'military', indeed, more than once the division of responsibilities caused delays and poor management of resources.

The aforementioned *Hofkriegsrat* (Aulic War Council) was established as permanent in 1556 by Ferdinand I in response to the perennial Ottoman attacks. Its formation marked the actual turning point of Austrian military policy. During the 16th and the first half of the 17th century, the Aulic War Council extended its activity in the Habsburg domains through a net of provincial war councils. Because to form larger armies required revenue, and the court was dependent on grants by the Estates, even the provincial war councils was bitterly opposed by these latter; however, because of the

---

but other expenses occurred in the following months due to the ongoing revision of the alliance treaty requested by the Poles. Besides the renunciation of the credits that Vienna had towards Poland, Leopold also renounced the mortgage on the salt mines south of Cracow, assigned to the Silesian Estates. See in Stoye, *The Siege of Vienna*, p. 102

19 The Austrian historian Hochedlinger focuses on the 'incomplete establishment' of the Imperial military: 'While, elsewhere in Europe, at least among the major continental powers, there was a direct connection between the increasing size of armies in the 17th and 18th centuries and the articulation of a stranger central government, this tendency appears to have been much less explicit in the Habsburg Monarchy. Indeed, Vienna managed to build up a formidable army without a full centralisation of military organisation. Between the survival of private involvement at all levels of the army and the persistently strong influence of the provincial Estates there seemed to be little scope for governmental responsibility and functions. It was only in the 1740s that this half private, half Estates-dominated system had to give way to resolute modernisation.' See in *Austria's War of Emergence*, p. 111.

perennial threat posed by the Ottoman Empire, the civil authorities usually co-operated in military defence matters. Larger armies, coupled with monetary inflation, increased the Habsburgs' need for revenue and dependence on grants by the Estates, since ordinary taxes could not be imposed on their own subjects without their consent.

Based in Vienna, the Aulic War Council was headed by a president – 'the eye of the Emperor in the army' – alongside the major commander, the general commissar, and some five to seven members from the nobility or the clergy. Adjutants, copyists and other employees in bureaucratic positions also worked in the council. Its major function concerned the co-ordination and centralisation of all the military affairs of the Habsburg territories. This matter included primary duties that centred on co-ordinating provisioning and equipment in wartime, appointment of commanders and generals and organising the maintenance of fortresses on the military frontier and in the cities of Vienna and Prague. Throughout the 17th century, the Aulic War Council extended its influence also within the Empire, but the establishment of a standing army enormously increased the burden upon the Hereditary domains.

Concerned with the matters of organisation and administration, the Aulic War Council was also the supreme legal authority for the army. In 1657, in the first year of Leopold I's reign, a new and more detailed draft of regulations was established which set the council's responsibilities in the following activities: 1) the control of the state of force, number of men and regiments were in conformity with the provisions of the ordinances; 2) the proposal of candidates assigned to the command of the armies and their adjutants, including the proposals of promotion to the higher grades for the officers, the conferment of the licenses for the rank of colonel, and the compilation of the main instructions for the army commanders; 3) mediation between the commanders and the Emperor concerning requests, reforms and transmission of the final dispositions; 4) the completion of the army in wartime, the supply of war materials and provisioning, the composition of the armies and the direct command of the regiments in peacetime and in winter quarters; 5) organisation and compilation of the main instructions for the army train; 6) control of the arsenals, technicians and the artillery of the fortresses; 7) the direction of the service of the fortifications, military bridges, garrisons and the Danube's fleet; 8) surveillance on matters concerning justice, and compliance with the judicial regulations issued by the ordinances. The last four assignments were carried out through specific offices, while all the activities were coordinated alongside the General War Commissar and the Aulic Chamber meeting in special commissions. The commissions concerning the affairs relating to quarters and supplies for the army, arsenals, the frontier, fleet and military regulations were permanent commissions, while for the other cases extraordinary meetings were held.[20]

---

20 K.u.K. Kriegsarchiv, *Feldzüge des Prinzen Eugen von Savoyen. Nach den Feldacten und anderen authentischen Quellen hrsg. von der Abtheilung für Kriegsgeschichte des K.K. Kriegs-Archives*, (Vienna, 1876–92), vol. I, p. 182.

THE ARMY OF THE EMPEROR

The principal and also the major work managed by the Aulic War Council derived from the fact that during the winter quarters, all the matters regarding the regiments had to be taken care of by the council in the absence of the commander-in-chief. The colonels of the regiments, wherever their troops were stationed, corresponded with Vienna for every problem of supply or money, as well as for the review, and for all the usual activities of which the army general staff was responsible. From this scenario derived the fact that even the claims of lower officers to their superiors and other minor service issues had to be examined by the highest military authority, with understandable loss of time and slowing down of other activities. It would hardly have been possible to carry out this immense work without the proverbial obstinacy that distinguished the presidents of the Aulic War Council. The charge of president was conferred with a renewable term every two years, but almost always the office lasted for life. In 1665, the appointment to the office of president of the secret council interrupted the career of Prince Lobkowicz, but after him, the Marquis Annibale Gonzaga held the position until his death in 1688 and the same occurred for Montecuccoli and the Margrave Hermann of Baden-Baden, appointed after Montecuccoli, until 1691. The Italian *generalissimo* had served as president and commander-in-chief of the army, but the two offices were not always united in one person and after him. In fact, the two positions were joined in a single personality only by Prince Eugene of Savoy in 1704–36 and Leopold Joseph von Daun in 1762–66.[21]

Margrave Hermann von Baden-Baden (1628–1691), here in a 1664 portrait. The Margrave was appointed as general commander of the Imperial contingent in October 1663. He became later a prominent military leader of the *Reich* against the French in the War of 1672-78, and in 1681, he succeeded to Montecuccoli as president of the Aulic War Council. (Author's collection)

Even though with the Imperial War Council the Emperor exercised his control over the army, the raising and provisioning of troops, and the upkeep of fortifications along the military border with the Ottomans were still largely in the hands of the provincial war councils. Together with the Aulic War Council of Vienna there was another based in Graz, which continued its activity until 1705. It was the *Innerösterreichischer Hofkriegsrat* (Aulic War Council for Inner Austria), created in 1578 to better manage the military affairs on the south-eastern border. The activities of this council were the same as the Viennese one, and included

---

21　The non-coincidence of these offices was also a source of discontent at the top of the army: 'Hermann of Baden, the younger son of the staunchly Catholic ruler of Baden, had, like the Emperor, been destined for the Church, the fate of many younger sons of ruling families. He was aged fifty-five in 1683, and had been promoted to succeed Montecuccoli as President of the War Council in 1680. But he resented the fact that he had not gained the other post, as the field commander, which the Emperor gave to Lorraine. A tall and strikingly imposing figure, a loyal patron but a bad enemy, most of the senior officers were dependent upon his goodwill. Unsurprisingly, they usually parroted his views, very much the best strategy for an ambitious soldier.' Wheatcroft, *The Enemy at the Gate*, p. 113.

the matters concerning the border militia in Croatia.[22] As a consequence, the command and administration of the defence system against the Ottomans was divided in two until the beginning of the 18th century. The principal purpose of the arrangement was to deliver financial support to the theatre of war as speedily and efficiently as possible. Unfortunately, a recurring shortage of funds blighted Habsburg military history during the whole period, limiting its success. Another similar office operated in Innsbruck, known as *Militärdirektorium*, who managed the military matters of the recently acquired Tyrol, even its authority was minimal and before of the council of Graz, this was placed under the control of the Aulic War Council in Vienna.

It is difficult to form a comprehensible picture of military expense in the period 1660–80, because too much documentation has been lost. However, finance remained a very delicate topic for the House of Austria in late 17th century. The increasing specialisation of the offices in charge of managing the army and the growth of the military forces also increased the need for money. Montecuccoli reassumed this in his famous sentence 'war needs three main resources: 1: money, 2: money and 3: money.'[23]

Although the Habsburgs had a strong sense of their Imperial status and destiny, their material resources were more limited than their aspirations. German historiography of the 19th century has always insisted on the conditions of deep economic crisis of the Habsburg domains and how it was exacerbated by the antiquated tax system, which, in addition to naturally weighing on the subordinate classes of the bourgeoisie and peasants, strongly conditioned every action of government. The incomes flowed into the Aulic Chamber's coffers through two types of contributions: the revenues deriving from the Imperial property, the so-called 'cameral' and the actual taxes, called 'contributional'.[24] These latter were calculated every year depending on the estimated expenditure and divided among the hereditary domains. As there was no actual financial balance and taxes were conditioned by the concept that each entry must have a definite purpose, Austria's financial policy was living for the day. Moreover, the provincial Estates took months to negotiate the payment and the quota assigned to them was not always paid in a single operation. Therefore, in absence of a planned balance of expenditure, every financial support became uncertain, forcing the Aulic Chamber into a meticulous search for the smallest source of income. Because the funds for the army were paid through the 'contributional' tax imposed on the Estates, this exhausting scenario of precariousness and emergency influenced the

---

22 In 1699, when the danger of Ottoman incursion had considerably shifted away from the Austrian borders, the activity of the War Council of Graz was reduced in importance. At the suggestion of Prince Eugene of Savoy, the Emperor disbanded the council and from 1704 all the activities were transferred to Vienna. See in K.u.K. Kriegsarchiv, 'Feldzüge des Prinzen Eugen', vol. I, p. 184
23 Montecuccoli, *Memorie*, vol. I.
24 The 'cameral' financed the court and the state's apparatus, and was drawn from the ruler's domains from indirect taxes, duties, tolls, monopolies and, overall, from the gold and silver mines in Hungary–Slovakia. The 'contribution' was voted by the Estates and served to finance the war with the taxation on private properties or goods.

effectiveness of military policy. Naturally, the financial shortage conditioned also the ordinary existence of the regiments, and therefore continued without interruption the practice of raising regiments that after two, or at most three years, were disbanded for lack of resources. The crisis sharpened in the 1670s, and reading the economic accounts published two centuries later,[25] it seems almost impossible that Vienna managed to keep an army, which was among the largest in Europe, in such a disastrous economic scenario. Though still financing the standing army, gradually the Estates no longer had any direct control over it. In the second half of the 17th century, the origin of this military tax was still clearly visible, as it went back to the requirement to provision the Imperial troops quartered in the Habsburgs' domains. The military tax at first consisted of money, most notably to cover recruitment cost as well as food and fodder, though such contributions in kind could be, and increasingly were, commuted into cash, when during the second half of the 17th century the troops were increasingly quartered on the borders or in enemy territory.[26] In order to allocate the total amount necessary, the ratio which had been agreed in 1542 for the war subsidies against the Ottomans, albeit slightly reformed at times, was still in place in the 1680s. The established proportion demanded of the Bohemian kingdom 65.3 percent and of the Austrian provinces 34.7 percent.[27] Hungary and Croatia, Tyrol, Anterior Austria and Gorizia-Gradisca remained *extra proportionem* and thus did not contribute on a regular basis to the financing of the army.[28]

During the entire reign of Leopold I, the financing of the war machine continued to be one of the most critical issues. The need for money to meet the continuous military commitments caused a dramatic increase of the debt. Gradually, every source of income was burdened with ever increasing taxes and even the state's properties ended up under heavy mortgages. Practically, the economic scenario that had occurred at the beginning of the Thirty Years' War became an even greater nightmare for the Viennese court. At the end of the century, the overall debt mounted to 11 million florins.[29] A very

---

25 In 1678, the total debt of the treasury had risen by three or even four times compared to three million florins 'certified' by the Aulic Chamber in 1665. A difference so remarkable between one estimate and another was also because not even the *Hofkammer* could calculate exactly how much the debt amounted to. K.u.K. Kriegsarchiv, 'Feldzüge des Prinzen Eugen', vol. I, p. 260.
26 Obviously, the provinces that had been affected by war campaigns were the ones to suffer the most. For instance, according to what was declared in the late 17th century by the Kingdom's Palatine, Pál Ezsterhazy, Hungary paid more money in two years of campaigning than in 100 years under Ottoman rule. N. Asztalos and A. Petho, *Storia dell'Ungheria* (Milano, 1937), p. 239.
27 M. Hochedlinger, *Austria's Wars of Emergence*, p. 109.
28 A new area of army expense was introduced in 1697 and established at 12 millions florins. Now Hungary and the recently conquered Transylvania paid four million and one million respectively. In 1697 Boemia paid 2,284,722 florins; Moravia 761,577; Silesia 1,523,148; Inner Austria 1,215,278; Upper Austria 405,090; Lower Austria 810,185. K.u.K. Kriegsarchiv, 'Feldzüge des Prinzen Eugen', vol. I, p. 261.
29 Other estimates, more pessimistic, calculated at 14 millions florins the debt accumulated by the Aulic Chamber. It is singular that the exact figure of the state's debt was not indicated precisely, as if not even the financial authority of the Imperial finances were able to establish it with certainty. Perhaps certain sources exaggerate the economic conditions of the Habsburg domains, however the collateral phenomena represented by the requisitions and thefts committed by the

catastrophic scenario, as a result of years of uninterrupted wars, but also for corruption and misappropriation.[30] Small wonder that the Aulic War Council was more focused on solving the problem of supply and salaries for the army than formulating a sophisticated military strategy. Financial expedients and foreign subsidies granted the Emperor to keep the war machine going. The Spanish Habsburgs had provided economic support for the war of 1663–64 and in the 1670s, but busy with their own bitter struggle against France, soon faded into financial insignificance. The principal source of external financing came from Italy, and specifically from Rome. In 1683, Pope Innocenzo XI granted subsidies for an overall 5 million florins until 1699, and authorised special taxes to be levied on the Austrian clergy. The Holy See's support was instrumental in nailing the Emperor down to the Hungarian theatre of war.

The Habsburg finances, controlled by the aforementioned Aulic Chamber – the treasury – was responsible for paying the troops and co-operated with the Aulic War Council in all financial matters relating to the army. After financial mishandling during the Thirty Years' War, any expenditure could be authorised only with the permission of the treasury. All military funding became subject to continuous checks and inspections in order to avoid any mistakes or attempts at financial misappropriation. In order to manage this affair, from 1650 all the funds destined for the army became administered by an independent office of the *General Kriegscommissariats-Amt* (General War-Commissar's Office) under the direction of a *General Kriegscommissar* appointed by the Emperor. He and the Aulic Chamber supervised the work of the commissars, whose principal duty was to control the payment after the reviews of regimental strength, the supplies for the army and fortresses as well as the payment of the soldiers' salary. The office of general war-commissary was established in Vienna and the appointment increased in importance until at the end of the century it became a court position. This office was responsible for the supervision of all the supplies destined for the troops, the inspection of the state of force of the regiments and the control of the payments to the soldiers. The general war commissar had under his command one or more *Obrist-Kriegscommissar* (colonel war commissar): while the general remained in Vienna, the latter went to the armies as directors of the *Feldzug Commissariats-Amts-Directeur* (field commissariat office). In Vienna also served three secretaries, one protocol writer, one accountant with one adjutant, plus a certain number of bureaucrats. After 1680, there was a colonel war-commissar in Upper Austria, one in Lower Austria and one for the Empire, one in Moravia and one in Bohemia together with two *Kriegscommissar* as adjutants. There was one colonel war-commissar and two war-commissars in the Aulic War Council of Graz, respectively in charge of the counties of Krain and Carinthia. In the late 17th century, Hungary and Croatia were divided in seven districts where the respective war-commissars operated.

Imperial troops due to the scarcity of resources, are widely documented by the chronicles of late 17th century. See in K.u.K. Kriegsarchiv, 'Feldzüge del Prinzen Eugen", vol. II, p. 65.

30 In the late 17th century, some investigations conducted by the War Commissariat revealed that: 'from the hands of certain officers, money arrived in the army like drops of water through a dirty rag.' Ibidem, p. 66.

The main task of the war-commissars consisted in verifying the muster of forces for the states, carried out in the regiments or in the garrison when the soldiers were located. In order to ascertain the exact amount of money for the payment to the troops, the commissar had to send to the Vienna office the reports of the general reviews, to be carried out twice a year. Furthermore, each month the war commissioners received reports on the strength of the individual companies from the regimental commissars. Also the recruits who came to the army were presented to the war-commissar, who had the last word on the suitability of the new arrivals. The two general annual reviews, one carried out during the winter quarters and the other – the most important, called the *Haupt-Musterung* – performed before the war campaign, took place under the supervision of the war-commissar. During the muster, all the anomalous cases eventually found were recorded and then transmitted to Vienna to the General War Commissar.[31]

In conjunction with the Aulic War Council and the War Commissariat, further major offices managed further military matters. After 1668, the *Obrist Mustermeister-Amt* (muster office) was charged with the strength review and provisioning of the military border militia. In the same period began operating also the *General Feld-Kriegauditoriats-Amt* (general office of the military court of justice); the *Obrist Land und Haus Zeug-Amt*, (office for the arsenals); the *Fortifications Bau-Zahl-Amt* (administrative office for construction and maintenance of fortresses); and the *Obrist Schiff und Brücken-Amt* (office for pontoons and river flotillas).

An important task of modern warfare was the provision of victuals for garrisons and field armies. Regarding this, for decades great concerns accompanied the Imperial troops on campaign, as the absence of a regular supply network caused disastrous results. Shortage of money and the rapacious attitude of soldiers and even officers, become a very unpopular characteristic of the Imperial army, whose transit was feared by enemies as well as friends. This scenario also generated paradoxical outcomes. In 1662, during the campaign in Transylvania preceding the war of 1663–64, most of the communities refused to provide supplies to the army. The town of Szeben-Hermannstadt (today Sibiu in Romania) closed the gate and refused any negotiation even when the Imperialists threatened to fire the suburban villages.[32] Disputes between the commanders and the provincial Estates happened on several occasions, especially when the latter could appeal to their privileges. In 1663, the campaign in Hungary began in very unfavourable conditions concerning supplies. On 6 May 1663, the archbishop

---

31 Since the payments to the regiments were calculated on the sum of the competences established in the last monthly review, the most frequent irregularities consisted of the attempts to present a force superior to reality, which often happened through the abuse of the so-called *Blinde Leute* (literally blind people, or 'dead wages'), or *Strohmann* (straw men), namely the simulacra of soldiers used in training. See also in K.u.K Kriegsarchiv, 'Feldzüge des Prinzen Eugen', vol. I, p. 262.

32 An event that later really happened. See in G. Gualdo-Priorato, *Historia di Leopoldo Cesare, contenente le cose più memorabili successe in Europa dal 1656 al 1670* (Vienna, 1670), vol. II, p. 95.

of Esztergom, in the name of the Hungarian Estates, declared that the country could not sustain the Imperial troops and informed the Emperor that:

> The Hungarians are ready to call for the general mobilisation of the Royal Army, but they implore you not to introduce the German soldiers, because forage is scarce and everything would be consumed before time, the inhabitants fled and the general mobilisation thwarted. If his majesty intended to place troops into the fortresses, although [the Estates] disagreed, the troops should be transported by river and supplied by magazines without ever touching the country.[33]

In late 1663, acting on Montecuccoli's recommendations, the *Proviant-Amt* (provision office) was fully overhauled to better coordinate supply operations in Hungary. This decision proved to be very useful for the crucial campaign of 1664. The main task of the office was the supplying of the field storage network in the provinces and the administration of money for the purchase of foodstuffs. During the winter months, the provision office devoted its activity to the preparation of the stocks for the following year. In 1670, the office gained the new title of *Obrist Proviant-Amt*. On campaign, a general baggage train staff was organised, led by a *Proviantmeister* with some adjutants, who cooperated with the army commissars directly for supplies. Budgetary problems did not allow these offices to function properly.

The supply of foodstuffs for the army consisted essentially of bread for troops and fodder for horses and other draft animals. The most common supply method was that offered by the *Subarrendatoren*, namely by the wholesalers who operated near the war theatre and who usually had their business with the army. However, this system was not always feasible, since in poor countries, resources were almost always scarce, and it was necessary to transport stocks from far away and then collect them together in magazines. In this way, the supply for the army in Hungary was carried out in full by the *Proviant* office in Vienna, which stipulated the contracts with the Austrian wholesalers and directed their works. However, this method had many negative sides. It often happened that the goods arrived damaged, either because of the long journey or because of attempts at fraud and illicit speculation, but above all because the Aulic Chamber's delaying of payments left the province at the mercy of wholesalers.[34]

During the Franco-Dutch war the question of supplies reached dramatic levels. Soon, in the popular imagination, the Imperial soldier became the archetypal profaner of property and insatiable plunderer. Considering that all sources of funding were drying up and the states near the war theatre were now devastated, the easiest solution to follow was to rely on private financiers. These characters began to occupy an increasingly important position as early as the 1680s. The greatest creditor of the House of Habsburg was Samuel Oppenheimer, Heidelberg's banker. Oppenheimer was a financier, a merchant and at the same time an intermediary and connoisseur of all the German markets. A typical figure of his time, the financier was

---

33 *Ibidem*, p. 226.
34 K.u.K. Kriegsarchiv, 'Feldzüge des Prinzen Eugen' vol. I, p. 188.

the only Jew who was allowed to reside in Vienna, despite a law from 1670 forcing Jews to abandon Austria.[35] The rise of Oppenheimer, from a simple merchant to *Hof-Commissar* and *Hof-Jud*, had begun in 1677, when – due to the excellent services rendered to the Imperial army during the siege of Philippsburg – he had become the main supplier of the Imperial army. In a completely disastrous economic scenario and in a chaotic monetary situation, Oppenheimer succeeded in asserting himself in the midst of all the risks and problems that an activity such as his entailed. Over the years, the Heidelberg financier and the Aulic Chamber had entered a real vicious circle: as the debt grew, the position of the creditor increased in importance, to the point that to get any supplies they had to turn to the omnipresent Oppenheimer. After 1685, there was no article that the financier did not deal with; Oppenheimer supplied the army of all kinds of goods, from flour to the buttons for the uniforms.

Because the duties of the *Proviant-Amt* became ever more complex, in the late 1680s the workload of the provision office was shared by several *Land Proviant-Amt* (Provincial provision offices) for Styria, Lower Austria, Bohemia, Moravia and Hungary. Each province organised its own office for the baggage train and supply, directed by one *Land Proviant Administrateur* with one *Proviant Commissar*, both under the *Proviantmeister*'s direction when the army was marching on campaign. However, the office had to deal with difficulties of all kinds, among the most important namely the lack of money to provide the rations for the troops.

The coordination of the resources destined for the theatres of war were also managed through the *Generalschaft* (generalty).[36] Although there were no regional commands in the modern sense, the generalties had been established for the coordination of forces in the regions most exposed to an external attack. The generalties were based in the major strategic centres and housed corps of permanent troops or hosted the command of the provincial militia, the *Landwehr*. Each generalty was divided into districts or *Directorium*, under the orders of general officers appointed by Vienna. In the 1670s, the largest number of generalties were in Hungary and Croatia, with Győr, Komárom, Kassa, Tokay, Karlstadt, Petrinja and Varaždin, but in the west there was a generalty for Anterior Austria in Freiburg. The command of the fortresses where the generalty had its location was entrusted to the office's holder, but in the case of large garrisons command was usually held by a commander of a higher rank.

---

35 Although the Jews had been expelled from Vienna in 1670, the Emperor permitted Oppenheimer to settle there, together with his *Gesinde* (followers), who included a number of German and Austrian Jewish families. He even received the privilege of building a mansion in the heart of Vienna. He was appointed *Oberfaktor* and court Jew with the recommendation of Margrave Ludwig of Baden. See in P. Johnson, *A History of the Jews* (London: Phoenix, 1996), pp. 256–258.

36 These generalties should not be confused with the ones on the border, which are dealt with in another chapter.

The High Command

There was also a high command in other armies of the time, even though the Imperial army was the one in which the engagment of the officers was not necessarily connected to the high aristocracy. During the wars against the French and the Ottomans, no military operation was directed by a Habsburg prince.[37] Compared to the army of their main adversary, Louis XIV, Leopold I exercised the appointment of Imperial commanders without ever distinguishing between officers belonging to the great families of the Empire and those coming from the lesser nobility, while in France command in the army was considered an inalienable right of the great aristocracy.

In this period the modern 'general staff' did not yet exist and the origin of the ranks of general derived from the still-surviving terminology introduced by Emperor Maximilian I. Originally, in fact, the rank of *Feldzeugmeister* mainly identified the commander of the artillery, while the *General Wachtmeister* was responsible for sentinels and reconnaissance. All officers comparable to the rank of general and all personnel assigned to the administration of an army belonged to the *General-Stab*, divided into *Gross General-Stab* and *Klein General-Stab*. The former included all the generals and the senior officers, while the latter comprised adjutants and assistant personnel for logistics and services.

The highest rank in the Imperial Army was the *General-Lieutenant*. He represented the Emperor in the army and was invested with the supreme command, holding full authority over all troops and officers. Immediately afterwards followed the *Feldmarschall*, and this was normally the rank of the army commanders. In campaign it was not unusual to have two field marshals at the same time, one of whom was the *Adlatus* (literally 'at the side') of the commander-in-chief and assisted him in the direction of large armies. More often the presence of two, or sometimes three field marshals, was dictated for political reasons.

The *Feldmarschall* was followed by the *General der Cavallerie* and by the aforementioned *Feldzeugmeister*, both equivalent in hierarchical line and distinguished exclusively by the fact that to the first rank were appointed officers with greater experience in the direction of cavalry, while the second qualified the general of infantry and artillery. Both of them could be in command of combined corps of foot and horse, even in autonomy, as occurred in 1657 with *Feldzeugmeister* Jean-Louis Raduit de Souches, during the campaign in Poland. The rank of *Feldzeugmeister* still retained something of its original technical qualification, as he could be consulted by the commander-in-chief as a consultant for siege operations or for the defence of a fortress. For this reason, the officers who, in the judgement of the *Hofkriegsrat*, had gained a sufficient understanding of these matters, entered the rank. The *Feldzeugmeister* was also the highest rank in the artillery and this extended his authority independently from the general commanders.

---

37 Before the war against the Porte of 1737–39, this happened only in September 1704 at the siege of Landau, when the operation was directed by Archduke, later Emperor, Joseph I.

THE ARMY OF THE EMPEROR

Count Jean-Louis Raduit de Souches (1608–1682), was the son of a French Huguenot nobleman, who left France in 1620. Having fought against Louis XIII at the siege of La Rochelle, Souches entered the Swedish Army in 1630. Four years later he felt insulted by the Swedish general Torsten Stålhandske, and challenged him to a duel. As regulations forbade challenging a superior officer, Souches joined the Imperial army to continue the feud and distinguished himself during the defence of Brno in 1645. He performed valiantly in the war against Sweden of 1657–60 and also in 1664, during the short campaign against the Ottomans in Upper Hungary, achieving two important victories at Szent Benedek and Léva. In 1674, he replaced the indisposed Montecuccoli as commander of the Imperial army alongside Bournonville. The contradictory instructions received from Vienna conditioned his actions in the Flanders campaign. Here, after a long debate, Souches joined the Dutch-Spaniards and on 11 August was involved in the battle of Seneffe. After further exhausting discussion, on 16 September he agreed to support the allies in the capture of Oudenarde; the conquest seemed achievable, but three days later Souches suddenly ordered his troops to leave the trenches, and the following night retreated with his entire field artillery and all munitions. These unprecedented actions caused a storm of indignation in The Hague. Dutch 'Grand Pensionary' Gaspar Fagel ordered the States-General's envoy in Vienna to lodge an official protest with the Emperor, and William III no longer wanted to serve in the same army with Souches. (Author's collection)

Both as commanders of separate corps and under the orders of the commander-in-chief, *General der Cavallerie* and *Feldzeugmeister* were engaged in the monthly muster together with the war commissars and, in turn, they remained with the troops in winter quarters. All this group of senior officers took part in the *Kriegsrat* (war council), which met at the beginning of the campaigns or before any major operation. This practice was expressly recommended by the Aulic War Council and failure to comply with this was considered a serious and prejudicial event for the regular conduct of an army. In the war council could exceptionally participate in suborder further officers, but this happened only if requested by the general commander, or if the number of senior officers was insufficient, or finally if there were allied troops in the army, whose commander had no degree equivalent to the *Feldzeugmeister* or *General der Cavallerie*.

The next ranks of general were the *Feldmarschall-Lieutenant* and the *General-Wachtmeister*, who in battle had usually the command of corps of infantry or cavalry. Rarely, he could be in command of autonomous corps, but in campaign the *Feldmarschall-Lieutenant* led the vanguard or rearguard of the army and for this, promotion to this rank represented the first concrete recognition for a general, as well as a reward for the service he provided. The *General-Wachtmeister* occupied the first step in the Imperial hierarchical order and usually he had command of small corps of 2–5 battalions or squadrons, or of a certain number of artillery batteries. In general, the latter constituted the indistinct mass of the general officers, provided with training and experience which were in most cases not homogeneous, as was a characteristic of other major contemporary armies.

Promotions were granted very frequently, thanks to the always benign attitude of Emperor Leopold I for his generals. In fact, at his death in 1705, the Imperial army had 22 *Feldmarschalls*, 11 *Generals der Cavallerie*, 11 *Feldzeugmeisters*, 36 *Feldmarschall-Lieutenants* and 60 *General Wachtmeisters*, of which at least a third remained without assignments, both for reasons of seniority and because their numbers were actually higher than needed.

In the *Gross General-Stab* also operated the *General Quartiermeister*, in charge of the direction of the logistical services of the army. He held the important task of tracing the march of the army and choosing the roads, and therefore he was constantly in contact with the commander-in-chief. The *General Quartiermeister* participated in the war councils and had on its orders a *General Quartiermeister-Lieutenant*, belonging to the *Klein General-Stab*. The General Staff was completed with the presence of the *General Auditor* for legal matters, the *Proviant-Meister*, and the *General-Stab Pater*, in charge of religious affairs. If the army was of large proportions, a *General Wagenmeister* was also assigned, assisted by the *Wagenmeister Lieutenant*, belonging however to the *Klein General Stab*. These officers were in charge of all the affairs concerning the army train, vehicles, drivers and draft animals, as well as the coordination of the regimental train.

The *General-Stab*'s chancellery was entrusted to the *Feldkriegs Secretar*, while the work relating to the generals' quarters belonged to the *General-Stab Quartiermeister*. The *General Gewaltiger* followed in the hierarchical line of the *Klein General-Stab*. He was subordinate to the *General Auditor* for the arrest of officers who committed violations of service. Finally, among the members of the *Klein General-Stab*, there were the *Feld-Hauptmann* and the *Feld-Lieutenant*, adjutant of the *General Gewaltiger*, and in charge of the medical service of the *General-Stab*. Sometimes, among these latter officers there were also the pharmacists. The *General-Gewaltiger* had among his subordinates the captain of the guides, who, in particular in the Hungarian war theatre, was in charge of gathering information and collaborated with the *General Quartiermeister* in choosing the roads to be travelled. But the largest group of officers belonging to the *Klein-General Stab* consisted of the *General Adjutants*, whose number was not regulated by any order and when it was considered insufficient, the commander-in-chief could require officers from the regiments. This rank served as a strong point of attraction for a large number of young aristocrats, eager to undertake the profession of arms under the orders of some famous captain.

In Austria there was no school or military institute in the modern sense, so all the officers learned the functions of their rank in the companies and, if they entered the higher ranks, continued the training within the regiments or the *General-Stab*. Both were and would have remained the 'forge of the commanders' for a long time and in fact, scrolling through the biographies of the officers in the service of the House of Austria, it can be seen that careers develop through very similar contexts, which – in all probability – allow us to form a fairly homogeneous range of cases, especially for the foreign officers. Not only economic reasons explain the presence of so many foreign

THE ARMY OF THE EMPEROR

aristocrats in the Habsburg army. Of great importance also was the desire for glory and adventure typical of the period as well as political convenience, and both acted as a strong incentive for some military careers. Several members of the ruling families of the Empire served as officers in the Imperial Army and their presence was useful to strengthen alliances and agreements between Vienna and territorial princes such as Schleswig-Holstein, Pfalz-Neuburg, Württemberg and Baden. It is interesting to focus on their presence in the Imperial army to follow the political support of the major ruling German houses to the Habsburgs.

During the 1660s and 1670s, Italian officers occupied key roles in the Imperial army. This situation led to the reaction of Imperial natives against Italian predominance. In 1677 a duel also occurred between the *Obristwachtmeister* Giovanni Andrea Corbelli and the equally ranked Friedrich Ferdinand von Reich. This event had great resonance in Vienna and fortunately ended without serious injury for the contenders. Corbelli later become *Obrist Inhaber* of a cuirassier regiment and closed his career in 1704 with the rank of *General der Cavallerie*. (Author's collection)

Luigi Ferdinando Marsili (or Marsigli, 1658–1730), here portrayed by Antonio Zanchi and Antonio Calza, possibly after his appointment as *Obrist Inhaber* of an infantry regiment in 1688. Note the Ottoman bridle and saddle covered with tiger fur. As many other volunteers arrived in Austria on the eve of the war, his career proceeded along an unchanged trajectory: the volunteer left the hometown comforted by the applause of the most conspicuous citizens; his letters passed from hand to hand and career progress flattered municipal pride. Notices, prints, poems, ceremonies emphasised his successes, or pitied his death in battle. The volunteer, in turn, continued relations with his city of origin, and relatives, friends and fellow citizens tried to join him. In general, he spent his life in the countries of the Empire and usually married local women. After a period as secretary of the Venetian *bailo* (ambassador) at Constantinople, Marsili entered the Imperial army in 1682 as a volunteer, just in time to be captured by the Ottomans and employed as a servant during the siege of Vienna. He was later ransomed and resumed the military career, becoming *General Wachtmeister*. On 4 February 1704, Marsili was expelled after a trial which condemned him for the surrender of Alt-Breisach. He left the fundamental *Stato Militare dell'Imperio Ottomanno* which constitutes an inestimable source on the Ottoman army of the 17th and early 18th centuries. (Author's collection)

In general they were cadets whom hereditary circumstances forced to make an almost obligatory choice, in the sense that the only worthy alternative was offered by the religious career. However, for the majority of the young nobles, economic motivations were decisive for choosing a military career. The biographers often keep silent about – or do not want to discuss – the economic conditions of many of the officers belonging to the lesser aristocracy of the 17th century, as well as the poor prospects offered by life in their states of origin, and this was especially true for the Italians. Other motivations are to be found in religious faith and in the struggle against Ottoman expansionism. The victory of Szentgotthárd, and later the triumph of Vienna and the capture of Buda aroused in the whole Peninsula what is not improper to call mass enthusiasm, so much so as to constitute an element of decisive call to choose the profession of arms.[38] Soon, clientelist relations widened the pool of candidates to the position of officer. Italians had a long tradition that started before the Thirty Years' War. They had gained prizes and properties in Bohemia, succeeding to the exiled Protestant nobles. In the 1680s, the same scheme was about to be repeated in the 1680s, in Hungary, where the properties of the rebel nobility would certainly have been confiscated. The Italian presence was considerable at all levels of rank. Between 1648 and 1690, 58 *Feldmarschalls* were appointed and 12 came from Italy. In the same period, 40 Italian officers had served as colonels of infantry and cavalry, making them as the most represented foreign nation of the Imperial army.[39] The presence

---

38 In this context, the career of Count Antonio Carafa is exemplary, whose actions in Hungary in the 1680s are marked by the harshness of the behaviour used towards the local population sympathetic to the Thököly cause. It is possible to identify regional factions limited to four macro-regions, namely the Italians of Austria – the ones from Trentino and Carnia – Emilians, Tuscans, and Lombard-Neapolitans, already subjects of the Habsburgs of Spain. The link that many aristocratic families had with important captains such as Montecuccoli, Piccolomini and Grana del Carretto, are all easily identifiable. Taking as an example the regiment of cuirassiers of Count Antonio Caprara, it is possible to see at the end of the 17th century the relevant number of officers, whose relations with the family of the Emilian captain had long been consolidated. Although their presence was at times intrusive and there were episodes of open conflict with the Austrian commanders, the Imperial army maintained a good number of excellent Italian officers.

39 Without claiming to provide a complete list, a significant group of Italian officers who milited in the Imperial army between the 1670s and the 1680s has been extrapolated from the *Dizionario Biografico degli Italiani*, and the *Enciclopedia Militare* by A.Valori, *Condottieri e Generali del XVII secolo*, (Rome 1943), both works largely obsolete but full of interesting details: Amerighi Paolo, Archinto di Trainate Carlo, Archinto di Trainate Ludovico, Arrighetti, D'Aste Michele (killed in action in 1686 at Buda), Bia, Bolognini Francesco, Caprara Francesco, Caprara Ludovico Girolamo, Caprara Silvio (killed in action in 1685), Castelli Giovan Battista, Cavalcante, Contarini, Corbelli Giovanni Andrea, Doria Giovan Battista, Fontana Giovanni Domenico, Gabrielli Gabriele, Ginnasi Domenico, Gonzaga Annibale, Gonzaga Carlo, Gonzaga Claudio, Gonzaga Ferdinando, Gonzaga Luigi, Madruzzo Ferdinando, Maffei Alessandro, Malvezzi Antonio, Mancini Salvatore, Marsili Ferdinando, Medici di Marignano Giovanni Battista, Medici di Marignano Giusto Antonio (killed in action in 1688 at Belgrade), Montecuccoli Ercole, Monte Santa Maria Orazio, Nigrelli Ottavio, Nelli Camillo, Nomis Evandro, Obizzi Pio Enea, Orlandi Francesco, Pace Carlo Maria, Parella, Pico della Mirandola Francesco (killed in action in 1684 at Esztergom), Piccolomini Alessandro, Piccolomini Enea, Piccolomini D'Aragona Francesco (killed in action in 1686 at Buda), Piccolomini Giovanni Norberto (killed in action in 1689), Pini,

THE ARMY OF THE EMPEROR

of so many Italian officers provoked reactions among the 'Germans', but Leopold I continued to hold in high esteem the *Welsches* (Italian, in Aulic German). In this regard, in 1693, an officer informed a colleague that despite the refusals of the President of the Aulic War Council, Count Ernst Rüdiger von Starhemberg, 'always little favourable to the Italian nation [...] with our great jubilation, three vacant regiments have been conferred to Italians!'[40]

Gradually, the Italian presence was counterbalanced by Lorraine officers, destined to increase in importance in the late 17th century until equalling the Italian predominance. One of the most famous commanders to come from Lorraine was undoubtedly Prince Charles François de Lorraine-Elbeuf de Commercy (1661–1702). He entered the Imperial army at a very young age following his uncle, Duke Charles V, and soon became famous for his courage and determination in combat, collecting a long series of wounds. With him also, officers without ties of kinship with Duke Charles V gained positions in the army, such as *General der Cavallerie* Louis d'Herbeville (1634?–1709), qualified as 'dragoon for vocation' by his contemporaries and still in service aged 75.[41]

Further French-speaking officers came from the Spanish Low Countries. In 1672, Brussels-born Alexandre de Bournonville (1616–1690) was appointed at the rank of *Feldmarschall* after a career begun as a cavalry officer in the 1640s. The same provenance for another Walloon cavalry officer who entered the Imperial army in 1683, aged 17, and destined to a glorious career: Claude Florimond de Mercy (1666–1734). He was a member of a dynasty of Imperial officers that began in the Thirty Years' War with Baron François de Mercy. The young Claude served as volunteer during the siege of Vienna alongside his cousin Pierre (1641–1686) who

Ernst Rüdiger von Starhemberg (1638–1701). The strong commander during the siege of Vienna, here portrayed in 1680, wears a fashionable coat-*Koller* with short sleeves without cuffs, under a three-quarter black-polished armour with golden accessories. The red sash with gold fringes was the main distinctive mark of all the Imperial officers and remained unchanged until 1700. (Author's collection)

Porzia Gian Silvio, Rocco Ottavio, Roverella Valerio, Salvatori Orazio, Sartori, Savoia Luigi Giulio (brother of Eugene, killed in action in 1683 at Petronell), Sereni Carlo, Solari, Sormani Antonio, Spinola Domenico, Stella Rocco, Strassoldo Orazio, Strassoldo Nicolò, Tacchi, Torre Gian Filippo, Torre Lodovico, Torre Luigi Antonio, Torre Nicolò, Visconti Annibale, Vitelli Vimes Francesco.

40 *Autobiografia di Ferdinando Marsili*, edited by E. Lovarini (Bologna 1938), p. 168.
41 F. Rákóczi, *Autobiographie*, edited by B. Kôpeczi (Budapest: Corvina, 1977), p. 118.

served as *General Wachtmeister* from 1682. Alongside the Walloons, also native French acquired high positions in Austria, such as *Feldmarschall* Jean-Louis Raduit de Souches (1608–1682) and Charles Eugène de Croÿ (1651–1702). This latter had an adventurous life that brought him into Imperial service in 1682 after service in the Danish army. In 1694 he left Austria for Russia, where he received the army command in Livonia from Tsar Peter I Romanov.[42] Often the French in Imperial service were frondists who served under Condé for Spain and did not ask for pardon. This was the case for Gaspard de Chavaignac (or Chavagnac, 1624–1695) who served with Spain until 1665, and after that militated for the elector of Cologne in 1672–73, and entered the Imperial service in 1674 as colonel of cavalry. He closed his military career in 1680 as *Feldmarschall Lieutenant*, when he was appointed as ambassador in Poland.

Obviously, an important place was also occupied by the Austro-Bohemian aristocracy. The overall picture was far from homogeneous, as it included both officers from pre-eminent families such as Liechtenstein, Kaunitz and Dietrichstein along with those of the small rural nobility, known by the not always positive term of *Junker*.[43]

Clearly, officers in the Imperial army were rather cosmopolitan, and the great variety of Habsburg domains made the officer corps a babble of different languages and cultures. The aristocracy adopted for official relations the court language of the 17th century, namely French. The German language, while still used to give orders to troops, was confined to private and informal talk, while the Hungarian nobility also used Latin, which was the political language of the kingdom. The Hungarians were little represented in the second half of the 17th century. Just one Hungarian, count Adam Forgách de Ghymes, obtained the rank of *Feldmarschall*. Other native Hungarians served as colonels in the light cavalry except two officers of the Pálffy family, János Károly, who was appointed colonel of a cuirassier regiment in 1675 and Nikolaus, who held the same rank of the first *Hayducken* regiment from 1688. Alongside the Pálffy, other great families loyal to the Emperor occupied place of command in the Royal Army, like Batthyány and Eszterházy, but compared to the variegated corps of officers, the Hungarians appeared like warriors of the Barbarian era. To this address, the description of the Hungarian aristocracy by an intelligent contemporary observer reveals much more than it apparently seems:

---

42 He led the Russian forces in the Battle of Narva on 20 November 1700 when he surrendered and was taken prisoner by the Swedes. He died in Reval (Tallinn) as a prisoner of war. On the demand of his creditors, his body, which rested at St. Nicholas' Church, was not buried for more than 190 years, and, when mummified, was exhibited as a curiosity.

43 The esteem in which the aristocracy of the Habsburgs domains was held was terrible. A satirical tale from Silesia provides a description of a young noble made by his mother: 'The rascal already knows he is a *Junker*, so he does not want to study and prefers riding with his servants. Eventually I will be forced to buy him a syllabus. If only it cost little and if the boys didn't need so many books to learn something. Someone told me that in other countries there are no nobles like those who live here.' P. Winckler, 'Der Edelmann', published in 1697, in *The Cambridge Modern History*, p. 560.

THE ARMY OF THE EMPEROR

[The Hungarians] are bellicose, bold, brave, but also fickle, inconstant and irreconcilable in revenge [...] They do not sympathise with the Germans, if not for the abundant drinks [...] they are generally not very clean, great eaters and lazy [...] they have the terrible look and the expression of fury always painted on the face.[44]

The Upper Hungary uprising and Montecuccoli's strong hostility towards them, contributed to relegating the Hungarian officers to a minor role, at least until the end of the century.[45] Even the Spaniards, once numerous, had just one senior officer between the 1660s and 1680s, the *General Wachtmeister* Juan Batista de Areyzaga (1620?–1694).

The Scottish, and even more the Irish, who had militated in the Imperial army since 1618, transfused new blood into the middle and senior officer class, achieved a prominent position with Count Jacob Leslie (1635?–1692) – son of the Thirty Years' War general Count Walter – promoted *Feldmarschall* in 1683, and Viscount Francis Taaffe (1639–1704), 3rd Earl of Carlingford. This latter was greatly esteemed by Charles V of Lorraine and became his best friend.[46] Taaffe was later promoted to *General der Cavallerie* in 1687 and later *Feldmarschall*. In 1698 he was appointed vice-president of the Aulic War Council.[47]

The *Obrist-Inhaber*

In Austria, perhaps even more than in other countries, the *Obrist-Inhaber* (colonel proprietor) represented the key figure of the military structure. In several respects, this rank preserved many prerogatives of the warlords of the previous centuries, especially in matters of administration and the judiciary, as well as training, recruitment and equipment.

Appointment as a colonel had a not irrelevant meaning, given that each could be considered lieutenant of the Emperor, and invested with the sovereign's authority within his own regiment. There were no rank

Hungarian infantryman, end of the 17th century, from Christoph Weigel's *Neu-eröffnete Welt-Galeria*, printed in Nuremberg. Austrian and other western historians, with few exceptions, have neglected to recognise the Hungarian military contribution, focusing exclusively on a few episodes, such as Zrínyi's enterprises in the war against the Porte of 1663–64. Foreign historians, probably due to language barriers, have omitted from their studies the role of the Royal Hungarian army, which did not disappear as an organisation. The Hungarian elites which strengthened relations with the Habsburg officers, such as the Eszterházy, Nádasdy, Pálffy and Zrínyi families, felt that the national identity survived in the army and that their subjects recognised in military service a common spirit of membership. Though disbanded before the end of the year, in 1664 seven *Husaren* regiments from the Hungarian and Croatian Royal Militia were recruited and incorporated into the Imperial army. (Author's collection)

---

44 Jean de Vanel, in Cardini, *Il Turco a Vienna*, p. 191.
45 The merciless judgement that the Italian general gave about the Hungarians clearly shows how irreducible was the hostility towards them: 'nothing else will appear to the minds of these people (the Hungarians), who like many Proteus, who now love and then do not love, immediately exalt and then depress, and want and do not want, and in a thousand contradictions they act.' Montecuccoli, *L'Ungheria nell'anno MDCLXXIII*.
46 In 1677, Lorraine ceded to Taaffe the property of his cuirassier regiment, see in Wrede, *Geschichte der K. und K. Wehrmacht*, vol. III, part two, p. 579.
47 The Taaffes were devoted Catholics. The call to ward off the Islamic invasion naturally had a strong appeal for them, especially for Francis, who performed succesful actions in Hungary between 1683 and 1690. Further reading: R. Ní Mheara, 'The Wild Geese in Austria', in *Seanchas Ardmhacha: Journal of the Armagh Diocesan Historical Society*, vol. 16, No. 1 (1994), pp. 76–92.

differences between one regiment and another and seniority was taken into consideration only to establish the position of the unit during the reviews, in battle or in the marching order. Unlike almost all European armies, the Habsburg Emperor did not have a Life Corps of infantry or cavalry,[48] and each regiment belonged to the respective colonel proprietor, designated by the Emperor through the Aulic War Council, which issued an attestation of nomination called 'patent of obedience'. The regiment was indicated by the name of the colonel's family, or of his own noble rank, as for instance for the regiment of Count Ludwig Anton von Pfalz-Neuburg (II-76), known as *Pfalzgraf zu Fuss*. When two Inhabers came from the same family, the unit belonging to the colonel with the greatest seniority added the adjective *Alt* to his name, while the other was preceded by *Jung*. Compared to other European armies, where among the colonels there were teenagers – even women – belonging to the families of the high German aristocracy, in the Imperial one the encomiastic appointments had completely disappeared. Out of 100 and more colonels who succeeded between 1657 and 1687, all had held a rank in the army. Most of them came from the rank of adjutant, while others had entered very young with the rank of ensign or lieutenant; moreover, almost all the colonels had served in some military office or held a position in the general-staff of an army. Most of the colonels belonged to the middle and small rural nobility, or to those who had ennobled themselves through the military profession. In the middle of the 17th century there were actual consolidated dynasties of colonels. Among the most famous, there were the Starhembergs, who numbered four infantry colonels and one president of the Aulic War Council between 1657 and 1690; and also the Souches, Montecuccoli, Piccolomini, Herberstein and Metternich placed two or more exponents as colonels of infantry or cavalry.

Throughout the 17th century the ownership of a regiment constituted a significant source of income and in relation to the infantry, the cavalry colonels could obtain higher profits thanks to a larger number of items to issue. Together with these economic privileges, the colonels exercised the right of appointment and promotion of officers up to the rank of captain, which usually could be granted after payment or regalia. Furthermore the colonel could accord licenses and marriage permits with any restrictions. However, belonging to the cavalry was considered a higher privilege to which most of the nobility aspired and the added value attributed to an officer of a cavalry regiment can be seen in the *Cartell* for the exchange of prisoners, stipulated in 1673. An officer of cuirassiers or dragoons was worth 20 percent more of one of infantry.[49] Another index of the highest level of consideration enjoyed by the officers of the Imperial cavalry is represented

---

48 The only Imperial 'Guards' unit was the company of *Trabanten* who served as palace corps in Vienna. At this regard, there is also a further couple of elite units, represented by the *Leibguardie* formed for escorting in campaign the commanders-in-chief. In 1657, one Life Corps of 150 horsemen accompanied *General-Lieutenant* Mechior von Hatzfeld (ic-i) in Poland, until disbanded in 1658. A similar unit of 120 horsemen (ic-ii) was formed in 1664 for escorting Raimondo Montecuccoli in the Hungarian campaign.

49 *Theatrum Europaeum*, vol. XI, p. 421.

by the fact that of the nine *Feldmarschalls* in charge in 1684, five came from the horse regiments. The line of demarcation always remained very clear between those who began their careers in infantry or cavalry and in fact obtaining the transfer from infantry to cavalry was a rarity.

The appointment to the rank of colonel represent often a prize awarded to worthy officers, who received from the Emperor a congruous and generous salary.[50] However, when, in addition to the rank of colonel, the candidate was granted the creation of a new regiment, the lack of financial support could prove to be problematic, because, it exposed him to an uncertain and risky investment. In the late 17th century, the newly appointed colonels had usually to advance the money for the recruitment of half the regiment. Some of these *Capitulationen* specifies further details of this kind of contract. Usually, the Emperor requested that at least 'two companies should be enlisted as soon as possible, according to the promise received and to advance the money for waggons and other material, including flags and spears for the Frisian horses.'[51] The new regiments always received a certain number of companies composed of more or less veteran soldiers extracted from other regiments. The colonels of these latter received a refund from the Aulic Chamber or from the newly appointed colonel.[52] The 'regiment market' included a number of diversified cases and usually the government tried to employ recruits from dissolved regiments, at least when it was possible.

Until 1698, the Aulic Chamber assumed the expense only for weapons and equipment, and when the Imperial treasury lacked resources, the *Capitulation* could require of the colonel advance money for recruiting the whole regiment. The colonels involved in this cases benefited from the 'special recommendation' from the Emperors, '… to have a unique *reflexion* … for the regiment, in the event of a reform or reduction'.[53] However, these initiatives could result in a failure. In January 1685 the newly appointed Colonel D'Erbey signed a contract for recruiting one regiment of infantry of 1,500 men, of whom 1,000 had to be recruited in the Habsburgs' domains. Unfortunately, in December, the regiment consisted of less than 1,000 men and therefore the recruits were amalgamated into other regiments.[54]

Between 1657 and 1689, relatively few regiments were disbanded following the casualties suffered in campaigns. In fact, the disbanding of regiments always stemmed from financial contingencies in periods of peace. Of course, there was special attention paid to the regiments owned by prominent commanders or belonging to princes of the Empire, but as soon

---

50 The infantry colonel's salary was 90,000 florins a year, the salary for a dragoon or cuirassier colonel 95,000 florins a year. K.u.K. Kriegsarchiv, 'Feldzüge des Prinzen Eugen', vol. I, p. 268.
51 K.u.K. Kriegsarchiv, 'Feldzüge des Prinzen Eugen', vol. I, p. 355.
52 In this regard, there was no precise rule. So for instance, in 1661, for the formation of the regiment *Spieck zu Fuss* (II-44), just two companies were extracted from the infantry regiment *Montevergues* (II-3), while the cuirassier regiment *Sachsen-Lauenburg* (IC-42), raised in 1682, received two companies from regiment *Metternich* (IC-35) and one from regiment *Dünewald* (IC-26). In the same year, the infantry regiment *Aspremont* (II-85), merged 800 men from regiments *Grana* (II-12), *Scherffenberg* (II-7) and *Strassoldo* (II-40). Wrede, *Geschichte der K. und K. Wehrmacht*, vol. I, p. 281; vol. III, part one, p. 182 and vol. II, p. 165.
53 K.u.K. Kriegsarchiv, 'Feldzüge des Prinzen Eugen', vol. I, p. 671.
54 Wrede, *Geschichte der K. und K. Wehrmacht*, vol. II, p. 168.

as certain considerations ceased to exist, budgetary requirements affected regiments indifferently, without taking into account seniority.[55] Minor concerns existed with regard to the regiments of hussars and Croats, whose existence was usually very short.

For various reasons, colonel proprietors could name his own substitute, especially if held the command of a larger corps or the army. Usually, the colonel proprietor delegated the command to another senior officer appointed as *Regiments Commandant*. More often the command in the absence of the colonel proprietor was entrusted to the *Obristlieutenant* (lieutenant-colonel), who in the cavalry also exercised the function of instructor of the regimental tribunal. He made sure that the disciplinary penalties and preventative arrests were carried out and urged trials when he believed that the number of subjects awaiting trial was too high. In trials, the lieutenant-colonel held the function of defence attorney and, as specified by the 19th century editors of the Austrian *Kriegsarchiv*: 'he had to take an interest for the delinquents'.[56] In the Imperial army the right of punishment was an emanation of the colonel's privileges. Notwithstanding there was a differentiation between crimes to be punished with disciplinary measures and judicial ones, military laws of the time were not very accurate in this regard. In general, small-scale crimes sanctioned through the courts were treated with less severe measures than those applied by disciplinary means. However, this often caused abuses of authority, as the colonels applied disciplinary punishments in order to proceed quickly at their discretion. The crimes subjected to judicial examination had to be examined by a military tribunal, but on campaign the colonels exercised this authority through the so-called *jus gladi et aggratiandi*. Cuirassiers were not subject to this authority, because they derived from the ancient cavalry corps and therefore enjoyed the prerogative of not being subjected to the colonels at trial. In their case, the tribunal had to be appointed by the Aulic War Council or, on campaign, by the commander-in-chief of the army.

Generally, the privileges retained by the colonel constituted a serious obstacle to reforms, since the rank reflected the spirit of independence of the aristocracy and all the colonels considered it normal to oppose attempts to limit their authority by the Aulic War Council or the leaders of an army. Obviously this situation caused various frictions between commanders and colonels, but any setback could be resolved very simply, at least in the opinion of Colonel Maximilian Ludwig von Regal: 'When a commander wants to impose his own methods and new systems in the army, these will be adopted as long as he remains in command, but then the colonel can go back to doing as before.'[57]

The colonel proprietor acted also as a significant figure for the recruitment of the soldiers. He managed the pickets dispatched to recruit volunteers, appointing the officers destined to this task. The picket usually comprised

---

55 In 1679, the cuirassier regiment *Bournonville* (IC-2), the second in the rank of seniority, was reduced to six companies, but all the officers and NCOs remained in service. Then, in 1682, the regiment was re-established ato the official strength. *Ibidem*, vol. III, part one, p. 133.
56 K.u.K. Kriegsarchiv, 'Feldzüge des Prinzen Eugen', vol. I, p. 292.
57 M. l. von Regal, *Reglement Uber ein Kayserliches Regiment zu Fuss* (Nurnberg, 1728), p. 144.

also one non-commissioned officer, one musician and two or three soldiers chosen among the most representative. The pickets had no restrictions for recruiting volunteers, except the prohibition against enlisting gipsies and Jews. Nor could clergymen, monks and friars be admitted as soldiers. German individuals were usually preferred, but also Swiss, French and other foreigners were accepted without particular restrictions. Instead, Hungarians and Croatians were not allowed to enlist in the 'German' infantry regiments.

Before the opening of a campaign in wartime, the pickets were sent to recruitment locations assigned by the Aulic War Council, or by the tradition of the regiment.[58] Unfortunately, there were cases in which the pickets had to travel several miles before reaching the destination, since some regiments were allowed to recruit in locations all over Germany. Enlistment in the states of the Empire depended naturally on the consent of the respective prince, while the Imperial cities allowed recruitment as a traditional right of the Emperor. The granting of the enrolment license in the Empire was often the cause of delays and all kinds of difficulties due to the changing political situation, but despite the drawbacks, this method was never completely abandoned. Criticism grew in the 1670s, both because of political obstacles and above all because of the delay with which the money for the recruitment arrived with the regiments. The pickets were often forced to start their job in the first months of the year, or even when the campaign was already underway. Moreover, the delays accumulated by the recruits before reaching the regiments meant they had little time left for basic training. It often happened that the recruits arrived with the regiments when the campaign had ended, and so the reinforcements expected in the spring filled the gaps with one year's delay. This was another reason why the effective strength of the Imperial regiments was always far lower than the official one.

In 1682, the urgent need of manpower for the incoming war against the Porte forced the Aulic War Council to advance a new plan for finding recruits in a short time. The Habsburg provinces were called to supply a quota of recruits directly, instead of paying the equivalent through 'contributional' taxation. The new system provided that at the end of the campaign, the *General Kriegs-Commissar* calculated the total of recruits needed for the next year. The new system, called *Landrekrutenstellung*, had to provide at least a third of the recruits before the summer of 1683. The initial intention was that recruitment would continued to be voluntary, but soon compulsion had to be employed to secure the number required. However, there were numerous exclusions: priests and religious personnel in general; professionals, but also the servants of nobles; public service employees, the sons of widowed mothers, and fathers of families; moreover, those who were extracted could avoid military service by paying an exemption fee, or presenting a substitute.

---

58 Some regiments had their traditional places of recruitment since the beginning of the century, such as the infantry regiment *Mers* (II-3), which recruited in Nurnberg. Infantry regiment *Starhemberg* (II-6) had sent its pickets to the Electoral-Rhenish circle since the 1670s, while infantry regiment *Stadl* (II-71) recruited in Würzburg and Bamberg. In March 1659, the elector of Cologne agreed the recruitment of 15 companies for the new Imperial infantry regiment *Nath* (II-33). However, the recruitment assembled just 500 men who were destined to a newly formed cuirassier regiment. See in Wrede, *Geschichte der K. und K. Wehrmacht*, vol. II, p. 136.

Given these arrangements, it is easy to understand that the sons of peasants and artisans of low status and other subjects without sustenance remained in the trap of compulsory military service. At the present stage of research, it is still difficult to reconstruct a social picture of recruits of the Imperial army in this age. Normally, in the urban centres it was easier to find volunteers among the many unemployed attracted by the cities, while in the countryside it was easier to find the protection of a noble who declared the subject irreplaceable. Certainly, there was also the contrary occurrence, namely that in this way landowners could comfortably get rid of subjects they disliked. To act as a lever of this mechanism there was finally the particular police regime of the society of those years, in which – for the report of some informer or the malice of a police officer – someone could turn to a military career to avoid a prison sentence.

Provincial Estates could also sub-contract the recruitment of the men required. If the Estates did not wish to burden their province with the recruitment of soldiers, the required quota of footmen and horsemen *in natura* could still be replaced by a lump sum which enabled the regiments to enlist the recruits themselves, preferably in the Empire and especially in the places that proved the most fertile hunting grounds for recruiting pickets from all across Europe. Provincial recruitment increased in the following years and at the end of the century covered 60 percent of the overall need for recruits. This system was certainly more effective and faster than recruitment by regiments, however, the *Landrekruten* were held to be more liable to desert, and their physical condition often left much to be desired.[59]

The provision of cavalry horses was equally problematic to that of recruits. Until the Thirty Years' War every cavalryman apparently had been obliged to bring his own horses – a custom which died out exactly as did the obligation for troopers to provide their own equipment. Both regiments and, on a larger scale, the Aulic Chamber, bought horses from private sellers. Besides, warhorse breeding was not fully developed in the Habsburg domains, so the purchase of horses had to be partly done abroad, especially in Brunswick, Holstein, and Poland, through intermediaries.

Logistics and Quartering

As the armies increased their size and became permanent, a major collateral effect was the provision of accommodation for the troops in peacetime. Given the absence of barracks, the problem could be solved only by quartering officers and men on town-dwellers and the rural population. This system was based upon the experiences that had become established during the Thirty Years' War, when a significant percentage of troops were no longer

---

59 Regarding the more or less forced recruitment, Montecuccoli stated: 'The men to be enlisted are not the ones from the scum of the people nor by chance, but chosen among the best […] who are healthy, bold, robust, in their prime, hardened in the hardships of the fields or of the tiring crafts, not lazy, not effeminate, not vicious', 'Della guerra col Turco in Ungheria', in Luraghi, *Le Opere di Raimondo Montecuccoli*, vol. II, pp. 262–263.

disbanded at the end of a campaign, but accommodated in winter quarters, either in enemy territory or, if the strategic situation made this impossible, in the Habsburgs' domains or in allied territory. More or less voluntarily, the provincial Estates collaborated with the commanders ensuring that the troops quartered there behaved in a decent manner and were well provided for in return, being given 'accommodation' – namely bed and board – and 'service' – wood, salt and bed – as well as food and wine or beer. In absence of these latter, the Estates had to pay a certain amount of money to allow the soldier to buy his daily provision, the *Mundportion* (mouth portion). Additionally, horses had to be given oats, hay and straw as *Pferdportion* (horse – fodder ration). Officers received several times the mouth and fodder portions of private soldiers, depending on their rank.[60] The Imperial ordinances continued to confirm the right of soldiers billeted to participate in the meals of the rural population, which reduced their salary accordingly. This system of quartering continued until 1699.

The provincial Estates were called to cooperate also with the army train, especially for long marches. They supplied draft horses, additional transport facilities and provisions in kind along the route of march, while commissioners sent by the provincial Estates supervised both the soldiers' quartering and their march through the territory. Understandably, the principal goal of the Estates was always to get the soldiery out of the region as quickly as possible.

The daily rations of bread, tents and other equipment such as the beams and boar spears for the *chevaux-de-frise*, as well as the personal property of the soldiers and officers had to be transported, if the regiment was in the field or on the move to new quarters. As a rule, soldiers carried provisions for three days, further rations being transported on the waggons. In the 1670s, 1,000 foot were calculated to need 30–35 carts for baggage and sutlers alone, not counting those for provisions and private use. The baggage increased for cavalry to 80 waggons for every 1,000 troopers. The train required many draft animals, which in turn increased its size with further carts. Usually the train had been provided by a private supplier, while the horses and mules belonged to the regiments.

A large baggage train also required additional horses and waggons, and mobility suffered accordingly. Montecuccoli and after him Charles V of Lorraine tried to reduce the size of the train, limiting the amount of private baggage, especially that of the officers, but the definitive reform of the train took place only at the beginning of the new century thanks to Prince Eugene of Savoy.

Logistical problems were amplified by the presence of non-combatant personnel who accompanied the army. In campaign, the army's baggage often increased with further waggons for wives and children as well as other camp followers and suppliers. The Imperial soldier of the 17th century was far from leading a life of celibacy. The colonel proprietors, managing the marriage permits, could encourage at will a proportion of women among the

---

60 Towards the end of the 17th century, an infantry colonel received the equivalent money for some 50 mouth portions and 12 fodder portions; 17 fodder portions in the cavalry. K.u.K. Kriegsarchiv, 'Feldzüge des Prinzen Eugen', vol. I, p. 268.

Portrait of Count Johann von Sporck (1595–1679). In 1664 he held the rank of commander of the Imperial cavalry at the Battle of Szentgotthárd. Sporck had been a veteran of the Thirty Years' War, and despite his advanced age demonstrated extraordinary energy and skill as a cavalry commander. He later took part in the campaign against the Hungarian insurgents in 1672 and later in the war against France until 1675. In late 17th century aristocrats maintained leading positions in the army; as they were slowly transformed into professional officers serving the state, they were joined by a growing number of non-nobles who were gradually encouraged to serve as soldiers in a permanent Habsburg army by the career prospects and material rewards it offered. The same process took place in the other German territories that engaged actively in the war, regardless of which side they chose. As elsewhere in Europe, the growth in army size and the greater reliance on mercenary infantry troops broke the nobility's monopoly over warfare. (Author's collection)

Count Antonio Carafa di Stigliano (1646–1693), was an archetypal figure of the Italian aristocrat in Imperial service. The Neapolitan count arrived in Austria in 1655 through the good offices of his relative, Cardinal Carlo Carafa della Spina, Papal legate in Vienna. In 1664, Carafa entered the army and eight years later obtained the appointment at colonel of a cuirassier regiment. He fought in Alsace and Upper Rhine during the Franco-Dutch War and successively in Hungary against the Ottomans. Here, Carafa become the implacable enemy of the Hungarian rebels, leading a very cruel struggle against the communities which supported the *Kuruc* league, and leaving a very tragic legacy around his name. From 1691 to 1693, Carafa held the command of the Imperial corps in Piedmont. On his death, his grandson Adriano sent the archive of the uncle to his tutor, Giovambattista Vico, to write a biography. The Neapolitan philosopher accomplished this work entitled *De Rebus Gestis Antonj Caraphei*, far from being objective about the actions of the Count, and certainly not the best of his works. (Author's collection)

troops. They were employed for cleaning the camp or quarters, cooking, laundry and needlework, nursing and other tasks. The percentage of married soldiers seems to be particularly high in the period 1650–1660, as a relic of the Imperial mercenary army of the Thirty Years' War. The massive presence of women and children is documented in a report dated 1650, when 500 Imperial soldiers marched into Styria accompanied by 400 women and 200 children.[61] The situation changed little in the next decade. On 12 May 1672, the Imperial command in Upper Hungary outlined that the 9,000 soldiers marching under general Johan von Sporck were mostly married people, who had with them twice their number of women and children.[62]

---

61 Hochedlinger, *Austria's Wars of Emergence*, p. 133.
62 J. Bánlaky, *A Magyar Nemzet Hadtörténelme* (Budapest, 1928–1942), vol. XVI, p. 308.

Sometimes the large number of troops with families to be quartered was used as a deterrent against rioter communities, such as the case of the Hungarians. Ultimately, this method was not very different from the contemporary French *Dragonnades*. Salaries in the Imperial army – meagre on an international scale and by definition only intended to provide for the soldiers – were insufficient to support a family. Similarly, it would have meant an unbearable burden on the provincial Estates if both soldiers and their families had been billeted on them. As a result, in the 1670s the enlistment was open preferably to single men and only a small percentage of married soldiers was now tolerated. Even junior officers' marriage came to be restricted for the same reason. Furthermore, the Estates also had to take care of a deceased officer's family, since impoverished and beggar widows were considered a particular disgrace to the reputation of the Imperial army.[63]

Women in the army contributed also to the care of wounded and sick soldiers. As early as 1649–50, every infantry or cavalry company usually had its own *Feldscher* (surgeon) with his adjutants, who not only shaved the men twice a week, but also rendered first aid in battle. Further personnel operated in campaign under the direction of their own *Regiment-Feldscher* in the infantry and *Regiment-Chirurg* in the cuirassiers. Trained medical personnel could be found in the headquarters and in the improvised field hospitals prepared after a battle. These were the only sanitary services existing in the Imperial army until the 18th century. There is not much information relating to health services for the private soldier in this age, but everything suggests that they were very bad. Furthermore, the General War Commissar, which was in charge of the financial funds of the medical service, always ordered that the use of pharmacy and drugs was paramount, expensive medicines and special cures being reserved only for officers.[64] Traditionally, the supervision of the army medical service lay in the hands of the Emperor's own personal physician,[65] but more often it was the commanders-in-chief who held this task. Montecuccoli and later Charles V of Lorraine introduced some improvements to alleviate the suffering of soldiers. They took care of several details concerning field hospitals, ambulances, hygiene, food, blankets and shelter. Both commanders insisted that the camp be kept clean and provided with water in order to limit the spread of diseases.

---

63 Hochedlinger, *Austria's Wars of Emergence*, p. 133.
64 K.u.K. Kriegsarchiv, 'Feldzüge des Prinzen Eugen', vol. I, p. 277.
65 Hochedlinger, *Austria's Wars of Emergence*, p. 135.

Infantry Organisation

In 1650, a regular infantry regiment was organised into 10 companies of 200 men, for an overall force of 2,031 or 2,033 men.[66]

Regimental staffs were formed as follows:

1 *Obrist Inhaber* or *Obrist Kommandant* (colonel proprietors or colonel commander)
1 *Obrist Lieutenant* (lieutenant-colonel)
1 *Obrist Wachtmeister* (major)
1 *Caplan* (chaplain)
1 *Regiment Quartiermeister* (regimental quartermaster)
1 *Regiment Schultheiss* (administrator)
1 *Regiment Feldscher* (surgeon)
1 *Profoss* 'cum suis' (*provost* with 8–10 guards)
1 *Regiments-Tambour* (drum-major)

Each company had a staff, the so-called *prima plana* ('first page')[67] composed as following:

1 *Hauptmann* (captain)
1 *Lieutenant* (lieutenant)
1 *Fahnrich* (ensign)
1 *Feldwebel* (sergeant major)
2 *Führern* (sergeants)
1 *Musterschreiber* (secretary)
1 *Fourier* (quartermaster)
1 *Feldscher* (surgeon)

Rank and file included:

1 *Gefreiter-Corporal* (exempt corporal)
8 *Corporalen* (corporals)
10 *Gefreite* (exempts)
6/8 *Spielleuten* (musicians)
164 *Gemeine* (privates)

In 1661, the Aulic War Council established for each company a strength of 114 musketeers and *Gefreite*, and 60 pikemen.[68] The companies maintained this establishment until 1672, when the number of pikemen decreased to 56. The strength grew to 205 men because of the introduction of eight *Grenadieren*. In wartime, the company would increase to 250 men, with a further 15

---

66 Wrede, *Geschichte der K. und K. Wehrmacht*, vol. I, p. 34.
67 Namely the officer and other ranks recorded on the first page of the muster roll.
68 F. Müller, *Die Kaiserl. Königl Österreichische Armee, seit Errichtung der stehenden Kriegsheere bis auf die neueste Zeit* (Prague, 1845), pp. 17–18.

pikemen, 29 musketeers and one corporal.[69] Pikemen were not diminished in number before the 1690s, but in the Hungarian war theatre they disappeared after 1688, converted to musketeers by order of *Feldmarschall* Ludwig von Baden.

The first company of each regiment was the *Leib-Compagnie*; the second company was the *Obrist Lieutenant Compagnie* and the third was called the *Obrist Wachtmeister Compagnie*. The other companies were identified by numbers starting from 4 to 10, or by the captain's name. The rule that required to keep the number of companies to 10 was not always respected, both because of the physical losses suffered in campaign and because of the amalgamation of companies from disbanded regiments. Thus in the 1660s, there were regiments that deployed for a while 12 or 16 companies.[70] In the late 1680s, in the infantry companies were established 3 or 4 *Furierschützen*, who served as guards for the officers, in order to regularise a rank that had previously been informally performed at the discretion of the colonels.

As discussed in the previous chapter, the standing regiments attempted to deploy their full strength in wartime, but in the Habsburg army the difference between its actual fighting force and theoretical regular strength was always very high. For instance in 1658, when the Imperial contingent resumed the campaign in Poland, the nine infantry regiments under Souches totalled 8,130 men and averaged 677 per battalion.[71] When on campaign, numbers were always reduced by combat injuries, fatalities, disease or desertion, but in the Imperial army the full fighting strength seems never to have been fully realised in the first place. When in the spring of 1664, *Feldmarschall* Montecuccoli led the army in the second Hungarian campaign, infantry battalion strength numbered 4–500 men each on average; only three regiments out of seven could deploy two tactical battalions,[72] the rest having been employed in garrison duties or dissolved. Further contemporary evidences confirm that in Hungary the actual basic strength always fluctuated considerably during 1660–64. Some units registered every year the loss of half of their manpower due to illness or desertion. In the Rhine campaign of 1675, the average size of the infantry regiments was 1,400 men and in the following years, the regiment often coincided with the tactical battalion of 1,000 men on average.[73]

Enlistment of units coming from the Empire occurred several time in this age and usually these regiments had a different establishment. In 1674, the Imperial army incorporated the infantry regiment of the Count of Reuss-Plauen (II-71), which had been capitulated for a strength of 1,000 men in eight companies. The muster executed in October registered 980 rank and

---

69 H. Meynert, *Geschichte der K. K. Österreichischen Armee, ihrer Heranbildung und Organisation, so wie ihrer Schicksale, Thaten und Feldzüge, von der frühesten bis auf die jetzige Zeit* (Vienna, 1854) vol. III, pp. 157–158.
70 Wrede, *Geschichte der K. und K. Wehrmacht*, vol. I, p. 35.
71 *Haupttabella der Infanteria*, 1658, in E. Opitz, *Österreich und Brandenburg im Schwedisch-Polnischen Krieg 1655–1660* (Boppard am Rhein: Harald Boldt, 1970), p. 75.
72 Österreichische Staatsarchiv-Kriegsarchiv, *Alte Feldakten* (Ungarn 1664/89).
73 Marr, 'Der Feldzug 1676 in Deutschland mit Benützung österreichischer Originalquellen', in *Österreichische Militärische Zeitschrift*, Vol. III–1844, p. 11.

file, but when the regiment arrived at the Rhine, the strength had deceased to just 324.[74]

Another source of enlistment for infantry regiments was offered by disbanding foreign units. In 1661, the infantry regiment *Sparr* (II-41) had been acquired from Brandenburg as reinforcement for the Imperial corps in Transylvania, while another regiment, *Wolframsdorff zu Fuss* (II-43), was sold by the electorate of Trier and destined for the same front.

These regiments, even if recruited abroad, were considered as the other 'German' infantry regiments. In this period, any 'foreign' unit served in the Imperial army, despite several foreigners usually being enlisted in the regiments. This occurred often during the campaigns against the Swedes in 1657–60, when some enemy garrisons in Pomerania and Denmark surrendered and entered Imperial service. In 1672 is registered the presence of Swiss soldiers, belonging to the regiment *Strein zu Fuss* (II-68), originally recruited in Tyrol and Carinthia. According to some alternative sources, the regiment was completed with the Swiss who served as Life Guards of the Archduke of Habsburg-Tyrol since 1664.[75]

In 1678, the need for infantry forced the Emperor to turn to the Dutch Republic. As the war against France ended, the provinces licensed part of their troops, but the House of Austria was still engaged in the conflict. Therefore, in late summer, a regiment of 2,000 men was raised with former soldiers of the Dutch army under Colonel Carl Mias (II-78). Seven years later, taking advantage of the reduction of strength voted by the States-General, the Emperor appointed the Walloon François Guillaume de Maigret as colonel proprietor, with the task of recruiting an infantry regiment with former Dutch soldiers (II-98). Unfortunately, the commission did not progress and the regiment was disbanded, leaving the companies already recruited to be amalgamated into the infantry engaged in Hungary against the Ottomans.

Another project for recruiting further regiments with soldiers from foreign armies took place in 1689, turning to the soldiers of the disbanded English army of James II Stuart. The assignment was entrusted to a certain Tadhg O'Hussy, who was a member of the Viennese Civic Guards. He had distinguished himself during the siege of 1683 and was quickly dispatched to Hamburg to make contact with the Jacobite exiles for recruiting a complete Irish regiment of 1,800 men.[76] Unfortunately, O'Hussy only managed to round up half of the original strength, because the men physically able were well on their way to France, in an endeavour to rejoin the Jacobite Forces there. Local Irishmen's warnings about the recruit being 'sent to the ally of William of Orange to battle with the Janissaries' were clearly now the public opinion, and considered no joke in Ireland.[77] O'Hussy led these recruits –

---

74 Marr, 'Der Feldzüg im Jahre 1675 in Deutschland', in *Österreichische Militärische Zeitschrift*, vol. III, 1839, p. 283.
75 In 1683, *Die Mölkerbastei*, XI, 1976. The regiment was disbanded in 1679.
76 Wrede, *Geschichte der K. und K. Wehrmacht*, vol. II, p. 170.
77 Mheara, 'The Wild Geese in Austria', p. 83: 'The fact that "the most Catholic king of all", as the French monarch liked to call himself, was secretly aiding and abetting the Turks assaulting

sick, starved, badly equipped, devoid of all motivation, herded across Europe from Hamburg to Hungary, and keeping up a state of revolt all the way. Here the men were placed under colonel and Jacobite former officer Jacob Wilson (II-92). The regiment continued to be registered among the Imperial infantry in Hungary, until disbanded in 1693.

The state of emergency in 1683 forced the Aulic War Council to turn to the militia. This decision involved the *Landregiment* of Silesia, which was incorporated into the regular infantry in early 1684 as *Houchin zu Fuss* (II-94). Most of these units hastily recruited from disparate sources had a short life, on the contrary this regiment inaugurated a history destined to end in 1918.[78]

The *Frei-Compagnien* of infantry (Free Companies of Foot), raised from retired soldiers and invalids, represented other permanent infantry. In 1663, there was at least one *Frei-Compagnie* in Érsekúivár and others in Sopron, Pressburg, Győr and Komáron.[79] The usefulness of these units was largely limited to garrison duties, explaining the reason for their absence from the calculations of fighting force. Free Companies continued to be active in the next decade, although their contribution against the Hungarian rebellion in the 1670s and the war against the Porte was limited to garrison duties.

As late as the second half of the century, the Imperial infantry fought in large formations up to eight ranks deep. This was the better way to conduct the troops in battle, which were composed of many untrained soldiers, despite that the unwieldy nature of it had become apparent even before the Thirty Years' War. Gradually, the massive columns were reconfigured to linear formations of six ranks. After the disappearance of the pike, the four-rank formation became dominant.

Montecuccoli introduced several tactical changes for the infantry, the actual meaning of which has been little researched. Though the six-rank battalion was Montecuccoli's favourite infantry formation, he deployed the infantry in a large variety of dispositions. Especially against the Ottomans, he adopted a much less profound alignment than is normally thought. In 1664, at Szentgotthárd, for the final assault that decided the victory, he deployed the troops alternating the infantry with the cavalry. The deployment of units is described as follows: 'pikemen on three ranks, with musketeers in two ranks on each wing; one musketeer "sleeve" of 24 men between the cavalry squadrons. Infantry was not to fire by individual ranks, nor the infantry and cavalry divided […] in the space between the infantry had to advance the horsemen at the command.'[80] These was the instructions for the deployment of a small army, and the minimal ranks helped the allies to extend to the maximum the space occupied by the troops. Although the European trend

---

the Pope's own Holy Empire had as yet failed to register in the minds of the Irish people, too preoccupied with disasters of their own.'
78 Disbanded in 1918 as I.R. N. 36; Wrede, *Geschichte der K. und K. Wehrmacht*, vol. I, p. 374.
79 *Deutsche Frei-Compagnie* Mayer; see in Wrede, *Geschichte der K. und K. Wehrmacht*, vol. II, p. 561.
80 Montecuccoli, Libro II, *Aforismi applicati alla guerra possibile col Turco in Ungheria*, p. 76.

was towards fewer ranks, two ranks of musketeers was very unusual in 1664. Certainly, in 1664, Montecuccoli could rely on troops generally well trained (at least the Imperial and the French ones), because while these thin formations made better use of firepower, the front line came to be extended to the detriment of manoeuvrability. In the following decades, the shallower infantry formation transformed the engagements in the static exchange of volleys. To limit this outcome, Montecuccoli, as well as his successors, introduced at a larger scale the deployment of two *Treffen* (battles), usually formed with infantry in the centre and two wings of cavalry, and a tactical reserve.

Infantry fire differed depending on whether it was facing the Ottomans or some 'Western' enemy. Against the Ottomans particular care was taken to keep up uninterrupted fire, since they were wont to use the pause for storming against the enemy. To address this, in 1688, Margrave Ludwig von Baden prescribed training in platoon firing for all the infantry of the field army in Hungary.[81] Against Swedes and French volley fire was preferred.

The increasing importance of firing contributed to form regular battalions of identical strength. Under Montecuccoli, each regiment had to deploy in campaign at least two tactical battalions with a strength of 1,000 men each, usually formed by five companies, but very frequently the regular size of the regimen was lower. When the regiment deployed less than one battalion, its companies were joined to other regiments to form a tactical unit of at least 500 men. Tactically, the Imperial bataillon formed a *corps de bataille* (centre) and two wings, all together as known *Haupt-Divisionen,* each under the command of a captain with a lieutenant or ensign as adjutant and a sergeant major. Pikeman were distributed at the centre of the battalion with musketeers at both sides.

Each division was divided again in two *Halb-Flügel* (half wings) each formed by two *Züge* (platoons). To each platoon was assigned a corporal with another three who were placed at both sides of the formation. The soldiers were placed inside the division by order of seniority, and then the veterans took their places in the last rows and the tallest in the wings. If the grenadiers remained within their company, they occupied the right wing in single platoons, otherwise each battalion formed a 'sleeve' of 30 or 40 grenadiers on the right wing. More groups of grenadiers were usually assembled in storming companies during the siege. The ensigns took their places in the centre of the battalion, with a lieutenant or a senior ensign in command of a 'guard' formed by a half dozen sergeants and exempts. Musicians formed a group in the centre of the battalion behind the last rank. In battle, officers and NCOs entered the ranks in the first line. Under assault of cavalry, the pikemen deployed themselves in the first rank with the pike butt on the ground, turned against the approaching enemy, and leaving space for the musketeers to fire above their heads. When muskets replaced pikes, each battalion formed a square, placing Frisian horses on the corners as additional defence.

---

81   K.u.K. Kriegsarchiv, 'Feldzüge des Prinzen Eugen', vol. I, p. 704.

In the normal position the soldier kept his feet half a step distant from the next man, pinned forward, body and head straight. With the left hand he held the weapon on his shoulder, musketeers and grenadiers with the trigger lever pointing down. The right arm stretched out to the powder flask. In case of rain, the musket was carried under the left armpit, held to the body with the elbow. If the musketeer was also armed with a *Schweinsfeder* (a musket rest with a spike), he held it with his left hand secured to a strap, and with the right held the weapon obliquely in front of his chest. A corporal held the halberd to the left side, a sergeant and sergeant major to the right.

Cavalry Organisation

In 1650, cuirassiers and dragoons were organised into eight companies. It was the original peacetime strength, because after 1657, companies increased to 10, with an overall 1,018 cuirassiers and 918 dragoons.[82] In the field, two companies formed one tactical squadron.

Cuirassier company staff (*prima plana*):
1 *Rittermeister* (captain)
1 *Lieutenant* (lieutenant)
1 *Kornett* (standard bearer)
1 *Wachtmeister* (brigadier sergeant)
1 *Trompeter* (trumpeter)
3 *Korporalen* (corporals)
89 *Einspännigen* (privates)

In a non-combatant role were included 1 *Fourier* (quartermaster), 1 *Musterschreiber* (secretary), 1 *Sattler* (saddler), 1 *Schmied* (smith) and 1 *Feldscher* (surgeon).

Regimental staff included:

1 *Obrist Inhaber* or *Obrist Kommandant* (proprietor colonel or colonel commander)
1 *Obrist-Lieutenant* (lieutenant-colonel)
1 *Obrist-Wachtmeister* (major)
1 *Adjutant* (warrant officer)
1 *Pauker* (drummer)
1 *Auditor* (auditor)
1 *Regimentschirurg* (surgeon)
1 *Profoss* (provost)

The full basic cuirassier regiment numbered 1,018 men with 977 horses. Dragoon regiments had 10 companies, but the strength included just 79 *Gemeine Dragoner*. Company ranks were the same for cuirassiers, except one

---

82 Wrede, *Geschichte der K. und K. Wehrmacht*, vol. III, part one, p. 43 and p. 51.

Hauptmann (captain), one *Fahnrich* (ensign), one *Pfeiffer* or *Hautbois*, one *Tambour* and one *Feldwebel* replaced the *Rittermeister, Cornett, Trompeter* and *Wachtmeister*. Furthermore, the dragoon regimental staff did not include an *Auditor* or *Pauker*. The regiment of dragoons resulted in a full strength of 918 men with 874 horses.

For cuirrasiers, as occurred also with the infantry, exceptions in strength were common. In 1672, the regiment *Gallas* (IC-32) joined the field army with just six companies, while three years later *Poiger Cuirassieren* (IC-36) marched to Upper Hungary with half of the regular force.[83]

The Imperial army deployed in this age one of the higher percentages of cavalry compared to other European armies. In 1662, notwithstanding the disbanding of many regiments, cuirassiers, dragoons and light cavalrymen, represented 32 percent of the regular army strength. In the following years, this percentage never dropped below 35 percent. The need for cavalry stemmed from the nature of the warfare. The Hungarian war theatre required many cavalry not only to face Ottoman superiority, but also because horsemen were the best instrument in a battlefield almost deprived of roads. In the 17th century, cavalry represented the 'frame of the army' and in the 1670s Montecuccoli still recommended that 'ideal army' of 50,000 men would have comprised at least 22,000 horsemen.[84]

Due to the fact that their use involved the horse in almost every circumstance, the cuirassiers constituted the first force of battle in the field. The cuirassier was the iconic Imperial cavalryman and usually recruited in the Habsburg domains or in the Empire, but there was also one regiment recruited in the Spanish domains of the Low Countries and Italy. This was the regiment *Fabbri Cuirassieren* (IC-23), raised in 1659 and later, in 1664, ceded to Spain.[85] Another 'Italian' cuirassier regiment was raised by the Pope in 1663, for the war against the Porte in Hungary. The funds to raise it came from Italy, but the recruits were ethnic Germans (and Bohemian-Moravians) and just the colonel, Giuliano Braida (IC-27), and some junior officers had been appointed among Roman aristocrats. The initiative encountered some difficulties because in 1664 the regiment was far from complete. In September the war ended, and therefore all the companies were disbanded. External initiatives like this were usually welcomed by the Emperor, however the Imperial cavalry incorporated also regiments from other states. In 1662, the hired cuirassier regiment of Münster *Post* (IC-25) entered Imperial service for Transylvania. Then in 1674, the Emperor integrated the cuirassier regiment of Cologne *Chavaignac* (IC34). A second regiment was incorporated in the same year, *Bayreuth Cuirassieren* (IC-33), from the Franconian circle, and a third in 1676, when the regiment *Sachsen Cuirassieren* (IC-39) was acquired from electoral Saxony. Enlisted as cuirassiers, 600 polish horsemen under Lubomirski (IC-48) entered Imperial service after the battle of Vienna, while in 1684 further two

---

83 *Ibidem*, vol. III, part two, p. 539.
84 Luraghi, 'Le Opere di Raimondo Montecuccoli', vol. I, p. 109.
85 Wrede, *Geschichte der K. und K. Wehrmacht*, vol. III, part two, p. 535.

cuirassier regiments came from the bishopric of Osnabrück, *Hanover* (IC-49) and the Electorate of Cologne, *Füstenberg* (IC-50).

Cuirassiers represented an elite force of the Imperial cavalry, but they were also the most expansive. Equipment and tall horses contributed to increase the cost of the armoured trooper and only in the 1670s did the Aulic War Council take into consideration the alternative offered by dragoons. In 1660, there were just a couple of dragoon regiments, after the disbanding of two regiments raised in 1657. Another regiment was raised in 1662 increasing the number to three. Especially renowned as commanders of dragoons were the French, Walloon or Lorraine officers and it was certainly no coincidence that in 1664, two of the three dragoon regiments had colonels and many of the regimental and company staffs coming from these countries. Dragoons were a relative novelty in the Imperial army, but if they were essentially infantrymen who fought on foot but moved on horseback, now – especially after the experiences of the Swedish and French armies – they were turning into soldiers capable of operating both as horsemen and infantry. This new approach was adopted also in the Imperial army, especially against the Hungarian rebels; nine *Frei-Compagnien* of dragoons were raised for Upper Hungary in 1675–1679. Dragoons were an acceptable compromise for countering the rebels in this war theatre and in fact, in 1678 they represented half of the mounted force in Hungary. The dragoons gradually increased their number with new regiments, and in 1688 totalled nine regiments. Among these was included also the regiment *Lodron* (ID-8), raised in 1674 but sometimes qualified as *Croater*. The regiment had been effectively recruited in Croatia and for this reason it appeared under this denomination. Almost certainly, this unit was equipped differently from other dragoon regiments, at least until the 1680s.

Croats and Hussars, who had increased in both number and importance in the Thirty Years' War, almost disappeared in the wake of the army reduction of 1649–50. It was not until 1657 to establish new regiments of light cavalry, *Croater* regiments *Gutschenich* (IHc-1) and *Lubetich* (IHc-2), were raised for the incoming campaign in Poland, but disbanded respectively in 1665 and 1660. In 1664, four regiments of *Husaren* were raised enlisting 4,000 Hungarian *Insurrectionis* militiamen. Regiments *Nádasdy* (IHc-4) and *Batthyáni* (IHc-5) each had eight *Husaren* companies and four *Hajduken* (footmen) companies. The other regiments, *Koháry* (IHc-6) and *Bercsény* (IHc-7) had a strength of 500 horsemen.[86] Hussars and Croats continued for a long time to represent a kind of poor relative of the Imperial cavalry, and apart from a few cases, they remained incomplete[87] and frequently disbanded, also because the endemic rebellions in Hungary continued until 1697.

In 1672, the Aulic War Council established a 'war strength' of at least 900 horses for all the cavalry at the beginning of the campaign, not including the regimental staff.[88] Each cavalry company deployed 82 privates and eight

---

86 Wrede, *Geschichte der K. und K. Wehrmacht*, vol. III, part two, p. 787.
87 In 1684, the newly established regiment *Zichy Husaren* (IHc-14) numbered just five companies. Ibidem, p. 793.
88 Meynert, *Geschichte der K. K. Österreichiscen Armee*, vol. III, p. 120.

officers and NCOs. The difference between the theoretical and effective strength remained usual, and in 1675, the cavalry regiment's average registered strength was 800 troopers.[89]

In the second half of the 17th century, the cuirassiers were the only cavalry tactically organised in squadrons, while dragoons and light cavalry were usually determined in companies. As in the infantry, also in the cavalry there existed a strict separation between administrative and tactical units, regulated by the *Feld-Ordennanz* which emanated from Montecuccoli, which – except for the adaptations occurred later – remained until 1740. The tactical deployment of the squadrons took the name of *Ordennanz* (ordinance). In the cuirassier regiments, the *Leib-compagnie* and the fourth company formed the first squadron, which took the name of *Leibschwadron*; in turn, the second squadron was the *Obrist Lieutenant-Schwadron* and the third the *Obrist Wachtmeister-Schwadron*. The remaining two squadrons were identified with the name of the respective senior captain, who was responsible for the tactical command of the squadron within the ordinance. Tactically the squadron was divided into two *Züge* (platoons) – each commanded by a captain or a lieutenant – and each *Züge* in three *Mannschaft* (squads). Each squadron would be composed of the same number of men, and therefore on the field the membership of a specific company was no longer taken into account. At a higher level, cavalry brigades or corps were formed, which did not have a defined structure and tended to be formed only for short periods just for tactical use. The brigade, which could also have been a mixture of dragoons and cuirassiers, but rarely of hussars, consisted of at least eight squadrons and its use became more frequent with the increase of the size of the armies and consequently of the cavalry corps. The positioning of the officers in the battle order followed established rules. The officers of the companies were located in front of the squadron 'five steps forward in the middle of the line' (one step was equivalent to 65/70 cm.).[90] While the squadron commanders were 10 paces ahead; the colonel had the adjutant or the lieutenant at his side, five steps back. On their side, five steps to the right or left, there was a trumpeter. The kettledrums of the regiment were instead placed behind the *Leibschwadron*, from which a guard was formed with 12 troopers and one corporal. The standards of the companies, in the ranks of the first line, occupied the central position of the squadron; the non-commissioned officers were instead placed on the wings and behind the ordinance. Between the squadrons an interval of 10 to 40 steps was left depending on the terrain. All these divisions had as their reference base the *Ordennanz Flügel* (wing of the ordinance) therefore, if a regiment occupied the left wing, its ordinance wing was the left one.

The same disposition was later adopted by the dragoons, who in foot combat followed the same tactical scheme of the infantry. Therefore they deployed a *Corp de Bataille* and two *Flügel* wings. On the field, a regiment of dragoons was tactically equivalent to a single infantry battalion.

---

89 Marr, 'Der Feldzug im Jahre 1675 in Deutschland. Nach österreichischen Originalquellen', in *Österreichische Militärische Zeitschrift*, Vol. I – 1840, p. 140.
90 K.u.K. Kriegsarchiv, 'Feldzüge des Prinzen Eugen', vol. I, p. 360.

The threat coming from the Porte was considered more dangerous and this decisively conditioned the cavalry tactical doctrine. The employment of the cavalry in campaign reflected the war experiences gained in the wars against the Ottomans and therefore favoured the mass rather than mobility and the constant volume of fire instead of the assault. This approach, which had procured so many victories, conditioned the use of the cavalry also against the Western adversaries. The cuirassiers and the cavalry in general, charged the enemy in closed order proceeding at low speed, while the gallop was then used only to pursuit enemies in retreat.

Depending on the adversaries encountered on the different fronts, there were considerable differences in the order of battle, especially in the deployment of squadrons, which against the *Erbfeind* (the hereditary enemy, the Ottomans), were deployed in three lines in order to have greater compactness. Against 'regular' enemies like the French, the squadrons were deployed in two lines only. In the ordinance at a standstill, the distance between the lines had to be five steps and the intervals between the rows such as the horses did not touch and hinder the action of the horseman. Regardless of the type of enemy, the dragoons were deployed in three lines, both on horseback and on foot. The three-line deployment was ultimately the one preferred by the Imperial cavalry commanders, because it was tactically more flexible; it also allowed for a simpler manoeuvre, and at the same time it offered an acceptable compromise between speed and covering of the terrain.

The training of cuirassiers still included many of the complex tactical manoeuvres developed by the Imperial cavalry schools at the beginning of the 17th century and perfected under Montecuccoli. Officers were obliged to train their horses in the Spanish manner and the education of their men focused on evolutions, conversions, the handling of weapons and horse fire. The importance of manoeuvring in the field derived from the typically 17th century discipline which considered cavalry as the mobile element inserted in the linear order, in support of the infantry. The result of this conception attributed an increasing importance to the volume of fire, and besides the cuirassiers was the main product of the transformation that occurred within the cavalry. The belief of many commanders of the need to maintain cohesion and symmetry in the battle order was the foundation of the art of the war in the 17th century.

The use of firearms, considered as the best method to face faster and more numerous enemies, continued to be the most important training. On horseback, cuirassiers and dragoons held the sword hanging to the right hand, and at the command of the non-commissioned officers, they extracted the left pistol from the holster ready to fire. The motions continued by extracting the other pistol and then the musket in the case of the dragoons. The cuirassiers, if included in the equipment, finally shot with the short musket, although the use of these weapons took place mainly in the service on foot, which happened much more frequently than one might normally think. In fact, in addition to normal quarters operations such as pickets, sentinels etc, executed without being on horseback, the possibility of performing actions on foot even in combat was far from remote and for this reason it was necessary for the cuirassier to have an armament capable of being transformed into a footman or, rather, in a dragoon. Moreover, the service on foot happened for lack of horse, a circumstance occurring many times, such as during the siege of Vienna in 1683, when about 100 cuirassiers of the regiment *Dupigny* (IC-2) joined the garrison as footmen.

Against the Ottoman and Tatar cavalry, both cuirassiers and dragoons were instructed to recharge on horseback. The training also included firing motions to support the infantry movement. When firing, the horsemen had to aim at the belly and to facilitate this the dragoons – who normally mounted smaller horses – rose on the stirrups. The fire was always carried out at the normal step, with the lines tightly closed, making the horses of the second line advance until they touched those in front with the chest. To keep the volume of fire constant, it was executed half a rank at a time.

The chronic condition of numerical inferiority against the Ottomans forced the Imperial cavalry to introduce specific formations such as the cavalry square. This type of formation was considered the most effective countermeasure to support the assaults of the enemies, especially if sustained by isolated corps. The complex series of manoeuvres to be performed to form a square was executed in step or in trot in case of imminent danger. To form a square of six squadrons, five different manoeuvres were required. The depth of the formation was established on two lines and each side fired in half ranks. Thus formed, the square had to be able to move in every direction keeping itself cohesive and on several occasions the cuirassiers as well as the dragoons sustained fights against Ottomans and Tatars for a long time, marching in that way for hours.

Notwithstanding that dragoons and Croat hussars were not considered actual cavalry, some tactical differences became less apparent in the 1680s, especially regarding the dragoons. Both specialties continued to reflect their difference in tactical discipline and training, however, the tactical flexibility of the cavalry received a decisive impulse from the experiences accumulated in the conflicts of the late 17th century.[91] Even the hussars, long considered irregular cavalry and numerically of little importance, achieved remarkable successes and their employment extended also on the fronts of Western Europe. Light cavalrymen from East Europe were well known in the West since 1618, but their presence had been often episodic. The Habsburgs recruited several units of Croats during the Thirty Years' War, but the actual start of the permanent presence of this kind of cavalry in the Imperial army was the late 17th century. The tactics developed on the Hungarian battlefields, establishing a model destined to last until the Napoleonic wars. The hussars continued to perform tasks completely different from the rest of the cavalry, especially in relation to their tactical use for which they represented a specialty. The hussars were not trained to fight in close order, nor to exploit the mass with a charge, but compared to the other light cavalry they were equipped with a more varied tactical repertoire. They were asked to perform

---

91 Montecuccoli, in 1645, stated: 'Dragoons fight as infantry, and as such must be used, even if they move on horseback.' *Delle Battaglie* (first treaty), in Luraghi 'Le Opere di raimondo Montecuccoli', vol. II, p. 48. About 28 years later, in his second treaty, he did not repeat this statement.

different tasks that required uncommon flexibility of use. This ability to adapt to different war scenarios shows well the transformation that occurred regarding the tactical doctrines of the light cavalry. In 1676, two regiments of hussars joined the field army on the Upper Rhine. There is little information about their employment until 1678, but some exaggeratedly optimistic reports related about their actions against the French in Alsace.[92] Here, one of the main functions performed by the light cavalry was reconnaissance and the gathering of information. Although military operations took place slowly and, on many occasions, the armies stopped for weeks in front of each other making reconnaissance superfluous, the Imperial side gave much importance to the detailed knowledge of the adversary. The accounts of the operations reported news of encounters and skirmishes with the capture of prisoners. Even when there were no large-scale actions in the open field, the hussars were used unceasingly in surprises, ambushes, alarms, destruction of bridges, capture of convoys, cattle and horses. These actions anticipated the exploits performed in Germany and in Italy in the War of the Spanish Succession, but evidently the hussars had gained a certain reputation already in the 1670s, since their presence in foreign armies began a few years later.

The raids carried out by the hussars also served to secure the land around the armies and inflict indirect losses on their opponent, taking prisoners, preying on horses and destroying magazines and supply trains. Furthermore, these actions had the task of discovering places where to forage and carry out requisition, as well as to deprive the enemy of resources by destroying everything that could not be transported. These actions differed little from the tasks carried out by their traditional enemies, the Ottoman *dely* and the Tatars.

In addition to reconnaissance and covert activities, the hussars could be used in battle as skirmishers against the enemy cavalry or infantry, using their firearms and avoiding the adversary's impact thanks to the greater agility of their horses. The armament used by the hussars to counter the enemy cavalry included the use of a particular weapon, the *Hegyesztor* (in German *Panzerschrecker*, the long blade saddle weapon), useful against armoured enemies. To counter the Ottoman and the Tatar cavalry, at least until the last years of the century, they also employed the lance.

The marching order of the cavalry was regulated according to the tactical scenario and therefore dragoons and cuirassiers performed the ordinary march in column and another *en Bataille*. In this latter the squadrons moved forward or backward, maintaining the order of battle. The ordinary paces were the step and the little trot. In order to march in column, the squadrons were arranged according to the width of the roads and therefore columns could be had for squad, platoon or squadron, while on paths the march proceeded for half-squad or single horseman. Usually the light cavalry preceded the marching columns advanced in open order and detached small parties of five or 10 men to patrol the terrain and ensure transit through fords, woods and other less easy passages. In the

---

92 Gustav von Kortzfleisch, *Der oberelsässische Winterfeldzug 1674–65 und das Treffen bei Türkheim* (Strasbourg: J.H.E .Heitz, 1904), p. 28.

Hungarian war theatre, which was characterised by a terrain crossed by water meadows and swamps, the presence of the cavalry for securing the march of the army was indispensable, so it was not rare that cuirassiers and dragoons were required to perform tasks of exploration, detaching a number of *Bereitschaft* (patrol party) before to the marching columns, in charge of the medium-range patrol. The employment of small parties of cavalry for this kind of operation was a common practice in the Imperial army even before the presence of regular regiments of hussars, and throughout the 17th century the *Bereitschaft* of cuirassiers or dragoons was used for this purpose, not only in Hungary, but everywhere the ground could hide a threat. The *Bereitschaft* also performed more specific offensive tasks, especially in raids and ambush, but it served mainly to protect convoys and marching columns and small parties were usually formed for escorting prisoners. The classic *Bereitschaft* acted under the orders of a sergeant or a corporal and consisted of about 20–30 horsemen who lined up on a front about 100 paces wide on open ground, with a pair of men posted further ahead within reach of the main group.

Artillery Organisation

In the second half of the 17th century, the military professions experienced a further transformation, as now armies consisted not only of professional soldiers but also of specialists, of which an artilleryman was the specialist par excellence. All over Western Europe, the artillery continued to maintain an independent status separate from the rest of the army. In the Imperial army terms, functions, and even ranks and assignments were used that were quite different from the other specialities. The *General Feldzeugmeister*, the commander of artillery, did not have the same obligations as other senior officers and even his subordinates were not subject to the authority of other army commanders, including, on occasion, the commander-in-chief. All the personnel involved were trained professionals belonging to a tight-knit, closed group, often passing down their job within a limited number of families, creating family dynasties of artillerymen. In the composition of the corps there were defined ranks less comparable with the infantry and cavalry units. The *Constabler* held the function of chief of the piece, directed by the *Hauptmann*, who was in charge the direction of a battery, usually formed by six guns. The ordinary artilleryman, known as a *Büchsenmeister*, formed the personnel who handled the artillery pieces, guns as well as mortars.

Artillery officers recruited additional personnel depending on the organisation of the artillery train for the campaign. In 1660, artillery personnel included those whom we would now consider as belonging to the engineering staff, sappers, or the arsenal crew, like the *Bindenmeister* (wheelwright), *Pulverhüter* (gunpowder holder) and *Schlossermeister* (locksmith). During the war against the Swedes in 1657–60, other ranks also mentioned included the *Kriegsbuch-Halter* (military accountant), *Comiss-Metzger* (ordnance butcher), *Comiss-Bäck und Müller* (ordnance miller and baker) and *Kroater-fahnrich*, who led the light cavalry troop forming the protective escort for artillery trains. Drivers and all draft animals were recruited separately, or supplied by private contractors with a *Patent* as for the ordinary regiments.

In 1661 the artillery deployed 12 companies of *Büchsenmeister* who increased with further four companies recruited in 1664. The regular strength of a single company was 150 rank and file. In the campaign of 1664, the Imperialists deployed 24 bronze field pieces with a calibre between eight and 12 pounds; the artillery crew numbered about 400 men, including the drivers.[93] From 1663 onwards, the artillery corps included a company of 100 *Grenadieren* and *Minierern* (miners), recruited and trained by the *Land-Haus und Zeugmaiester* Count Traun.[94]

In 1666, the permanent artillery strength decreased to 12 companies again.[95] This force diminished to just 142 artillerists with 68 drivers and 497 horses in 1672.[96] Three years later, Montecuccoli had 180 *Constabler* and *Büchsenmeister*,[97] and in the war against the Ottomans, six companies with 600 artillerymen supported the field army in campaign in 1685.[98] On campaign, the artillery drew authority from the commander-in-chief, who usually appointed as director another general chosen among the most experienced in matter of artillery and siege warfare.

Since 1657, all the guns were cast and processed in the Imperial arsenal of Seilerstätte in Vienna. In the same year models, patterns, calibres and ammunition were also finally standardised. Generally the categorisation took into account the length of the barrel in relation to the calibre. Thus the piece with a lower ratio was the *Kartaune* (cannon), followed by the longer *Feldschlange* (culverin) and finally by the fixed artillery and *Wallmuskete* (rampart muskets).

The Imperial artillery park was divided into two categories: *Feldstücke* (field guns) and *Batteriestücke* (fixed artillery), which also included fortress and siege artillery. This distinction was not always respected, because on campaign both were employed, but usually the *Feldstücke* included the artillery pieces ranging from 6 to 12 lb and the lighter 2- or 3-pounder field pieces.

The most common classification of the artillery pieces in the mid 17th century is summarised below:

---

93 W. Nottebohm, 'Montecuccoli und die Legende von St. Gotthard (1664)', in *Wissenschaftliche Beilage zum Programm des Friedrich Werderschen Gymnasiums zu Berlin* (Berlin, 1887), p. 32.
94 Wrede, *Geschichte der K. und K. Wehrmacht*, vol. III, part two, p. 269.
95 A. Dolleczek, *Geschichte der Österreichischen Artillerie von den frühesten Zeiten bis zur Gegenwart* (Vienna, 1887), p. 209.
96 Dolleczek, *Geschichte der Österreichischen Artillerie*, p. 210.
97 Marr, 'Der Feldzug im Jahre 1675 in Deutschland. Nach österreichischen Originalquellen', in *Österreichische Militärische Zeitschrift*, Vol. III – 1839, p. 283.
98 Dolleczek, *Geschichte der Österreichischen Artillerie*, p. 210.

Artillery piece:	Calibre in Austrian lb*	Barrel length	Weight in kg.	Artillerists	Assistants	Draft Animal	Shot frequency in 24 hours
Ganze Kartaune	48	380	6,800	4	12–16	24	50
Dreiviertel Kartaune	36	380	5,300	3–4	12–14	20	60
Halbe Kartaune	24	370	4,300	3	10–12	16	80
Viertel Kartaune, or *Ganze Feldstück*	12	320	2,500	2	6–8	8–10	100
Einhalbsviertel Kartaune	6	290	1,400	1	3–4	6	100
Einsviertel Feldstück	3	110–150	400	1	2–-4	4–6	100
Ganze Feldschlange	18	460	3,200	3	9–10	14	80
Halbe Feldschlange	8–9	400–420	1,900–2,000	2	6	8–10	90
Viertel Feldschlange, or *Falkaune*	5–6	250–260	1,700	1	4	6	100
Halbe Quartierschlange	1–1.5	200–230	680	1	1–2	4	100
Falconet	2–3	260–290	800	1	1–2	4	100
Halbes Falconet	1	220	480	1	1	1–2	**
Serpentinel, or *Kleins Schlängel*	0.5	160	300	1	1	1–2	**

* The 17th century Austrian lb was equivalent to the Nuremberg lb of 682 grams.
** Limitless shot.

Since the last years of the Thirty Years' War, the Imperial commanders had adopted the Swedish concept of regimental light artillery, deploying 3 lb or 4 lb guns in the first line to support the infantry fire.[99] To improve the firing rate, in the 1670s the Imperial arsenal introduced the first *Geschwindgeschütze-Stücke* (fast fire pieces). These cannon had a fire chamber projected to receive a prepared charge including powder and projectile. This pieces were known also as *canon à la Suédoise* and the expedient was basically the same for the grapeshot. In the same period appeared also the last multi-barrel guns, less employed in field engagements and mostly confined to the forts.[100]

Mortars were employed as siege artillery and classified alongside the howitzers. Mortars existed up to 1,000 lb, but the largest calibre mortar used was 300 lb. The other calibres normally used, and most widespread, were the 100 lb and 50 lb. The howitzer replaced the old *Kammer-Geschütze*, and the calibres most widespread and employed were the 8, 10, 12, 15, 20 and 30 lb.

---

99 Montecuccoli, *Delle Battaglie* (first treaty), in Luraghi 'Opere di Raimondo Montecuccoli', vol. II, p. 47.
100 One 50 multi-barrel gun, dated 1678, is preserved in the *Wiener Waffensamlung*. The barrels are mounted in two layers.

THE ARMY OF THE EMPEROR

The Royal Hungarian Army and the *Militärgrenze*

Alongside the standing army, the Emperor had the power to deploy the Hungarian crown's militia, a relic of the feudal age, as a first line defence against Ottoman incursion. During its centuries-old history, the House of Austria clashed with the Ottoman Empire in eight separate conflicts, but before 1660, the Emperor had faced the 'hereditary enemy' only in the 'Long War' of 1593–1606 and earlier in the conflicts between 1527 and 1566. All the clashes were fought on the same terrain of Hungary, Croatia and Transylvania. On each occasion, the Ottomans threatened Vienna. In 1529 they laid siege to the capital for the first time as well as menacing the provinces with devastating raids in Austria, Styria, Krain and Moravia. Although the aim to take the Austrian capital had failed, the Porte had historically always militarily prevailed: three-quarters of Hungary was ruled by a Turkish *paşa* sent from Constantinople. As a result, the Habsburgs maintained only a narrow strip of territory in the northern area of the Drina and Raab rivers, leaving them dangerously exposed to enemy attacks. Even when modest territorial gains had been achieved, the Sultan had always managed to impose his political conditions on the Emperor.

The Royal Army was as yet structured on ancient territorial lines, where the *comitates* (counties) were the main units of administration. Although their role changed over the years from being administrative, royal centres for regional tax collection for the nobility living on the territories, the counties maintained their traditional military function in the seventeenth century.

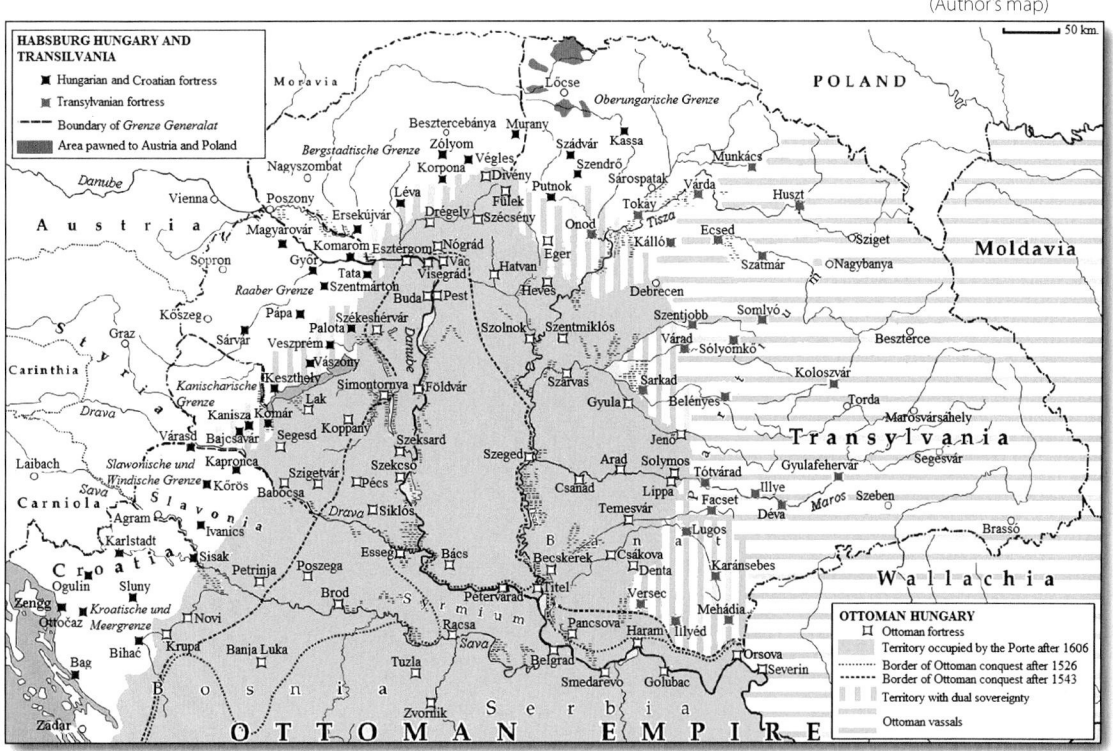

The Hungarian and Croatian *Militärgrenze*, 1662. (Author's map)

For decades, the defence of the Hungarian kingdom lay in the hands of the increasingly outdated feudal style system with general levies of troops being raised by counties and free royal cities, alongside the contingents of the provinces. The original Hungarian military structure comprised three sections: nobles' troops, *Militia Portalis*, and general levies (called *insurrectionis*). Every Hungarian and Croatian aristocrat was obligated to military service, the so-called *Primipilus*, and was also charged with the duty of recruiting certain soldiers dependent on the value of his property. For every 20 farms or *masserias* – *portae* – one cavalryman and infantryman had to be equipped for the militia, and these troops were originally identified as *Militia Portalis*. If the Parliament voted for a general call to arms, each farm would add an additional horseman and one foot soldier to join the army. Since the previous century, the Austrian *Hofkriegsrat* had tried to progressively reduce the aristocratic influence on the militia, maintaining only the formal existence of the 'Insurrection'. The long period of peace from 1606 to 1663 influenced the Kingdom of Hungary's defence policy, causing a deep stagnation in military matters. If, theoretically, the *Insurrectionis* could assemble more than 80,000 men in 1660, only 15–20,000 were actually suitable for a campaign.

On 14 July 1663, the Hungarian 'army' encamped on the left bank of the Danube between Bratislava and Érsekújvár totalled just 9,000 poorly-equipped men. Montecuccoli described them as 'for the most part inexperienced villains, forcibly detained and therefore ready to flee from the field […] or not accustomed to facing the enemy, poorly armed and obliged to stay in the country for only a few days.'[101] One year after, Count Ferenc Nádasdy led a force of 12,000 militiamen who, however, joined the field army the day after the battle of Szentgotthárd. The military discipline of this hastily equipped and trained levy remained erratic and often low. However, on some occasions, particularly in defensive actions and led by capable officers, the Hungarian and Croatian militia behaved valiantly, fighting alongside the best equipped and trained *Grenzer* bordersmen or professional soldiers.

For decades, the Habsburgs possessed few field officers and commanders who were experienced in warfare or diplomacy against the Ottomans; nor were they familiar with the geography and strategic conditions of Hungary or Croatia. Hungarian and Croatian officers, knowledgeable of the terrain and experienced in Ottoman warfare, made up in some way for the shortcomings of the Lower Austrian nobles who showed a lack of familiarity with Hungarian conditions. This class of officers became increasingly relevant as commanders of the *Militärgrenze* (military border).

The main Hungarian defensive strategy comprised a line of frontier fortresses extending from the Adriatic Sea to Transylvania. This chain of 100–120 large and small fortresses was organisationally divided into six *Grenzgeneralat* (border generalties). Each generalty came under the command of a border captain general (*Grenzgeneral* or *Grenzoberst*) quartered in the main regional fortress or fortified city of the province. Smaller demesnes

---

101 Montecuccoli, *Della Guerra col Turco in Ungheria*, in Luraghi 'Le Opere di Raimondo Montecuccoli', vol. II, p. 412.

fell under the direction of larger fortresses, in accordance with uniform principles. The keystone of the six military borders and the most important linchpin in the defensive line was at Komárom (today Komárno in Slovakia), a strongly fortified town along the Danube. Straddling the major military highway, the fortress was of critical strategic importance in the defence of the Habsburgs' hereditary provinces, and especially Vienna. The fortress was the command centre for the Danube flotilla and its general captain answered directly to Vienna.

For a long while, the military border had preserved Vienna from Ottoman attacks, but already in the 1660s several border fortresses needed restoration, enlargement and defensive improvement, especially on its eastern side. The eastern military border had served a dual function. Firstly, it acted as a protective bastion, not only against the Ottomans, but also against the Porte's vassal states, where Tatars riders were usually quartered. Here, the newly modernised border fortress of Szatmár was a crucial hub for the control of the Tisza River area, and played a special role in the defence system of Upper Hungary by impeding attacks from the north-east. Therefore, after 1606, when Szatmár became a Transylvanian possession, Habsburg Hungary had been dangerously exposed. Hungary's policy of active defence required much work in transforming fortified border towns into modern fortresses; examples include the transformation of Győr and Komárom into *Festungsstädte* (town fortresses). Minor outposts in the south-west were reinforced, along with the building of modern fortifications at Érsekújvár (today Nové Zámky in Slovakia). In the southern section of the border, between the middle of the River Drava and the middle of the Sava, and through Croatia to the Adriatic, the mountains formed natural defences, so Karlstadt was the only new large fortress constructed along this line.

As mentioned before, the direction centre and key element of the frontier defence system was the *Grenzgeneralat* (border generality). There were four of these generalities, all functioning within the *Militärgrenze*. The main ones were situated in the Banate of Croatia–Slavonia, in Transdanubia and in Cisdanubia, extending from Pozsony to Gomor County, and in Upper Hungary. The defence force was represented by the recruitment of a semi-regular force assigned to the *Militärgrenze*. Command of the southern border fortresses was taken over by the Inner Austrian War Council of Graz.

The principal fortresses were massively enlarged, and had garrisons of 1,000–1,500 men. These strongholds constituted the pillars of the defence system and the centres of *Militärgrenze*. Next, these key strongholds were followed by large fortresses containing garrisons of 400 to 600 men, and then finally by smaller stone or palisade fortifications (*palánka*) garrisoning 100 to 300 soldiers. There were also minor guard and patrol posts with only a dozen soldiers, but they had important functions too, such as the surveillance of enemy detachments and the provisioning of mounted messengers. All these contingents were assigned to various fortresses or private castles and thus participated in the defence of outlying areas. South of the River Drava they helped in establishing a separate defence zone. Since the 16th century the Habsburgs had welcomed new communities in the region, bordering the Ottoman Empire, which could be resettled with new populations hostile to the Porte. These early settlements were modest, but led to the creation of a new kind of soldier. Initially, the new population was classified indistinctly as the *Walaken*, but in the early 17th century they became known as the *Grenzer*. Other communities escaping from the Ottoman domains settled on the border in the 1660s. They were mainly Serbian 'zadrugas' (clans) which anticipated the massive exodus of 20 years later. These communities enjoyed a wider autonomy with the aristocracy and local clergy, remaining subservient only to the Emperor. Vienna confirmed this status to each subject living in the *Militärgrenze*. The *Grenzer* were granted property rights of field and pasture and exemption from taxation for three years if they accepted military service as armed frontiersmen. The officers of each unit were proposed by the communities and all the members registered in a role of service, from the age of 17 upwards. Only the rank of *Grenzgeneral* was to be appointed by the Emperor. This position could only be held by a person who was *Nativi Hungarie*, namely a Hungarian aristocrat, since his salary was paid for by a war tax voted for by the Hungarian Estates. This was also true for the *Banus*' position in Croatia-Slavonia. However, a foreigner could only be named to it, if he first received a Hungarian diploma of *indigenatus*.

The *Grenzer* were trained weekly by their respective officers. Weapons, and eventually horses, issued became their property, with only ammunition being provided by the Imperial arsenals. The units, organised by company, were led by a *Capitaneus* or *Kápitan* with a *Hadnagy* in Hungary and a *Waida* in Croatia and Slavonia as a junior officer. The *Grenzer* served within their district without receiving any wages, but if mobilised for more than 14 days across the border received wages that were lower than their professional counterpart, namely the regular soldier.

By the second half of the 17th century, approximately 18–20,000 soldiers served in the border defence system against the Ottomans. This force is particularly significant if compared to the deployment of regular troops in southern Hungary and Croatia of 28–30,000 men in the mid 17th century.[102] About 7,000 frontier soldiers were provided by the *Banal* and *Wendish-Bajcsavar Grenzgeneralat*, whilst 11–13,000 belonged to the other four generalties. In detail, in 1657, 1,248 men were mustered in the Karlstadt generalty. They operated under the *General-Obrist* who managed a little secretary office with four employees. He had also a life corps of 100 *Arquebusieren* and four horsemen who were employed as messengers. The mounted troops comprised a further 100 *Husaren*. The main force was composed of 1,023 footmen and 13 artillerymen, who supplied the garrisons for eight border outposts. The *Meergrenze* deployed just 530 men in two companies with a staff of eight adjutants and secretaries.[103]

This manpower was not completely available for operating outside its region, because approximately one third was formed by reservists, who manned the outposts on the border as static defence troops. In 1683,

---

102 K.u.K. Kriegsarchiv, 'Feldzüge des Prinzen Eugen', vol. I, p. 424.
103 F. Vanicek, *Specialgeschichte der Militärgrenze aus Originalquellen und Quellenwerken geschöpft* (Vienna, 1875), vol.I, p. 102.

THE ARMY OF THE EMPEROR

the overall force should have increased considerably. The information comes from neutral observers such as the French ambassador Sebeville and his information seems very accurate. He informed Louis XIV that the border posts amounted to 112 infantry companies, corresponding to 20,848 Grenzers, and another 11,158 on horseback, to which should be added for Hungary alone another 4,950 'reservists' with 70 pieces of artillery, 60 carts of ammunition, 30 food carts and 800 draft horses.[104]

The Croatian *Grenzer* were mainly light infantrymen, but at least one third were horsemen. In Hungary the percentage ratio of cavalry was higher and in some districts there was a horseman for every foot soldier or *Hayduk*. The Hungarian-Croatian *Militärgrenze* was an impressive force, especially when compared to the total population of the Kingdom of Hungary and Croatia in the mid 17th century, which numbered only 2,500,000 inhabitants.

The *Grenzer* provided a valuable force during the war of 1663–64. Croatian *banus* Miklós Zrínyi[105] managed a mobile force of 4,000 *Petrinjaner* and *Warasdiner* who on 17 October 1663 defeated a corps of 7–8,000 Ottoman and Bosnian irregulars near Zrínyivár. Further encounters happened in the following months, and the *Grenzer* achived successes engaging the enemy forces at Časma and other site along the border. Contemporary records claimed these victories were always achieved against a much higher enemy force. On 10 November, with just 600 *Grenzer* from Varaždin supported by

Miklós Zrínyi (1620–1664). The talented commander of the Imperial *Militärgrenze* and arch-enemy of Montecuccoli was also an inspired writer and poet. He is the author of the first epic poem in Hungarian literature. Beside his poetic works, Zrínyi is also a forerunner of Croatian and Hungarian political thinking and military science. In his essays and manifestos, such as *Ne bántsd a magyart – Az török áfium ellen való orvosság* (Do not hurt the Hungarians – An antidote to the Turkish poison) or *Mátyás király életéről való elmélkedések* (Reflections on the life of King Matthias) he proposed the creation of a standing army, the moral renewal of the nation, the re-establishment of the national kingdom, the unification of Royal Hungary with Transylvania, and the ousting of the Ottoman occupants. (Author's collection)

---

104 Cited by Cardini, in *Il Turco a Vienna*, p. 565.
105 'Numerous historians have portrayed both Zrínyis, the hero of 1556 and his great-grandson with the same name, as Hungarian freedom warriors. Few people in Hungary ever discovered that just as many generations of Croat school children were taught to regard the two Zrínyis as perhaps the greatest heroes of their national history. In fact both sides were right. The Zrinskis – their original name was Šubić – belonged to those ancient Croat families with which the Hungarian king Coloman had concluded the contract of union at the beginning of the 12th century. They adopted the name *Zrinski* in the mid 16th century on being given the large estate in the Muraköz with the fortress of Csáktornya (Cakovec) by Emperor Ferdinand I. Zríny, or Zrinski, Miklós spoke Hungarian; his family lived in Croatia, and there is no doubt that his mother-tongue was Croat. On the other hand, Croatia at that time had already been an integral part of Hungary for 400 years, albeit under a special administration. As a member of the high nobility, Zrínyi therefore belonged to the *Natio Hungarica*, the political nation of Hungary which, however, was not an ethnic but a juridic-political category. In 1566, Zrínyi-Zrinski's ancestor fell as a Croat nobleman in the war against the Turks for the Emperor, who was at the same time crowned king of Royal Hungary and he died as a Croat for Hungary. At that time his ethnic affiliation had nothing to do with language, as it would in contemporary Hungary.' Lendvai, *The Hungarians*, p. 126.

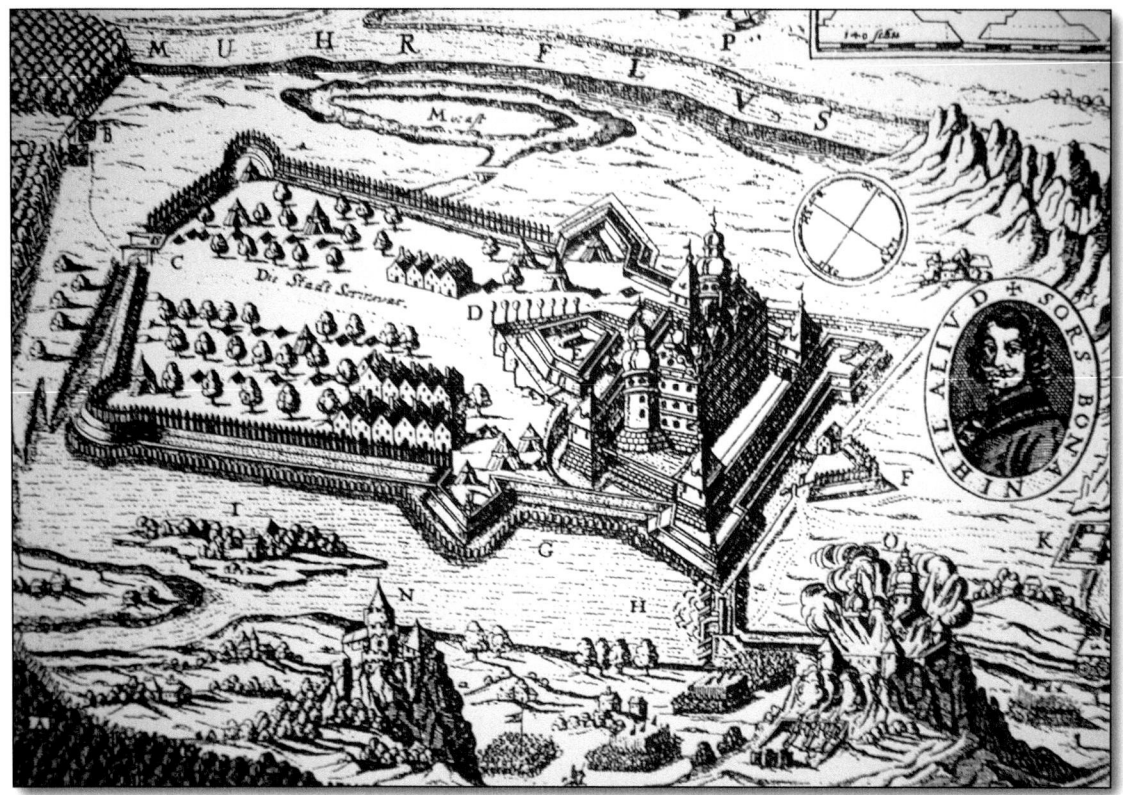

The new-built fortress of Zrínyivár on the River Mur was the main operational base in the south west area of the *Militärgrenze*. In August 1663, Ottoman cavalry raided the stronghold, but were repulsed by the *Grenzer* under Miklós Zrínyi. Successively, the fortress was besieged and finally destroyed in July 1664. The loss of the stronghold turned again on the controversies over Raimondo Montecuccoli. Many historians have debated the behaviour of the Italian general and the criticism of the Croatian-Hungarian commander. Mutual distrust and a lack of understanding of the resources available, generated misconceptions and a manipulation of each other's positions seems to have contributed to distort the facts. (Author's collection)

militiamen of the Royal Army, Zrínyi intercepted a column of 9,000 Ottomans in enemy territory and defeated them, inflicting heavy casualties.[106]

Also the Hungarian *Grenzer* performed successful actions in the war of 1663–64, showing a special aptitude in night actions. The chronicles register several episodes in which the border's troops received praise from the Imperial generals, such as in September 1663, before the siege of Érsekújvár, when some companies of *Raaber* frontiersman secretly swam the Niytra River twice to reach the garrison in the fortress.[107]

Twenty years after, the *Militärgrenze* was involved again to counter the Ottoman advance to Vienna. Several actions engaged the Hungarian frontiersmen against the enemy vanguards. The major concerns regarded the border on the Rába River, but also in Croatia significant episodes occurred. The *banus* János Pálffy-Erdödy organised a mobile force of 5,000 men from Varaždin, Karlstadt and Petrinja. In 1684, this number operated under *Feldzeugmeister* Jabob Leslie alongside the regular troops in the conquest of Verovitica in July. Leslie's offensive resumed in 1685 with the conquest of Eszék, wich engaged 2,000 *Warasdiner*.[108]

---

106 The encounter was recorded as the battle of Aililikapasha, in Vanicek, *Specialgeschichte der Militärgrenze*, vol. I, p. 296.
107 Gualdo-Priorato, *Historia*, vol. II, p. 243.
108 Vanicek, *Specialgeschichte der Militärgrenze*, vol. I, p. 304.

THE ARMY OF THE EMPEROR

The legacy of the ancient military corps inspired also in Austria the revival of the past with historical parades and carousels. Uniforms and equipment were more or less exact copies of the surviving original items that in the early 20th century were much abundant than today. The picture represents officers and troopers of the *Piccolomini* cuirassier regiment in mid 17th century, participating at this re-enactment dated 1901. (Author's collection).

The Provincial Militia

The Thirty Years' War inflicted serious damage to the regular service of the militia, especially in Bohemia and Moravia, which in the middle of the century had to be completely reconstituted. However, this institution could boast an established tradition. The history of the Habsburgs' provincial militia dated back to 1511, when Emperor Maximilian I issued the *Libellen* that forced the Estates to form the *Zuzugwesen* (contingents) for the defence of the country. This act constituted the basis which, with a few modifications, regulated the organisation of the militia in an almost homogeneous manner, though variously conducted according to the local conditions of the provinces. Particularly in places like the Tyrol or Hungary, where the power of the Estates and local privileges were strongest, such territorial defence was long to remain the most important, if not only, form of military organisation.

The militia existed everywhere through compulsory service operated by the Estates and directed by the *Landes Obrist* (provincial colonels) and *Landes Hauptleute* (provincial captains) with a variable number of adjutants and war advisors. Despite provincial variations, the home defence system already followed the same general principle in most Habsburg lands. Depending on the level of danger every 30th, 20th, 10th, or 5th man could be called up in times of need; the general levy, the conscription of all able-bodied man, being restricted to situations of extreme emergency. In the 17th century, the levy of the militia assumed the title of *Landwehr* and *Landsturm* when that call to the arms concerned the whole male population. Arms and armour came from arsenals specially set up by the Estates. In case of enemy attack, home defence units as well as the civilian population were warned by a special system of beacons and signal shots. The civilians then had to take refuge in castles, fortified villages and churches.

The provincial levies of the second half of the 17th century rested on two main pillars, the 30th-man conscripts on foot and the *Gülreiter* or horseman. Both were known as *Auszug* or *Ausschluss* and were supposed to train regularly and be mustered annually to be available if necessary. Regular shooting contests on Sunday and holy days served to train the civilian population, as did schemes in Inner and Lower Austria to send part of the contingent in rotation to the Ottoman border. Indeed the Ottoman threat meant that the *Landwehr* increasingly had to operate outside their own provinces. Usually, active service lasted from one week to three months. Obviously this commitment was a burden for most militiamen. The garrison of border posts forced them on a march that sometimes lasted a week for the militiamen who came from farther away. Therefore, an active seven-day service lasted three weeks and for many militiamen this commitment represented an often unsustainable absence from work, especially for peasants. For this reason, the contingents were afflicted by a high rate of desertion or more or less justified absences.[109]

The distinction between the home defence system run by the Estates and the growing of the permanent army controlled by the Emperor had been blurred during the Thirty Years' War, when militia forces increasingly had to serve as a recruitment pool for the regular army. To address this, at different stages of the conflict against the Porte in 1683–99, the Estates set up quasi-regular units, the so-called *Landregimenter*, officered by members of the provincial aristocracy, which defended the provinces alongside or instead of the unwieldy levies, and could also serve abroad when required. These regiments were used in whole or in part to fill up the ranks in the Emperor's standing army. This method, though common practice in several European armies, was legally flawed and also led to mutiny of units unwilling to be conscripted into the regular army. From the second half of the 17th century onward the infrastructure set up by the provincial Estates for calling up their levies was used to solve the manpower deficiency of the standing army.[110]

The militia's commitment differed depending on the involvement of the provinces in the conflicts fought by the House of Austria starting from 1657. In Lower Austria, the militia had remained inactive since 1683. However, the sudden Ottoman offensive prevented mobilisation and the population was employed exclusively in the construction of the field defences.

In Upper Austria, the militia was established in two infantry corps, formed by one able man in every five. The first corps, the *Auszug*, was maintained in activity and then replaced in rotation by the second corps, the reserve. Depite the accurate regulation introduced in this province, the militia was almost ineffective and employed in secondary tasks, such as guarding bridges and mountain passes.

In Anterior Austria the Estates had to gather an *Auszug* of 3,000 foot militiamen divided into *Landfahnen* (companies) from the 23 provinces' districts. This force was divided into four *Zug* (corps) with an active strength of 4–500 men. The Anterior Austria *Landwehr* had its own company organisation, which comprised one captain, one lieutenant, one ensign, one first sergeant, two sergeants, one *Wachtmeister*, one quartermaster, one secretary, one trench master, one surgeon, four fifes, six drums, and six *Trabanten*. The local militia was constantly in alarm from 1674, and in 1676

---

109 K.u.K. Kriegsarchiv, 'Feldzüge des Prinzen Eugen', vol. I, p. 405.
110 See in chapter 3, the case of the Silesian militia regiment that became *Houchin zu Fuss* (II-94) in 1684.

faced with poor results the French offensive in Breisgau. In the course of the campaign, the Anterior Austria militia sustained a major engagement against a regular force during the defence of Freiburg, which resulted in a surrender on 16 November.

Inner Austria militia followed the scheme of the *Auszug* calling 30th, 20th, 10th or 5th man depending on the emergency. In 1677, a corps of militiamen from Stiria marched to secure the border against the incursions of the Hungarian rebels, continuing to serve there in rotation until 1680. In 1683, about 2,000 militiamen were called to arms and assembled in Graz, Leibnitz and Pettau, employed alongside local peasants for the digging of trenches. They secured the places destined to receive the civil population fleeing from the Ottoman advance, and manned the border forts of Radkersburg, Fürstenberg and other minor posts until the winter 1683–84.

In Tyrol, due to the province's extraordinary status within the Habsburg monarchy preserved also after extinction of the archducal line in 1668, traditional home defence run by the Estates managed to survive, and retained the anachronistic prerogative of having to provide only for the defence of its own territory. The local militia was under the command of an *Obrist-Feldhauptmann* (field captain-colonel), supported by a *Defensionsrat* (council of defence) that from Innsbruck coordinated the fortification works in case of need. The regulation was continuously updated, and all the Tyrolean male population was minutely registered. Usually, the mobilisation depended on the level of threat. In case of low emergency, the call committed 10,000 men; then 15,000 and finally 20,000 if the threat was serious. In the third case, the numbers of men gathered were higher, because they comprised NCOs and officers, and numbered 20,934 militiamen. The mobilisation engaged all classes, but in Tyrol the militiamen could be enlisted by turning to volunteer recruits. Clergy and aristocracy had to provide 3,600 men for the first call, 4,500 for the second, and 7,200 for the third. Nobles were obliged to serve as officers, leading their servants in case of a general call, and the same duty regarded also the churchmen's servants. Pratically, the Tyrolean *Landwehr* included all able men aged 15 to 60, divided into three categories.

In order to maintain this force at a good level of efficiency, the militiamen were gathered in permanent regiments on a territorial basis. In 1668, the militia deployed four infantry regiments with six companies of 200 or 350 men, who received a salary half from the Tyrolean Estates and half from Vienna.[111] The colonels mustered the companies in spring and autumn, and in the same events trained the men, assembling their regiments. Further training was performed every Sunday at company level.

In Bohemia the militia was no longer mobilised after 1648. The relative distance from the southern borders and consequently from the Ottoman threat, led to little interest from the local Estates in organise its own defence.

---

111 The first regiment included companies from the Upper and Lower Inn Valley, the second gathered militiamen from Wippthal, Upper and Lower Pusterthal, and from the Eisack region, the third had companies from Nonstal, Sole Valley, Upper Adige Valley and Vinschgau, the fourth assembled the companies from the Lower Adige Valley. *Ibidem*, p. 407.

Moreover, the Bohemian peasant rebellion in 1680 persuaded the local officials to avoid the military involvement of the civilians.[112]

Also in Moravia there was no active militia and only in September 1663 the Estates organised a defence to face the Tatar incursions. Further commitments engaged the militiamen in 1677 and 1682 against the Hungarian rebels. The levy for the footmen was calculated on the number of farms: every 10, five or three depending on the emergency, while one mounted militiaman had to be mobilised every 50, 30 or 15 farms. The militiamen received equipment and weapons from the Estates, and in 1677 Moravia deployed a strength of 1,100 Foot in 10 companies and 500 'dragoons' in five companies. The year after this force decreased to five infantry companies and two mounted companies. Not all the province's militia was regulated by the farm method, which mainly concerned the countryside. The cities participated in territorial defence with manual labour and in-kind supplies of artillery material and supplies for the army. The privileges granted to the city of Olomuc, a bishopric, allowed the city council to organise its own militia. In this city, a corps of *Scharfschützen* (marksmen) had been formed and regularly trained since the 1660s.

Also Silesia was interested by the Tatar incursion in 1663. The local militiamen could offer some sporadic resistance against the aggressive enemy raids, but in late October, under the *Obrist Feldhauptmann* Georg von Liegnitz-Brieg, they repulsed the Tatar horsemen who tried to force the pass of Jablunka. In Silesia the militia followed the Moravian scheme. In 1683, the active companies were joined together in the *Landregiment zu Fuss*.

Often associated with the militia, major cities and fortresses and even some larger townships, raised their own urban guards, mostly used in the maintenance of public order, but in case of emergency these units could also be used in military actions. The most numerous was the *Wiener Stadt-Guardia*, formed in 1618, with a strength of 800 men divided into four companies as the *Viertel* (district) of the city: *Stuben-Viertel*, *Kärnthner-Viertel*, *Widmer-Viertel* and *Schotten-Viertel*. In the spring of 1663, regimental strength increased to 2,000 men, half of which were sent to Hungary in the following autumn, to join the field army, under their *Obrist*, Marchese Annibale Gonzaga, president of the Aulic War Council. The regiment returned to its

---

112 The rebellion centered on Northern Bohemia, in the districts of Caslau, Elbogen, Leitmeritz (Litomerice in Czech Republic) and Bunzlau, both in areas inhabited by Czechs and by Germans. In May 1680 rebel peasants drew up a list of 43 demands. Imperial cavalry under *Obrist* Enea Silvio Piccolomini contained and finally suppressed the rebellion. The peasants were poorly armed and without experienced leadership. When troops approached, the rebels of Zwickau (Cvikov) fled to the Grünberg (Zeleny vrch), a mountain hideout; surrounded and hungry, they surrendered there after two days of resistance. In late May 1680, the first rebel leaders were hanged in Aussig (Usti na Labem). In August 1680, a commission charged with punishing the rebel leaders was sent into the region, they finished their report on 29 August, the last rebel leaders were executed the day after. In German, the rebellion is referred to as the *Robotaufstand* of 1680. In Czech it is referred to as *Selske Rebelie roku*. See in J. Koči, 'Der Widerstand der Leibeigenen im Gebiet Friedland 1679– 1689. Ein Beitrag zur Geschichte des Aufstandes der Leibeigenen in Böhmen im Jahre 1680', in *De Gruyter Jahrbuch für Wirtschaftsgeschichte* (edited by D. Ziegler), N. 6 – 2018.

original role in late 1664. In 1676, the regiment provided again troops for the regular army, ceding 500 'volunteers' for the regiment *Serény zu Fuss*.[113]

In 1683 four new companies were added, called *Jung-Stuben, Jung-Kärnthner* etc., together one company of *Schützen,* one of artillery and a small corps of mounted guardsmen.

In Prague there were 12 companies of urban militia. In 1665, the Emperor granted them an annual prize for the weekly training that took place in the Pražské Benátky. Finally, a company of militia operated in Trieste, in charge of the coastal defence.

---

113 Wrede, *Geschichte der K.und K. Wehrmacht*, vol. I, p. 277.

4

The *Reichsarmee*

The complex and fragmented political structure of the Holy Roman Empire caused the main indeterminacy in all affairs; the army was no exception. In 1650, the army of the Empire was a quite fragmented and almost theoretical reality. Some aspects and particularities of the military structure had been inherited from previous centuries, whilst other recently introduced reforms contributed to establish the classic *Reichsarmee* of the later 17th century onwards. As always in history, changes were neither instant nor total, and some interesting aspects of the Imperial 'military' are the survival of old elements combined with the new.

As experienced in the past, in military affairs the Emperors remained largely bound by the Imperial Diet and from the prince-electors, both of whom determined the total amount of cash available for the army and its maintenance on campaign. Though their formal influences were limited, the presence of France and Sweden as external guarantors of the Osnabrück treaty signalled the internationalisation of Imperial politics, which was to grow as the century progressed.[1] Already Denmark had substantial territory in north Germany, entitling it to a formal presence in the constitution, while the Dutch retained garrisons in a number of Westphalian and Rhenish towns occupied during the Thirty Years' War. The implementation of the peace treaty did secure the withdrawal of Swedish and French troops by 1653, but had serious repercussions for the Burgundian circle west of the Rhine, which had been excluded from Münster's agreement on the grounds that it consisted nearly entirely of Spanish territory. The Austrian Habsburgs were forbidden to use their hold on the Imperial title to facilitate German assistance to Spain, which remained at war with France, reinforcing the general intention that the *Reich* was to remain non-aligned with regard to its great power relations. On the other hand, the main aim of the Westphalia Treaty was to avoid other devastating wars within the Empire's territory. The military structure of the

---

1   In addition to foreign interference in Imperial affairs, Habsburg and Hohenzollern (Brandenburg) possessions outside the formal *Reich* boundaries extended German interests into other parts of Europe; a factor that was to increase with the involvement of other dynasties in international affairs.

Reich evolved to this end, with the emphasis being on peaceful, diplomatic resolutions and defensive cooperation.

The mechanisms developed to mobilise territorial resources for internal peacekeeping and peace-enforcement were adapted to provide defence against external threats, whilst denying the Emperor the opportunity to exploit them for his own offensive operations.[2] The Treaty of Osnabrück imposed additional restrictions obliging him to seek *Reichstag* approval, before sanctioning a full Imperial war effort in the so-called *Reichskrieg*. The need for money to defend the *Reich* against the Porte was the primary reason why the Habsburg emperors convened the *Reichstag* to back up their demands relating to *Reichstürkensteuer* (the Imperial Turkish tax). The subventions for the defences from the 'Ottoman scourge' were the subject of the usual haggling and wrangling in the Diets and in the Circles of the Empire. These latter established the military order of the Empire since 1521. In fact, the circles had been formed to facilitate the setting up of the army, in accordance to the maintenance of the internal peace.

The appointment of the *Kreis* military commander as *Kreisoberst*, along with the nomination of the region's judges in the *Reichskammergericht* (Court Chamber of the Empire), as well as the subdivisions of tax and other burdens assigned it by the Diet, were all subject to approval from the assembly. How this worked in practice depended on the territorial composition and geographical location of each *Kreis*, particularly as the formal structure had evolved in response to circumstances, allowing for considerable variations across the Empire.

The *Reichsmatricel*

Each circle had to supply its aliquot of soldiers to form the *Reichsarmee*. This aliquot was known as *Reichsmatricel*. In 1564, the Diet of Worms established in case of war the *quota in duplum*, then in 1566, in Augsburg, the Diet voted the *Türkenhülfe*, who modified the size of contingents to the triple of the original *Reichsmatricel* figures, every time the Empire engaged in war with the Porte. In 1648, the Diet of Regensburg fixed for each circle the division *in simplum* of the *Reichsmatricel* for an overall 4,000 horse and 12,000 foot.[3] These figures were obviously inadequate to perform any serious military task. In 1663, the Ottoman offensive in Hungary, and the following raid in Moravia, persuaded the Diet to vote for a new *Matricel*.[4]

Only on 4th February 1664 the Empire agree to raise an army, based on the triplum of the 1521 Matricul of Worms, for the war against the Porte. However, the mobilisation of the *Reichsarmee* already displayed many of the

---

2   Prohibitions to this effect were written into the electoral agreements – the *Wahlkapitulationen* – containing concessions wrung from each new Emperor by the electors. See in Wilson, *German Armies*, p. 14.
3   K.u.K. Kriegsarchiv, 'Feldzüge des Prinzen Eugen', vol I, p. 438.
4   See for details in the Appendix chapter, the *Reichsmatricel* of 1663.

Friedrich IV, Margrave of Baden-Durlach (1617–1677). In 1663, the Margrave was the principal organiser of the Swabian contingent for the war against the Porte in Hungary. Alongside his Catholic cousin, the Margrave of Baden-Baden, he gathered one horse and two foot regiments recruited with the participation of almost all the 92 states composing the circle. Margrave Friedrich contributed also with further contingents for the Burgundian circle. In the war against France of 1674–78, he held the rank of *Feldmarschall*. (Author's collection)

Prince Friedrich Karl von Württemberg (1652–1698). The Prince was colonel of a Swabian infantry regiment between 1674 and 1677, and later become one of the leading military entrepreneurs of Germany. As regent of the Duchy, in the 1680s he supplied mercenary troops to Venice, the Dutch Republic, and the Emperor. (Author's collection)

The Swabian circle's infantry *Compagnie Fahne* (company colours), late 17th century. Black and yellow flames, green laurel with red ribbon; black lions on yellow and white cross on black. Flags with the same colours but with vertical flames were also common. (Author's illustration)

features that were to characterise collective security in the coming years.[5] First, the official strength of 30,000 decreed on 4th February 1664 was cut by the decision to deduct the contingents already serving in Hungary. The remaining 20,993 men were apportioned to the individual circles, anticipating later mobilisation arrangements, with the Austrian circle omitted because the Emperor already had soldiers in the field. In the spring of 1664, the effective strength was, in several circles, still short of the established *Reichsmatricel*. Nonetheless, the composite formation of the contingents remained a characteristic of the corps raised by the circles. *Reich*'s war participation was fairly impressive. In the fall of 1663 the circle of Franconia – the Catholic majority – demonstrated greater involvement in the preparations for war. Since autumn, the first contingents began to march to Hungary, taking over winter quarters in Pressburg and in the Schütt area. The infantry regiment (Colonel Johann Plettern, FI-1) deployed 10 companies for 1,821 men overall on paper; the cavalry regiment (Johann Wilhelm Zobel zu Giebelsted, FC-1) had a strength of 629 rank and file organised in six companies. The Franconian regiments were followed by other troops from Westphalia and Swabia. Apart from a few cases, in both circles there were no States large enough to have a permanent army, that were ready to be quickly mobilised for war. This resulted in a number of quite significant drawbacks. The major problems were caused by the patchwork pattern of the regiments. Especially in the case of the Swabian contingent, which was assembled from more than 92 States:

---

5   The total decreased before 1669 to 2,568 horse and 12,406 foot. See in K.u.K Kriegsarchiv, 'Feldzüge des Prinzen Eugen', Vienna, 1876–91; vol. I, p. 438.

THE *REICHSARMEE*

Imperial cities, secular princes and religious rulers, further divided by Catholics and Protestants.[6] After the Diet on 28 January 1664, the Swabian circle granted a voluntary *Erste Armatur* (first-armed force) as aid to the Emperor. The Catholic regiment *Fugger zu Fuss* (SI-2), under *Obrist* Count Franz von Fugger, was formed comprising seven companies containing a total of 1,555 men. The ratio of pike-musket was 1 to 2. The regiment included recruits provided by the Swabian imperial knights, who agreed to the inclusion of their 220 footmen, although they were under no obligation to co-operate. The Protestant regiment (SI-1), commanded by *Obrist* Christian *Pfalzgraf* von Zweibrücken-Birkenfeld-Bischweiler, deployed eight companies, organised slightly differently to the Catholic unit, with a pike to musket ration of 1 to 3. The Swabian cavalry had a strength of 486 men to four troops under the *Obrist-Lieutenant* Count Maximilian Franz zu Fürstenberg (SC-1). However, the Swabian *Kreis* was not able to assemble a complete cavalry regiment, because the Duke of Württemberg joined his 170 horsemen, led by prince Ulrich, with the new-formed and independent army of the German Alliance. In the following months, other troops narched to Hungary from Mecklenburg, Holstein-Gottorp, Hildesheim, Pfalz-Neuburg, Münster, Osnabrück and Paderborn, representing the circles of Westphalia and Lower Saxony. The Westphalian circle raised three infantry regiments of foot for 3,712 men overall. Regiments *Hochstatten* (WI-2), recruited by Pfalz-Neuburg, and *Post* (WI-3) from Münster, had a strength of 1,000 men with eight companies. The third regiment, *Uffeln* (WI-1), recruited by the prince-bishop of Paderborn and other smaller states, deployed 12 companies with 1,712 rank and file on paper. The cavalry regiment, under *Obrist* Lothar von Post zu Bosfeld (WC-1), had eight companies with 713 men from Münster.

The Upper Rhine circle delayed the formation of its quota until May and mustered the first troops on 24 June.[7] The cavalry regiment of *Obrist* Walrad von Nassau-Usingen (OrC-1) had a strength of four companies, three of 76 troopers and one of 77, for 305 troopers overall.[8] Days later the infantry regiment *Nassau-Idstein* (OrI-1) deployed 5 companies with 173, 170, 169, 174 and 170 men, for 856 soldiers in all.[9] The second infantry regiment, under

Leib-standard of the Lower Saxony circle's cavalry regiment *Rauchhaupt* (NsC-1), 1664. Gold embroideries and green laurel on white background. This regiment belonged to the Lower Saxony circle and participated with Count Hohenlohe's corps in the 1664 campaigns under Zrínyi Miklós, culminating in the sieges of Kanisza. The war cost the German contingents a very high number of casualties, the contingents for the most part formed by soldiers unaccustomed to the severe conditions of the Hungarian war theatre, and in several cases the circle's contingent lost two thirds of its force. (After 'Von Celle nach St. Gotthard, 1163–1664 für das Reich gegen die Türken', in *Alte und Neue Zinnfiguren*, 1974)

---

6. The Swabian states with the major quote of recruits were the Imperial cities of Augsburg and Ulm, with 150 foot and 25 horse, while 15 states recruited fewer than five infantrymen. See the *Reichsmatricel* of 1663 in the Appendix.
7. 'The Elector of Mainz was present in his position as bishop of Worms and *Kreisdirector* with the Prince of Pfalz-Simmern as vicedirector. The deputies of the major estates were also present to witness the muster', *Theatrum Europaeum*, vol. XI, p. 1099.
8. *Ibidem*: According to *Theatrum Europaeum* the life company, 76 men, comprised troops from Hanau-Münzenberg with 30 men, Hanau-Lichtenberg 18, Solms 24, Nassau 4; the second, 77 men, had troopers from Strasbourg 50, Colmar 8, Schlettstadt 8, Landau 4, Ober-Ehnheim 4, Speyer 3; the third company, 76 men, Fulda 51, Isenburg 18, Wittgenstein 7; fourt company, 76 men, Frankfurt 60, Sponheim 6, Pfalz-Simmern 6, Pfalz-Veldenz 4.
9. *Ibidem*, *Leib Compagnie*: Nassau 88, PfalzSimmern 20, Bishopric Speyer 30, Sponheim 20, Kaisersberg (town) 15; the second company had 170 men from the bishopric of Speyer; third company: Speyer (town) 60, Worms (town) 45, Weissenburg 22, Landau 36, Rossheim 6;

WARS AND SOLDIERS IN THE EARLY REIGN OF LOUIS XIV – VOLUME 2

Parade of the Ulm contingent for the Swabian circle, 31 March 1677, Ulmer Museum. The picture shows the infantry recruited by the Imperial city for the regiment *Baden-Durlach* (SI-3). The contingent seems to be composed only of musketeers with NCOs. Private soldiers wear a dark grey coat apparently with carmine red stockings. The NCO wears the same coat or buff leather *koller* coat with stockings as the private soldiers (Author's collection)

A musketeer and NCO, Swabian circle regiment *Baden-Durlach zu Fuss* (SI-3), 1677. Author's reconstruction after the painting in the Ulmer Museum. In the Franco-Dutch war the contribution of the Imperial circles was intermittent. Apart from the arbitrariness suffered from the allies, the contingents arrived on campaign often outnumbered and with poor equipment. According to some reports, companies of the same regiment were equipped with muskets of different calibres. In 1676, the Upper-Rhenish contingent garrisoned in Heidelberg and other places had several musketeers without firearms and therefore they served with half pikes and *Morgenstern*.

Colonel Philipp von Solms (OrI-2), deployed 850 men with five companies.[10] The last unit mustered was the artillery, which consisted of four 3-pounder guns, two each from Frankfurt am Main and Strasbourg.[11] A third regiment, *Zobel* (OrI-3), came from the Hessian states and numbered 810 men in five companies. The fragmentation of the Upper-Rhenish contingent was the result of a political dispute, which affected also military affairs. Both colonels, Nassau-Idstein and Solms, considered themselves as a commander-in-chief and the dispute remained unresolved until the end of the campaign.

The separation between major and minor states was also evident in the Lower-Saxony Circle, which assembled one cavalry and two infantry regiments. The regiment of Foot *Ende* (NsI-2) was composed of nine companies of 100 men each, two of which had been recruited by the bishop and the town of Magdeburg; one each from Lübeck, Mecklenburg, Holstein-Gottorp, Sachsen-Lauenburg and Denmark, as ruler of Schleswig; the last company was a combined unit of troops provided by the Imperial towns of Goslar, Mühlhausen and Nordhausen. The infantry regiment under *Obrist* Job Bernhard von Muchlen (NsI-1) was raised by Brunswick-Lüneburg, and deployed six companies with 810 men. The cavalry regiment *Rauchhaupt* (NsC-1) – comprising 420 horse – included soldiers from the duchies of Brunswick-Wolfenbüttel, Kalemberg and Celle.[12] A second cavalry regiment of just 352 men in four companies was raised by the minor circle members and sent to Hungary under *Oberstleutanant* Claus Josias von Schack (NsI-2).

In contrast, the highly fragmented circle of Rhine-Electoral formed its cavalry from only two states, joining 400 electoral Palatine troops and another 76 from Cologne. On the eve of the battle of Szentgotthárd-Mogersdorf, the Rhine-Electoral circle sent to Hungary one of cavalry and three of infantry, which joined the infantry raised the year before, for an overall force of 7,600 men on paper, including 200 artillerymen with 14 guns.[13]

The Bavarian circle formed a contingent of two battalions, regiment *Flettinger* (BI-2) with seven companies for an overall force calculated as 1,050 men. Six companies were supplied by Salzburg and one from Passau. In addition the circle provided the auxiliary single battalion infantry regiment *Freising* (BI-3).[14]

---

fourth company: Hanau 156, Falkenstein with Oberstein 6, Pfalz-Veldenz 8, Leiningen 4; fifth company: Colmar 60, Schlettstadt 48, Oberehnheim 25, Münster (for Gregorienthal) 24, Dürningheim 10.

10 *Ibidem*, *Leib Compagnie*, 176 men: Solms 126, Leiningen-Daxburg 14, Rheingrafen 36; second company, 170 men: Isenburg 60, Frankfurt am Main 80, Wetzlar 12, Friedberg 18; third company, 164 men: Fulda 150, Leiningen-Hartenburg 14; fourth company and fifth company had 170 each from Frankfurt am Main.

11 *Ibidem*, The ammunition included 100 balls, 50 grapeshot, 8 hundredweight of gun powder and 4 hundredweight of matches for each, in addition to 200 filled hand-grenades, 60 shovels, 90 hacks and picks.

12 The first company, Wolfenbüttel, had 136 troopers; second company, Celle, 155 troopers; third, Kalemberg-Hannover, 129 troopers. 'Von Celle nach St. Gotthard, 1163–1664 für das Reich gegen die Türken', in *Alte und Neue Zinnfiguren*, XI-November 1974.

13 H. Forst, 'Die Reichstruppen im Türkenkrieg', in *Mitteilungen des Instituts für österreichische Geschichtsforschung*, vol. IV – 1901.

14 Wilson, 'German Armies', p. 77.

Some of these troops had received their baptism of fire in January 1664, when they were in action at the siege of Pécs. Then in the spring of 1664 the infantry of the *Reichsarmee* was placed under the command of Margrave Hermann of Baden-Baden.

It was unlikely from the outset that these contingents would operate effectively in action due to a chronic deficiency of cavalry that hindered them (it was usual to replace the cavalry quota with three foot for each horse). Apart from the Burgundian circle – which appeared with a single 900-man foot regiment of 12 companies in June 1664, followed in July by another of 600 horse divided in 10 companies, both supplied with an agreement with the Margrave of Baden-Baden[15] – the other *Kreis* turned out to complete the contingent with a further 5,000 soldiers, largely accounted for by the fact that Brandenburg, Saxony and Bavaria refused to integrate their troops with the *Kreistruppen* with few exceptions. This situation evolved partially when Ferdinand Maria von Wittelsbach, prince-elector of Bavaria, sent the battalion- and squadron-size regiments *Puech zu Fuss* and *Höning Cavallerie* as the Bavarian electoral contingent contribution.[16] These troops fought under Montecuccoli at Szentgotthárd but they operated independently from the Bavarian circle.

Despite all these contradictions, in the campaign of 1664 the appearance of the *Reichsarmee* in the field represented a considerable achievement for a force that had largely to be raised quickly and from scratch. Moreover, the mobilisation of 1663–64 represented a politically relevant fact, since after 60 years the circles had formed contingents of a significant size to be sent to support the Emperor.[17]

The war against the Ottomans ended with a glorious outcome, but the price paid by the troops of the circles was very high. Apart from the desertions and the battle casualties, diseases afflicted the troops little accustomed to the Hungarian climate. When the troops were engaged in the battle of Szentgotthárd, the circles' infantry deployed six regiments but with a strength of just a battalion each. The *Reichs'* troops lost in average from half to two thirds of their original strength.[18] Even the Upper-Rhenish contingent, which did not perform any fighting, claimed significant losses, returning to its states with half of the original force.[19]

---

15 G. Tessin, 'Reicharmee und Allianzkorps in Turkenfeldzug 1663–64', in *Zeitschrift für Heereskunder* 308/309, 1983; pp. 133–137.

16 F. Münich, *Geschichte der Entwicklung der bayerishen Armee set zwei Jahrhunderten*, Munich, 1866 (Osnabrück: 1984), pp. 24–25.

17 The last time the circles had raised their own contingent to the aid of the Habsburgs had been in 1606, when a regiment of cavalry under the *Obrist* Mannsfeld had been sent in Hungary by the Swabian circle. G. Tessin *Die Regimenter der europäischen Staaten im Ancien Régime des XVI bis XVIII Jahrhunderts* – Teil 1, Biblio Verlag: Osnabrück, 1986.

18 The infantry regiment *Ende* (NsI-2), from Lower Saxony, returned in its states with just 10 officers, 23 NCOs and 178 private soldiers. '1663–1664, für das Reich gegen die Türken', in *Neu und Alte Zinnfiguren*, VI – June 1975.

19 Infantry regiment *Solms* (OrI-2) was mustered in Frankfurt with only 772 men instead of the planned 850. On the march the regiment lost 96 men and at Sopron further 122 men left the regiment, so that it numbered only 559 effectives. On 15th August the army left the quarters at Sopron and on 30 August laid the camp two miles from Bratislava. By now the regiment had

No further military involvement affected the Empire until 1674. Not even in 1668–69, during the War of Devolution between France and Spain, did the external circles consider the need to raise a defence force as a priority.[20] The absence of external threat caused also a significant reduction of the *Matricel*. In 1669, the Diet agreed a strength *in simplum* of 12,406 foot and 2,568 horse.[21] Austrian delegates, supported by the external circles, persuaded the Diet that this figure was inadequate to perform any serious military task. Before the end of the year, the *Reichsarmee* would swell to 30,000 men overall, but this number was not obtained with a new *Matricel*. The Diet supported a general agreement between the circles, which assumed to divide the difference among their states. The agreement remained completely theoretical, because no permanent contingent still existed.

The *Reich* in War, 1674–1678

The Franco-Dutch War acted as an accelerator for the formation of a new *Armatur* in late 1672. The circle of Franconia voted for the formation of two regiments of infantry, two of cuirassiers[22] and one of dragoons, followed by Swabia and Upper Rhine. Though the first contingents had been formed in 1672 and 1673, their participation in the war against France started in late 1674, a long time after the declaration of the 'Imperial War' by the Diet of 31 March. Furthermore, when the first troops began to arrive at the theatre of war, other circles had not yet formed their units. The absence of the Westphalian troops is at best explainable by the proximity of the Low Countries war theatre, although the princes did not provide any active assistance there either. In October 1674, Elector Friedrich Wilhelm of Brandenburg warned in Vienna that the Westphalian circle may also be obliged to do his duty, but private interests prevailed. Similar circumstances affected the Electoral-Rhenish circle, where rivalry, suspicions and the strong pro-French party supported by several princes made it difficult to gather troops for the *Reichsarmee*. Elector Maximilian Heinrich of Cologne, who had reluctantly renounced the French alliance, held his troops away from the war. The bishop of Trier, who kept his militia ready to march, carefully avoided active intervention and protested to the Diet when the Imperial troops crossed his domains in 1675 and 1676. Reciprocal discourtesy occurred also among the states. In late 1674, Duke Wilhelm Ludwig of Württemberg openly refused to march

---

only 400 effectives. Concerning the cavalry, the company of Nassau-Hanau had only 60 men instead 76; a further four troopers had deserted in September, the other casualties were probably due to sickness. G. Tessin, 'Reichsarmee und Allianzkorps im Türkenfeldzug 1663/64', in *Zeitschrift für Heereskunde*, VII- 1983.

20 At the beginning of the War of Devolution the Upper Rhine circle's *Kreisdirector*, Lothar Friedrich von Metternich, archbishop and prince-elector of Mainz, refused to call the Diet, despite the presence of the armies near the border of states comprised in the circle. See in Whaley, *Germany and the Holy Roman Empire*, p. 33.
21 K.u.K Kriegsarchiv 'Feldzüge des Prinzen Eugen', vol I, p 438.
22 In 1674, one Franconian cuirassier regiment was ceded to the Emperor. See in Wrede, *Geschichte der K.und K. Wehrmacht*, vol. III, part two, p. 550.

A 19th century reconstruction of the uniform of Swabian cuirassier regiment *Hönstett* (SC-5) in 1683, source for figure 2 on Plate H. (Author's collection)

across the bridges on the Neckar to the approaching contingents from north Germany.[23] Furthermore, the diplomatic action of the pro-France German princes contributed to slow down the mobilisation of the Empire's troops, and advanced the request to open peace negotiations.

Even the directly threatened states were only temporarily and weakly represented in the field army assembled for the protection of the Empire. For the campaign of 1674, Elector Karl Ludwig of the Palatinate sent his 2,000 troops to the field army but at the beginning of December, after the arrival of the Brandenburg corps, called back them across the Rhine. His main aim was to preserve his country from new damage, bearing in mind the turmoil of Turenne's ravages in the summer. In June 1674, The Upper Rhine circle has called for a negotiation to discuss the new *Armatur* for the oncoming war against France, following a general invitation sent to all the circle's states. The Diet met in Friedberg and agreed to form an initial contingent of troops[24] including only the northern states of the circle, namely Hessen-Kassel, Hessen-Darmstadt, Nassau-Idstein, Nassau-Usingen, Nassau-Weilburg, Hanau-Münzenberg, Solms, Isenburg, Leiningen-Westerburg, Wittgenstein, Waldeck, the abbey of Fulda and the Imperial cities of Frankfurt am Main, Friedberg and Wetzlar. The contingent had to amount 1,400 foot and 700 horse, under Count Moritz of Solms.[25] The result was less than hoped, because the troops from Kassel and Darmstadt did not join the corps. The troops marched to the Rhine and then quartered in Alsace in the winter 1674–75. The Diet discussed new troops and applied a quota to raise two regiments of infantry and one regiment of cavalry. However, as the regiment of cavalry had left the circle for Hungary, only two foot regiments remained available for the Rhenish theatre, overall 1,573 rank and file. Of them, only the regiment *Nassau-Idstein* (OrI-4) joined the field army,[26] while the regiment *Solms* (OrI-5) arrived in the war theatre in early 1675 and was assigned to the reserve corps under Margrave

---

23 See Kortzfleisch, *Der Oberelsässische Winterfeldzug 1674–75*, p. 24.
24 The treaty was known as *Partikularallianz* (particular alliance). G. Tessin 'Die Oberrheinische-Kreis und seine Kreistruppen', in *Zeitschrift für Heereskunde* 1-1985.
25 T. Schüler, 'Die Nassauer unter den Truppen des Oberrheinischen Kreises im Reichskrieg gegen Frankreich 1674–79', in *Alt-Nassau* (VII, 87), 1917.
26 *Ibidem*. The regiment *Nassau-Idstein* marched off in August 1674. When it arrived in Dudenhofen it was discovered that the muskets of the Hanau company had a smaller calibre than the rule. The Fulda company, on the assumption that they would receive their pay etc. directly from the circle's chest, had not brought any money with them. On 26 November 1674 news came from Kehl that the Nassau company now had a strength of 144 men. The contingent of Nassau-Idstein-Wiesbaden consisted of 1 sergeant, 4 corporals, 1 *Fourierschütz* and 29 men; of them 6 had deserted and 4 were in the hospital. The Waldeck contingent comprised 1 sergeant, 1 Fourier, 1 corporal, 4 corporals, 38 men, of these 8 had deserted, 3 were sick, 3 dead and 1 missing.

Hermann of Baden.[27] The Upper-Rhenish troops were quartered as garrisons in Kehl, Heidelberg, Hanau and other minor places. Poor discipline and and other inconveniences considerably reduced the strength. In the same period, the regiment *Nassau-Idstein* had just 232 rank and file instead the 758 of original force.[28]

As 10 years before, the *Reichstruppen* appeared a mosaic of loosely arranged and never uniformly equipped units. Although the Swabian and Franconian circles had promptly assembled their units, they also followed this pattern and when the campaign of 1674 started, the circles deployed 5,000 men in all. The Franconian contingent was far from complete. In late 1674 only the cuirassier regiment had been fully mobilised and sent on campaign. The first complete infantry regiment arrived in March 1675 at Heilbronn under Lieutenant Colonel Roth (FI-2); then further companies from Ansbach-Bayreuth, Kulmbach and Würzburg joined the field army in mid December 1675 at Heilbronn and Pforzheim, to be assembled in the infantry regiment *Thüngen* (FI-3).[29] Both Franconian infantry regiments deployed 1,000 rank and file, but *Roth* had 10 companies, and *Thüngen* only five. The cuirassier regiment *Bayreuth* (FC-2) had a strength of 800 troopers with eigth companies.

Elector of Saxony Johann Georg sent a strong contingent to the Rhine,[30] but after it joined the field army in September 1674, he did not allow it to cross the river. The Elector had been a great admirer of Louis XIV and therefore in Vienna considered his actions with suspect and aimed only 'pour rentrer dans le bon party'.[31] Of the Thuringian states, only Saxony-Gotha was represented by 300 men as a contingent of the Upper Saxony circle, while one foot regiment from Reuss-Plauen entered Imperial service in late 1674. The Lower Saxony troops came slowly to the Rhine; but they did not completely fail. Even such an outspoken friend of France as Johann Friedrich of Hannover mobilised two infantry companies for the Lower Saxony circle. However, they left home only at the beginning of November 1674, together with two Mecklenburg companies, three Holstein companies, and the troops of Sachsen-Lauenburg and Lübeck. Duke Georg Wilhelm of Brunswick-Celle as *Kreis-Obrist* of the circle, eagerly but unsuccessfully tried to enforce the union. Among the northern German prince-bishoprics, only Osnabrück and Münster participated in the 'Imperial War', though the latter not spontaneously but under the threat of the allied arms. The Bishop of Paderborn did his utmost to maintain relationship with France, but in summer

---

27 According to Kortzfleisch, *Der Oberelsässische Winterfeldzug 1674–75*, p. 22. the fifth company of the infantry regiment *Solms* (OrI-5) had been raised by the Imperial cities of Upper Alsace, although they were under French threat. Colmar had paid for the recruitment of 61 soldiers, Schlettstadt 48, Münster 24, Türkheim 10 and further 28 men from other states in the Upper Rhine circle.
28 Schüler, 'Die Nassauer unter den Truppen des Oberrheinischen Kreises', in *Alt-Nassau* (VII, 87) 1917; p. 22.
29 *Ibidem*, p. 23.
30 Two infantry regiments, two cavalry regiments and four dragoons companies. See in Beust *Feldzüge der Kursäcshishen Armee*, (Hamburg, 1803), vol. II, pp. 6–7.
31 Kortzfleisch, *Der Oberelsässische Winterfeldzug 1674–75*, p. 25.

Count Johann Karl von Thüngen (1648–1708), marble bust by an anonymous sculptor. The *Reichsarmee* provided also several good officers for the Imperial army. Thüngen began his military career in Spanish service and later in the Franconian infantry as officer of the Würzburg contingent, becoming colonel in 1675. The loss of his right eye dates back to this first phase of his life; a wound that surgeons tried to remedy with an unlikely prosthesis. In 1688, he was appointed commander in chief of the Franconian troops and two years later entered Imperial service as *Feldmarschall-Lieutenant*. In 1696, he was finally promoted *Feldmarschall*. Thüngen continued to hold positions in the Franconian circle and for a time he was also in the service of the Elector of Mainz. His aversion to Louis XIV was well known, to the point that for the baptism of his sons he imposed, together with the oath of renunciation to Satan, an additional one against France. (Author's photograph)

1674 had to change sides, even avoiding any military support to the *Reichsarmee*. Notwithstanding these shadows, following the *Kreis* mobilisation and the Emperor's second agreement with Brandenburg, the common army had risen to over 50,000 men by December 1674, making it the largest single force assembled by the *Reich* since 1648.[32]

Though Franconia, Swabia, Upper Saxony and Upper Rhine sent forces to the Rhine in the following campaigns, contributions from the Bavarian, Westphalian, Burgundian, Lower Saxon and Electoral-Rhenish circles remained virtually nonexistent in the following years, due to the presence of French sympathisers, the elector of Bavaria amongst the most important. The circles' contribution to the 'Imperial War' continued to be alternate and often limited to a single campaign. Westphalia maintained its contingent of 1,200 men from 1675 to 1678 as garrison in Cologne; Upper Saxony did the same with its 1,000 infantry and Bavaria with 600 men from Salzburg. However the major contributions came from Franconia, which in 1675 increased its contingent to 3,100 men, raising one dragoon regiment of three companies (300 men), Swabia with 2,600 and Upper Rhine 2,100.[33] Despite the difficulties faced by the circles in the formation of their contingents, the 10,600 *Kreistruppen* in the field by summer 1675 were far from insignificant, especially when seen in conjunction with at least as many militiamen and garrison troops retained for territorial defence, many of whom were performing vital frontline duty in outposts along the Rhine and first line fortresses such as Mainz, Koblenz, Bonn and Cologne.

As well as the Emperor's army, also the *Reichstruppen* remained critically subjected to financial shortage. According to contemporary records, in late

---

32 Wilson, *German Armies*, p. 50.
33 H. Weigel, *Die Kriegsverfassung des alten deutschen Reiches von der Wormser Matrikel bis zur Auflösung* (Bamberg, 1912); A. Marr, 'Der Herbstfeldzug Montecuccolis gegen Condé, 1675 am Rheine und an der Mosel', *in Österreichische Militärische Zeitschrift*, vol II – 1842, and 'Der Feldzug 1676 in Deutschland mit Benützung österreichischer Originalquellen', in *Österreichische Militärische Zeitschrift*, vol. III – 1844.

winter 1675, the actual force of the the circle's regiments was decreased to just 4,500 men 'poorly prepared and deprived of any martial attributes […] they lacked of discipline and were almost useless in campaigns.'[34] In the opening phase of the war, the *Reichsarmee* consisted of soldiers and officers who had voluntarily entered the service for the duration of the war, and especially for the latter, the poor career prospects in a small organisation like the circles' contingents contributed to produce negative effects. Letters and accounts referred to the appalling state of the regiments and the tendency of many soldiers to desert, crossing the Rhine to enlist in the French army. Moreover, the behaviour of the larger states' troops in campaign was hardly better than that of the French enemy and caused much bad feeling among the smaller states, which became victims of plundering and requisition.[35] Subsidies were scarcely lucrative, and though they paid for initial mobilisation, they rarely covered the cost of long-term involvement. Barely able to pay its own army, Spain quickly defaulted on the money it promised, while the Dutch only agreed to cover half Brandenburg's expenses in their treaty of May 1672. Given the number of men they were obliged to contribute – Brandenburg was to field 20,000 – most states quickly experienced serious difficulties, especially as their foreign partners sought to reserve the best billets for their own men. Increasingly, the rulers of Brandenburg, Brunswick, Celle, Saxony and later Hanover began demanding billets and contributions from neighbouring German territories on the grounds that these were not pulling their weight for the common cause. The war was causing disastrous side effects in the smaller states. The cost sustained for quartering the troops accelerated a political crisis, as the existing mechanism of mobilising collective defence proved incapable of meeting the French challenge, pushing the Emperor into a number of dangerous expedients at the expense of the weaker, unarmed states, identified with the explicit terms *Nicht Armierten*, opposing to the largest and power ones, the *Armierten*. The largest states were those that could most easily set up an armed force and supply the quota of recruits required by the *Reichsmatricel* also for the smaller states. This gave them a considerable advantage because, in return, the unarmed states agreed to contribute financially to their maintenance in campaign. From the theoretical point of view the agreement seemed fair, but it did not take into account the variables that inevitably occurred in every conflict. Faced with the need to assert his influence and obtain urgently needed additional forces, Leopold I made a virtue of necessity by capitalising on his prerogative to assign billets and arbitrate inter-territorial disputes. To be successful, this tactic depended on balancing concessions to the armed princes with the need to maintain the loyalty of their unarmed victims, something that became very difficult after January 1675.[36] The billeting of winter 1674–75 represented a considerable burden, with the cost of accommodating 12 Brandenburg regiments in Franconia for four months amounting to no less than 400,000 rix-dollars, or nearly three times the annual tax contribute of

---

34 Marr, 'Der Feldzug im Jahre 1675', in *Österreichische Militärische Zeitschrift* (1842), p. 126.
35 *Ibidem*.
36 Wilson, *German Armies*, p. 47.

Ansbach and Bayreuth combined. The Swabian states were even worse hit, with their unwelcome guests extracting well over 500,000 florins more than they were entitled to from just 12 of the 92 member territories.[37] Moreover, the procedure set a precedent that was followed in the four subsequent winters of the war, because with the exception of 1675–76, the Imperial and allied armies failed to secure quarters outside the Empire.[38] Already in 1674, Würzburg, Bamberg, Eisenach, Gotha and Hessen Darmstadt made bilateral arrangements, supplying auxiliary troops for the Emperor on the Rhine in return for limited cash assistance and exemption from billeting and provision of allied and circles' troops.[39] The withdrawal of these territories from collective defence naturally angered their neighbours, who were still participating in the circle structure, while their exemption from billeting reduced the areas available for the Imperial and allied troops. Matters reached crisis by October 1676, as the shortage of assigned quarters and contributions began to undermine the decisive Brandenburg's war effort. Believing that they were being sacrificed to preserve the Emperor's relations with Brandenburg, the circles of Franconia and Swabia decided to pull out of the war altogether, withdrawing their troops by April 1677 and unilaterally declaring their neutrality. Adding insult to injury, the requests of the quartered troops became increasingly exorbitant towards their hosts, as happened in September 1677 with the retreating Saxon auxiliary corps, which simply commandeered the Swabians' field artillery.

The experience of 1674–78 demonstrated that though possessed of sufficient human and material resources, the Empire continued to be scarcely able to defend itself, because it lacked the central co-ordination necessary to manage its disparate elements. Constant internal feuding and rivalry further weakened the cohesion of the Empire, contributing to the excesses of the Franco-Dutch War, which only served to widen the gap between it and its western European neighbours. Most subsequent commentators agreed that the lack of a strong hereditary monarchy was a fundamental weakness, condemning Germany to a largely passive international role, until Prussia and Austria acquired sufficient power to act independently and emerge as

---

37 W. Dotzauer, *Die deutschen Reichskreise in der Verfassung des alten Reiches und ihr Eigenleben* (1500–1806) (Munich: Wissenschaftliche Buchgesellschaft, 1989), p. 161.

38 Wilson, *German Armies*, p. 51: 'While costs in Swabia remained roughly constant at 2–3 million florins each time, they rose in Franconia to 2.1 million in 1675–6 and the subsequent winter. Altogether, billeting made up at least 8 million florins of Swabia's total 21 million florins war costs and dwarfed the annual cost of maintaining the 3,000 Kreistruppen which stood at 500,000 florins.'

39 *Ibidem*: 'Other states followed different ways to save their territory from the heavy billets required. Since Vienna defaulted on his subsidy and still assigned Imperial troops for winter quarter to Würzburg and Bamberg in 1675–76, bishop Peter Philipp von Dernbach realised that four auxiliary regiments cost only 265,000 florins annually compared with 1,050,000 florins spent previously in just six months for foreign billets. Imperial and Papal support also compelled the querulous canons to suspend their opposition to Dernbach's absolutist domestic measures. Unable to reach an agreement with the Emperor directly, regent Hedwig Sophie of Hessen-Kassel made a separate treaty with Denmark to achieve armed status by fielding 2,000 auxiliaries for the campaign against Sweden in April 1677. As these were destroyed by the enemy, a second force of 1,300 was despatched the following April, this time with formal Imperial approval extending to exemption from billets.'

rivals for political leadership. Though familiar, this view no longer holds true with contemporary military historians, as several scholars rightly outline.[40] Unlike other European states, centralisation at national level in the *Reich* was paralleled by a similar development in the component territories, prolonging the medieval fragmentation of political and military power. As the Emperor sought to assimilate power under his own command as supreme overlord for the entire area, individual territorial rulers were attempting to do the same within their own domains. Control over the central mechanisms for raising money and soldiers was shared between both the Emperor and princes and minor rulers. However, the cost of preserving Habsburg influence was considerable. Continued postponement of defence reform left the mobilisation dependent on the existing circle structure, where it could be derailed by the major princes. As a result, after the Peace of Nijmegen, the circles licensed their troops and in 1679 no regiment or minor unit had remained active.

The 'Laxenburg Alliance'

In 1679, memory of the war contributions and the devastation caused by the allied armies were still alive, and considered as looting of an enemy. More serious for the immediate conduct of the defence of the Empire had been the continuing disagreement over how defence should be organised. The failure to agree on defence reform meant that the Diet could only mobilise the forces of the Imperial circles in the traditional manner. This worked reasonably well in the circles nearest the front line, which were in any case dominated by small and relatively defenceless states. Hence Swabia, Upper Rhine and Franconia, the most vulnerable of the so-called *Vordere Kreise* (forward circles), were conscientious in raising their share of troops from the outset. In the circles that contained one or more 'armed princes', the system did not work so well: initially because some of those princes sympathised with France, then because they preferred to send their troops as auxiliaries under contract in return for much needed cash, rather than as part of a regular circle contingent. Some even argued that these contingents should be dispensed with altogether and that their auxiliaries should serve as the official forces of the Empire. Relieved of their obligation to raise troops themselves, the unarmed territories had made heavy cash payments to support the troops of their armed neighbours. The circles had mustered between 10,000 and 12,000 men in 1675, 1676, and 1677, but the total raised by eight major armed princes in the same period was between 50,000 and 60,000.[41] Their costs, moreover, were not adequately met by subsidy payments, even where the subsiding power did not delay or even default. The far greater contribution made by the armed princes and the immeasurably greater costs they incurred led some to argue that the burden of defence was being unequally distributed and to demand billets and contributions from their neighbours.

---
40   *Ibidem.*
41   Whaley, *Germany and the Holy Roman Empire*, p. 36.

However, this situation, combined with the growing threat represented by French and Ottoman expansionism, favoured the establishment of permanent contingents administered by the circles. This process began in 1679 on the initiative of Count Georg Friedrich von Waldeck. He was the ruler of a little state of the Upper Rhine circle and obviously the Count was interested to preserve the integrity of his domain. Waldeck was also a talented general who had successfully served in the *Reichsarmee* in 1664 and in the Dutch army during the war of 1672–78, and he looked at the Dutch 'military' as a model. The Dutch Republic, with its peculiarities and differences between one province and another, was quite similar to the Empire, but this had not prevented the Republic from deploying a modern army capable of facing in the field the feared French army. According to Waldeck, a relatively large but permanent army, well trained and supported by modern fortresses, would have been able to offer enough resistance against an invasion, avoiding looting and war contributions. The Waldeck proposal saw the adherence of other princes and cities equally interested in avoiding the costly provisioning of troops. This first association assumed the name of *Wetterau Bund* or *Frankfurt Allianz*. The initiative appeared interesting because of the unprecedented military organisation devised: instead of resorting to the contingents deployed by the stronger 'armed states', each member of a circle committed to contribute for the formation of a war treasury – to be established in Frankfurt am Main – proportional to its size, sufficient to maintain a single armed force uniformly equipped, regularly trained, and subjected to a unified high command. Soon, the proposal met the favour of other princes of the Empire, both Catholic and Protestant, and was also examined by the Emperor's chancellery. The diplomatic action of the prince-bishop of Würzburg, Peter Philipp von Dernbach, was instrumental in the alliance, acting as an intermediary between Waldeck, Vienna and the princes of the Empire. Waldeck's project was an evolution of the one already introduced by external circles in 1674, but now it also contemplated the possibility of establishing units to be maintained permanently also in peacetime. Thanks to the efforts of Dernbach and Waldeck, the original union was transformed in 1680 into the *Laxenburg Allianz*, which joined together the circles of Swabia, Franconia and Upper Rhine. Encouraged by the success of his initiative, Waldeck proposed to the Diet to extend the project to the whole Empire, calculating – optimistically – to gather at least 90,000 men recruited within the circle and under the orders of a general staff appointed by the Diet. The Emperor's representatives managed to take advantage of the Laxenburg Alliance to their advantage, using it to counterbalance the power of electoral princes and the other armed states. The final project, presented to the Diet in January 1681, was similar in many respects to the original, but contained details that concealed the Emperor's political intent. Despite Leopold's unconditional support for the formation of central treasury and unified command, some questions related to armaments – in particular the siege artillery – were left unresolved as well as the appointments of the commander generals. With these limitations, it became possible to keep in awe the military structure assembled by the circles and conveniently exploit the resulting power. To obtain this result, concessions were necessary and the endless discussions that threatened to take the initiative to a blind alley were to be avoided. A revision of the *Reichsmatricel* was therefore discussed and the respective circles' Diets were allowed to divide the quotas among the states. The work of the Viennese chancellery gave Leopold I a decisive advantage over the major states, in particular due to the fact that his proposal left the structure of the circles intact, fuelling the ambitions of hegemony of the major components. Moreover, the Imperial diplomacy was able to avoid the self-sufficiency of the Alliance, because the lack of an agreement regarding the artillery left the circles' contingent subordinate to the Emperor's field army.

In 1681, the Diet of Regensburg voted for the *Dritte Armatur* establishing a new *Reichsmatricel*:

Circle:	Horse	Foot
Austrian and Bohemian	2,522	5,507
Bourgogne	1,321	2,708
Franconia	980	1,902
Swabia	1,321	2,707
Upper Rhine	491	2,853
Rhine-Electoral	600	2,707
Bavaria	800	1,494
Westphalia	1,321	2,708
Lower Saxony	1,322	2,707
Upper Saxony	1,322	2,707

Overall 12,000 horse and 28,000 Foot *in simplum*, which could increase to 120,000 men in the case of war against the Ottomans.

Regarding the total number, this time also the actual results were lower than expected, and concerning the formation of permanent units, only the circles of Franconia and Swabia raised the first regiments between 1681 and 1683, followed by Bavaria in 1683.[42] However, this decision formed the basis of the *Reichsarmee* for the following century and remained unchanged until the dissolution of the Empire in 1804.

The establishment of these permanent corps allowed the circles of Franconia, Swabia and Bavaria to send their troops in 1683 to relieve Vienna and subsequently to Hungary, where in 1685 they were joined by the Upper-Rheinish contingent. About 10–11,000 troops from the circles served alongside the Imperial army in Hungary until 1688, when the reopening of the war against France forced them to hastily return in Germany.

---

42 Franconia formed the first infantry regiment, *Andlau* (FI-4) with the participation of Nurnberg, Würzburg-Bamberg, Ansbach, Rothenburg, Bayreuth, Hohenlohe, Henneberg Schleusingen, Eichstaett, Schweinfurth, Windsheim and Weissenburg. The second regiment, *Avila* (FI-5), comprised Würzburg-Bamberg, Nurnberg, Bayreuth, Ansbach, Geyer, Rothenburg and the Teutonic Order. The circle reconstituted the cavalry regiment disbanded in 1676, cuirassier regiment *Bayreuth* (FC-3), which resulted formed by these companies: *Leibkompanie* by Bayreuth; 2nd and 10th by Nurnberg; 3rd and 8th by Würzburg; 4th by Bamberg; 5th by Rieneck, Geyer, Rothenburg, Windsheim and Weissenburg; 6th by Eichstätt, Henneberg-Schleusingen, Henneberg-Röhmild, Henneberg-Schmalkalden and Erbach; 7th by Eichstätt and Dernbach; 9th by Ansbach, Schwarzenberg and Seinsheim. Dotzauer 'Die deutschen Reichskreise', p. 188.

5

The Imperial Army on Campaign

'After the battle, you either win or lose. In victory, thank God, bury the dead, spread the news, exaggerate it, continue it, pursuit the enemy's defeated army, do not give him time to rally the troops.'

Montecuccoli, *Aforismi dell'Arte Bellica*

The Habsburg Monarchy, with its strategically exposed and vulnerable location in Central Europe, was surrounded by numerous neighbours and potential foes, against whom simultaneous defence was impossible within the resources which could be mobilised with its own forces. Despite this unfavourable scenario, the Imperial army faced enemies on four different fronts, though not always concurrently. Alongside the traditional fronts in Hungary against the Ottomans and the Rhine against France, the Imperial commanders led their troops also in Poland–Pomerania and Denmark in 1657–1660 and also in Italy. The clauses of the Peace of Westphalia, supported by the Rhenish Alliance, obliged the Emperor not to intervene militarily in defence of the Spanish domains on the Rhine and in the Low Countries, which remained battlefields until 1659, but in Italy he was free to support his Madrid cousin. Military historiography rarely deals with the Italian campaigns of the Franco-Spanish war. Though on this front there were no encounters comparable to those of Valenciennes and the Dunes, the French attempts to invade the Milanese continued until 1659. Seven infantry regiments and four cuirassier regiments marched from Austria to the *Estado de Milan* between 1657 and 1659, to support the Spanish troops who faced the French in northern Italy and engaged France in battle during the siege of Alessandria in 1657, and in the encounter of San Giorgio di Mantova in 1658.[1]

---

1   Wrede, *Geschichte der K. und K. Wehrmacht*, vol. II, pp. 121–137.

THE IMPERIAL ARMY ON CAMPAIGN

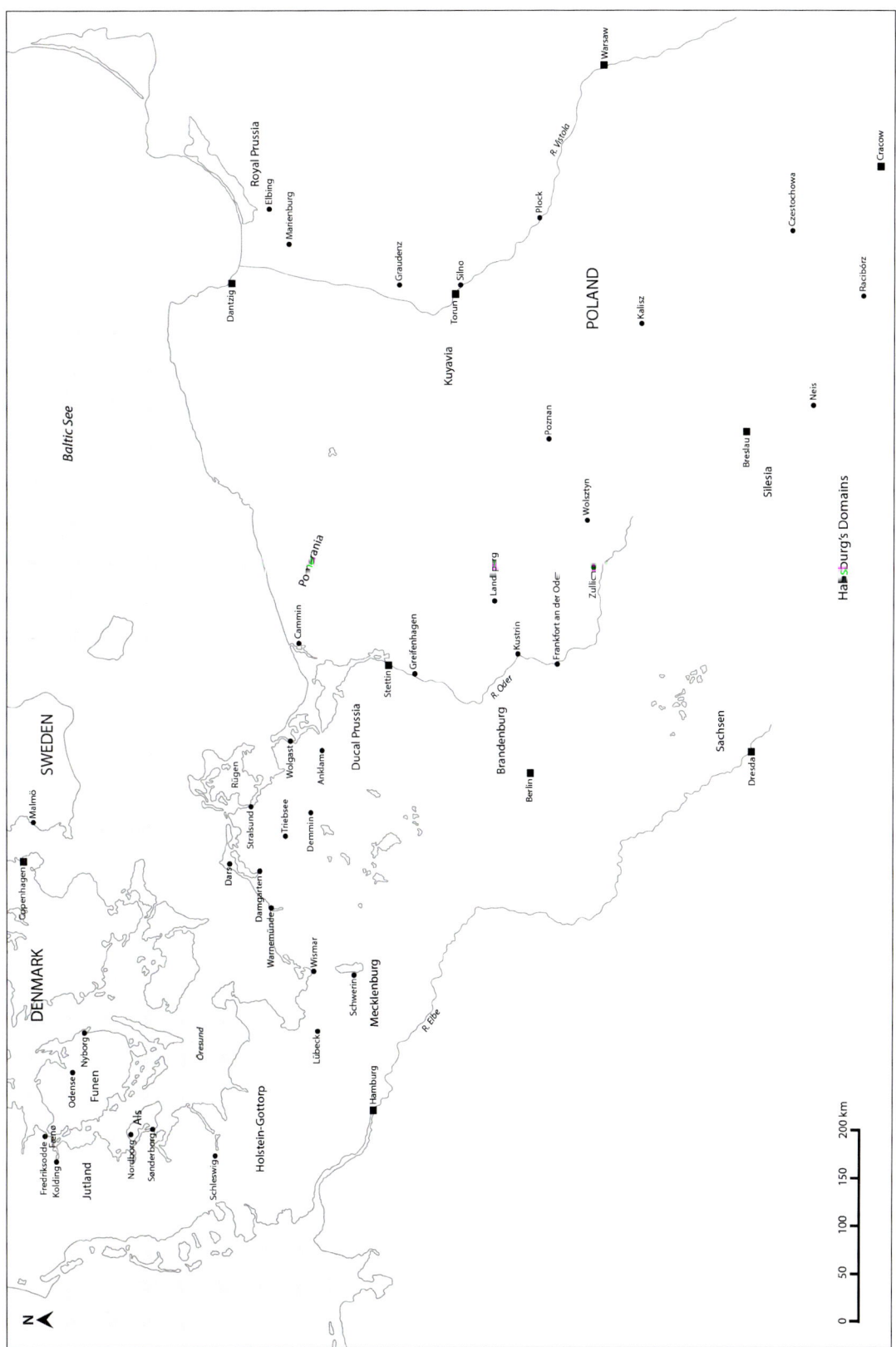

Theatre of war in Poland, Denmark and Pomerania, 1657–1660.

Poland, Jutland and Pomerania, 1657–60

In 1657, the decision to move against Carl X of Sweden in Poland interrupted the isolation of the Habsburgs after the Treaties of Westphalia. The expedition of a relief army to Poland was not an easy task, considering all the difficulties that had to be faced by sending troops to regions far away from their quarters. Despite these concerns, the campaign began in the spring of 1657 with the departure of the Imperial troops gathered near Breslau, in Silesia. The aged *General-Lieutenant* Melchior von Hatzfeld was the commander-in-chief, alongside *General der Cavallerie* Raimondo Montecuccoli as vice-commander. The forces numbered 16,550 men,[2] who had the task of engaging the enemy exclusively in Poland, avoiding any involvement inside the *Reich* territory, in order to not infringe the Peace of Westphalia. In exchange for military aid, Poland would grant the Imperialists the revenues of the cities of Cracow, Poznan and another city to be established.[3]

On 6 June 1657, the army crossed the border at Neis (today Nysa in Poland) and continued the march along the road to Cracow. Hatzfeld had timed the departures to meet the king of Poland, Jan II Casimir of Wasa, at Racibórz. Here, the allies planned to join the armies at Tarnowskie and then to lay siege to Cracow.[4] The Imperial army arrived at the meeting point on 14 June, waiting for the arrival of the Poles coming from Warsaw. Three days after, the two armies joined. On the same day, *Feldmarschall-Lieutenant* Johann von Sporck advanced to Cracow with 3,000 foot and 3,000 horse to surround the city. The Transylvanian cavalry, which had the task of surveying the roads to Cracow, withdrew without offering resistance. News revealed that both the Transylvanians and the Swedes were withdrawing, concerned by the approach of the Tatars from east and the involvement of Denmark and Brandenburg to the north.

Having freed some fortified villages nearby, the allied army arrived at Cracow on 18 July. The Polish king took quarters in a convent outside the city, bringing with him all the court and ministers. The besiegers could deploy 30,000 soldiers, while the defenders numbered 5,500 men in all. The city had an ancient curtain wall reinforced by a few modern works and described in relations such as 'imperfect in many points'.[5] On 20 July, Hatzfeld opened the line of circumvallation, but the Poles considered it too far from the city. Furthermore, the siege operations were delayed by the lack of artillery, which was still on the way. The Polish court complained to the Imperial general, who they said acted too slowly, and sent letters to Vienna

---

2   9,700 foot and 6,850 horse; *Theatrum Europaeum, vol. VIII, Friedens- und Kriegs-Beschreibung, Von Anfang des 1657sten, biß an das 1661* (Frankfurt am Main, 1693), pp. 110–111.
3   G. Gualdo-Priorato, *Historia di Leopoldo Cesare* (Vienna, 1670), vol. I, p. 26.
4   After the 'deluge' a new Royal Polish army had been formed in April thanks to the effort of the great marshal Lubomirski, the royal chancellor Goricinski, the bishop of Premysla Trzebiski, the palatine of Poznan Leczinski, the court marshall Opalinski and others; but excluding some German mercenary regiments, most of the Polish army consisted of untrained recruits with poor armaments. See in Klaje, *Der Feldzug der Kaiserlichen unter Souches nach Pommern im Jahre 1659*, p. 19.
5   Gualdo-Priorato, *Historia*, vol. I, p. 27.

to ask for a replacement. With the great joy of the Poles, the direction of the operations was carried out by Montecuccoli, who ordered a new, and less extensive, line of circumvallation.

The first clash occurred at the end of July, when the Imperialists assaulted some external buildings manned by the Swedes. The action was performed by two infantry battalions from the regiments *Souches* (II 4) and *Baden* (II 7) flanked by the cuirassiers of the regiment *Gonzaga* (IC 1).[6] It was the first time since 1648 that the Imperialists and Swedes engaged in fighting. The action was more demanding than expected, and after an initial success by the besiegers the Swedes launched a counter-attack, immediately rejected by the Imperialists, who sent another two battalions from the regiments *Kaiserstein* (II 15) and *Holstein* (II 24). Until now the artillery had been inactive, but now from the city it opened fire on the Imperial cavalry to allow the retreat of the defenders into Cracow. Consequently, the besiegers' battery located on this side responded to the fire, burning some houses. This fight would remain the only one of the entire siege, as in mid August the besieged garrison opened the negotiations and finally agreed to evacuate the city on 24 August.[7] Hatzfeld left in Cracow some infantry companies of the regiments *Souches* and *Kaiserstein*, and then prepared the army for a march north. In the meantime, more news had arrived informing that the Transylvanians had been surrounded and captured by the Tatars at Skalat,[8] and the Swedish field army was marching northward, leaving only some garrisons in the larger cities.

However, favourable news was balanced by disputes arising between the Poles and Imperialists in the aftermath of the conquest of Cracow, due to Count Lubomirski's complaint: he claimed to be appointed military governor of the city in place of *General Wachtmeister* Johann Paul von Kaiserstein. The dispute lasted a long time and involved the chancelleries of the two sovereigns, until a compromise was found, which allowed Lubomirski to install his own garrison in the castle and leave the city to Kaiserstein.

The Imperial army rested until 30 August before to resume the campaign. The troops marched to north undisturbed, with stops at Czestochowa and Kalisz. In late September the Imperialists took Poznan, abandoned by the Swedes, and in early October moved to Royal Prussia (Prussia under Polish rule), crossing the Vistula on boats made available by the town of Plock. The campaign had been a triumphal march, however the information gathered confirmed that the Swedes had arrested their retreat, using the Vistula as

---

6   *Ibidem*, p. 29.
7   *Ibidem*, p. 30. About 3,000 Swedes left the city after six days with their carriages escorted by the Imperial infantry. Alongside the Swedes, 2,000 Transylvanians left Cracow two days before, even in the absence of agreements with the Poles, who wanted to take them prisoner and deprive them of any property and weapons. In fact, on 23 July 1657 Rákóczi had signed a peace treaty with the Polish Commonwealth, in which he promised to break the alliance with Sweden, withdraw his troops from Poland, and pay 200,000 rix-dollars for the damage inflicted by his army. In mid August, the payment had not yet paid and therefore the Poles wanted to retaliate on the surrendered Transylvanians.
8   On 20 July 1657 the Transylvanian-Cossack army was defeated at the Battle of Czarny Ostrów by Poles, forcing Prince Rákóczi to sign the truce. On 26 July, at Skalat, in Ukraine, the Crimean Tatars surrounded the retreating remnants of the Transylvanian army. The Tatars killed 500 Transylvanians and captured 11,000 prisoners including the commander-in-chief János Kemény.

an obstacle between them and the allies, and that they were reorganising in Royal Prussia. On 15 October, with 1,500 cuirassiers and 500 dragoons, Montecuccoli advanced boldly to the north-east, eluding the enemy and conquering some castles and mills near Torun. The mounted force surprised some parties of Swedish infantrymen, and on 17 October finally arrived before Torun. The escaped soldiers alarmed the city's garrison and the commander ordered the suburbs fired, to prevent the Imperialists from occupying the posts.

During the march, several problems arose between the Imperialists and Poles regarding supplies, which were deemed insufficient. The dispute caused bad feelings between the Imperial commanders and the Polish court. The king's ministers tried to reassure Hatzfeld that the supplies would arrive by river and that the delays were due to storms on the waterways, but in the following weeks the situation had not improved. Probably for the veterans of the Thirty Years' War, the scenario must have seemed familiar. The commanders protested for the lack of resources and the civil authorities of the allied country looked for any excuse to escape their duties. Hatzfeld declared it impossible to lay siege to Torun, due to the lack of resources and horses for the artillery, because the train for feeding the troops had been lost. A war council was summoned, the elector of Brandenburg, the Imperial ambassador Lisola, the king of Poland and Hatzfeld were also present, and it was agreed to besiege Torun before the winter, which was expected to be very cold. All the necessary supplies were promised, including horses for the artillery, but again reality denied fulfilment of the agreements. On 30 October, Hatzfeld ordered the army to cross the Vistula again to take winter quarters. His message to the commanders contained these bitter considerations: 'I see well that the designs of the people who are against us is that they would like to see such beautiful troops dead. Our Emperor has sent here his soldiers with good faith to help such ungrateful people.'[9] However, the dispute seemed resolved again, and in fact the Imperial officers, knowing that Hatzfeld often returned to his decisions, had held their troops north of the river, but for the third time the promised supplies did not arrive and finally the campaign ended. The infantry took winter quarters between Plock and Warsaw, while the cavalry was sent further south, where the forage was more abundant. Hatzfeld left command to Montecuccoli and went back to Silesia, where he died on 9 January 1658.

The march to winter quarters was also marred by accidents and delays and lasted until 30 December. Hatzfeld's death obliged Montecuccoli to take on diplomatic assignments that took him to Berlin, to discuss the details of the military alliance with Brandenburg. Command in Poland passed to *Feldmarschall-lieutenant* Louis Raduit de Souches, in charge to negotiate the terms for the future campaign with the Polish court transferred at Poznan.[10] Here, the Imperial general also negotiated the sending of supplies, which

---

9   Gualdo-Priorato, *Historia*, vol. I, p. 398.
10 Troubled and mutual rudeness marked the meetings in Posen. The Queen, Marie Louise of Gonzaga-Nevers, openly hostile to the Imperialists, declared to Souches that all the Poles wanted the Austrians to leave the country. It even went so far as to evoke the existence of a plan

THE IMPERIAL ARMY ON CAMPAIGN

were eventually granted under the terms of the Vienna Treaty of the previous year, but accorded only after a long negotiation. During the winter, accidents inevitably occurred with the civilian population, caused by the constraints in which the soldiers found themselves, and this served as a pretext for the Polish commissars to suspend the sending of supply. The difficult conditions obviously influenced discipline. Casualties due to fighting and illnesses had been until then minimal, but now the desertions provoked many voids in the regiments.[11]

There were no major clashes during this period, except for an ambush against the Imperial cavalry in late February, in which the Swedes captured count Gottfried von Heister, *General Wachtmeister* and colonel proprietor of a cuirassier regiment.[12] In April, the allied war council agreed to block Torun with the minimum of necessary troops, and to head in the direction of Marienburg (today Malbork, in Poland), where the Swedes had set up their main camp. The conquest of the strategic posts between Elbing (Elblag in Poland) and Marienburg would force the Swedish garrisons in the area to surrender. The plan appeared promising, because Marienburg had just an old curtain wall and Elbing, isolated in the swamp, could be easily conquered blocking the communication roads and channels.

The council had been continually interrupted by the suspicions of the Poles about the allies and their real goals. The regularity of supplies always represented the biggest problem, so much so as to induce Montecuccoli to request the sending of money from Vienna, so as to be able to purchase necessities on site without waiting for the Poles. However, the artillery officers had to return to Cracow to recover the siege artillery, and conduct it by river to Plock. Montecuccoli, with 8,000 troops, had to perform against the main targets in Royal Prussia, while Souches with approximately 5,200 men was entrusted to the blockade of Torun alongside the Poles.

In early May, the Imperials marched in two separate columns. The cuirassier regiment *Heister* (IC-9) formed the vanguard, supported by a corps of Tatar cavalry send by King Jan Casimir.[13] This corps headed to Torun without being discovered and on 14 May camped a few miles from the city. The Tatars performed well, capturing a spy sent from Torun and 300 Swedish infantryman after a sortie in the area.

The defensive curtain of Torun consisted of an external wall of medieval origin to which two less elevated ramparts had been added in the 16th century to flank the gates. The whole perimeter was surrounded by a shallow ditch, devoid of water. Some suburbs stood not far from the walls. The Swedes had no interest in guarding the external curtain, considered as indefensible and therefore they had concentrated the garrison in both ramparts and in the fortress, which extended into the city in a dominant position. This fortress

---

to kill the Imperial general and immediately afterwards forcibly expel his troops. Klaje, *Der Feldzug der Kaiserlichen unter Souches nach Pommern im Jahre 1659*, p. 23.

11 According to Gualdo-Priorato, from October 1657 to May 1658 the overall strength had decreased to 13,200 men; see in *Historia*, vol. I, p. 422.

12 *Ibidem*, p. 404.

13 *Ibidem*, p. 405. These Tatars came from Lithuania, and are described in the source as 'less barbaric compared to Crimean Tatars.'

had high towers, a well-designed rampart with a palisade and a ditch with deeper water.

Souches took quarters in the village of Silno, a few miles from Torun, fortified the encampment and threw a pontoon bridge on the Vistula, waiting for the arrival of the main corps, which crossed the river one day after with 4,000 infantrymen, 600 dragoons and a huge train, enhanced by the requisitions. Souches planned a surprise assault, trusting that the Torun garrison was still unaware of his presence. On May 16, before dawn, a mixed corps of Imperialists and Tatars approached the city without being discovered and took up a position in a friars' cloister not far from the city's gate. At dawn, the Tatars tried to attract the Swedes out of the city, approaching the foragers coming from Torun, but the action failed when the Swedish sentinels alarmed their comrades. In vain, the Imperialists waited for two hours for the garrison to come out to disperse the Tatars, and finally they left the cloister to move in front of the city. Meanwhile Colonel Spankau with 300 cuirassiers and 200 dragoons assaulted a fortified village near the Vistula, but the Swedes offered fierce resistance and the action ended. The surprise had vanished, and Souches awaited for the arrival of the Polish allies, and – above all – the artillery for a regular siege. However, the Poles arrived only in late July with the troops under Prince Radziwill, who resumed the assault against the fortified village, conquering it on 26 July. The Imperialists built a second pontoon bridge on the Vistula and finally, on 6 August, further Polish forces led by generals Sapieha and Grogeski arrived in the area.

Now the besiegers deployed 12–13,000 foot and horse in two main camps around Torun, supported by a battery of artillery. Inside the city, under the talented general Bengt Oxenstierna, there was a garrison of 5,000 regular soldiers and 600 militiamen recruited by the pro-Swedish leading citizens.[14] The regular siege began on 10 August, when the defenders launched two sorties, engaging the enemies for the whole day. Two days later a new sortie involved an Imperial outpost built near a water mill, defended by 100 dragoons, who were saved after two hours of hard fighting by a relief force of cuirassiers under Souches and Polish horsemen under Sapieha. On 13 August Colonel Heister, disguised as a peasant, arrived in the allied camp after evading Marienburg days earlier. More fighting occurred in August, including an Imperial attempt to fire a bridge manned by the Swedes. However, the decisive event occurred near Graudenz (Grudziądz in Poland), when on 30 August the palatine Czarniecki intercepted and defeated the Swedish relief corps marching from Marienburg.

On 23 September the troops under King Jan Casimir and Lubomirski arrived, numbering 10,000 soldiers with some small pieces of artillery; the queen and court were with him. The presence of the sovereign caused great agitation in the besieging camp. The King never missed an opportunity to show his courage by exposing himself to the risks of a siege along with his magnificent procession. It happened that during his inspection to the Imperial entrenchments, which were near the Swedish artillery, the King

---

14 *Ibidem*, p. 407.

risked being killed by a bullet, which mortally wounded some of his entourage and amputated a leg of a Polish officer.[15]

Before September, new complaints came from the Polish court when the King received news concerning the arrival of further Imperial troops in Poland. This was in accordance with the treaty of alliance to bring the number of soldiers back to 20,000: a very unfortunate event in the opinion of the councillors of Jan II Casimir, who insinuated that the Emperor wanted in this way to quarter his troops in the country and burden Poland with their maintenance.[16] Slowly the situation stabilised when it became clear that these troops were not destined for Poland,[17] and in this climate of mutual suspicion, the council of war began to meet.

For the planned assault, to be carried out from two sides, the problem of the ditch that protected the sector occupied by the defenders had to be solved. The immediate solution was to prepare enough fascines to throw into the ditch, as proposed by Souches, and to assault the external ramparts and then occupy both these sectors with the artillery in order to cover the attack against the fortress. The external walls, although imperfect, would have allowed the hiding of enough infantry and even cavalry, to be launched into the breach once it was ready. Although from the beginning the understanding between Lubomirski and Souches had been excellent, the King's councillors opposed the Imperial general's proposal, believing that a direct attack would cause too many losses to the besiegers, and therefore Lubomirski opted for a slow assault to be conducted with entrenched approaches. While Souches wanted to complete the Torun conquest as soon as possible and then re-join Montecuccoli, the Polish allies preferred to take all the time they needed to conquer the city. The impatience of the Imperial general was understandable. Concerning supplies, the Imperialists continued to depend on the Poles. However, Souches had received from Montecuccoli a modest sum in cash to use in case of emergency. Moreover, to increase the scarce economic resources, he had instituted a tax on all the waggons crossing the pontoon bridges built by the Imperialists.[18]

On 26 September the Imperialists positioned a battery with six heavy guns, which targeted the city. The Swedes responded with three heavy cannons that fired from one of the external ramparts. On the same day, the allies opened the approach trenches. The siege turned into a war of position, slowed by Swedish sorties launched three times between the end of September and the first half of the following month. On 14 October the approaches had progressed close to the external ditch, where Souches

---

15 *Theatrum Europaeum*, vol VIII, p. 138. In the following days, the Queen also risked her life when her carriage was hit by the Swedish artillery.
16 The King threatened to order all the governors to call up the militia to close all the frontier's posts; see in Gualdo-Priorato, *Historia*, vol. I, p. 418.
17 The chronicles of the Imperial side do not report that a part of these troops actually went to Torun and participated in the siege under Souches. See also in Wrede, *Geschichte der K. und K. Wehrmacht*, vol. II, pp. 121–137.
18 The sum collected was modest, but the tax provoked the protests of the Queen, who declared it was unheard of that foreigners claimed money in her own country. Gualdo-Priorato, *Historia*, vol. I, p. 414.

ordered the artillery moved, to open a breach in the curtain. On 21 October, the Poles assaulted the external ramparts, chasing the Swedes, and the day after maintained both, rejecting a counter-attack. The war council planned the general assault on 16 November, despite the oncoming of the winter, announced as being very cold. To overcome the ditches the besiegers prepared 10,000 fascines, and to facilitate the approaches to the inner fortress the action was planned for the night. Mortars and howitzers had to support the assault. Two cannon shots gave the assault signal at two in the morning. The bombardment was intense and lasted three hours, but the darkness hindered the attackers as well as the defenders and any objective was eventually achieved. The Imperialists suffered considerable casualties, especially the infantry regiment *Nicola* (II-11), which tried to cross a breach but was repulsed with the loss of a company alongside its captain.[19]

In the aftermath of the failed assault, the Poles and Imperialists reproached each other. Polish commanders criticised the Imperial artillery, which failed to open the breaches, while Souches complained at the poor attitude of the Poles in the siegework.

The inertia of the Poles at Torun was also due to the strategic change that occurred at the end of August. The initial plan had been thwarted by the move of the Swedish king, who had transferred the army from Royal Prussia to turn it against Denmark, disregarding the armistice signed at Roskilde in March 1658. Though the move was unexpected and Denmark was unprepared to face the threat, the strategic scenario offered the possibility of attacking the Swedes from behind, occupying its rear areas in Pomerania and Royal Prussia.[20] Informed of the news by a messenger sent from Berlin, on 30 August Montecuccoli stopped the march of the army at Wolsztyn and soon headed to Zullich (today Sulechów in Poland), entering Brandenburg. A new war council was convened with Polish and Brandenburg commanders in order to join the respective forces. On 5 September the allied army gathered in Küstrin. The Polish corps, under Czarniecki, numbered 3,000 soldiers, further 8,000 from Brandenburg under general Sparr, and finally the same figure of Imperialists under Montecuccoli.[21] With him there were as commander officers the *Feldzeugmeister* Leopold Wilhelm of Baden-Baden, *Feldmarshall-Lieutenant*s Prince Ruprecht of Palatinate-Sulzbach,[22] and Johann von Sporck, and *General-Wachtmeister*s Sigmund von Götz and Christoph von Ronst.

---

19 *Ibidem*, p. 420, *Hauptmann* Thüngen, relative of the future Imperial *Feldmarschall* Johann Carl von Thüngen (1648–1709).
20 The new situation and the involvement in the war of the *Reich*'s territories alarmed also the Imperial Diet, called to reply by the duchies of Brunswick. Klaje, *Der Feldzug der Kaiserlichen unter Souches nach Pommern im Jahre 1659*, p. 29.
21 Gualdo-Priorato, *Historia*, vol. I, pp. 421–422.
22 He was colonel of an Imperial cuirassier regiment since 1657; his brother Philipp was the Swedish commander in Funen. This latter, in 1660, entered service with Venice and two years after for the Habsburg Emperor. In the Hungarian campaign of 1664, he played an important role as *Feldmarschall* and cavalry commander in the successful battle of Szentgotthárd. See in A.B. Michaelis and J.W. Hamberge, *Einleitung zu einer vollständigen Geschichte der Chur- und Fürstlichen Häuser* (Lemgo, 1760) vol. II, p. 121.

On 9 September the three columns crossed the Oder, and marching through Mecklenburg entered Holstein-Gottorp. Both the duchies proclaimed their neutrality, but the Imperialists occupied the castle of Gottorp, where they left a garrison. Montecuccoli was unconvinced of the neutrality of Mecklenburg and Holstein-Gottorp, both linked to Sweden by kinship. Furthermore, negotiations had begun to reach a peace with Charles X, promoted by the elector of Brandenburg, whose ambiguous behaviour did not reassure the Imperial commander. It is also noteworthy that the internal situation of the coalition seemed unsafe because, although they had stopped hostilities at the beginning of 1657, Brandenburg and Poland had not yet signed a peace treaty and therefore were not bound to pursue a common action.[23]

Meanwhile, Montecuccoli gathered the troops arrived from Silesia and Bohemia as reinforcements for his army, which climbed to 10,600 men.[24] News coming from Denmark reported that the Swedes were advancing unopposed and further troops had been assembled in Scania for an assault on Copenhagen. The naval battle in the Öresund, fought on 29 October 1658 and won by the Dutch fleet, brought temporary relief to Denmark, but the threat to Copenhagen was only postponed.

Discussions and disagreements, as well as diplomatic interference, marked the campaign and therefore the military operations suffered several pauses and resumed only at the end of November. Despite the cold season Montecuccoli headed the army north, crossing the Danish borders, and on 14 December ordered the assault on the Island of Als, occupied by the Swedes in early September. The action had to be executed by the Imperial and Electoral troops with the Poles as reserve. The village of Sønderborg was the first objective, separated from Holstein by a stretch of sea of about 180 metres. On the island, the Swedes had a garrison of 4–5,000 horse and foot, quartered in Sønderborg and Nordborg. The allied infantry crossed the sea on boats, but the cavalry reached the island by swimming, despite the almost prohibitive temperature. At Sønderborg the Swedes offered a short resistance and then took refuge inside a coastal fort. Before the arrival of the Imperial artillery they were rescued by the Swedish fleet, but leaving the horses, numbering 3,000, the sick, and all the baggage.[25] The day after, the small Swedish garrison of Nordborg surrendered and agreed to enter Imperial service. After this action the allies conquered Kolding, extorting contribution in Holstein, which suffered greatly from occupation and looting, especially from the Poles. In January, finally the allied troops transferred their winter quarters to Jutland.

Meanwhile at Torun, the quarrelsome allies had convened a new council of war after the failed assault performed on 16 November. The enemy garrison remained under constant artillery fire, and finally a new general assault was planned for the end of December. However, worried about the exhaustion of ammunition and supplies, Oxenstierna asked for a negotiation and finally surrendered on 21 December 1658.

---

23 The treaty was finally signed on 6 October 1658.
24 The reinforcements were two regiments of infantry and two of cavalry; see in Wrede, *Geschichte der K. und K. Wehrmacht*.
25 Gualdo-Priorato, *Historia*, vol. I, p. 424.

Fredriksodde was the main Swedish fortress in Jutland and surrendered to the Imperialists on 27 May 1659. Montecuccoli considered this action as one of the most important strategic successes of the entire war. (Author's collection)

Charles X of Sweden was determined to break the Danish resistance and did not cease to move his armies on several fronts, invading Courland to threaten Lithuania and forcing the Poles to withdraw from the war, clashing with the Russians in Estonia and finally attacking in Norway to engage the Danes far from Copenhagen. In this eventful scenario, Montecuccoli managed to move the army further north, in order to remove the Swedish presence in Denmark. The war council, now including also the Danish commanders, discussed the plan for the following year. The objectives for the campaign of 1659 were then Fredriksodde (today Fredericia) and Funen. For this last objective it was necessary to gather as many troops as possible, given that the Swedes would offer a strong resistance to protect the army engaged in the siege at Copenhagen. Once he achieved the conquest of Funen, for Montecuccoli it was necessary to transfer 25,000 men to Pomerania in order to remove the Swedes from that region, includin the port of Stettin. Simultaneously, from the south, the Poles supported by a strong Imperial corps had to advance in Prussia and besiege the fortresses of Marienburg and Elbing. To achieve this, which could considerably reduce the Swedish threat to Germany, they needed at least another 8,000 Imperial soldiers to send half to Pomerania and half to Prussia. The Aulic War Council agreed to Montecuccoli's demands and sent new troops to Denmark and Poland. Here, Souches held always the command of the Imperial corps, and continued to face a very critical situation, because public opinion in Poland had swung strongly against the Habsburg alliance, as the Imperial army demanded ever-larger sums of money to support it.

By January the Swedes reduced their garrison in Jutland, concentrating the troops on the siege at Copenhagen. In the same month, a sortie by the

THE IMPERIAL ARMY ON CAMPAIGN

The landing at Kerteminde, on Funen Island, painting of the Danish artist Christian Ferdinand Andreas Mølsted (1862–30). The action occurred on 2 November 1659 by an allied corps consisting of Danish, Polish and Dutch troops under Field Marshal Hans Schack. Swedish cavalry is seen coming from the right side of the picture attacking the landing forces. These were soon pushed away and the landing secured, leading to the battle of Nyborg on 14 November, where the Swedes found themselves decisively defeated. In this battle, the Imperial contingent was represented by a cavalry corps of 2,500 cuirassiers under *Feldmarschall-Lieutenant* Herberstein. (Author's collection)

Imperial cavalry intercepted a column of Swedes marching from Fredriksodde and captured most of them after a short fight.

No further encounters occurred until May, when the campaign opened as soon as the grass was sufficient for fodder. The Imperial army increased its strength with the arrival of further regiments,[26] now totalling 17,000 men. With this force, on 24 May Montecuccoli headed to Fredriksodde, almost deprived of soldiers, and after three days of siege the besiegers penetrated into the city; while the Swedish garrison took refuge in the citadel and from there left the city on boats during the night. Fredriksodde represented a major success for the allies, and inside the town they captured several pieces of artillery, tons of gunpowder and the magazines full of flour.

The following step was landing on Fænø Island, which the Swedes had left without a strong garrison to block the allied offensive in Jutland. The action had the dual purpose of threatening the Swedes who besieged Copenhagen and making use of the island as a bridgehead for the campaign on Funen. On 12 June the allies landed on Fænø and conquered the island notwithstanding the enemy resistance and reinforcements coming from Funen. At that point, there were no more obstacles to the landing on Funen. However, the allied fleet commanders were not in favour of risking their ships by facing Swedish batteries closely. Moreover, the island was well guarded and therefore the first attempts at invasion failed.[27] It was therefore necessary to plan the landing during a favourable moment.

---

26 Wrede, *Geschichte der K. und K. Wehrmacht*, vol. II, pp. 121–137.
27 It is interesting to read Montecuccoli's commentary on the Danish campaign, also because it is one of the few testimonies of the great Imperial general on the war of 1657–60: 'We were in Jutland, trying to pass in Funen to fight against the army that the king of Sweden had sent

The operations were planned down to the smallest detail by Montecuccoli, who displayed his exceptional qualities as an organiser. This was a very challenging action in which, for the first time, he held the autonomous command of a coalition force. The assault was conducted with three corps, with the Imperialists to the right, Danes in the centre and the Brandenburg corps to the left, taking up ground simultaneously with the support of the fleet. The sector chosen for the landing was the beach in front of Fænø, where nearby was a dense wood that could provide cover for the infantry, which had to land first to prepare an entrenchment. To this end, each corps carried *chevaux-de-frise*, fascines, hoes, axes and other useful tools for this purpose. Some of the troops had to take care of the work, while the rest were to secure the bridgehead deploying the pikemen lined up in the front line. The cavalry had to be deployed in small groups of 50 troopers, with the task of supporting the infantry only if the enemy broke through into their sector. Montecuccoli recommended the officers to avoid any possible confusion: each battalion had to distribute its own tools without loss of time and the three landing corps did not mix. For this purpose each boat was identified by a coloured flag, red for the Imperialists. Once the first landing was completed, the boats had to immediately return to Fænø and take on the reserve troops and the supplies. The landing was scheduled for early July, as soon as the wind was favourable.

Finally, on 3 July, the assault started. The changing winds did not allow the attackers to land simultaneously, but despite the violent Swedish artillery fire, the action was successful.[28] The allies consolidated their bridgehead in Funen and waited all summer before advancing within the island, prevailing slowly against the dogged defence offered by the Swedes. In early August, Montecuccoli left in Funen a corps of 2,500 Imperial cuirassiers from the regiments *Mattei* (IC-16), *Nath* (IC-19), *Carafa* (IC-21) and *Piccolomini* (IC-5) under *Feldmarschall-Lieutenant* Herberstein, and then he moved the army back to Jutland and then to Pomerania.[29] However, the defeat of a (largely cavalry) Swedish corps at Nyborg on 24 November finally forced the evacuation of the island.

Montecuccoli's backward path served to threaten the Swedes in Pomerania from the west, allowing Souches to transfer the Imperial troops

---

under Gustav Wrangel. It was an important design and consequent of capital interest, but of difficult execution. As in a siege, we had to cross a sea like a ditch and overcome a beach like a parapet, garnished with forts and batteries, protected by an army deployed in battle [...] We were subjected to the changeable winds and, worse, to use the fleet, whose captains did not lead to floods, because they had not agreed with this enterprise. This did not mean that he attempted the assault with value, fortunately without too many losses, but always being rejected.' Cited by Luraghi, 'Le Opere di Raimondo Montecuccoli', vol. II, p. 309.

28 Gualdo-Priorato, *Historia*, vol. I p. 495. The vessel on which Montecuccoli was located was hit by a bullet in the forecastle, right where the Imperial general was observing the operations. Montecuccoli was struck by the fragments of wood from the planking, remaining slightly wounded in one leg.

29 Concerning his plan, Montecuccoli declared that 'the best way to capture Funen was to move away from there, and the shortest way to get into Funen was to turn around and that the door to invade the island was through Pomerania' Luraghi, 'Le Opere di Raimondo Montecuccoli', vol. II, p. 310.

quartered in Poland (more precisely in the voivodate of Kuyavia) to Royal Prussia, joining them with the reinforcements (10,000 foot and 2,000 horse) camped near Breslau.[30] In Poland, with the Palatine Lubomirski, remained only the cuirassier regiments *Heister* (IC-9) and *Ratschin* (IC-20), the dragoon regiments *Flettinger* (ID-3) and *Spankau* (ID-4) and the infantry regiment *Mers* (II-3).[31]

On 30 June, Souches was ready to move from Breslau with his army to join the troops coming from Poland. Some regiments were still incomplete, but the greatest deficiencies concerned the artillery, especially the lack of horses for the train. In early June came the packhorses, but sufficient only for the field artillery. The march to Pomerania had been the subject of negotiations with the Brandenburg ambassador, who was understandably worried about the damage that could occur during the passage of the Imperial troops, whose poor reputation was well known. Finally, it was agreed they would march through the states of the elector of Saxony, who consented only after receiving guarantees from the Emperor. The Imperial commissars accompanied the army until Frankfurt an der Oder, taking care that everything needed was prepared. To minimise problems, the columns marched divided into multiple corps and along different roads. Souches succeeded in shortening the march by crossing the swamps south of Küstrin, benefiting from the dry soil. The place of conjunction was established at Landsperg (today Gorzów Wielkopolski in Poland). Here, on 15 August, the Imperial *Feldzeugmeister* mustered the army, which included the new-raised cuirassier regiments *Salis* (IC-15), *Holstein* (IC-17), *Pfalz-Sulzbach* (IC-14) and the veteran *Schneidau* (IC 10); the *croater* (light horse) regiment *Gutschenich* (IHc-1) and *Lubetich* (IHc 2); the new-formed infantry regiments *Lichtenstein* (II 23), *Stallnacher* (II-29) *Schlebusch* (II-27), *Montavergues* (II-28), and the newly formed *Starhemberg* (II-6), *Wallis* (II-16), *Strozzi* (II-12), and *Cob* (II-8).

Two days later, the Imperialists crossed the border and assaulted the castle of Wildenburg and the town of Greifenhagen (Gryfino in Poland), which surrendered immediately.[32] Greifenhagen became the centre for collecting the supplies for the army on campaign, but the march of the Imperialists was marked by thefts and requisitions that ruined the crops in the countryside and obviously attracted the hostility of the population. In vain, Souches tried to repress these acts, which were often led by the officers of the companies.

In late 17 century, the countryside south of Stettin was surrounded by vast swamps that the Imperialists crossed on rafts. Before reaching Stettin, on which Montecuccoli was also converging, Souches conquered several places, including the fortified town of Wollin north-east of the city. This place fell on 6 September after fierce fighting, which destroyed most of the

---

30 The *Historia* of Gualdo-Priorato says 'Bratislava', but obviously the Silesian city is the actual location where the Imperial troops had been gathered.
31 In the second half of 1659, these regiments participated under *General Wachtmeister* Heister at the sieges of Brodnica, Marienburg and Elbing. See in Wrede, *Geschichte der K. und K. Wehrmacht*, vol. II, p. 124.
32 The conquest of Greifenhagen and Wildenburg was directed by Colonel Jakob von Salis, who had received from Souches the order to prevent the looting, which instead was performed with considerable obstinacy. Gualdo-Priorato, *Historia*, vol. I, p. 565.

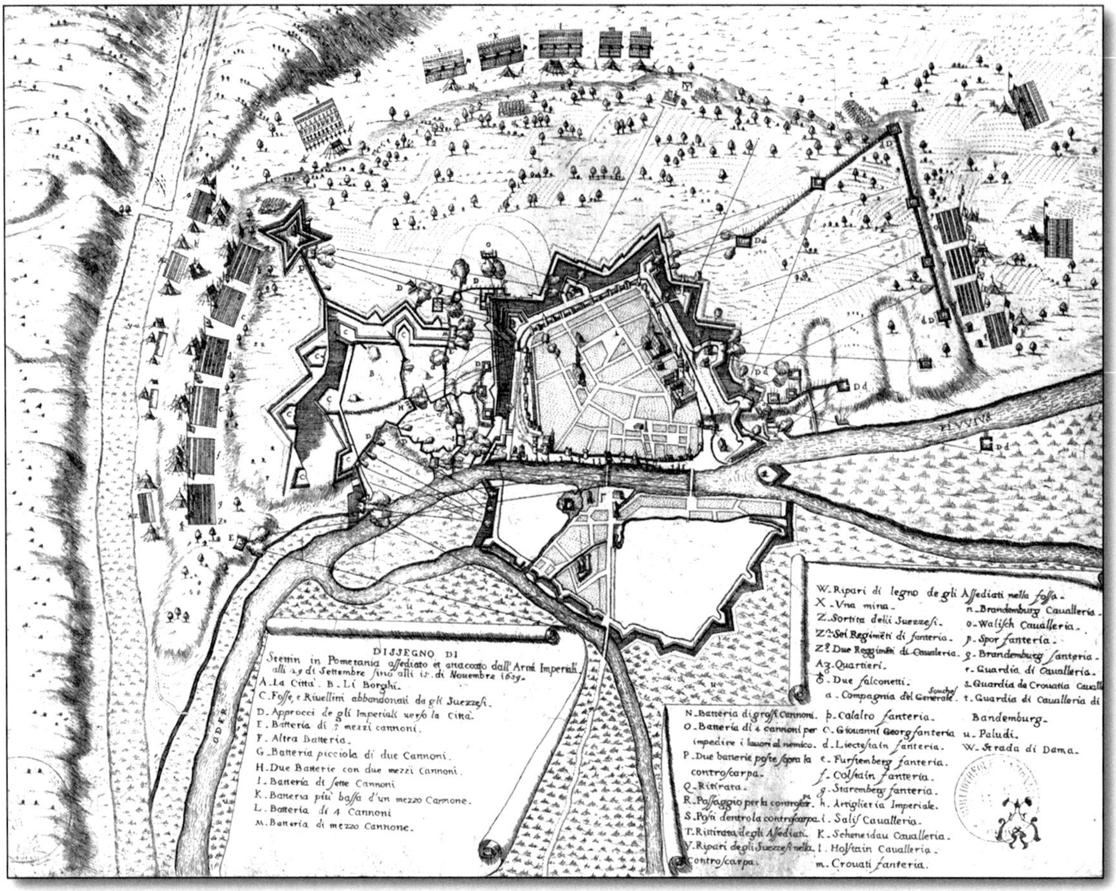

WARS AND SOLDIERS IN THE EARLY REIGN OF LOUIS XIV – VOLUME 2

Siege of Stettin in 1659. Imperial and Brandenburg troops besieged the town from 18 September, but left on 30 November after a fierce struggle. (Author's collection)

Imperial troops in Poland, 1657–58, from the series of prints preserved in the Biblioteka Narodowa of Warsaw. A doublet with short breeches and *Koller* appear as the typical dress for officers and NCOs in this period. Note the high 'Puritan'-style broad-brimmed hat.

houses.³³ Montecuccoli dispatched a third corps under *General Wachtmeister* Johann Reichard Starhemberg, in charge of assaulting some minor places. On 29 August, Starhemberg took Cammin (today Kamień Pomorski) without resistance and then crossed the Oder on boats. He approached the entrenchments that guarded a channel from the Baltic Sea to Cammin. On 7 September, Montecuccoli crossed the border at Troppau, entering West Pomerania after establishing in Glogau a base to collect supplies. The Imperial commander maintained the general direction of the campaign, which intended to isolate Stettin in order to push the Swedish garrison to surrender. It had seemed like a viable option, to be achieved by cutting off all land communication routes to the city and, with the Danish fleet's support, even blocking the sea route. However, the conquest of Stettin appeared a very difficult task that required time and resources. The city was well fortified and surrounded by a large number of channels making a regular approach with trenches problematic. The garrison was estimated to be at least 4,000 men, not counting the militia. If the land routes could be manned, the Swedes always had the option of bringing supplies and reinforcements to the city at night, carrying them with boats that could easily escape the naval blockade. The Swedes were in retreat on all fronts, but it was obvious that Charles X Gustav would do everything to preserve the possession of Stettin, which granted him control of Pomerania. How important Stettin was for Sweden, was readily understood by the commander appointed by the king for the regional defence: Carl Gustav Wrangel. Brandenburg's support was necessary to complete the ring around the city, but both Montecuccoli and Souches doubted the elector's willingness to engage his forces in a siege of uncertain outcome.³⁴ Finally, September had already begun and therefore another winter campaign was on the way, with all the negative consequences for the performance of the troops. All Swedish fortresses in Western Pomerania, except Stralsund, could be conquered coherently with the plan of campaign, but it remained necessary to engage the Stettin garrison with a regular siege. Between September and October Montecuccoli ejected the Swedes from Troppau, Triebsee, Damgarten, Spandau and Demmin. The Swedish garrisons surrendered on terms, and only Demmin resisted longer. However, Montecuccoli led the siege with great speed and even the latter place surrendered after three days. In early November the Swedish controlled only the city-port of Stralsund, and the towns of Wolgast and Anklam. The loss of these latter would probably have also accelerated the surrender of Stettin, therefore Wolgast was besieged by Electoral troops, while Anklam was blocked by the Imperial *Holstein* cuirassier regiment.

On 18 September, before Stettin, supported by 13,000 Brandenburg soldiers under general Dohna, Souches occupied the suburb of Damm (Dabje) on the south-east side of the West Oder, after two days of hard fighting.³⁵

---

33 In Wollin the Imperialists captured 800 infantrymen and 400 horsemen; see in *Theatrum Europaeum*, vol. VIII, p. 577.
34 Gualdo-Priorato, *Historia*, vol. I, pp. 580–581.
35 The surrender was granted on terms: the defenders could retreat to Stettin, but without ammunitions and artillery, and thus remained in the hands of the besiegers 29 guns, 50 quintals

The Swedes did not remain inactive, and before the end of September they tried to recapture Wollin. Then, in early October, they also began to engage the besiegers with effective sorties and on one of these, the Imperial colonel Jakob von Salis was mortally wounded by an artillery shot.[36] On 4 October, the besieging camp was tormented by a strong wind that swept away all the tents, while from the city the artillery incessantly targeted the trenches and also the pavilion of the Imperial commander, which was struck on 5 October, severely wounding one of his adjutants and damaging his chaise.

Souches realised that without siege artillery it was difficult to effectively counter the enemy batteries that constantly targeted the approaches. This came only at the end of October, but with ammunition limited to 100 projectiles per cannon. A battery was then set up, also reinforced by some mortars to hit the bastion on the right side facing the suburb of Damm. A trench dug by the *Starhemberg* infantry regiment advanced against this defence. This sector appeared to be the most promising for such an attack, given that the bastion was not wide and the ditch less deep. The approach of the *Starhemberg* was supported by another prepared by the regiment *Liechtenstein*. On 30 October, the Imperialists launched an assault that succeeded in conquering the bastion's counterscarp. The fighting was extremely hard and cost the life of several soldiers, including the colonel commander of the *Montavergues* regiment. The Imperialists held the position until 5 November, notwithstanding the high casualties, when finally a strong Swedish sortie with 2,000 men surprised the *Liechtenstein* infantrymen and forced the besiegers to retreat. According to some sources, it seems that the Swedish sortie was successful because the trenches were unguarded and the officers gathered for lunch to celebrate St. Martin's day.[37] The retreat almost turned into a rout, and endangered the deposits of ammunition and food, miraculously saved by the providential arrival of a squadron of the *Gonzaga* cuirassiers who were escorting a gunpowder convoy. The Imperialists lost 70 men and further 60 were captured, among them one captain, two lieutenants and one engineer. The Swedes nailed nine cannons but only four irreversibly.[38] Carelessness and negligence were also the result of the harsh weather conditions and, not any less importantly, the delayed payment of salaries and the scarcity of food. Although the delivery of supplies was skilfully managed by Colonel Mers from Greifenhagen and Glogau, the besieging camp began to suffer from the lack of flour. Montecuccoli sent 7,000 florins to Souches for the salaries, while after an action carried by the Croats near Anklam, many cattle were acquired to supply the army with meat. In the following days, two other sorties were carried out by the Swedes, and in the second they destroyed the flour stores of the Brandenburg troops. The allies called all the available forces to maintain the ring around Stettin and neutralise the enemy sorties, but the Swedish resistance and the increasing cold induced Souches and Dohna to suspend the siege in late November.

---

of gunpowder, projectiles and matches. Among the 1,500 soldiers of the garrison, many of the Germans deserted to enlist in the Imperial regiments. *Ibidem*, p. 572.
36 Wrede, *Geschichte der K. und K. Wehrmacht*, vol. II, p. 134.
37 Gualdo-Priorato, *Historia, vol.* I, p. 581.
38 Klaje, *Der Feldzug der Kaiserlichen unter Souches nach Pommern im Jahre 1659*, p.120.

Meanwhile, since September French and English diplomatas had been promoting peace negotiations. Charles X Gustav had appealed against the treaties of Westphalia, denouncing the Emperor for bringing the war into the Empire, but the complaints remained unheard. On 23 January 1660, the sudden death of the Swedish king accelerated the negotiations that led to the peace of Oliva, signed the following 3 May. Before the signing of the treaty, Montecuccoli achieved further results with the conquest of Wismar, Darss and Warnemünde in late April. On 29 May, the Imperialists abandoned Pomerania and transferred all the troops to Moravia and Mecklenburg, including those from Poland, Prussia and Funen.

The Ottoman War of 1663–64 and the Miracle of Szentgotthárd

The long period of peace that existed in Hungary between 1606 and 1663 offered little in the way of military details. The only exception was the slow, continuous upgrading by the Habsburg 'military', which involved the strengthening of the Hungarian defence system through the modernising of fortresses and garrisons. In the field, the Imperialists might have had superiority over their Ottoman enemies in weaponry and battlefield tactics; however, in terms of war resources the general scenario was more favourable to the Porte. Because of the composite nature of the Habsburg monarchy throughout the war, the Imperial army had to depend for money, supplies, carts and draught animals on subsidies granted by the Austrian, Bohemian, Moravian and Silesian estates, because the Hungarian ones refused more than once to support the Imperial army on campaign. The slowness with which subsidies were provided paralysed the Imperial forces on many occasions. Thus it took less time for the Ottoman forces to get from Constantinople or Edirne to Buda than it took for the Imperial forces to reach their encampments on the nearby Austrian–Hungarian border.

The principal achievement accomplished in the 16th century by the Habsburgs, was to stop the Ottoman advance, although this was only possible by losing much of Hungary and by mobilising all the available military and financial resources of the Habsburg domains. Campaigns began to be marked by the clash of smaller forces dispersed along the front line in a succession of rapidly executed attacks and sieges spread across a wide territory, as happened in Transylvania after 1657. In the 17th century, the Ottoman army conducted a more fluid, exploratory and opportunistic style of engagement that shared many common features with the *Klein Krieg* warfare, where a concentration of huge opposing armies massing on a single battlefield became increasingly uncommon. This elusive warfare represented a serious problem for the Imperialists, to whose analysis Montecuccoli himself dedicated a substantial part of his theoretical writings.

Heavy rains or unseasonable weather affected attackers and defenders in siege warfare in disproportionate ways. The effect of unforeseen or freak weather conditions on land campaigns could be dramatic, turning imminent victory into sudden rout. The initial campaigns of the war show a dynamic trend, with deep advances enemy territory achieving important strategic goals. Using this strategy, the Ottoman cavalry, with superior strength, played a significant role, especially when the Tatar horsemen joined the army on campaign. In August 1657, Köprülü Mehmed launched a disciplinary Tatar offensive in Transylvania against the rebel great-prince György II Rákóczi, who had joined the Swedes in the war against Poland. If Rákóczi had quickly turned around and taken his intact army home, his losses would have been great, but tolerable and recoverable. He did not realise, however, that fortune had abandoned him, and he now committed an unpardonable mistake. He and a few hundred of his soldiers returned to Transylvania, but left behind the main force, about 20,000 troops, in Poland. They were surrounded by the Poles and Tatars, captured and taken to the slave markets in Crimea; the majority of these soldiers never returned home. The golden age of Transylvania ended in one fell swoop. The prince was forced to accept a demeaning peace agreement, paying enormous compensation for his failed coup. During the next two years, Rákóczi was forced to abdicate twice. In the meantime, Transylvania became a battleground both internally and externally.

In the spring of 1658, Rákóczi reformed the army after he eliminated Ferenc Rhédey de Kisréde,[39] who had been established as a new *kiral* (great-prince). The Porte reacted by getting Ákos Barcsay elected as new ruler. The war ravaged in the princedom inflicting bitter suffering on the inhabitants. In 1658, the extensive Ottoman punitive campaign is estimated to have cost the lives of 100,000 people with as many again deported as captives by the Tatars.[40] Rákóczi fought valiantly against the Ottomans and Tatars, but after some initial successes, was finally defeated at Szászfenes on 22 May 1660. Seriously wounded in battle, he died two weeks later in the besieged Várad. Kemény János, Rákóczi's second in command in the Polish campaign, negotiated with Leopold I for help. He also renewed the offer to cede *Partium* to the Emperor and some western Transylvanian towns, including the strategic strongholds of Tokay and Szatmár, as a sign good faith.

The absence of an active Ottoman threat after 1606 had given the Emperor a free hand during the Thirty Years' War, but it also undermined German support for him. Now, the renewed Ottoman advance after 1658 reawakened German fears and permitted Leopold to wear the traditional Imperial mantle as defender of Christendom, a task that he took seriously, through personal conviction. Furthermore, intervention in Transylvania represented for Vienna the opportunity to occupy a place of strategic relevance in the region. Due to its geographical position, the control of the princedom made possible the complete and secure control of Upper Hungary and at the same time ensured a military outpost in Moldavia and Wallachia, two states that openly showed their lack of allegiance to the sultan. Creating a platform for the Imperial eagle in these provinces provided also an opportunity to reaffirm the primacy of the House of Austria over the turbulent Calvinist Hungarian

---

39   From November 1657 to January 1658 the princedom was ruled by Ferenc Rhédey de Kisréde. Rákóczi forced him to abdicate and then ordered his death.
40   G. Payer, *Armati Hungarorum* (Munich: Körösi Csoma Sándor, 1985), p. 106.

nobility, and show the large majority of the population a renewed respect for Catholicism.

However, it seemed that even with divine blessing, victory would prove hard to achieve. To have any chance of success against the Ottomans there was an urgent need for a rapid conclusion to the war, an event that the Austrian court considered likely, because since 1645, the sultan had been already fighting a second war in Crete against Venice. Further east, on the border of the Persian Empire, the risk of a resumption of hostilities with the Safavids could discourage the Ottomans from stepping up the struggle in Transylvania. On the contrary, the Porte did not appear intimidated and, unfortunately for Vienna, the Ottomans accepted the challenge with unexpected energy. The Austrian policy encountered several problems as soon as Leopold began his interference in Transylvania. With the intention of curbing Ottoman influence in Transylvanian affairs, in May 1660 the Emperor sent 15,000 men under the new appointed *Feldmarschall* Souches to support his own candidate Kemény as prince. Two separate Diets then elected two different princes. As a result, the war turned into a chaotic civil struggle between the two factions, the one supported by the Porte and the other by the Emperor.

The struggle for power resulted in a bitter and devastating conflict, further aggravated by a plague epidemic propagated from Hungary, which ended only in 1666. In summer 1661, Kemény prevailed on Barcsay,[41] but he could not face the *paşa* of Buda's forces, estimated at about 25,000 men. On 14 November, four years after the fiasco of the Polish campaign and the dissolution of the Transylvanian princedom, the Diet crowned Apafy Mihály I as its prince with the military support of the Ottomans.

Meanwhile, the Imperial troops manned the fortresses in *Partium* and immediately this news caused the Porte to complain. Austrian ambassador Gonzaga tried to reassure the Ottoman court that the presence of the Emperor's soldiers only served to restore peace in the princedom, but few believed his words. Soon in June 1661, a large corps of Ottoman riders crossed the border at Nagybanya (today Baia Mare in Romania) and looted the Habsburg-Hungarian domains south of Ungvár (Užhorod, in Ukraine). On the west side of the border, seeing the conflict approaching, the Croatian *banus* Miklós Zrínyi began to fortify the site which took the name of Zrínyivár and from which he began to direct the actions of pillaging across the frontier. Now, even though the war had not been formally declared, hostile actions took on an increasingly threatening character, and in the Imperial side, the most determined to act was certainly Miklós Zrínyi.

He was the son of a family who had already fought against the Ottomans for four generations, therefore, it seems to have been almost a foregone conclusion that the young Miklós was destined to become a soldier. He was born in 1620 and studied in the Jesuits school of Graz, Vienna and Nagyszombat (today Trnava in Slovakia) in a spirit faithful to the Habsburg monarchy. From 1635 to 1637, he toured Italy and studied philosophy at the University of

---

41 Barcsay was later assassinated on the order of Kemény on 3 July 1661.

Bologna. Although his humanistic education and intellect made him the first real Hungarian philosopher in history, as well as a renowned poet, upon his return from Italy he chose a military career because 'the buried bones and the ghost of Hungarian heroes won't let me sleep'.[42] After a few years of border-guard duties as *Grenzhauptmann* on the Croatian frontier, he took part in the Thirty Years' War. In 1646 he fought in Bohemia against the Swedish troops of Lennart Torstensson. Zrínyi took his duties very seriously and Emperor Ferdinand III rewarded him with flattering titles and positions. He became initially the Governor of Legrad and Murakoz, then later the military governor of Zala and Somogy counties, and finally the 'Master of the Royal Stable' (in other words the cavalry commander of the Hungarian Royal Army). In 1655, he was awarded the position of a Croatian *banus*, or military general governor. On several occasions, Zrínyi replied to every breach of the peace by the Ottoman cavalry with incursions into Ottoman-occupied territories, which gained him widespread fame as a talented cavalry commander. His name became well known not only in Croatia and Hungary, but also in the German Empire. It is possible to get an idea of Zrínyi's personality through his writings, his letters, and his achievements, as recorded by contemporary witnesses. On the whole, Zrínyi appears to have been a sympathetic and interesting person, a dynamic, vigorous and generally healthy man, but it is possible he suffered from depression. His tireless vitality and his prodigious activity amazed his peers. He brought a sense of duty to his career to the point of selflessness. Zrínyi was indeed entirely devoted to the Habsburg family, whom he identified with his country. The absolute and sacred power of the monarch was the only thing that he never questioned. He sacrificed his private life to his duty and served with total loyalty and unselfishness. He showed his superiors a respectful though not a slavish devotion, never fawning and never hesitating to express his ideas, mixing criticism and anger with plain speech and sometimes with stubbornness. As a man of action, he felt more at ease on the battlefield, leading his troops in person regardless of his own personal safety. With time, he wrote more and more about history, politics and the economy, subjects that on occasion irritated his superiors and even the Emperor himself. His life gradually became marked with bitterness, sadness and disappointment. Two Emperors showered him with rewards and titles leading Zrínyi to expect that upon the death of the Palatine of Hungary, Pál Pálffy, he would be promoted to very high rank. The Hungarian Estates, however, passed him by and appointed the magnate Ferenc Wesselényi as Palatine. Deeply hurt, Zrínyi retired to his estates and began to study the art of war, adding his own military experiences and writing several excellent treatises on strategy and tactics.

The Swedish model particularly interested Miklós Zrínyi. He thought that a national army could perform extraordinary deeds. Its officers could seek decisive action in battle, instead of trying to avoid risk by forcing the enemy to surrender through clever, but time-consuming manoeuvres. Zrínyi, studying the Habsburg as well as the Swedish military structure, concluded that against

---

42 Lendvai, *The Hungarians*, p. 127.

the Ottomans, a Hungarian general could rely on the emotional strength of the troops. Equipped with modern weapons, and adding good training and discipline, Zrínyi believed, the Hungarians could liberate themselves from the Ottoman yoke without outside help. Furthermore, he realised that the Habsburg will to liberate Hungary from the Ottomans would always depend on the situation in the West. Over time, he became also suspicious of the Habsburgs' design concerning the future of a liberated Hungary. Zrínyi accused Montecuccoli of excessive caution and to have failed to exploit his successes. The ideological differences and rivalry between Montecuccoli and the Hungarian general turned to a mutually reciprocated enmity.[43]

Montecuccoli assumed the command of the Imperial army in Transylvania in July 1661 In Komáron he discovered the poor state of the army. Of 14–15,000 soldiers who were in Transylvania from the spring of 1660, only 6,000 were able to undertake a campaign.[44] The regiments were greatly reduced by plague and dysentery that struck rank and file; in some fortresses the garrison comprised solely of sick men.[45] Though Montecuccoli detailed the shortage of resources and soldiers to explain his inaction, some historians have alluded to secret Imperial instructions to maintain a defensive position. Montecuccoli described the situation in a revealing account:

> It is a deplorable thing that the health of so many people rests in the virtue of so few soldiers. And what should I do as I am the commander? Should I attack the enemy like a Croat with only a band of 4,000 horses? With the rank of General and with my long service it is not appropriate. Complain to the Emperor? He lay ill with smallpox. Should I leave the service with the deference and loyalty that is my due? I protested. I did. I sacrificed.[46]

Thus decimated by plague, dysentery and shortage of supply, the Imperial army proved no match for the Ottoman offensive and the strategic situation turned in favour of the Porte. In August 1661, the Transylvanian *Saxons*[47] declared their allegiance to Apafy as their only prince. Kemény and Montecuccoli joined forces, advanced in September 1661 and occupied Kolozsvár (Cluy-Napoca in Romania), but, one after the other, the Transylvanian Estates

---

43 Among the most important contributions about the long controversy between Montecuccoli and Zrínyi, see in Luraghi, 'Le Opere di Raimondo Montecuccoli', and G. Perjés: *Zrínyi Miklós és kora* (Budapest: Gondolat Könyvkiadó, 1965). Of the latter author see also the articles 'A Metodiszmus', in *Századok* 95, (1961) pp. 507–533, 'Zrínyi, Montecuccoli, ki volt igaz?', in *Századok* 96 (1962), pp. 25–44, and 'A Zrínyi-Montecuccoli vita', in: *A korai stratégiai gondolkodás*, Budapest, 2005. Among the more recent works see L. Nagy, 'Montecuccoli, a magyarok és Szentgotthárd', in *MTA Bölcsészettudományi Kutatóközpont*, Budapest, 2017, pp. 107–121.
44 K. Peball, 'Die Schlacht bei St. Gotthard-Mogersdorf, 1664', in *Militärhistorische Schriftensreihe*, Vienna, 1964.
45 Österreichische Staatsarchiv-Kriegsarchiv, Alte Feldakten, 1661–64/81, dispatch from Komárom, July 1661.
46 Montecuccoli's letters, cited in Cesare Campori, *Montecuccoli, la sua famiglia e i suoi tempi* (Modena, 1876), pp. 14–17.
47 The *Saxons* were German inhabitants of Transylvania, settled in the central region with Hermannstadt (today Sibiu in Romania), Kronstadt (Brasov) and Schässburg (Sighişoara) as their main cities.

declared their support for Apafy. The allied occupation of Kolozsvár lasted only three days. On 16 September, Ottomans appeared in front of the city and everyone thought that the clash was imminent, and with it the war not yet declared between the Porte and the Emperor would have begun. The two sides faced each other for two days, then on 18 September the Ottomans retreated, but lacking resources and hearing the news about the riots in Hungary, where the peasants assaulted the isolated Imperial garrisons, urged Montecuccoli to move back, leaving Kemény alone. On 22 January 1662, the fate of the unfortunate Transylvanian pro-Habsburg pretender was sealed with his defeat at Nagyszőllős. Over 2,000 heads were sent as trophies to Constantinople, including the prince's. It is not unlikely that Vienna was displeased by the defeat of Kemény's party, but evidently was trying to avoid a military confrontation with the Porte at this time. The situation was becoming critical for the Imperialists. The excessive confidence in a bloodless solution of the Transylvanian crisis had led to the licensing of many regiments previously recruited for the war against Sweden. On paper, the Emperor could deploy a force of 24,000 infantry, 11,000 cuirassiers, 3,000 dragoons and 1,000 of light cavalrymen, but the actual strength was even lower than expected. In 1662, the Habsburg regular forces available in Hungary barely totalled only 20–23,000 men in all; even when backed by 15,000 native 'insurrectionists', they were no match for the Ottoman field army, which could easily swell to over 100,000 men with the arrival of the Moldavian, Wallachian and Tatar auxiliaries. Along with the shortage of troops, there was the chronic lack of money. The artillery was practically devoid of horses and many officers had been licensed for budgetary reasons. Many regiments claimed shortages of gunpowder and foodstuffs, but magazines and arsenals were now empty. In the spring of 1663, some money and even gunpowder were provided by the Pope and Tuscany; in Avignon, Alessandro VII recruited one regiment ready to march at the opening of the new year.[48] Predictably, the unfavourable outcome of the Transylvanian events and the defeat of Kemény became the object of new and fierce criticism of Zrínyi against Montecuccoli, but the Hungarian foreign policy of the Habsburgs did not include a war against the Ottoman Empire.[49]

The weakness of the Imperials convinced the Ottoman commanders to assume a more aggressive strategy but the Grand Vizier intended to test the Emperor's determination to engage an open conflict. Negotiations were opened to find an agreement. The Ottomans asked for the evacuation of the Imperial forces from all the Transylvanian fortresses, because the princedom

---

48 C. Campori, *Montecuccoli*, part II, chapter. III, p. 6. Budget problems delayed the calling of this regiment (II-57), until it was disbanded in October 1664.

49 When the Imperial army retreated from Transylvania, Zrínyi desperately urged Montecuccoli and the court to resist the Ottoman offensive, but the Hungarian Diet ignored his pleas. His passionate appeal concluded with this warning. 'If we Hungarians do not re-conquer Várad and if we lose Transylvania, then we are not Hungarians: we will have fled the country in shame. There is enough land in Brazil. Let us ask the Spanish king for a province, let us establish a colony, let us become citizens there! […] But those of you, who trust in God, love your fatherland and still have a drop of Hungarian blood left within you, do not give up but take up your weapons!', Lendvai, *The Hungarians*, p. 127.

was a vassal of the sultan and the Imperial army had violated the peace treaty by invading and occupying its western fortress. The Emperor wanted to keep at least the fortresses of Tokay and Szatmár. The Ottoman delegates replied that the border fortress of Zrínyivár, recently built, had to be dismantled in exchange.[50] However the Imperial diplomacy was slow to react, the decision-making process faltered and, as a result, open war broke out on 12 April 1663.

With great haste, all available Imperial forces were sent to the East, while recruits and new regiments hurriedly marched to Hungary.[51] In the winter of 1662–63, the Imperial forces facing the Ottomans were divided into three corps. All the wars against the Ottomans took place in a geo-strategic context that had the Danube region as the central area. The geography of the Hungarian plain offered other access routes that bypassed the extensive swamps between the Danube and the major rivers. To the west, Croatia was easily accessible through Ottoman Bosnia, while in the east, Transylvania had always been a base for invading Upper Hungary through the numerous passes with routes easily accessible by waggons. The Hungarian plain could be reached from Transylvania also via the Mureș River, which flows west. Altogether, the theatre of war extended for over 400 km with 20 large and medium-sized fortresses. Montecuccoli established three different gathering places for the troops destined for the war theatre. In Croatia, the *banus* Zrínyi Miklos had 16–18,000 *Grenzer* and militiamen with a few Imperial infantry; in Upper Hungary there were 8,500 regular soldiers under *Feldmarshall* Souches, in order to guard the pass from Transylvania. Unfortunately, although 25–30,000 troops under Montecuccoli's command were already based in Hungary, only 15–20,000 remained readily available for the field army.[52] Montecuccoli had reinforced the garrisons in Upper Hungary and Transylvania with 12 infantry battalions and five companies of dragoons; further infantry was despatched to Érsekújvár, Komárom, Győr, Veszprém and Fülek; finally one regiment of cuirassiers and two of infantry marched to Inner Austria to secure the access to Graz.

However, negotiations between Vienna and the Porte continued even after the start of hostilities. The Imperial delegates, Reininger and Goes, met Grand Vizier Köprülü Ahmed in Belgrade and later in Eszék (today Osijek in Croatia), following the march of the approaching Ottoman army. The last negotiations took place in Buda in July 1663, but this time the Imperial delegates held discussions with the governor of Silistra, Ali Paşa, while the Grand Vizier secretly listened to the talks, hidden behind a curtain. Ottoman demands were now not limited to the evacuation of the Transylvanian fortresses and the dismantling of Zrínyivár, but also included the handing over of Szatmár and Tokay as well as the re-establishment of an annual tribute of 30,000 gold ducats to the sultan.

The Ottoman army's initial opening gambit in the 1663 campaign was the siege of Érsekúivár, directed by Grand Vizier Köprülü Ahmed with the main

---

50 J. von Hammer-Purgstall, *Geschichte des osmanischen Reiches*, vol., XI, p. 158.
51 Before the end of 1662 and in the following year, eight infantry and four cavalry regiments were recruited. See in Wrede, *Geschichte der K. und K. Wehrmacht*, vol. I & III, part one.
52 Luraghi, 'Le Opere di Raimondo Montecuccoli', vol. I, p. 24.

army, whilst 6,000 horse launched a raid in Croatia against Zrínyivár. In late July, Köprülü Ahmed ordered his commander in Transylvania to join the main army in the siege of Érsekúivár. The 8,000-strong Ottoman vanguard corps advanced to Esztergom, where it crossed the Danube over a single bridge, confident enough not to form screens or outposts as defence. *Feldmarschall* Ádam Forgách de Ghymes, the Imperial commander of Érsekúivár, decided to take advantage of this, and the bottleneck of troops around the bridge. He assembled a force of 2,500–3,000 foot and horse *Grenzer* with 500 German infantry from the regiments *Starhemberg* (II-41) and *Strozzi* (II-12) to lead a sortie.[53] Alerted by *dely* scouts, who sighted the Imperial forces coming out from the fortress, the Ottomans sent 20,000 troops to intercept the enemy. On 7 August, the Ottomans crossed the Niytra River on boats and rafts, and assaulted Forgách near Párkány. The Imperialists suffered massive casualties, losing two thirds of their fighting force. Forgách himself was saved only by the skin of his teeth, before he fled to Érsekúivár chased by the Ottomans. About 700 *Grenzer* and Imperial captured soldiers were immediately put to the sword. The Grand Vizier had promised a bounty for each enemy soldier captured or even their head. Only 341 prisoners' lives were spared, and they were eventually marched to Buda under escort.

Even in this specific phase of the campaign, many historians have criticised Montecuccoli's inertia. The great Italian general was certainly more concerned with defending Vienna from an assault than risking a battle to rescue Érsekúivár. However, it is not correct to say that these events happened with the complicit passivity of the commander-in-chief. As soon as the news of the defeat suffered by Forgách, Montecuccoli sent to Érsekúivár two companies of infantry regiment *Cob* (II-8), and five of *Sparr* (II-41) with an escort of cuirassiers and dragoons from the posts on the Váh River. Other cavalry parties were sent to Érsekúivár even when the siege was in progress. The encounters were alternately in favour of one side or the other, however the Ottomans always prevented the entry of reinforcements and supplies into the besieged city.[54] In August, the Emperor authorised the call to arms of the Hungarian militia, through the 'insurrection' of the counties near Érsekúivár, but the result was disappointing. On 24 August, the Hungarian Palatine informed the Imperial command about the difficulties encountered in assembling the troops. Most of the towns declared the militia more necessary to guard their homes; Bratislava's magistrates declared that their militiamen had been defeated at Párkány or were already inside Érsekúivár, while Niytra, Papa and Honod refused to send their militia because, they insisted, the Ottomans were approaching the towns.[55]

The shortage of troops imposed a change of strategy, and therefore the hypothesis of erecting a fortified camp at Landschutz (Bernolákovo in Slovakia) was discarded, because this position exposed Bratislava to serious

---

53 J. von Hammer Purgstall, in *Geschichte des osmanischen Reiches* (Pest, 1829), vol., XI, p. 140, doubles the Hungarian force to more than 6,000 men, but this number is improbable, considering the whole force in Érsekúivár numbered 3,500 or 4,000.
54 According to Gualdo-Priorato, at least 5–600 dragoons entered Érsekúivár in August. Gualdo-Priorato *Historia*, vol. II, p. 248.
55 *Ibidem*, p. 242.

Plate A
1) Pikeman, unknown infantry regiment, 1657–60
2) Musketeer, Regiment *Strozzi zu Fuss*, 1663–64
3) Junior Officer, Regiment *Strozzi zu Fuss* (II-12), 1663–64
(Illustration by Bruno Mugnai © Helion & Company 2019)
See Colour Plate Commentaries for further information.

Plate B
1) *Feldwebel*, Regiment *Mannsfeld zu Fuss* (II-44), 1670–75
2) Musketeer, Regiment *Starhemberg zu Fuss* (II-41), 1675–80
3) Artillery, *Constabler*, 1671
(Illustration by Bruno Mugnai © Helion & Company 2019)
See Colour Plate Commentaries for further information.

Plate C
1) *Hauptmann* Regiment *Heister zu Fuss* (II-81), 1685
2) Pikeman, Regiment *Thüngen zu Fuss* (II-96), 1685–88
3) Grenadier, Regiment *Scherffenberg zu Fuss* (II-7), 1685
(Illustration by Bruno Mugnai © Helion & Company 2019)
See Colour Plate Commentaries for further information.

Plate D
1) Cuirassier Officer, 1660–64;
2) Cuirassier Trooper, 1658–64, unknown regiment
(Illustration by Bruno Mugnai © Helion & Company 2019)
See Colour Plate Commentaries for further information.

Plate E
1) Dragoon, Regiment *Gérard Dragoner* (ID-1), 1664
2) Dragoon NCO, Regiment *Trauttmansdorff Dragoner* (ID-7), 1672
(Illustration by Bruno Mugnai © Helion & Company 2019)
See Colour Plate Commentaries for further information.

Plate F
1) Dragoon Officer, unknown regiment, 1675–80
2) Dragoon, Regiment *Savoyen Dragoner* (ID-13), 1682
(Illustration by Bruno Mugnai © Helion & Company 2019)
See Colour Plate Commentaries for further information.

Plate G
1) Miklós Zrínyi (1620–1664)
2) Croat, Regiment *Gutschenich Croater* (IHc-1), 1664
3) Hungarian *Hayduk Grenzer*, late 17th century
*(Illustration by Bruno Mugnai © Helion & Company 2019)
See Colour Plate Commentaries for further information.*

Plate H
1) Musketeer, Regiment *Uffleln zu Fuss* (WI-1), Circle of Westphalia, 1664
2) Cuirassier, Regiment *Hönstett Cuirassieren* (SC-5), Circle of Swabia, 1683
3) *Tambour*, Regiment *Nassau-Idstein zu Fuss* (OrI-4), Circle of Upper-Rhine, 1674–78
(Illustration by Bruno Mugnai © Helion & Company 2019)
See Colour Plate Commentaries for further information.

Plate I
Imperial and Reichsarmee Colours
(Illustration by Bruno Mugnai © Helion & Company 2019)
See Colour Plate Commentaries for further information.

Plate J
Imperial Colours
(Illustration by Bruno Mugnai © Helion & Company 2019)
See Colour Plate Commentaries for further information.

Plate K
Imperial and Reichsarmee colours captured by the French at Friedlingen in 1702.
*From MSS 'Les Triomphes de Louis XIV dit le Grand, roy de France et de Navarre représentés par les Drapeaux, Guidons et Etendarts...' (Bibliothèque Nationale de France, Paris)
See Colour Plate Commentaries for further information.*

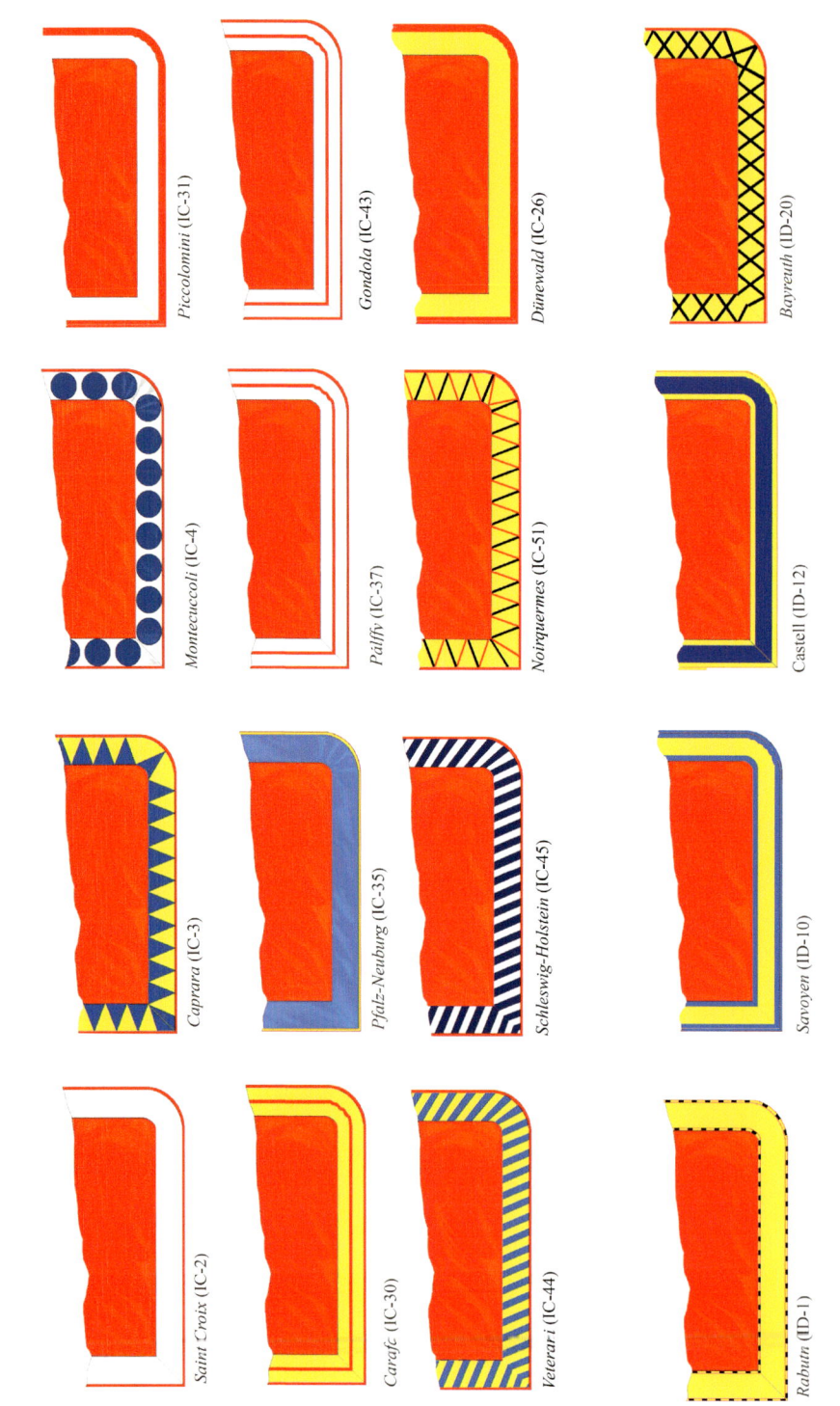

Plate L
Cuirassier and dragoon saddle covers, late 17th century.
(Graphics by Bruno Mugnai © Helion & Company 2019)
See Colour Plate Commentaries for further information.

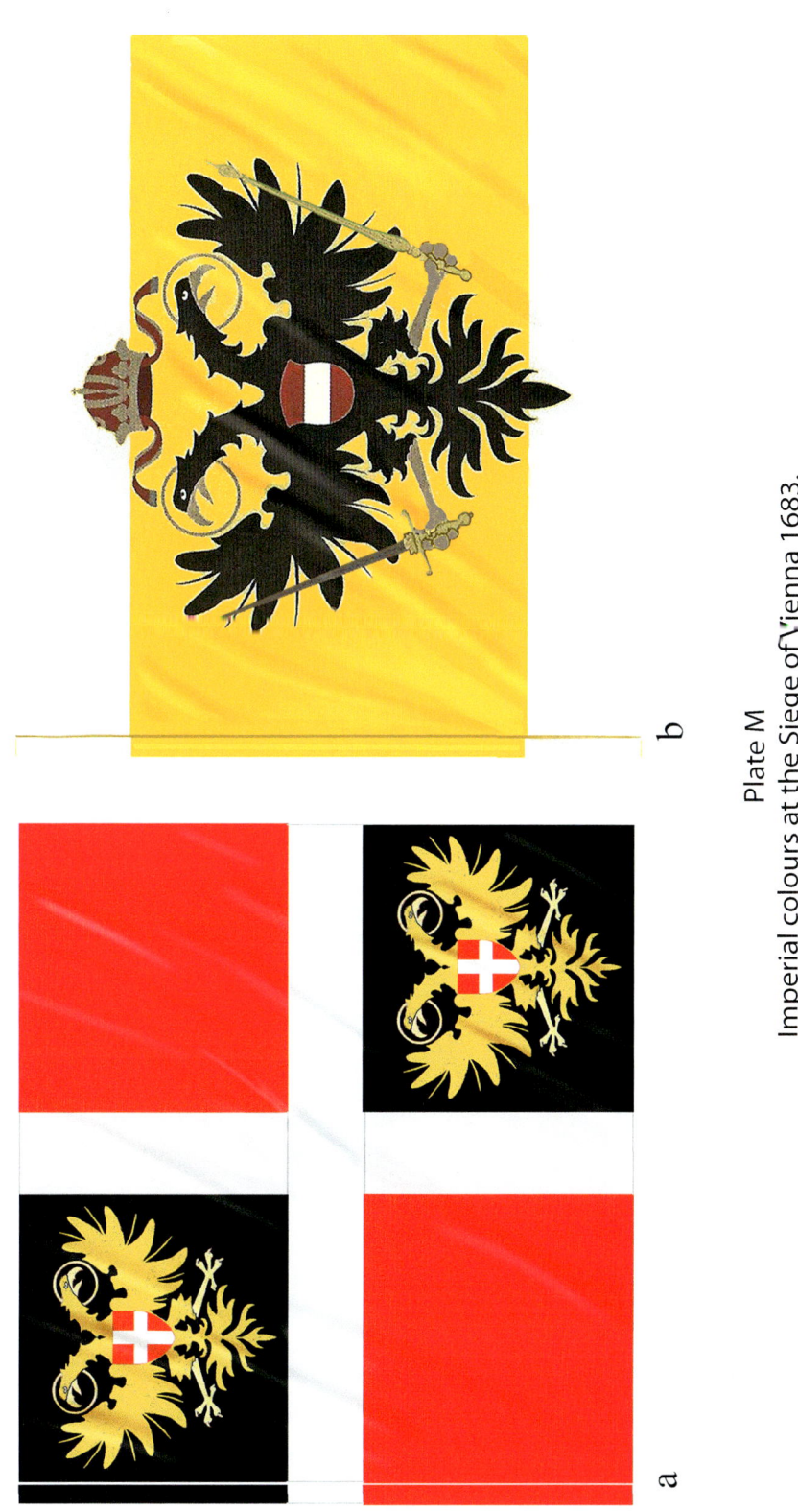

Plate M
Imperial colours at the Siege of Vienna 1683.
(Illustration by Bruno Mugnai © Helion & Company 2019)
See Colour Plate Commentaries for further information.

xiii

Plate N
Flags 1 and 2 are Imperial standards of a cuirassier regiment.
Flags 3 and 4 are the two sides of an Imperial Dragoon cornet.
Collection of the Armémuseum, Stockholm.
See Colour Plate Commentaries for further information.

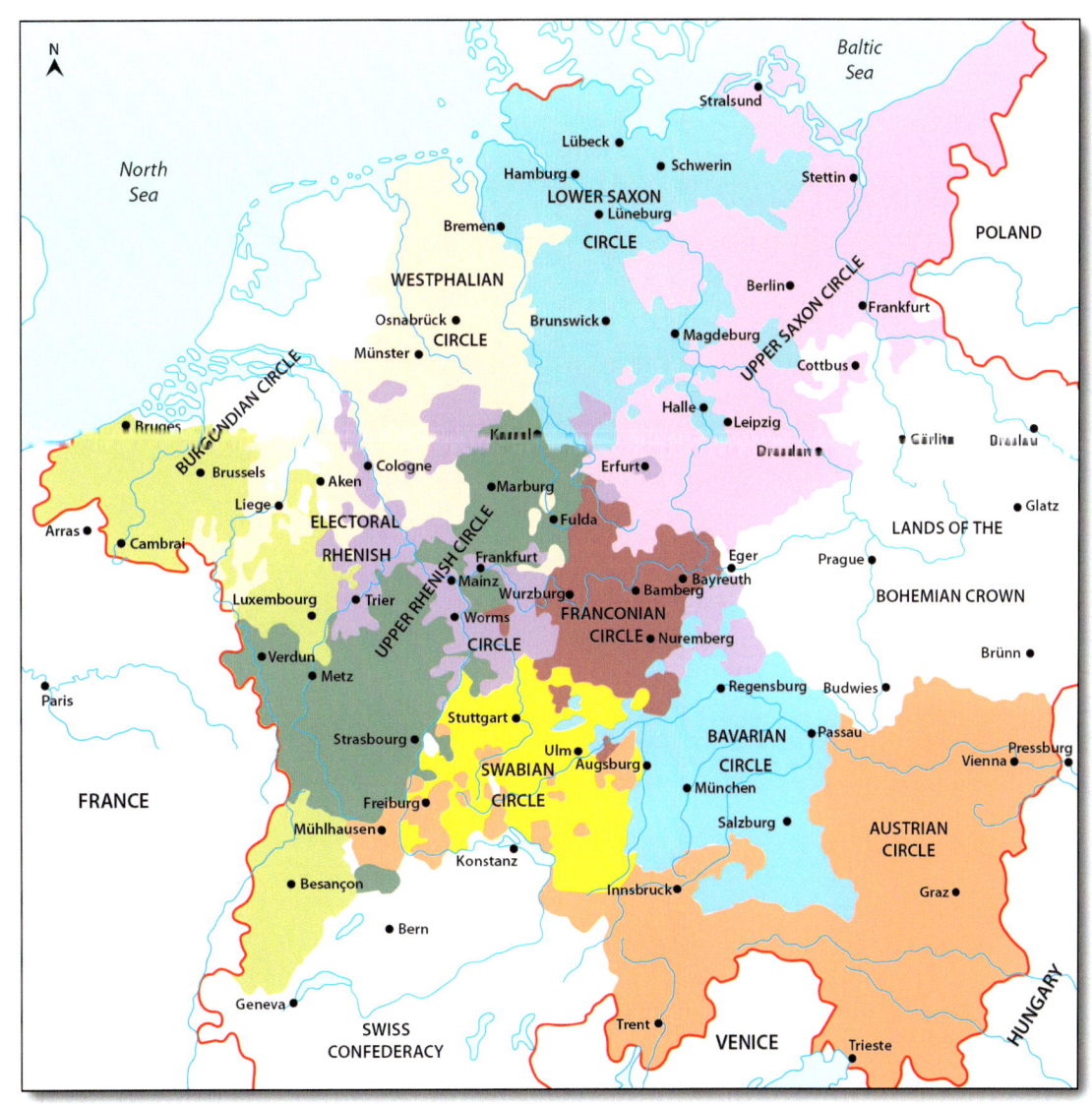

Plate O
The Imperial Circles.
(Illustration by Bruno Mugnai © Helion & Company 2019)
See Colour Plate Commentaries for further information.

Plate P
General-Lieutenant Raimondo Montecuccoli (1609–1680).
(Illustration by Bruno Mugnai © Helion & Company 2019)
See Colour Plate Commentaries for further information.

danger. Montecuccoli moved the army to an area closer to the Danube for better defending the Kingdom's capital. There was nothing left to do but keep contact with the enemy by surprise attacks using the cavalry and the *Grenzer*. For these actions, the infantry of the *Raaber Grenze* of Győr and Komárom was also employed, alongside the *Montecuccoli* (IC-4) and *Sporck* (IC-6) cuirassiers.

In mid August, the Grand Vizier employed the Tatars for a large incursion across the border. The Imperialists tried to intercept the Crimean horsemen with 2,000 cuirassiers and dragoons under *Feldmarschall-Lieutenant* Sporck. A first encounter occurred on 18 August, when a large corps of Ottoman horsemen with Wallachians and Moldavian auxiliaries crossed the Váh River north to Komárom in order to open the way to the Tatars. Further encounters happened the following day, involving the Imperial frontiersmen on foot and horse, as well as the regular cavalry. Finally, on 3 September, a large corps of Tatars penetrated Styria, eluding Sporck's persuing cavalry. Tartar incursions ravaged several villages in Styria and Moravia, causing great alarm. 70,000 people fled Vienna, as panic spread throughout the Habsburgs' domains and southern Germany.

The siege of Érsekújvár proceeded slowly but every phase was planned to perfection. Ottoman engineers diverted channels that filled the ditches of the fortress, while approach trenches were dug by soldiers and manpower recruited among the local peasants. Fighting was fierce with the Ottoman artillery firing an estimated 18,000 projectiles. The besiegers stormed the breached bastions three times, but each time they were repulsed. In early September, Köprülü Ahmed offered surrender terms to the Imperial garrison. Forgách, after convening a war council with both his wounded lieutenants, Enrico Grana del Carretto and Eriberto Pio di Savoia, discussed a conditional surrender. Considering the low morale of the inhabitants, and realising that the Imperial field army would not bring relief to the city, Forgách decided to accept the Ottoman proposals. On 26 September an honourable evacuation was agreed. The Grand Vizier wrote a declaration commending the valiant resistance put up by the besieged Imperial forces. According to Ottoman chronicles,[56] officers and soldiers were given leave to evacuate the fortress, not just with their personal belongings intact, but also were allowed to leave the fortress bearing arms. This concession represents a point of honour not commonly agreed by the Ottoman commander, despite the fact that the garrison had, at least for an initial period, offered determined resistance.

In the short period between the events of Érsekújvár and the final clash at Szentgotthárd, military activity followed a common pattern of strike and counter-strike operations, with the difference that in this instance reaction times were reduced to single days. Instead of returning to Constantinople – the regular practice in the absence of any significant threat of off-season counter-attacks – a part of the Ottoman army, including a proportion of the Tatar allies, remained in the field throughout winter, allowing a much faster response time.

---

56 Mühürdar's account, cited in R. Murphy, *Ottoman Warfare* (London: UCL Press, 1999), p. 127. This example of the surrender of Érsekújvár is an interesting precedent of the Ottomans' offering face-saving concessions to encourage local military figures to lay down their arms.

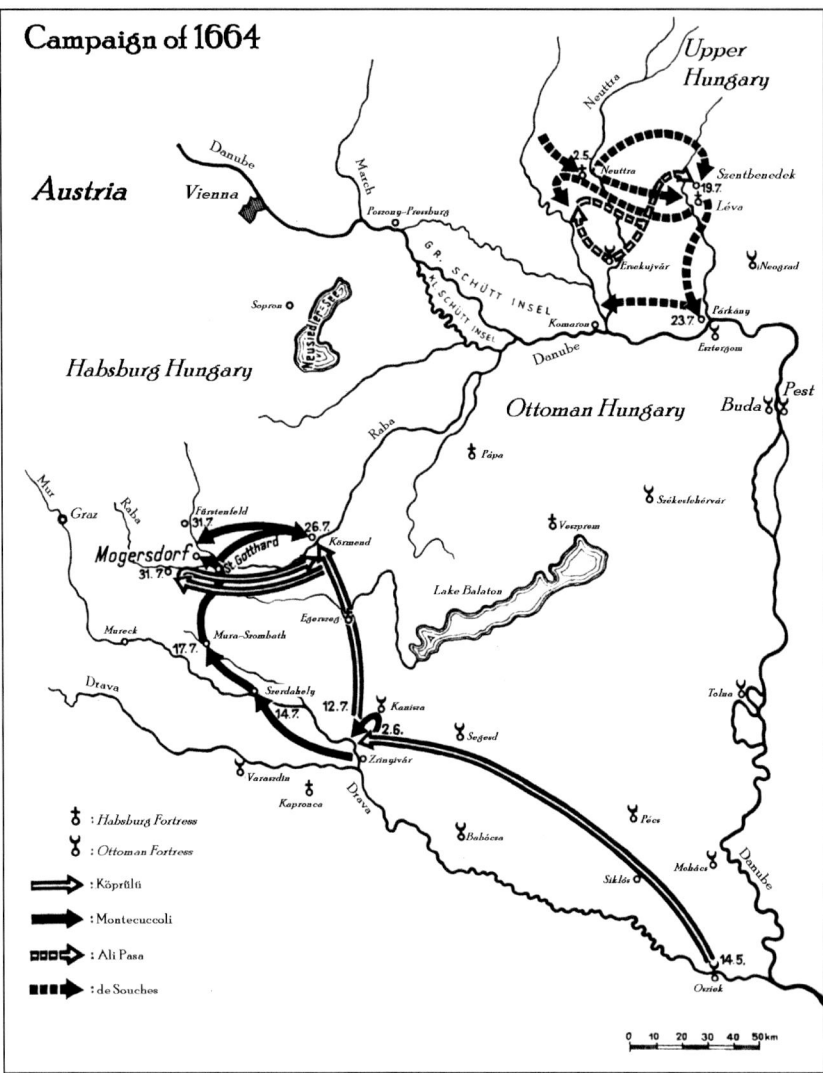

Campaign of 1664 in Hungary (after Peball, 'Die Schlacht bei St. Gotthard-Mogersdorf 1664', in *Militärhistorische Schriftenreihe*, III-1964).

The last phase of the war lasted for a 10-month period from autumn 1663 to early summer 1664. The period between the Ottoman conquest of Érsekúivár in late September 1663 and the battle of Szentgotthárd on 1st August 1664, saw most of the full variety of military activity that typifies eastern warfare. In the opinion of several scholars, after the conquest of Érsekúivár the Ottomans turned to a strategy of low-intensity warfare.[57] In this regard, someone quotes Montecuccoli's *Aforismi* when he declares: 'The Turk did short but great war.'[58] The idea that no important action took place in late 1663 reinforces the criticisms regarding the inertia of which Montecuccoli would have been guilty. On the contrary, this statement is questionable, especially examining the chronicles of the events that followed

---

57 *Ibidem*, p. 128.
58 Raimondo Montecuccoli, *Aforismi applicati alla guerra possibile col Turco in Ungheria*, chapter III, XIII aforisma.

during the autumn of 1663.[59] Part of the Ottoman conquest of the Upper Hungarian towns of Niytra and Nógrád occurred between October and November; after the surrender of Érsekúivár Köprülü Ahmed intensified the incursion into enemy territory until the end of October, faced by the Imperialists at Komarom and the fords on the Váh River.

During the winter 1663–64, the walls of Bratislava and other major strongholds were improved. Montecuccoli was aware that the outcome of the war would be decided during the oncoming campaign. He was aware also that a new enemy advance would expose not only Bratislava but Vienna itself to an assault, with catastrophic results.

Montecuccoli's writings on his scientific approach to strategy and tactical warfare resulted an illuminating study of the war, but for several scholars the efforts to justify his personal conduct did not make him immune to critics. His excessive caution in engaging the Ottomans remains undeniable. However, in his defence, shortage of supply continued to afflict the Imperial side, and in September 1663 Montecuccoli could only deploy approximately 29–30,000 men against an enemy army estimated at 90–100,000. Furthermore, historians have perhaps not paid enough attention to a second reason, which could have influenced Montecuccoli's decision in maintaining a defensive position. The Italian general had contacts with agents of both the Transylvanian prince Mihály Apafy, and the Prince of Moldavia George Ghica. Although they were on opposing sides, they had long kept the Imperials informed of the movements of the Ottoman army.[60] Montecuccoli knew, however, that this was a double game which often concealed conflicting interests. Some agents had revealed the existence of secret contacts passing information between the Palatine of Hungary, Ferenc Wesselényi, and the Transylvanian prince. Therefore, it is very likely that Montecuccoli was cautious about taking offensive action on such unreliable information.[61]

The Habsburg reply came swiftly. A winter offensive, led by Miklós Zrínyi, was launched from his fortified base of Zrínyivár. This offensive was planned and carried out on his own personal initiative, with assistance from local militias provided by the Croatian *Militärgrenze* and the Hungarian *Kanischarische Grenze*, with the magnate Pál Batthiany's hussars. These local resources were further augmented by the Imperial infantry under Jacob Leslie,[62] and the foot regiments with 14 guns just arrived from Germany under the Count of Hohenlohe. These troops brought Zrínyi's army up to 23,000 men, capable of undertaking the investment of Szigetvár, one of the Ottomans' principal bases in central Hungary. After an initial attack against the smaller forts of Berzence and Bobócsa, on 21 January Zrínyi moved quickly to assault Szigetvár on 25 January. Gürcü Mehmed, the Ottoman

---

59 Gualdo-Priorato, *Historia*, vol. II, p. 320.
60 Campori, *Montecuccoli*, part II, chapter III, p. 13.
61 Plots and betrayals affected also the fortress, as occurred on 6 January 1664: when the Imperial-held town of Szekelyhid rebelled against the German garrison and delivered it to the pro-Ottoman prince Apafy. Payer, *Armati Hungarorum*, p. 107.
62 One battalion from regiments *Tasso* (I-12 and *Sparr* (II-41), and two battalions from regiments *Alfonso Portia* (II-42) and *Spieck* (II-44), in Gualdo-Priorato, *Historia*, vol. II, p. 321.

officer in command of the winter quarters at Eszék, was ordered to organise a relief force drawing on local troops, because most of the army's main units had been assigned to winter quarters five to 10 days' march away. Although the Grand Vizier moved quickly from Belgrade to set up field headquarters at Zemun, across the Sava River, his whole force amounted to little more than an escort troop of 4,000 men. Infantry immediately available to Gürcü Mehmed's command were, when the alarm was first raised, no more than half that number.

Able to move more or less at will against his targets, Zrínyi, instead of concentrating his forces against Szigetvár, devised a two-pronged attack. On 29 January he mounted his first against Pécs, one of the Ottomans' most important regional bases in southern Hungary, and his second on 2 February against the bridges at Eszék, which guarded supply and communications between the Hungarian front and vital Ottoman resources and reinforcement links along the Danube. The Ottomans could do little more than helplessly watch while the enemy systematically destroyed the outer defences of Pécs. The destruction was so complete that Ottoman sources acknowledge the devastation resulting from a sustained enemy bombardment was 'wide enough to allow grazing animals to pass in and out of the city walls without obstruction.'[63] Although Zrínyi raised the siege of Pécs on 6 February, without having captured the inner citadel, the whole of the operation carried out between the last week of January and the first week of February cost the Ottomans dearly. Losses were great both in terms of the financial cost for repairs and the inevitable delays that would result in their spring campaign. This damage had been inflicted by a lightly-armed force composed mostly of irregulars, who advanced unopposed into Ottoman territory at a time when the Ottoman army had taken to its winter quarters.

On the Imperial side, this unexpected and clamorous series of victories gained by Zrínyi fed the dispute between the *banus* and Montecuccoli. Emperor Leopold I was too young not to be influenced by his advisors, Montecuccoli included. The proposal to strengthen the Hungarian Royal army found little enthusiasm in the court. The widely disparate convictions between Zrínyi and Montecuccoli did not end simply with the respective different strategic visions. The ideas of the Croatian *banus* looked ridiculous to the inflexible and pragmatic Montecuccoli. To give up manoeuvring and a traditional defensive strategy to go after field engagements, even accepting reasonable risks, seemed amateurish in the mind of the Italian general. Montecuccoli defended his strategy in an unsigned leaflet, accusing the Hungarian officer of being 'militarily illiterate and thus unable to understand modern military operations'.[64] Zrínyi publicly replied in another pamphlet. The *banus* called the Italian general *magnus cunctator* (great timekeeper), and after refuting Montecuccoli's charges, he ridiculed him with irony and contempt: 'You received a wonderful army and destroyed it without fighting the enemy. You molested your friends more than your enemies; you looked on passively as the Turks carried away over 100,000 Hungarians

---

63 Mühürdar's account, in Murphy, *Ottoman Warfare*, p. 131.
64 Lendvai, *The Hungarians*, pp. 127–128.

into captivity. Such behaviour is worse than that of a villainous hangman.'[65] Then he laid down those principles which he thought should be the basis for the strategy of an anti-Ottoman campaign. According to Zrínyi, the precondition of victory is not to manoeuvre so as to keep a safe distance from the adversary, but to advance with decision, forcing the enemy to engage in unfavourable conditions. A commander should not be concerned exclusively with numbers. Although the Hungarians in the Imperial army were inferior in number to Germans, the Emperor should have taken into consideration the fighting spirit of the Hungarian soldiers. Zrínyi believed that a good general should reward his subordinate commanders if they used their initiative to seek out and defeat the enemy. A general should search for those factors which in his judgement would make victory possible instead of looking for the impossible. A general should be the protector of the local population, gaining their support, which would benefit military operations. Courageous incursions into the rear of the enemy were considered to be of more worth than cautious manoeuvring at the front. In Zrínyi's opinion, only victorious battle could win the war.

After a season of engagements in Habsburg Hungary, the Ottoman troops were not very favourably disposed to listen to the Grand Vizier's urgent orders to reopen the campaign. In the spring of 1664 the full Ottoman army was redeployed to the sectors where immediate repairs were required, and to make good the damage inflicted in the winter raids carried out by the Croatian and Hungarian *Grenzers*. Lightning strikes were rapidly and effectively executed. However Grand Vizier Köprülü Ahmed had barely advanced beyond Mitrovica, the second stage for the Ottoman army after Belgrade. While the Ottoman army progressed in its march, the Imperial raiders had already withdrawn to their own bases beyond the Habsburg frontier. At the time of his return to Belgrade on 11 February 1664, the Grand Vizier had already set in motion plans for organising work crews to carry out the extensive repairs that would be required, before the critical bridges at Eszék could be restored.[66] As a result of Zrinyi's offensive, Ottoman engineers and pioneers were kept busy throughout the winter and beyond just restoring bridges and paths, let alone attending to preparations for the Ottoman counter-offensive. Seventy-five days later, the Ottoman pioneers were dispatched to Eszék. Even then, the arrival of the Grand Vizier with his assembled troops at the river crossing on 15 May 1664 still managed to coincide with a last-minute flurry of activity to complete the final phase of reconstruction of the bridge.

After a short delay, whilst he sought backing from the Imperial court in Vienna, Zrínyi resumed his offensive from the bases in Croatia with an early season attack on the strategic Ottoman frontier fortress of Kanisza in the

---

65 *Ibidem*.
66 The effect of the enemy's winter offensive in the early months of 1664 had been to eliminate a vitally important period of winter rest and recuperation. This normally stretched over a four and a half-month period beginning with the *Ruz-i Kasim* 'day of division' on 6 November, marking the end of summer and ending with the *nevruz*, equinox, on 21 March, which marked the end of winter, leading to the army mobilisation in springtime. See in Murphy, *Ottoman Warfare*, p. 133.

closing days of April 1664. The previous attacks carried out against Berzence, Babósca, Pécs and Darány and, most importantly, on the bridge at Eszék, had left Kanisza effectively cut off, not just from its immediate hinterlands, but from all practicable routes of approach for purposes of supply and reinforcement. The fortress was well manned and Zrínyi's 36-day siege of Kanisza ended in failure. Nevertheless, before they were able to move ahead with their own offensive plans, the Ottomans were once again burdened with the task of repairing the damage suffered to this fortress, which formed a key element of their border defences along that sector of the frontier. The scale of these repairs was such that, according to an Ottoman account,[67] even with input from civilian work crews mobilised from the outlying districts the work was not completed until 13 July, long after the normal start of summer operations. The immediate challenge facing Grand Vizier Köprülü Ahmed in the spring of 1664 was the mobilisation of his force in areas scattered throughout the Danube. Even after the bridges at Eszék had been finally restored, and regular army units attached to the Grand Vizier had crossed the river on 20 May, Ahmed Pasha had to advance slowly to allow time for his army's strength to build. He had only reached Szigetvár by 29 May. He was joined there by irregulars from Bosnia and Albania enlisted in place of regular units still lingering in their winter quarters. It should be said that swifter mobilisation was difficult due to the need for cavalry mounts – on whom the army would depend in the later phases of the campaign – to complete their spring pasturing before proceeding to the front. The Ottoman progress proceeded slowly, and the difficulty in assembling the army was clearly demonstrated when it was delayed for two days covering the 20 kilometres separating the army's base of departure at Szigetvár and its camp at Darány. In order to complete the march, the Ottomans had to construct bridges in four places to pass over marshy terrain. However, once the army was up to full strength and had brought the Kanisza relief operation to a successful conclusion, it was able to proceed with its real purpose, which was to launch an offensive of its own. The fortress of Zrínyivár, situated only two hours' march west of Kanisza, was the first objective. Zrínyivár's relatively sophisticated defences occupied Ottoman siege engineers for 21 days, before it finally yielded to an Ottoman frontal assault on 30 June. The Imperial garrison totalled 3,500 Croatian irregulars of foot and horse, and aliquots of German infantry from regiment *Strozzi* (II-12), *Sparr* (II-41), *Spieck* (II-44), *Wallis* (II-56), cuirassiers from regiment *Piccolomini* (IC-5), *Rappach* IC-8) and *Schneidau* (IC-10) and dragoons from regiment *Paconchay* (ID-2) and *Görtzky* (ID-5). The defenders offered a fierce resistance, but the outcome appeared unavoidable. On 7 July, the Ottoman miners triggered a mine and the explosions destroyed some parts of the walls making several breaches. The besiegers consequently rushed forward and penetrated the fortress. The surviving and enormously outnumbered defenders were forced to withdraw and to abandon the ruined stronghold under cover of night. The Imperial

---

67 Evliya Celeby, *Seyhatname*, vol. VI (Istanbul: Inkilap Kitabevi, ca. 1970), p. 522.

casualties totalled 900 men, including the valiant *Feldmarschall-Lieutenant* Pietro Strozzi, who was much mourned by Montecuccoli.

The loss of Zrínyivár caused new furious quarrels between the Croatian *banus* and the Italian *generalissimo*. Blockading the main roads to Vienna, Montecuccoli refused to send aid to the garrison which defended the besieged fortress. Montecuccoli's remark increased Zrínyi's aversion to him.[68] In mid July, Zrínyi travelled to Vienna to personally plead with the Emperor to adopt a more aggressive strategy. The Pope awarded Zrínyi a gold portrait; Emperor Leopold I also raised him to the rank of prince, but when Zrínyi realized the failure of his mission, he resigned his command, and returned to Croatia a frustrated and disappointed man.

After some further delays in overseeing the demolition of Zrínyivár, on the one hand, and the rebuilding of Kanisza on the other, the Grand Vizier decided to move against a new, previously untested region along the Hungarian frontier to the north of Kanisza towards the natural boundary formed by the Zala and Rába rivers. The Ottoman army set out on 14 July with its sights set on the lightly fortified central frontier zone that stretched for some 80 km between Kanisza, in the south, to Körmend, in the north. The Ottoman advance included numerous diversions during late July on both primary and secondary fronts, and some minor action in Upper Hungary from Transylvania. The Ottoman offensive involved a series of closely coordinated attacks, over a considerably wider territory. Most of the encounters during these two weeks of intense activity were extremely brief. In fact, of the seven small-to medium-sized forts which lay on or near the Ottomans' route of advance to the Rába in July 1664, only one, Pölöske, opposed resistance. The Imperial *Grenzer* acted on an initial determination

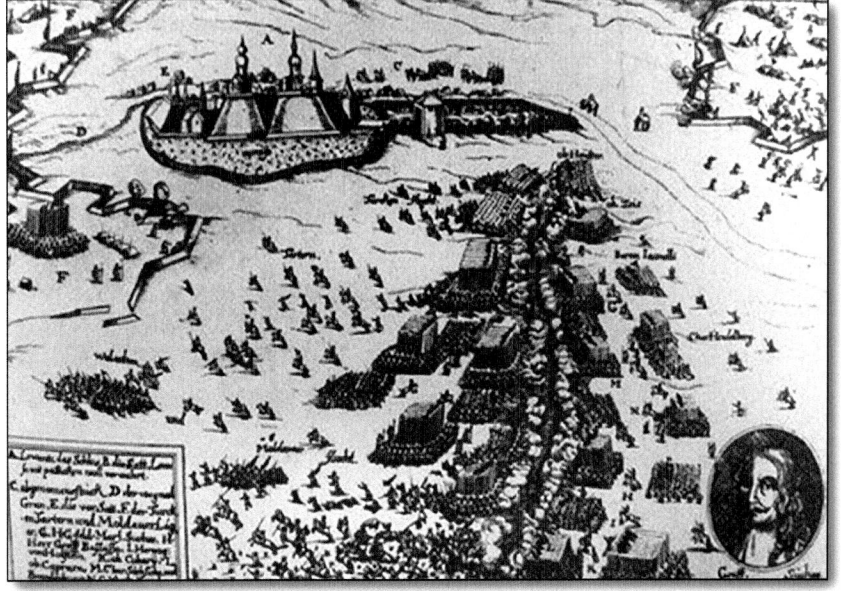

A contemporary print illustrating the battle of Léva, fought on 9 July 1664 between the Imperial army under Souches and the Ottomans with their allies under Ali Paşa of Temesvár. The Ottoman offensive in Upper Hungary had been planned to distract the Imperialists from the main theatre of war. The Ottomans and their allies outnumbered the Imperial force, but the battle ended in a complete disaster for their side. (Author's collection)

---

68 Montecuccoli would remark: 'The fortress was built on the wrong location. I knew it was undefendable.' However, this assertion is reported especially in the Hungarian works on Zrínyi. See in A. Komjathy, *A Thousand Years of the Hungarian Art of War* (Toronto: Rakoczi Foundation, 1982), p. 42.

to defend the fort, but it proved short-lived when the outbreak of artillery fire along the walls forming its outer defensive perimeter rendered its continued resistance useless. Minor outposts at Zalakomár, and Egervár, which lay 18 km north-west of Kanisza, surrendered on 14 and 22 July, while Zalaegerszeg was abandoned by the garrison on 17 July. All the fortresses were demolished or set on fire. On 25 July, Kemendollár voluntarily surrendered, while the garrisons of Nagykapornak and Zalaszentgrót fled before the Ottomans laid siege on 26 and 27 July. The latter forts were both set on fire.[69] The main purpose of this phase of the Ottoman campaign was not to extend the Ottoman frontier or conquer new territories, but to neutralise their potential as a base for counter-attacks aimed against their supply line.

Meanwhile, in Transylvania also the Ottomans were preparing for a new offensive. However, in early spring of 1664 the Imperialists succeeded in gaining the initiative in Upper Hungary, laying siege to Niytra. The town surrendered on 7 May, and on the 16th Souches defeated the Ottoman relief corps at Szent-Benedek. Reinforced with part of the contingents arrived from the Empire, Souches could deploy in late June about 10,000 regular soldiers and 2,600 irregulars with some artillery. Intelligence and reports from Montecuccoli informed him that the Ottomans were preparing a new assault in Upper Hungary. This happened punctually in early July against the fortress of Léva. On 9 July, Souches was able to attract the enemy vanguard, largely composed of irregular Tatar, Wallachian and Moldavian horsemen, isolating them from the rest of the army. After provoking their flight, the Imperial assault overwhelmed the disordered enemy troops. The victory was widely celebrated on the Imperial side because of the low casualties suffered,[70] about 500, compared to the enemy, who lost 4–5,000 men dead, wounded and taken prisoner.[71]

In early July 1664, the Imperial and allied forces assembled and set out in the camp near the Mura River. Montecuccoli was now planning for a decisive battle, as he wrote in his letters to Vienna when urging reinforcements.[72] Recruitment and reinforcements had increased the allied forces to 51,000 by the summer of 1664, supported by 15,000 Hungarians from the Royal Army who were slowly assembling between Győr and Komárom. However, disease and the need to garrison border fortresses reduced the effective combined fighting force to about 20,000 men with 24 field guns by the time Montecuccoli began the campaign of 1664. The Imperial commander was well aware that he could count on contingents of very unequal value. Excluding the 11,000 veterans of the Imperial regiments, the majority of the troops that arrived from Germany had never participated in a battle against

---

69 Murphy, *Ottoman Warfare*, p. 129. The author comments as the prevalence of voluntary surrender as a means of ending conflict is a striking feature of the pattern of military engagement.
70 J. Mailath, *Geschichte des Österreichischen Kaiserstaats* (Hamburg, 1848), p. 28.
71 Among the Imperial casualties, there was also the brave hussar's colonel Isztvan Koháry, killed while he was leading his regiment in the pursuit of the enemy. Banlaky, 'A Magyar Nemzet Hadtörténelme', vol. XVI, p. 141.
72 Luraghi, 'Le Opere di Raimondo Montecuccoli', vol. I, p. 25.

the Ottomans. He relied also on the arrival of the French troops sent by Louis XIV, who were still assembling in Bratislava.[73]

Meanwhile, on 14 June, Köprülü Ahmed moved the field army from Eszék, marching to Kanisza along the Mura River, deploying the troops on the left bank. It was a bold move, but from there he could cross the river and break the Imperial supply lines coming from Graz, or move to the nort-west along the Rába River and to threaten the enemy on that side, forcing it to retreat to Wiener Neustadt and then to march against Vienna.

Montecuccoli had already moved his scouts between the Mura and the Rába and had received detailed information on the position held by the Ottomans. He was still awaiting the arrival of troops and supplies that were indispensable to face an opponent estimated at at least 50–55,000 men. On 5 June, Montecuccoli had deployed the troops on the right bank of the Mura, a few hundred metres from the enemy camp on the opposite bank. From that position, the Imperialists could wait for supplies to arrive and observe the enemy's movements, waiting to strike at the most appropriate time. In the reports written at that time, Montecuccoli was worried about the pressures that led him from Vienna to engage in battle prematurely.[74] Although he awaited the arrival of the artillery, the infantry of the circles and French troops,[75] the Mura was swollen by rains, and for the Grand Vizier to cross the river against the allied army deployed in front was a suicidal option, which kept Montecuccoli safe from an eventual Ottoman attack. He was also protected behind by the Drava River, against an eventual assault from the rear. The Grand Vizier who made the first move. On 12 July, he left the camp and marched towards the Rába River. He hoped that Montecuccoli would follow him, and at that point he could decide to engage in battle with him in open field or continue the march towards the north, heading to Vienna. On 26 July the Ottomans had reached the Rába at Körmend, but on the opposite bank they found the allied army that prevented them from crossing. Montecuccoli had guessed the plan of the Grand Vizier, and marching north and taking advantage of the wooded terrain, he had kept the army protected behind the Mura River and finally crossed the Rába near Szentgotthárd, 30 km east of Körmend. At that point, Köprülü could not cross the river under enemy pressure. Montecuccoli expected that the Grand Vizier would try to open the road to the north and that he would look for an easily accessible ford, and the nearest point was near the monastery of Szentgotthárd.

---

73 The French contingent had a strength of 3,500 infantry and 1,900 cavalry, including 300 aristocratic volunteers with the cavalry. K. Peball: 'Die Schlacht bei St. Gotthard-Mogersdorf 1664', in *Militärhistorische Schriftenreihe*, III-1964.

74 Luraghi, 'Le Opere di Raimondo Montecuccoli', vol. I, p. 28. Luraghi's reconstruction of the battle of Szentgotthárd is the most accurate and based on the direct sources, like Montecuccoli's correspondence with Vienna, preserved in the Österreichisches Staatsarchiv-Kriegsarchiv. Before Luraghi's study, many inaccuracies persisted about Montecuccoli's intent to accept battle and on his command performance during the encounter of 1st August.

75 *Ibidem*. In early July Montecuccoli still awaited the arrival of other troops, as deduced from the letter to the Austrian Ambassador Gonzaga, dated 4 July 1664: 'I hope that the Margrave of Baden will arrive here in three or four days and alongside him [the infantry regiment of] Pio, the artillery and the French could be here, because in battle we will need everyone.' Österreichisches Staatsarchiv-Kriegsarchiv, Vienna, Alte Feldakten, 1661–1664, B. 89.

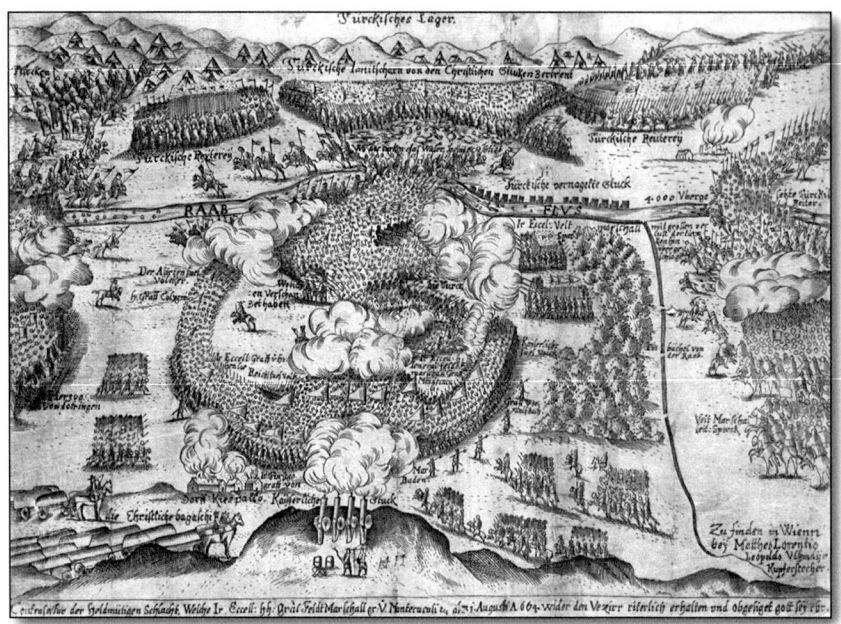

The final phase of the battle of Szentgotthárd-Mogersdorf in a contemporary German print of Matthäus Lorenz Leopold Ultzmayer. The Ottomans, pressed by the Imperialists and allies in the bend of the Rába River, are retreating in disorder. The high level of violence achieved in the wars against the Ottomans, alongside the mystical struggle for the defence of the faith remained long impressed in Central European culture, and in the 19th century both topics were transfigured by Rainer Maria Rilke in his *Die Weise von Liebe und Tod des Cornets Christoph Rilke*, which tells an introspective epic of the battle of Szentgotthárd. (Author's collection)

On 30 July, the both armies marched westward in parallel, keeping the river to their flank. The following day the Allies and Ottomans faced each other across the Rába River, between Szentgotthárd and Mogersdorf. In summer, the river was at its lowest ebb. During the night, the Ottoman artillery targeted the enemy camp, it caused no damage but evidently Köprülü aimed to create a state of tension and anxiety to weaken the enemy.

The Ottoman assault took place on 1 August at 9:00 a.m., after a diversion of the Ottoman cavalry against the allied right wing at dawn. Köprülü's plan was simple but effective. A considerable Ottoman force should be able to ford the river and penetrate into a space more than 800 metres wide, protected by wood and high marsh grass. The wide loop would protect the flank of the attacking force. The Ottomans did not encounter trouble crossing the Rába, about 10 metres wide at that point, and began to take up positions within the loop. Montecuccoli had deployed his troops since 31 July: the general's diary referred to the deployment. Like Hannibal at Cannae, the *Feldmarshall-General* placed the inexperienced *Reich* troops in the centre, the Imperialists to the right and the French to the left.

After the Imperial sentinels gave the alarm, the allied troops moved southbound to the narrow front to engage the enemies. Meanwhile on both the wings, with orders to keep in reserve, the French and the Imperial cavalry repulsed small groups of Ottoman horsemen spotted south of Mogersdorf and Szentgotthárd, but the decisive action happened in the centre. A well-planned series of Ottoman assaults and fake retreat caused the rout of the circles' infantry. The French and German troops counter-attacked from the left, while Montecuccoli's cavalry charged in from the right, just managing to stem the Turkish advance. After an hour of fierce fighting, the allies could restore the compactness of their front, but the casualties suffered by the Empire's troops were very high. Infantry regiments *Puech* (BI-1), *Uffeln* (WI-

1) and *Fugger* (SI-2) were almost annihilated and the survivors had lost weapons and equipment.⁷⁶

Moreover, Köprülü Ahmed's plan was progressing well. The Ottoman infantry began to entrench and did not stop the influx of troops through the fords on the Rába River. At 12:00 o'clock Montecuccoli convened his staff for a war council, introducing the situation in clear terms: to remain on the defensive while the Ottomans consolidated their bridgehead, or counter-attack immediately and repulse the enemies on the opposite bank of the river. For the second option, it was necessary to use all available forces, including the French contingent. At this point, the hesitations of Coligny, the French commander, manifested. He objected that his king had entrusted him with the best troops of France and he could not risk their destruction. The weaknesses of the coalition emerged and Montecuccoli did not have full authority over it. However, most commanders declared their favour for a general assault, including Coligny's lieutenants, La Feuillade and Beauvezé.⁷⁷ Montecuccoli ordered the assault in the early afternoon. The action progressed successfully and soon the allied pressure restricted the enemy's space for manoeuvre, the Ottomans crowded in all directions, until the increasing pressure caused the first failure in their line. Although 30,000 or more of his troops remained unengaged, the Grand Vizier sensed the battle going against him and decided to retreat, leaving the allies in possession of the battlefield.⁷⁸ After seven hours of fighting 2,000 allied soldiers, mainly Germans, had been lost, along with a similar number of deserters. Ottoman casualties are not known, but were probably higher.⁷⁹

The commemorative stone raised in 1964 by the Turkish, Austrian, and Hungarian governments, with the word 'peace' in the languages of all the nations who fought at Szentgotthárd on 1st August 1664. (Author's photograph)

---

76 Franconian infantry regiment *Pleitner* (FI-1) lost all its officers, while the Lower Saxony infantry regiments claimed 600 dead and wounded. In '1663–1664, für das Reich gegen die Türken', in *Neu und Alte Zinnfiguren*, March III – 1975.
77 *Ibidem*, p. 34.
78 Western sources on the battle outline the decisive effect of freak weather conditions during the engagement. Rycaut's commentary, cited by Murphy in *Ottoman Warfare*, p. 42, includes the following statement: 'As soon as the Turkish army had waded over the water, the night following so much rain, and such a deluge came pouring down from the mountains, that the river which was fordable the day before, did now over swell its banks and was not passable without floats and bridges.' Montecuccoli's performance also are examined with further opinions: 'By carrying out an exhaustive multi-lingual comparative analysis of existing accounts of the battle, including those by contemporary Ottoman historians, Nottebohm was able to dismiss some excessively adulatory accounts of Montecuccoli's generalship as the decisive factor in the victory by the allied forces; while at the same time giving emphasis to some of the exceptional operational difficulties under which the Ottoman forces performed as the battle unfolded.'
79 A lesser known source about the battle was published in Bologna in 1664, entitled *Nuova e Vera Relatione del sanguinoso Combattimento seguito tra gli Esserciti Imperiale e Ottomano al fiume Raab*. The anonymous author was certainly an eyewitness of the battle, as evidenced by several accurate descriptions of the facts and the detailed list of dead and wounded among the

The allies were exhausted and did not pursue the enemy, who retreated to Buda. On 2 August, the arrival of the 12,000 Royal Hungarian troops of the 'insurrection' did not change this situation. Neither could the Ottomans resume the offensive. Montecuccoli assembled the army at Győr and met the war council to plan the siege of Érsekújvár, but soon both sides agreed to negotiate a truce, which was concluded at Vasvár (or Eisenburg) on 10 August 1664.

It is not unreasonable to ask why, in view of these significant military improvements, the war of 1663–64 resulted only in a minor success for the Habsburgs, while the Porte gained an important strategic victory conquering Érsekújvár as well as achieving complete control over Transylvania. The war of 1663–64 did not bring significant territorial gain to the Habsburgs except for Tokay, Szatmár and some small fortresses in Upper Hungary and Transylvania. Signing the 20 years truce of Vasvár, the Emperor appeared very compliant to the Ottoman requests. Considering this unfavourable outcome, the conflict appears as a substantial Imperial defeat. History, however, seems to not agree with this opinion. The Emperor entered into a war convinced to close the question with little effort, trusting that the Porte would not fight on two fronts, namely against him in Transylvania and against Venice in the Mediterranean. Instead, the conflict turned into an expansive war: the problem was always money, and to a more limited extent the fragmented nature of the Habsburg domains. When the war took a different course from that intended, the House of Austria risked being overrun by the Ottoman sultan, because an assault on Vienna could result in a bitter end, considering that in 1664 the Austrian capital was much less fortified than 19 years later.

In the moment of greatest danger, the Habsburgs were able to offer a considerable resistance, joining their army with contingents from all over the Empire. This experience showed that even a heterogeneous force was able to resist a powerful opponent like the Ottoman army, if well directed by an excellent commander such as Raimondo Montecuccoli. Moreover, in the campaign of 1664 the Imperial army developed logistics that, more or less, were able to support in campaign an army of considerable size, even if compared to the numbers later achieved during the Franco-Dutch War. Most important detail for the Habsburgs' policy, the truce with the Porte endured, imperfect, but nothing happened that justified another war until 1683. From this point of view, the war of 1663–64 represented, for both sides, the general test for the decisive conflict that began in 1683 with the siege of Vienna.

After 1664, the 'Turkish War' returned to be a central point in the formation of the Imperial military leadership, and certainly it was not by chance that all the best Imperial commanders after Montecuccoli – Charles V of Lorraine, Ludwig of Baden and later Eugene of Savoy – had accomplished their apprenticeship in Hungary.[80]

---

allied officers. He relates the capture of 126 Ottoman ensigns, 19 guns, more than 5,000 sabres and several horses with rich harnesses. The author claims 8,000 death and wounded for the Ottoman side, and many prisoners.

80 Through these commanders derived the 'Age of Heroes', an invented tradition started in the 1690s and initially manufactured by the heroes themselves. Is possible to see ways in which

Like a thriller novel, the history of the war of 1663–64 also includes a poisonous epilogue. On 18 November 1664, Miklós Zrínyi was killed by a wounded boar whilst hunting. The death of 'the master of the *Klein Krieg*' seemed the crowning misfortune of a national tragedy, whilst Hungarians and Croatians were unable to regard it as a tragic accident.[81]

Insurgencies and Rebellions, 1670–1680

In 1664, the battle of Szentgotthárd had been a victory for the Emperor, but somewhat surprisingly Leopold I quickly agreed the terms of the Peace of Vasvár, recognising the Ottoman candidate in Transylvania and paying an indemnity of 200,000 florins to the sultan in return for a 20-year truce. The Hungarian magnates were furious, accusing him of wasting the victory, but Leopold was conscious of how narrow the margin had been between victory and defeat. Montecuccoli's army was already disintegrating, and though the Imperial Diet had granted military assistance for an unlimited period, the agreement with the *Rheinbund Allianz* had been for only one year. The Aulic Chamber had also run out of money and Leopold I wanted an excuse to remove the French from his territory, as he saw them as an affront to his dignity and an encouragement to the more independently-minded Hungarian nobles.

Ottoman preoccupations elsewhere ensured that the truce nearly lasted its term, despite growing Hungarian discontent, culminating in openly armed opposition against the Habsburg policy of absolutism in the 1670s, the period known as the 'Ten Dark Years'.

The conspiracy and rebellion against Vienna was entirely led by the aristocracy, with the Palatine Ferenc Wesselényi as principal leader, soon joined by dissatisfied members of the noble families from Croatia and Hungary, such as Fran Krsto Frankopan, the Croatian *banus* Petar Zrínyi, the high judge of Hungary Ferenc Nádasdy, Esztergom archbishop György Lippay and Johann Erasmus von Tattenbach, a feudal lord from Styria. Wesselényi died before the conspiracy was discovered while Zrínyi, Frankopan and Nádasdy were arrested in March 1670. Hungarian historians described the Habsburg retaliation as brutal: mass arrests, torture and persecution accompanied the violence acted by the army, which arbitrarily performed requisition and extortion. The repression extended also to Croatia. The Hungarian historians concur in describing the kingdom as a country collapsed in misery, terror and desperation. The aristocracy held the political direction of the uprising,

---

their myth was created, how it spread and how it survived. Montecuccoli was a less potent role model than his younger protégés, but he created the prototype. Furthermore, the Italian general's teaching contributed to form the 'glorious generation of 1683' who performed successfully in the following decades. See in Wheatcroft, *The Enemy at the Gate*, pp. 228–244.

81 Immediately, suspicions and legends flourished after the sudden death of the brave *banus*: 'Even for a literary historian as Antal Szerb, Zrinyi's hunting accident has remained "an eternal enigma". After hinting at the murder plot against Wallenstein, he recounts in his *Literary History* that a musket is allegedly kept in Vienna, labelled "this is the boar that killed Miklós Zrinyi".' Cited in Lendvai, *The Hungarians*, p. 130.

but the lowest class also reacted against Vienna. The common people, who suffered greatly for the Imperial soldiers' robberies, openly manifested their hate against the Habsburgs, and in the countryside the peasants claimed that 'the whole country would have taken to arms if it had a leader, or if it had the support of the Ottomans.'[82]

In 1670, the 'Hungarian tragedy' had gone. Upper Hungary became the base of the resistance against Leopold I. In early 1670, a tenth of Hungarian nobles led by magnate Ferenc I Rákóczi planned the first openly hostile act against the Habsburg rule. Ferenc I Rákóczi, the heir of Prince György of Transylvania, became the natural leader of the insurgents also for his parental links. Rákóczi had married a daughter of the Croatian *banus* Miklós Zrínyi, and still he had many supporters in Transylvania, although the Porte had decreed that any member of his family could once again access the throne of the princedom.[83] The action took place at Sárospatak on 10 April, when the Hungarian nobles arrested the Austrian commander of Tokay, Colonel Ernst Rüdiger von Starhemberg, invited by them for a meeting.

The episode at Sárospatak triggered the fire of rebellion and a larger action occurred on 12 April, when bands of insurgents besieged the Imperial garrison of Tokay. The number increased to 5–6,000 men when another Upper Hungary powerful magnate, Isztván Bocskay, joined the uprising. He immediately asked all the northern *comitates* (counties) to support the rebellion, but without artillery the insurgents could not achieve any significant result. Moreover, the scenario was complicated, because Ottoman military support appeared uncertain. Even regarding the strategy to be adopted for provoking the uprising there were conflicting opinions. In late April the insurgents seized Nagybánya (today Baia Mare in Romania), and in other places the rebels demanded the surrender of the Imperial garrisons, but at Szatmár, the Imperialists under Colonel Strassoldo repulsed the assault. Then, on 2 May, with 300 dragoons, Strassoldo captured the leader of the rebels of Nagybánya. Days later a field encounter occurred at Szatmár, when the Imperial cavalry under Colonel Johann von Dünewald engaged the rebels and dispersed them after a short fight. The defeat did not stop the insurgents, and on their return the Imperialists fell into an ambush suffering heavy casualties.[84] The lack of a unified plan and the impossibility of obtaining concrete support from the Porte undermined the cohesion of the insurgents. For a moment, Rákóczi thought that he would flee to Transylvania, but soon he hurried to his mother Sophia Báthory at Munkács and asked her to obtain forgiveness for him from Vienna.[85] The other leaders fled to Transylvania or negotiated for a general pardon, and as a sign of submission Starhemberg was released on 20 May. By now, the peace was restored. On 22 May, the rebel bands dispersed immediately when the news about the arrival of

---

82   Banlaky, 'A Magyar Nemzet Hadtörténelme', vol. XVI, p. 218.
83   Count Rákóczi was the father of Ferenc II, who led the Great Hungarian rebellion of 1703–11.
84   Historians attribute the plan for the ambush to Anna Lónyay, the widow of János Kemény. Banlaky, 'A Magyar Nemzet Hadtörténelme', vol. XVI, p. 222.
85   *Ibidem*, p. 231. Count Ferenc I Rákóczi was the only leading actor of the conspiracy whose life was spared, due to his mother Sophia Báthory's intervention and a ransom payment of 300,000 florins.

the Imperialists under *General der Cavallerie* Johan von Sporck spread in Upper Hungary.[86] The Imperial troops opened the way at Murányi in late May, charging the rebels with the cuirassiers of the regiment *Lothringen* (IC-7).[87] On 24 June Sárospatak opened its gates, while Ecséd, the other major insurgent stronghold, surrendered to the Imperialists days later. In Upper Hungary were quartered six infantry battalions, two regiments of cuirassiers and one of dragoons for 9,000 men overall.

In Vienna, most of the major councillors demanded the most unrestrained policy. However, Lobkowicz and Montecuccoli persuaded them to proclaim a policy of waiting for the weakness of the movement to emerge. Though they were afraid that the Emperor would face a huge national uprising, which could eventually gain support from the Porte, Poland, France or Transylvania, both also recommended acting cautiously. By the summer, however, the situation had changed. The most important factor to emerge was that the confused and over-hasty uprising of 1670 and its quick collapse provided the Viennese court with the excuse for introducing absolutism outright.[88] The decision to impose exemplary punishment prevailed and in this way the Imperial court engaged the process against the major leaders of the conspiracy arrested in March 1670. On 30 April 1671, in Vienna, Zrínyi, Nádasdy and Frankopán were sentenced to death; the same fate in Graz for Tattenbach the following December.[89]

All these facts increased the emigration of the Hungarians and, most of all, of the persecuted Protestants. Transylvania became their natural refuge because many of the nobles had relatives in the Princedom. Slowly but constantly, regions and towns like Maramureș, Kővár, Debrecen, but also some villages in *Partium* were full of refugees and wanted insurgents. The unrestrained imposition of taxes and the cruelty of religious persecution also forced the lowest classes, such as the poor nobility and the serf peasants, to

---

86 'In the countryside, the peasants deserted when the Germans passed. There was no resistance anywhere, even though 2–3,000 people would have been on their way between the counties of Liptó and Szepes, but panic and dread caught everyone and all ran across the woods.' Banlaky, 'A Magyar Nemzet Hadtörténelme', vol. XVI, p. 2323

87 In this action distinguished the 26-year-old *Feldmarshall-Lieutenant* Prince Charles of Lorraine-Bar. Wrede, *Geschichte der K. und K. Wehrmacht*, vol. III, part two, p. 581.

88 The Austrian government based its actions on the so-called *Verwirkungstheorie* that had been successfully applied in the 1620s in Bohemia. It suggested that the Hungarians should be punished collectively for their revolt. The Habsburgs' policy did not make it a secret, in any case, that they held all Hungarian governmental norms to be 'good-for-nothing and worthless' laws that 'should be burnt right on the head of the Hungarians'. Now they considered the time to be ripe for realising their objectives without any obstacle. See in L. Benczédi, 'Hungarian National Consciousness as Reflected in the Anti-Habsburg and Anti-Ottoman Struggles of the Late Seventeenth Century', in *Harvard Ukrainian Studies, Concepts of Nationhood in Early Modern Eastern Europe*, Vol. 10, No. 3/4 (December 1986), pp. 424–437.

89 'Zrínyi, Frankopán and Nádasdy had a separate court in his turn, which consisted of 11 members under Paul Hocher's presidency, but none of them were Hungarians. This court was held in the Imperial Palace of Vienna, and on 6 April 1671, Frankopán, on 11 April Nádasdy, and on 18 April Zrínyi, was sentenced to loss of head and properties. The punishment was exacerbated by preliminary hand mutilation. The Emperor approved the terrible verdict on 22 April 1671 and implemented it on 30 April at 9:00 in the morning. Hand mutilation was subsequently abandoned, but otherwise the sentence was executed in the said time.' Banlaky, 'A Magyar Nemzet Hadtörténelme', vol. XVI, p. 328.

leave Hungary. In 1672, the number of 'malcontent' refugees had increased to thousands. They were grouped in exile according to their social position. The alliance assumed the name of the *Kuruc* (Crusade) league. In the spring of 1672, the *Kuruc* leaders began to organise their forces for an attack against the Imperial garrisons. The goal was to expel the Imperialists from Upper Hungary and establish a protectorate under the Porte. It was a heterogeneous force with poor armament, but motivated and determined to reopen the game against the hated 'Germans'. The new leaders were Isztván Petróczy, Pál Szepessy, Mátyás Szuhay and Gábor Kende, who organised a reliable force of light cavalry in order to deeply strike into the enemy territory. The first large-scale incursion was carried out on 20 August against Nagyszöllös (today Vynohradiv in Ukraine), followed days later by another raid on Szatmár. The Imperial cavalry under *General Wachtmeister* Paris Spankau reacted with an expedition against Debrecen with 800 cuirassiers and 300 mounted *Grenzer*. He knew that the rebels used the city to avoid Imperial retaliation, because Debrecen formally lay in Ottoman territory, but like several counties along the border it had dual sovereignty with Transylvania. Therefore, every offensive action in this area could be considered as a hostile act against two neutral countries. However, the *Kuruc* had left Debrecen before the arrival of the Imperial cavalry. The tactics used by the insurgents was frustrating for the Imperialists, who could rarely could engage the fast-moving Hungarian riders in a closer fight. In vain, Spankau patrolled with his cavalry the fords on the Tisza River, and only once was almost about to intercept the enemy. However, the *Kuruc* did not limit its offensive to the raids. On 1 September it assaulted the fortified town of Kálló and penetrated inside, but the Imperial garrison took refuge in the citadel awaiting the arrival of the relief force. The actions of the Hungarian horsemen continued in the following weeks, but finally Spankau's constancy was rewarded on 13 September. A large column of about 5–6,000 enemy foot and horse was sighted while marching to Enyiczko (Haniska in Slovakia). The Imperialists had in the area only two squadrons of dragoons, but Spankau arrived just in time with 2,000 cavalry. The Imperialists did not take advantage of the surprise because Spankau failed to arrive unnoticed, but the *Kuruc* resistance was overwhelmed. However, this was not to be the first major Imperial victory in the open field against the insurgents, because the arrival on the battlefield of 2,000 mounted insurgents halted the Imperialists. The situation for the Imperial cavalry worsened further, because a downpour fell on the battlefield, preventing the use of firearms. Many Imperialists were captured and Spankau hardly escaped being a prisoner, reaching Kassa with the remains of his cavalry.[90]

The victory was highly celebrated by the insurgents and served mainly to arouse interest in their cause from the Prince of Transylvania, Mihály Apafi, who saw in the *Kuruc* struggle a way to gain political advantages in the region. Soon the Transylvanian governor of Kövar, Mihály Teleki, joined the Hungarian *Kuruc* with his troops, without the consent of the Estates. New raids and engagements occurred near Szatmár before the end of September,

---

90   Payer, *Armati Hungarorum*, p. 109.

until on 10 October 1672, Isztván Petróczi conquered Eperies after three weeks of siege.

Some little success had been achieved by the Imperialists before the end of 1672. On 19 September the commander of Szatmár, Adolf Löben, assaulted Teleky's corps encamped not far from the fortress and pursued the enemy to the Transylvanian border. In other counties, however, the rebellion was gaining support. In Autumn, numerous centres of Upper Hungary swore loyalty to the insurgents declaring the Habsburg monarchy decayed. On 10 October, at Árva (today Orava in Slovakia), peasants and citizens assaulted the small Imperial garrison and threw the soldiers into the river, while at Kálló the local garrison switched to the rebel side. The Imperialists achieved some success against the *Kuruc* at Görge on 24 November, while on the same day, General Sporck invested Árva and retook control of the rebel city. Days later, 24 insurgents were sentenced to death. The conflict turned into a bitter struggle without quarter, with the typical harshness of civil wars. In an attempt to annihilate every will of resistance, the Imperial soldiers committed acts considered excessive even for the mentality of the time. War prisoners, as well as every civilian suspected of helping the rebels, were always tortured and almost nobody survived the mistreatment. Reprisals did not have an effect at military level, and on the contrary they exasperated even more the Hungarians who saw an increase in external support for their cause. Money and weapons came not only from Transylvania but also from Poland and Ottoman Hungary.

The extraterritoriality of Debrecen guaranteed the rebels a place through which the elusive raiding corps could easily enter or exit from Upper Hungary. It was therefore necessary to prevent the *Kuruc* from using the city, which was also a propaganda centre of the Magyar Protestants against the Habsburgs and was considered 'the Geneva of East Europe'. In December 1672 an infantry corps under Strassoldo was therefore sent in order to seal any access from Debrecen. The blockade did not have any significant effect, indeed at the end of January 1673, a large corps of *Kuruc* entered from the north in Nyírség county and proceeded south, destroying the Imperial outposts at Szatmár, and finally repaired to Nyírbéltek in Ottoman Hungary with the passport of the local *beg*, who was eager to provide them with food and care.

The court at Vienna began to take in account of the escalation of the war unleashed by the *Kuruc* with culpable delay. The Imperial troops in Hungary, excluded the *Grenzer*, were approximately 7,500 infantry, 2,500 cuirassiers and 900 dragoons.[91] A further 2,000 foot and 1,000 cuirassiers were garrisoned in Silesia. The international scenario did not allow allocation of further troops in Hungary, while the opinion of Montecuccoli was to bring that figure to at least 18,000 regular soldiers. He suggested dealing with the Hungarians in a hurry as long as there was an army capable of breaking all ambition of resistance.[92] But the economic balance did not allow for an increase of the army with new regiments, and therefore in early 1673

---

91   Banlaky, 'A Magyar Nemzet Hadtörténelme', vol. XVI, p. 354.
92   Montecuccoli, *L'Ungheria nell'anno MDCLXXVII*, p. 24.

only 2,000 cuirassiers in all marched to join the army that was facing the rebellion.[93] If the military strength could not be increased, it was desirable to place in charge more experienced commanders, in order to better lead the operation until now performed by Spankau. The choice rewarded the candidates proposed by Montecuccoli, the *General der Cavallerie* Johann von Sporck, and *Feldmarschall-Lieutenant* Wolf Friedrich Cob von Neuding authority to operate simultaneously from north and south with two corps. They were considered veterans and both well knew the Hungarian scenario having served here since 1663. However there were some remarks concerning Cob, depicted as 'the most cruel among the harsh Imperial generals, and perhaps he was sent to Hungary particularly for his malicious attitude.'[94] General Spankau remained as a subordinate. The Imperial commanders were to be supported by 4,500 frontiersmen from Slavonia and the *Bergstadtische Grenze* under the *Kreis-Oberst* Pál Eszterházy.[95] Finally, in February 1673, when the war against France seemed ever closer, Leopold I created a new executive for Hungarian affairs, directed by the Grand Master of the Teutonic Order, Johann Kaspar von Ampringen, with the task of pursuing the policy of repression with full power.

However, restoring Imperial control in Upper Hungary remained a very difficult task, because the insurgents could operate from their safe bases in Transylvania, eluding Imperial attempts to engage them in the open field. Moreover, the rebel bases in *Partium* and Maramureş were located in a strategically favourable position for a prolonged defence, because a direct offensive against these places would have exposed the Imperial troops to sudden enemy assaults from the rear. Before freeing this area, it was necessary to secure the region by restoring the Imperial control in all the surrounding counties. To achieve this goal, however, more troops were needed, but now they were not available. Even having deprived the rebels of their strategic centres, the problem of the Transylvanian asylum persisted. Moreover, to resolve this, it would have been necessary to invade the princedom with the risk of a new war against the Porte: an occurrence to be avoided by all means, because the House of Austria could not fight two large-scale wars simultaneously.

In January 1673 the Imperialists achieved a success with the capture of Nagybánya, which had remained under rebel control since the previous year. Lack of manpower forced Sporck to order the destruction of the fortifications, at least depriving the *Kuruc* of a major stronghold. Shortly afterwards

---

93 Banlaky, 'A Magyar Nemzet Hadtörténelme', vol. XVI, p. 355.
94 'Already in the last war against the Porte, when he served as commander in Szatmár, Cob was close to being displaced by a complaint from the inhabitants', in 'Kriegs-Chronik Öst. Ungarns nevét következetesen Koppnak írja' cited in D. Angyal, *Késmárki Thököly Imre 1657–1705* (Budapest, 1888–89), vol. II, p. 65.
95 Count Pál Eszterházy was considered an able commander and a loyal man who served under Miklós Zrínyi. He was Roman Catholic and one of the major Hungarian nobles who remained loyal to the House of Austria. His loyalty procured him some complaints by the 19th century Hungarian historians, who depicted him as 'one of the worst egoists [...], who was ready to sacrifice his country, if he foresaw his interest. Already in 1670, he contributed to the repression of the insurgents at Árva.' In Banlaky, 'A Magyar Nemzet Hadtörténelme', vol. XVI, p. 356.

Feldmarschall-Lieutenant Cob, who was quartered at Kálló, was able to intercept an enemy incursion against Kassa capturing many prisoners. From February the duel turned into a war of position in which the Imperialists tried with the scarce troops available to restrict strategic manoeuvring space to the rebels. In May–June, Cob took back under Imperial control of some villages in *Partium*,[96] but no significant action occurred in 1673 because the *Kuruc* leaders reorganised their forces in Eger, under Ottoman protection, and in Transylvania.

The quiet period lasted until the grass grew in the fields and the woods resumed their foliage. Operating in small groups of 2–300 horsemen, to gather safely in the woods, in early June 1674 the *Kuruc* eluded Imperial surveillance. Soon, a series of devastating raids hit Moravia and Silesia; in July, the *Kuruc* horsemen appeared before Veszprém, in central Hungary. A series of skirmishes engaged the Imperial corps under Cob near Onod, but the rebels achieved a good success in early June, when they defeated the Imperial *Grenzer* under Pálffy, and on 21 June inflicted many casualties on the Imperialists who relied on besieged Tokay. In the summer and autumn, minor encounters engaged the Imperial garrisons of Tokay, Kassa and Szatmár. This latter fortress was the most coveted by the rebels, but until they had any artillery, it remained impossible to conquer it with an assault.

In 1675, the rebel offensive resumed with unprecedented violence thanks to aid coming from abroad, especially from Poland,[97] and above all from France. In April 1675 Louis XIV's emissaries in Poland promised a monthly allowance to the rebels in exchange for a general insurgence in Hungary, to divert the Imperialist forces engaged on the Rhine in the war against France. Money allowed the increase of the rebel army with mercenaries from Poland, Transylvania and even from Serbia.[98]

Moreover, the *Kuruc* had found a skilled and charming leader in the young Lutheran noble Imre Thököly. Safe in his possessions in Transylvania, he had cooperated to gather around him resources and volunteers exasperated with the violence of the Imperial troops and eager to join the struggle against the Emperor. From early 1675, he served under the high-commander of the *Kuruc* army, Pál Wesselényi, nephew of the Hungarian Palatine who had initiated the conspiracy, but soon he gained a growing popularity among the *Kuruc* leaders for his boldness and bravery.

In summer 1675 the *Kuruc* army launched a large offensive with a 7,000-man army, including Poles and Ottomans 'volunteers', conquering the forts of Szádvár and Torna (today Szikszó in Slovakia), but failed at Szatmár and Kálló, repulsed by the newly appointed *General Wachtmeister* Carlo Strassoldo. He continued to engage the enemy near Debrecen, and when he remained in Hungary as commander of the Imperial army in the absence of

---

96 At Diósgyőr, among the prisoners, were identified 15 former Imperial soldiers who had deserted to the rebels and were immediately sentenced to death. *Ibidem*, p. 360.
97 On 20 May 1674, Jan Sobieski had been elected king of the Polish-Lithuanian Commonwealth and one of his first acts in foreign affairs was the alliance with Transylvania and France. See in Cardini, *Il Turco a Vienna*, p. 187.
98 The alliance of France was perfected at Warsaw on 27 May 1677 and extended to Transylvania and Poland. Payer, *Armati Hungarorum*, p. 108.

Sporck and Cob, he occupied the city on 6 December with German troops and Croatian frontiersmen, imposing an extraordinary tribute of 80,000 florins. This act obviously provoked the Ottoman *paşa*'s reaction, but fortunately the grievance was limited only to letters of complaint.[99] Strassoldo's expedition against Debrecen saved the military financial situation in Hungary, but in October the city returned again to rebel control.

The *Kuruc* army was increasing ever more, while in early 1676 the Imperialists could deploy 9,000 soldiers in all.[100] The shortage of manpower forced the Imperial commanders to an exhausting defensive strategy, waiting for events. The forces available were assembled between Szatmár, Kálló, Tokay and Kassa, where Cob placed his headquarters, and a mobile force under Strassoldo behind the Tisza River. In March 1676 the *Kuruc* army besieged Szatmár and Onod again. Strassoldo gathered a force of 1,800 infantry, dragoons and *Grenzer* and planned an assault to interrupt the enemy supply lines, engaging the rebels near Onod, but he was defeated and seriously injured in the encounter. On 12 August another sudden *Kuruc* incursion clashed near Kálló with a corps of mounted *Grenzer* and German infantry which was escorting supplies to the city. The Imperialists prevailed, but the *Grenzer* incautiously pursued the fleeing enemies leaving the infantry isolated. The battle ended with an Imperial defeat and the loss of the supplies destined for Kálló. Raids and skirmishes continued during the summer and minor encounters occurred along the Tisza River and at Szatmár. The war continued with all its corollary of cruelty committed by both sides. In late 1676 *Feldmarschall-Lieutenant* Cob ordered the mass deportation of villagers who had provided aid to the *Kuruc* army, and this measure often happened without the existence of solid evidence. The rebels responded by intensifying the war without quarter against the Imperial garrisons. Incapable of facing the unpredictable moves of the *Kuruc* forces, in early 1677 the Imperialists were on the verge of collapse. If the increasingly unfavourable strategic scenario was not enough, there was the problem of money to make the situation even worse. Many garrisons had not received salaries for months, with had a very bad effect on discipline and loyalty.

In July the *Kuruc* army with 7,000 Hungarians and 4,000 Transylvanians and other mercenaries was assembling near Ecséd with the aim of seizing Szatmár. Cob realised that an eventual open field encounter was destined to fail, and avoiding the assault against Ecséd he delayed the enemy operations, because they expected an Imperial assault in order to have free hand on Szatmár. The Imperial commander ordered the retreat to Kassa of the available troops, abandoning all the minor outposts to the enemy. The Imperial troops crossed the Tisza River heading to Kassa and Tokay, facing continued enemy assaults. The action of the *Kuruc* cavalry further exasperated Cob, but retaliation was prevented because the Emperor had now dismissed him from command, replacing him with *Feldmarschall-Lieutenant* Georg Stephan von Freudenthal-Würbent as general commander. Informed about the Imperial retreat, on 22 November Wesselényı marched

---

99 *Ibidem*.
100 Banlaky, 'A Magyar Nemzet Hadtörténelme', vol. XVI, p. 366.

to Nagybánya and then besieged Munkács, but after failing to succeed, he moved the troops to Debrecen for the oncoming winter quarter.

In late 1677 the *Kuruc* army deployed 15,000 well-equipped soldiers with 10 siege artillery pieces. Spies in Poland informed Imperial headquarters that 2,000 French soldiers and specialists had joined the rebels,[101] while more Transylvanians, Poles, Cossacks and Ottomans were marching to Upper Hungary. The effects of the increased strength and effectiveness of the *Kuruc* army were revealed at Nyalábvár on 10 October 1677, when a mixed force of rebels and allies surprised the little Imperial field corps camped nearby and annihilated it.[102] The Imperial casualties were 1,200 (or 1,500) dead and wounded,[103] including the commander of Szatmár, the Count of Herberstein. On 22 November, Pál Wesselényi finally conquered Szatmár after two weeks of siege. Now the *Kuruc* army could move west from this major stronghold, which practically opened Upper Hungary to an easy advance.

In Vienna the ever worse news from Hungary was accompanied by that coming from the Rhine, where the war against France continued, drying up all the economic resources. It was therefore necessary to find a solution and avoid the loss of Upper Hungary, arresting an escalation that would provoke a new war against the Porte. However, the Hungarian question was inextricably linked to the European policy and that within the court of Vienna. The court parties expressed different thoughts, but finally the proposal to open a discussion with the *Kuruc* leaders prevailed. Regarding this option, opinions were nuanced and one suggested finding a solution by direct diplomacy with the rebels to divert the Ottomans from a new war against the Habsburgs, even finding a *modus vivendi* with the Hungarian rebels. This last point, if realised, could delete one of the major Ottoman pretexts for opening hostilities against the Emperor and at the same time would have isolated the rebels by forcing them to lay down their arms.

While diplomacy was trying to open the talks, the rebel offensive resumed in May 1678 after the conjunction of the rebel army under Thököly with the Transylvanians and Poles under Mihály Teleky. Soon the allies were joined by armed peasants who transformed the campaign into a triumphal march. Between June and July, Thököly advanced in the mountain counties and one by one the townships of Bodokö, Torna, Szalánc and Putnok surrendered to him. On 2 July the allies entered Szendrö and days later Murányi opened its gates. The Imperial garrisons in Upper Hungary surrendered before the end of summer after the granting of safe conduct. On 10 October Besztercebánya (today Banská Bystrica in Slovakia) also surrendered to Thököly, but on 1st November the rebels were arrested at Barsszentkereszt, where the Imperialists had assembled a force of 4,000 regular soldiers and *Grenzer*.

In February 1679 the war against France closed with the Peace of Nijmegen. Point 33 of the treaty included the peace between the Emperor and the Transylvanian prince Mihály I Apafi, allied to Louis XIV. It was also

---

101 Payer, *Armati Hungarorum*, p.110.
102 The cuirassier regiment *Poiger* (IC-36), formed in 1675 and still incomplete, was completely destroyed. See in Wrede, *Geschichte der K. und K. Wehrmacht*, vol. III, part two, p. 539.
103 Banlaky, 'A Magyar Nemzet Hadtörténelme', vol. XVI, p. 368.

expected that the negotiations opened in the assembly of Odenburg (Sopron, in West Hungary) would lead to a composition of the conflict in Upper Hungary. In the spring, new skirmishes involved Imperialists and rebels in central Hungary. On 11 April 1679 a strong Hungarian party was repulsed by the Imperial infantry at Torna. However, before negotiation could stop the fighting, the rebels achieved an important victory at Uifalu on 3 November 1679 followed by another incursion led by Thököly in Moravia in July 1680, and the conquest of Késmárk and Löcse (today Kežmarok and Levoča in Slovakia) in August.

On 15 November 1680, in Jolsva, both sides agreed the suspension of hostilities. Now the rebels could negotiate the truce from an advantageous position, while for Vienna the war had stopped later than hoped. Underestimating the ability of the rebels to wage a liberation war was one of the most serious errors committed by Imperial politics. The army had faced the struggle of an unfavourable situation due to the distance of the war theatre, which aggravated the chronic shortage of supply, and after 1672 it was unable to avoid the disastrous outcome of the campaigns. From the political point of view, the confrontation left too many questions unanswered, while on the geostrategic ground it was impossible to keep away the interference of the Porte, which was naturally interested in the Hungarian question. The negotiations stopped in February 1682: the duel with the Sultan was therefore destined to open, and this promptly happened 14 months later in 1683.

Duel on the Rhine, 1673–79

The military success of France against the Dutch Republic in the campaigns of 1672 reverberated in the diplomatic arena. On 25 July 1672, shortly afterwards the French invasion, the States General and the Emperor entered into a pact with the object of ensuring of the Peace of Cleves, signed in 1666 by Münster and the Dutch Republic. The treaty had to prevent any state acting something to the detriment of the Peace of Westphalia. At court, the 'Spanish party' strongly advocated this resolution, but among the councillors who opposed the war against France there were important personalities, such as the Court Council president Prince Lobkowicz.

Leopold I agreed with Prince William of Orange to send 16,000 troops under Montecuccoli on the Rhine,[104] and as soon as these troops were ready to march, they would be deployed against the French and their allies in conjunction with the Brandenburg army that was assembling for the same purpose. The arrival of this 36,000 men strong army on the left bank of

---

104 'Leopold's inability to do more indicated his underlying weakness. Montecuccoli's meagre force of 15,000 men represented all that could be spared in 1672–73, given the other pressing commitments in Hungary. In desperation, he resorted to illegal covert operations to neutralise troublemakers. In February 1673, Imperial agents unsuccessfully tried to assassinate the prince-bishop of Münster, who was still allied to France, while others did manage to abduct the chief minister of Cologne a year later.', Wilson, *German Armies*, p. 46.

THE IMPERIAL ARMY ON CAMPAIGN

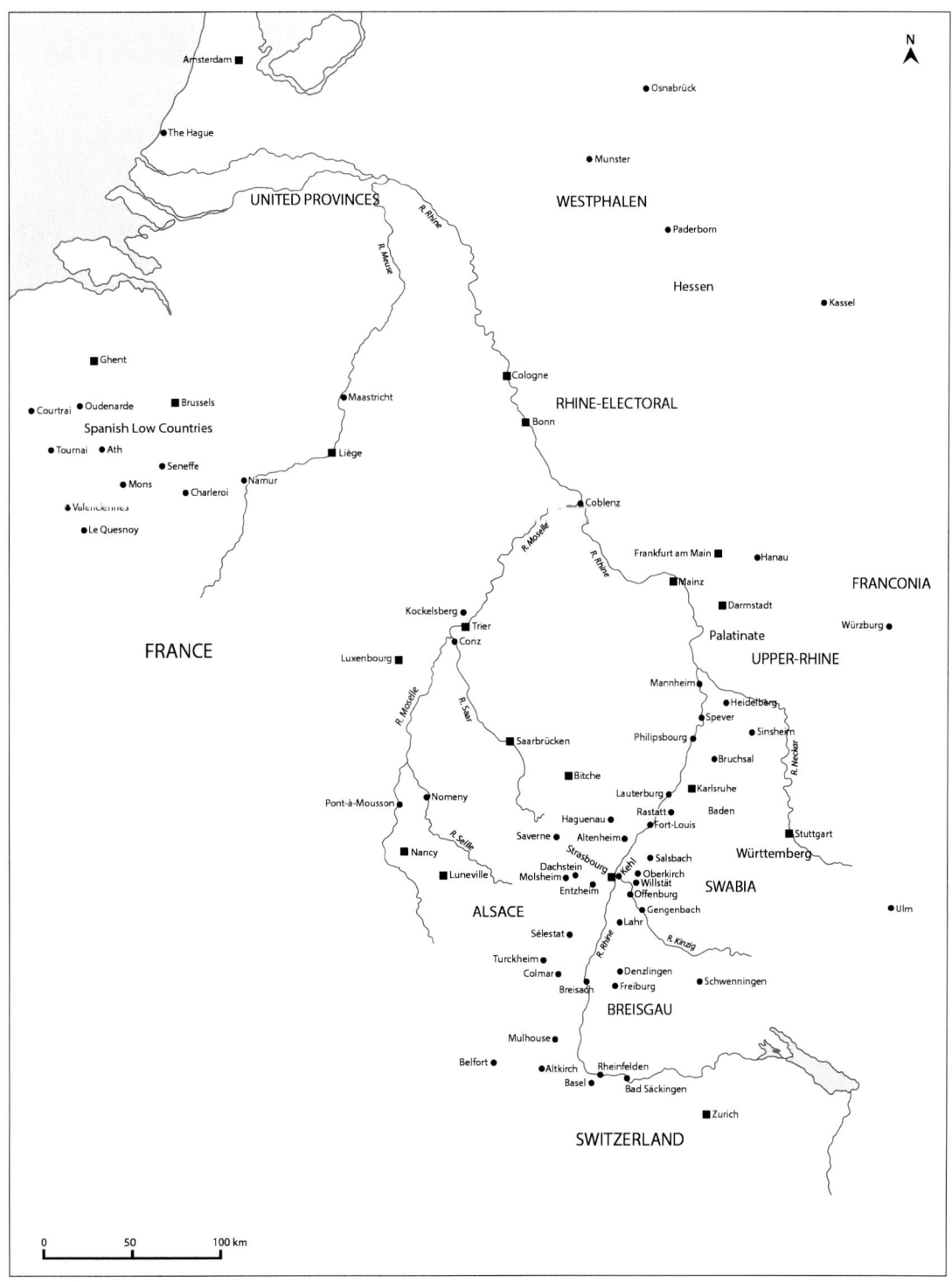

Theatre of War in Alsace, Rhineland and Spanish Low Countries, 1673–78.

the Rhine could permit the Dutch to emerge from behind the Water Line, because the French would have found themselves dangerously isolated and at the risk of losing their lines of communication, which passed through the territories of the German allies of Louis XIV, namely Cologne and Münster.

On 26 September 1672 the Imperial and Brandenburg armies were at last conjoined near Hildesheim. Much has been written about the actual Habsburg desire to limit the manoeuvring space of the French army on the Rhine, however it is certain that Montecuccoli had received 'secret instructions' to desist from anything except purely defensive action, while Leopold's counsellor Wenzel Lobkowicz assured Louis XIV there was really nothing to worry about.[105] In 1672, the Imperial army was not yet prepared to face open hostilities with France, but the Emperor wanted to prevent Brandenburg taking advantage of the enfeeblement of Cologne and Münster. Montecuccoli had to limit the campaign to a 'demonstration' along the Lower Rhine. But even this came to nothing because Turenne anticipated the allies' moves. The French commander had ordered the land on both sides of the Rhine from Wesel to Koblenz to be stripped bare, in order that Imperial and Brandenburg troops would find no more forage or foodstuff there. Rather than stand idle, Montecuccoli decided to head for Frankfurt am Main. The French would then at least have to be on the alert for an enemy advance along the Moselle or an incursion into Alsace. The march of the allied army to Frankfurt meant that the Dutch would have to manage without direct help from their allies, but now William III and his staff could take advantage of Turenne's departure to plan some offensive action before the winter. The most achievable target was Charleroi, one of the strategic crossroads of the French supply line. The success of the expedition to Charleroi ultimately hinged on the action that Montecuccoli undertook. If the Imperial *generalissimo* were to cross the Rhine with the Imperial–Brandenburg army and join forces with the Dutch-Spaniards, it would certainly be possible to conduct a siege with a reasonable prospect of success. In November, the Imperial army was camped between Frankfurt and Hanau. The order from Vienna was clear; moreover, the presence of Turenne on the Moselle did not allow bold actions. Yet the Dutch-Spaniards wanted to postpone the march to Charleroi until they were certain that Montecuccoli would cross the Rhine, and against the unfavourable news on the allies approach, they waited until mid December 1672. This delay frustrated the Dutch-Spanish hope to seize Charleroi. However, it was not an option to close the campaign while the Imperial–Brandenburg army was still in the field, because Leopold I would then be able to place the blame for the joint operation's abandonment.

Moreover, further disappointments came from Germany. Under threat of the devastation of his possessions in Westphalia, the elector of Brandenburg had in April 1673 been forced to sign the treaty of Vossem, interrupting his participation in the war against France. Despite this, in summer 1673, Leopold I finally decided to openly support the Dutch Republic. On 30 August 1673, a triple alliance was concluded with Spain and the United Provinces of

---

105 J. Whaley, *Germany and the Holy Roman Empire*, p. 35.

the Netherlands, in exchange of substantial subsidies.[106] With the resources coming from The Hague and Madrid, the Emperor could gather an army with an effective force of 40,000 men.[107] Troops and recruits were assembled near Eger (today Cheb, in Czech Republic) in western Bohemia. Leopold agreed to send his troops to the Rhine and to continue the war until the Dutch Republic had recaptured from France all the towns and fortresses lost after the invasion.

However, there were many contraindications that made the task very difficult for the Imperial army. After Westphalia, the Empire had lost its protective shield and the front line advanced to the upper area of the Rhine, where France now held the strategic advantage thanks to the possession of Philippsburg, Hagenau and Breisach. Thanks to the protection offered by these strongholds, the French could easily move troops, holding under threat Swabia, Lorraine and Upper Rhine. After the Peace of Westphalia, the Rhine had become the natural border between France and Germany. From the Swiss border in Basel, to Mannheim, the river then divided into numerous branches that formed islands and sandbanks. In this sector, the river was easily traversed with boats and pontoons, but in the area from Philippsburg to Bruchsal, there was extensive swamping on the right (German) bankwhich made crossing difficult. All along the course from Lake Constance to the Netherlands, there were only 10 fixed bridges. The most important were at Strasbourg–Kehl, Breisach and Philippsburg, while Mannheim, Mainz, Fort-Louis (near Hagenau) and other sites had just boat-bridges, which in winter were usually dismounted. At other points, there were several mobile bridges, pontoons and rafts, often unsuitable for cavalry and artillery. To the north-west, the war theatre was bordered by the Moselle, which crossed Lorraine and represented a strategically significant river route because it connected that region with Germany and the Netherlands. The Moselle was crossed by stable bridges in its lower course at Mainz, Trier and Koblenz. On the Saar, the most important of the Moselle's tributaries, there was a stable bridge at Conz. Control of these rivers could prevent communications between Lorraine and the states of Germany, which occurred regularly in any conflict between France and the Empire after Lorraine was regularly occupied.

The other major natural obstacles, mountains, were represented by the Black Forest and the Vosges, both situated to the south. In contrast to the Vosges, which were passable only east of Saverne and through the Belfort Gap, the Black Forest was traversed by several tortuous routes. While the French armies could manoeuvre on the broad Alsatian plain to defend their side of the river, the Germans were cramped on the narrow east bank, which was cut by numerous tributaries of the Rhine. Contemporary opinion concurred that immediate defence behind the Rhine was impracticable, and it was better to take up a central defensive position east of the Black Forest

---

106 The Dutch Republic agreed the payment of 50,000 rix-dollars a month and Spain promised a further 45,000. See in O. van Nimwegen, *The Dutch Army and the Military Revolution, 1588–1688* (Woodbrige, Boydell press, 2010), p. 462.

107 According to a contemporary source, the army mustered at Eger had a strength of 13,650 horse and 25,000 foot. See in *Theatrum Europaeum*, vol. XI, pp. 358–359.

to see where the enemy would cross, and then fall on him before he could deploy properly.[108] However, the French practice of raiding across the river to devastate the east bank made this politically impossible, since the Emperor could not afford to abandon the Rhinelanders to enemy depredations.

In early September the Imperial troops crossed the Bohemian border, marching to the High Palatinate. Some troops from the Rhine marched to Hungary, where the rebellion was increasing in intensity. Further troops were dispatched in Upper Austria to reinforce the *Landwehr*, to guard the frontier with the Electorate of Bavaria, who maintained an ambiguous neutrality.[109]

On 6 September 1673, Montecuccoli informed the Dutch-Spanish commander that he was marching west in order to make contact with them as soon as possible. Now the scenario slowly turned in favour of the allies. In the same period, the French had occupied Trier, but the Imperial army set out on their march west. To prevent the crossing of the Main River, Turenne occupied Aschaffenburg leaving a corps of 4,000 men. The French commander tried to hold back Montecuccoli, but the Imperial *General-Lieutenant* was more adept than anyone else in constantly staying one step ahead of his enemies. He anticipated Turenne, who tried to restrict his space to manoeuvre, with a series of marches and counter-marches, heading south to make him lose his trail. Then, on 15 September, Montecuccoli took a decisive advantage thanks to the bishop of Würzburg, who left him free access to cross the Main River. Without opposition from the French side, the Imperialists proceeded quickly to the north, heading to the Rhine. Now there was a real chance of a conjunction of the Dutch-Spanish army and the Imperial army. Montecuccoli agreed with William III and the Spanish governor Monterrey that they would jointly lay siege to Bonn, residence of the elector of Cologne. The conquest of this place would force prince-elector Maximilian Heinrich of Wittelsbach to switch allegiance, laying the bishopric of Münster open to an invasion, and to crown it all it would sever the lifeline between the French army in the Dutch Republic and Charleroi, and from there to the home bases.

More or less simultaneously, the French evacuated Utrecht and other small outposts, and headed for Maastricht with all available troops. If possible, Turenne and Luxembourg were to hamper the investment of Bonn. Montecuccoli proceeded successfully and anticipated the enemies. After a feint advance to Alsace, the Imperial army proceeded along the Main and on 6 October made camp between Höchst and Frankfurt am Main. Turenne expected that the Imperial army would have crossed the Rhine at Mainz, knowing the presence of the pontoons and boats assembled there.[110] Instead, on 12 October, Montecuccoli crossed the Rhine at Koblenz, and descending the river met the Dutch-Spaniards not far from Bonn. On 11 November 1673 the besiegers began to undermine the main rampart. Soon the French-Cologne garrison opened negotiations for a reasonable capitulation. The 1,200 defenders remaining were granted a free withdrawal to Neuss, but

---

108 Wilson, *German Armies*, p. 60.
109 This force was composed by the infantry regiment *Baden* (II-70) and five companies of dragoon regiment *Wopping* (ID-6). Kortzfleisch, *Der oberelsässische Winterfeldzug 1674–65*, p. 40.
110 J. Bérenger, *Turenne*, p. 399.

THE IMPERIAL ARMY ON CAMPAIGN

only a small portion actually arrived there because 'a great many of them have entered into service with the Imperial army'.[111] After the damage to Bonn's fortifications had been repaired, Montecuccoli and William III cleared away the remaining garrisons of troops from Cologne and France within the Electorate.

During the winter, negotiations continued in Cologne to avoid the extension of the war in Germany, but in February 1674 the French had invaded the Spanish province of Franche-Comté with 15,000 soldiers. Weeks later, when renewed French depredations in the Palatinate made it impossible to ignore the obligation to assist Emperor Leopold, the Imperial diet sidestepped the issue by expelling the French ambassador from Regensburg and informing Louis XIV in March that, by their actions, the French had made themselves an enemy of the *Reich*. This closed any residual hope of negotiation, and on 31 March 1674 the Diet declared 'Imperial War' against France. The importance of this decision lay primarily in the domain of the provision of troops: the declaration of war legitimised making circles' troops available to the Emperor for the new campaign on the Rhine.

In order to control Brandenburg, which was agitating to abandon its bilateral Peace of Vossem with France and re-enter the war, Leopold signed a new convention with the elector in July 1674, with which Friedrich Wilhelm had to send 16,000 troops to the Rhine. The war became general now.

According to Dutch-Spanish belief and intelligence, in 1674 Louis XIV would bring 65,000 men into the field, deployed across four fronts: the Low Countries, Alsace, Franche-Comté and Roussillon. On paper the allies could muster twice as many troops. Vienna, The Hague and Madrid determined the main thrust of an operational plan that covered all fronts. The Emperor and the German princes promised to mobilise two armies, one along the Upper Rhine and the other on the Moselle. The Imperial army's *Feldmarschall* Alexander Hippolyte Balthasar de Hennin, Prince of Bournonville, who replaced the indisposed Montecuccoli, with 40,000 men, held the task of preventing the French from dispatching the army from Franche-Comté to the Spanish Low Countries. The allied plan could work better by laying siege to Philippsburg, the stronghold on the Rhine which had been in French possession since 1648. The conquest of Philippsburg would provide Bournonville with a bridgehead for operations in Alsace. Alternatively, the Imperialists could assault Breisach, from which the French menaced Anterior Austria. Turenne held command in this region, and his army was estimated to be 13,000 strong at most, while its actual force was 4,000 lower.[112] The allies' expectation was that an Imperial advance into

Walloon General Alexandre Hippolythe Balthazar de Bournonville (1616–1690). He fought for the Emperor in the Thirty Years' War and then for Spain from 1655 to 1659, where he distinguished himself at the Battle of Arras (1654) and at Valenciennes (1656). In 1658, Philip IV of Spain awarded him the title Prince of Bournonville. In 1674, as Imperial commander in Alsace, he failed to achieve success notwithstanding the numerical superiority of the allied army, being defeated by Turenne at Entzheim, Mulhouse and Turckheim. (Author's collection)

---

111 Kortzfleisch, *Der oberelsässische Winterfeldzug 1674–65*, p. 467.
112 A. Cousine, 'La campagne de 1674–1675 du maréchal de Turenne', in *Troisième centenaire de la mort de Turenne. Actes du colloque international sur Turenne et l'art militaire*, Paris, 2–3 October 1975 (1978), pp. 221–234.

Alsace would compel Louis XIV to deploy his army in Franche-Comté for the defence of France's eastern border. The second German army was formed by 25,000 Imperial troops, 9,000 from Münster and 2,000 from Cologne, under the command of the veteran *Feldmarschall* Louis Raduit de Souches. His task was to operate along the Moselle to ensure the protection of Bournonville, and to be ready to join with him or with the Dutch-Spaniards in the Low Countries if required. The allied plan included also the siege of Charleroi, performed by Dutch-Spaniards, in order to interrupt the French supply line between the army and the homeland.

While the allies were still assembling the troops, on 21 May 1674 the French under the Duke of Enghien seized Besançon, completing the conquest of Franche-Comté. This unexpected rapid French conquest of the Spanish province complicated the allies' plans, because the enemy's campaign was effectively at an end, and the bulk of the 15,000-strong invading army was therefore available for operation elsewhere. With the campaign beginning so inauspiciously for the allies, divergences of opinion emerged between the commanders about the campaign in the Low Countries. In late May, the news about the assembling of a 40,000-strong army under Condé, instead of 30,000 as initially believed, posed a serious threat against Namur or Mons. This forced the Dutch-Spanish army to face the enemy advance, but to engage in a battle with numerical inferiority was out of the question. Therefore, there was no other option but to ask Souches to immediately join William III and Monterrey. The allied war council agreed that with more than 60,000 troops, the allies could engage Condé in an open field battle with a reasonable prospect of success. Furthermore, if Condé avoided the engagement, Charleroi could be invested with the Imperialists as an observation army to cover the siege.

William III was intent on seeking out the French and giving battle as soon as the Imperialists had crossed the Meuse at Namur and conjoined with the Dutch-Spanish army. Before the end of May, Souches received letters from the allies to move as soon as possible, but the Imperial commander replied that he would head to Namur, but not with the complete army, because the Aulic War Council was afraid that Louis XIV would further reinforce Turenne and with this army the enemy would subsequently launch an invasion into Anterior Austria or the Swabian circle. Moreover, Bournonville's army was still far from complete and by early June it numbered just 30,000 men. Souches was thus compelled to send part of the Münster contingent to the Upper Rhine, and his own force decreased to 11 infantry and 10 cavalry regiments – just 25,000 men or fewer[113] – because days later he informed the allies that half of the Münster troops had rebelled and deserted.[114]

While the Spaniards were exhorting Souches to move as fast as possible, Condé was amassing food and ammunitions in Le Quesnoy and Ath. Now the allied command expected that Condé could head not only on Mons or Namur, but also even against Ghent, and the fall of this fortress would have seriously put Brussel in danger. Several historians have claimed that

---

113 According to the *Militär-Conversations-Lexikon* (Adorf, 1839), vol. VII, p. 631, in August 1674 Souches would have commanded a force of 12,000 infantry and 15,000 cavalry.
114 A. Marr, 'Der Feldzug im Jahre 1675 in Deutschland…', p. 279.

THE IMPERIAL ARMY ON CAMPAIGN

Souches marched anything but fast and caused the delay of the allies' plan. Furthermore, as stated by Dutch and Spanish sources, he displayed little interest in crossing the Meuse to join the allied army. Obviously, there were more reasons to explain this behaviour. Primarily, shortage of food and fodder had afflicted Souches since April. The Imperial commander also refused to cross the Meuse because in early June Turenne had crossed the right bank of the Rhine at Philippsburg, in search of Bournonville. After this news, the Emperor had ordered Souches to remain on the Meuse's east bank.

For the Imperial side the main campaign was taking place on the German border along the Upper and Lower Rhine. The first encounter in this theatre occurred on 16 June at Sinsheim, between the French under Turenne and an Imperial corps coming from Bohemia. The battle involved 1,500 foot and 6,000 horse under *Feldmarschall-Lieutenant* Enea Silvio Caprara against a similar French force, which had crossed the Rhine at Philippsburg in order to survey the Imperial movements in the area. Turenne surprised the Imperial corps while marching to join the main army in Heidelberg and defeated it after a bitter fight.[115] The Imperial casualties were 2,000 dead and wounded, plus 600 prisoners. In July, the Imperial army was still camped between Frankfurt am Main and Heidelberg. Bournonville hesitated to start the campaign and was still waiting for the arrival of the *Reich* infantry. The delay in the assembling the troops caused serious concerns about supplies and soon the magazines were empty, forcing the soldiers to live from the countryside. Moreover, Bournonville was concerned for the discipline of the troops and their composite provenance:[116] alongside the Imperial troops, the army included contingents from Franconia, Upper Rhine, Münster, Kur-Sachsen, the Palatinate, Brunswick-Lüneburg Celle and Lorraine. The circles' troops were mostly inexperienced, while the Münster soldiers distinguished themselves for their high rate of desertion, so much so that it was necessary to send most of them to Hanau as a garrison.[117]

In July, the French were advancing to Heidelberg, and as soon as the cavalry reconnaissance reported to Bournonville the presence of the advancing enemies, the Imperialists crossed the Neckar and moved the camp north of the River Main. Turenne continued to manoeuvre in the Palatinate and in Upper Rhine, consuming the forage in order to deprive the enemy of this resource and exhorting contributions from towns and villages in the region. In addition to these actions, the French soldiery acted as self-interested marauders, exasperating the population to provoke rebellion. The devastation of the Palatinate of the summer 1674 represented the general test for the one of 1688–89.

In August, Bournonville call for a war council in Frankfurt, and after that Vienna and other German courts pressed him to start the campaign. Finally, in early September, the 36,000-strong army crossed the Rhine at Mainz heading

---

115 *Maréchal* Turenne, who directly participated at the battle, declared that he never saw such a fierce encounter. In Lynn, *The Wars of Louis XIV*, p. 176.
116 Kortzfleisch, *Der Oberelsässische Winterfeldzug 1674–75*, p. 18.
117 *Ibidem*, p. 19.

for Speyer, where it crossed the river again on 17 September. Bournonville led the army south and through the bridge of Kehl entered the Free Imperial City of Strasbourg. The Republic of Strasbourg participated in the formation of the Upper Rhine circle's contingent, but declared itself formally neutral. However, the city council opened the route to Alsace to the Imperialists. On 26 September the Imperial vanguard under Caprara cleared the way, dispersing a small French outpost. Strasbourg offered to Bournonville a good base for an advance into Alsace, but before ordering the march, he awaited the arrival of the 20,000 troops from elector Friedrich Wilhelm of Brandenburg. Bournonville no longer disposed the troops from Electoral Saxony, because the prince did not allow his soldiers to operate outside Germany. Despite this drawback, he expected to enter Alsace with a force larger than the enemy's. To prevent the invasion, Turenne prepared one of his finest masterpieces. The plan was typical of the man, but untypical of the period in imagination and sheer audacity. After his army had swelled to 22,000 men with 30 field guns, with the arrival of reinforcements from Franche-Comté, the great French *maréchal* engaged the enemy with an elusive skirmish and then performed a series of fast marches to confuse his opponent. On 4 October, after a night march, he deployed his army before the village of Holzheim, just four kilometres from Strasbourg, threatening the Imperial supply line coming from the city. Despite being outnumbered, Turenne decided to assault the enemy. In the morning, the French advanced on the opposite village of Entzheim, covered by a thick mist that gave way to rain. Turenne's infantry (which included the English regiments in French service) took advantage of a wood on the left flank to engage the enemy infantry. The Imperial cavalry under *Feldmarschall-Lieutenant* Caprara assaulted the French left flank, opening the way between a wine yard and a wood. The charge prevailed on the first enemy line of cavalry, but the second and third repulsed the Imperialists with a series of effective counter-charges. The battle remained indecisive, but Bournonville realised that the enemy infantry performed better than his troops on the left flank, which included the poorly trained *Reichstruppen*. Therefore, after suffering 3,000 casualties, Bournonville ordered a general retreat, and Turenne did not pursue him.

The Imperialists withdrew to Colmar to enter winter quarters, and finally in late October they gained an important achievement through the union with the Brandenburg army.

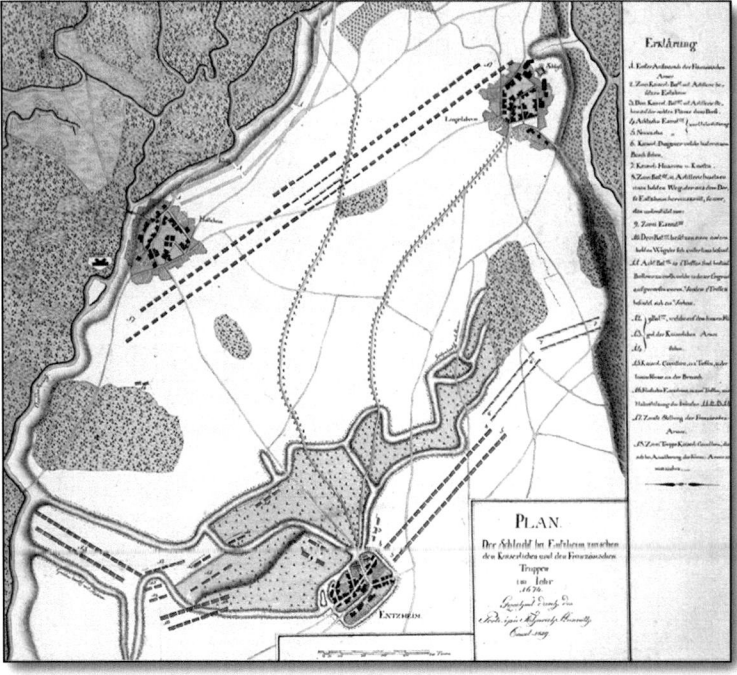

Map of the battle of Entzheim, fought on 4 October 1674, between the Imperialists and allies (above) under *Feldmarschall* Bournonville and the French under Turenne (below). The Imperialists outnumbered the French, but Turenne deployed his troops taking advantage of the natural defences on the ground, and soon prevailed against the less disciplined enemy. (Hessische Staatsarchiv, Marburg)

Bournonville and the Elector Friedrich Wilhelm of Brandenburg could number more than 55,000 men with 50 cannons. On 20 November Turenne, after destroying the castle of Hochfelden and fortifying the village of Saverne, moved to Lower Alsace's more extensive quarters behind the Moder River near Hagenau. The harsh season which had occurred seemed to inhibit the operations of both parts; nobody thought it possible to perform anything else, but Turenne, despite his 64 years, planned otherwise. In great secrecy he assembled all the troops available, and on 29 November, using the Vosges mountains and a cavalry screen to conceal his march, he led them towards the Belfort Gap.

Turenne's arrival took Bournonville by surprise, but the French commander did not take advantage of this, because the need to gather food forced him to halt. The Imperial army and its allies were concentrating in two corps between Colmar and Altkirch. Turenne received this information from interrogation of prisoners, and he determined to force his way between the two groups by advancing through Mulhouse, a free city associated with the Swiss cantons. He could take with him only 3,000 cavalry. A small force of infantry was to follow as rapidly as practicable.

Bournonville hoped to hold the line of the Ill River to gain time for his army to fully assemble. The delay in the French advance allowed the Imperial vanguard to occupy Mulhouse before Turenne arrived. This was part of a cavalry vanguard of 2,000 troops that was marching north from Altkirch towards Colmar under the command of Margrave Hermann of Baden. He was in command of a composite force, including Imperial, Lorraine and Münster cavalry.[118] On 29 December, as soon as Turenne reached the Ill River near Mulhouse, he ordered a reconnaissance of the enemy position. The river was fordable at several points, allowing the French to assault the foremost Imperial squadrons. The battle quickly escalated as Turenne and Baden sent reinforcements. Turenne deployed the cavalry on his right flank in a single line, giving the impression that the whole French army was arriving. The French cavalry advanced with as much sound as possible, with trumpets and kettledrums to deceive their opponents. Suddenly the Imperial cavalry turned and fled into Mulhouse. This led the whole force to withdraw in disorder in several directions; some fled toward Basel to take refuge in Switzerland. Turenne had lost just 60 men, including his cavalry general Montauban, who had been captured. Sources disagree about the Imperial casualties, but these appear to have numbered at least 40 dead and 100 prisoners.[119]

Turenne returned to his main force at Belfort. The French were finally ready to resume the advance in the first days of January. Turenne gathered the army, which now numbered more than 30,000 men, and moved on the enemy's winter quarters near Colmar. For the Imperial side the situation was getting worse day after day. After the defeat at Entzheim there were

---

118 French accounts double this number. See also Kortzfleisch, *Der Oberelsässische Winterfeldzug 1674–75*, p. 189. According to Austrian sources, the average strength of a squadron was about 50 troopers. The cavalry of Münster, formed by 15 companies, deployed just 400 cavalrymen and dragoons. A. Marr, 'Der Feldzug im Jahre 1675 in Deutschland…', p. 280.
119 A. Marr, 'Der Herbstfeldzug Montecuccolis gegen Condé …', p. 130.

just skirmishes between the two sides, but cold weather and inadequate food had considerably reduced the number of men available. The sick were several thousand and desertions took place in large numbers. Moreover, Franconian and Upper-Rhenish troops had been sent to Schwenningen to join the Swabian force. In fact, Turenne had reinforced the garrisons of Hagenau and Breisach. This movement had alarmed Bournonville who feared a French assault in Anterior Austria or in Swabia. Bournonville and the elector Friedrich Wilhelm estimated they could deploy 45,000 men in all. On the afternoon of 5 January 1675, reconnaissance parties informed the allied commanders that Turenne was approaching Colmar. Bournonville and the elector deployed the troops in a strong position, but their forces had not yet been supplied completely to be ready for battle. The French feigned an attack from the centre and then another from their right. While the allies were engaged to face the threat, the actual assault occurred in another sector. Turenne led a third of his army on a march around to his left flank. The movement skirted the mountains and was hidden from the enemy's view because of the terrain. The French captured the small village of Türckheim; the elector tried to retake the town but was defeated by heavy fire from French guns and an infantry charge. Turenne then fell against the extreme right of the enemy. The speed of the attack, which was executed without artillery fire, and the numerical superiority concentrated on a single point, disrupted and demoralised the allies, routing them after suffering 3,400 casualties.

Now, with their winter quarters threatened, the Imperial–Brandenburg army was forced to leave Alsace, and sought the safety of Strasbourg, where in mid January it crossed the Rhine to the right bank and into Germany. Turenne then completed his formidable campaign, taking the last Imperial outpost in Alsace. On 25 January the French advanced to Dachstein, where Bournonville had left a garrison of eight companies – about 1,000 soldiers – of the infantry regiment *Knigge* (II-3). Besieged by eight French battalions with strong artillery, the garrison resisted until 29 January, when finally the general French assault penetrated into Dachstein. All the survivors, 800 soldiers, were captured and transferred to Hagenau.

The campaign in Alsace closed with a substantial defeat. In the other sector, the outcome was equally negative. In July 1674 Souches continued to be reluctant to cross the Meuse to join the Dutch-Spaniards, and to not contravene the instructions received from Vienna. This stipulation conditioned the action of the Imperial *Feldmarschall* during the entire campaign. Though the excess of prudence can partially explain Souches' behaviour, he definitely represented more of an obstacle than a support for his Dutch-Spanish allies.[120] Finally, after an exhausting series of negotiations, in mid July the Imperial cavalry crossed the Meuse and joined the Dutch-Spaniards camped 18 kilometres north of Namur. Now the allies could deploy a very large army of 70,000 men with which to face the outnumbered Condé. After discussing several plans, the allied commanders agreed for an advance south to cross the border, in order to exact contributions in enemy

---

[120] See also in volume one of this series, *The Army of the United Provinces of Netherlands 1660–1687* (Solihull: Helion & Company, 2019), pp. 138–142.

territory and force Condé to accept a battle in unfavourable conditions.[121] This decision led to the bloody battle of Seneffe, fought on 11 August 1674. Because the encounter started with the French attack on the rear of the allied marching army, the Imperialists, who proceeded in the vanguard, were partially involved in the fight. The infantry remained unengaged except four regiments and just the cavalry actually participated in the action supporting the allies in the last phase of the battle. The Imperial losses were low, but the allies suffered heavy casualties. Dutch-Spaniards, Imperialists and French remained in their positions for almost a month; then, notwithstanding the terrible losses suffered at Seneffe, the allies resumed the campaign. On 9 September, after agreeing with William III to lay siege to Ath, Souches rejected this plan and offered to support the allies in besieging Oudenarde, but another time Souches caused the failure of the allied operations.[122] On 16 September 1674, the allied army arrived before Oudenarde and the opening of the trenches followed a day later. On 18 September, during the siege, Souches gave order to abandon the trenches, declaring the ammunition to be exhausted.

This unprecedented action caused consternation among the Dutch and Spaniards and their great indignation forced Leopold I to replace Souches with Montecuccoli, even in poor health. In 1675, the aged 66-year-old *Feldmarschall-General* took command on the Rhine, but for the incoming campaign there was no chance to support the allies in the Low Countries, because the Swedish attack on Brandenburg turned part of the available troops to this new war theatre.[123] Another Imperial corps, under Grana del Carretto, was assigned to the Moselle alongside Brunswick-Lüneburg and Lorraine troops.

The condition of the troops was very bad. In early February, Bournonville wrote to Vienna informing the Aulic War Council that the regiments were reduced to a miserable state.[124] After the departure of the Brandenburg army to face the Swedish invasion, the Imperial army numbered less than 10,000 men.[125] The optimistic expectations of the 1674 campaign had been cancelled. The French still held the strategic advantage derived from their possessions on the Rhine, to which they could add Trier, occupied since 1673. In February, Margrave Hermann of Baden had entrenched some villages leaving the

---

121 The Imperial *Feldmarschall* submitted an alternative plan. He proposed to invest Dinant, in the bishopric of Liége but held by the French, with his army and part of the Dutch-Spanish force. Both the Dutch and Spanish commanders rejected this proposal, because the conquest of Dinant would have no effect on the strategic situation in the Low Countries. William III proposed to reinforce the Imperial army with 17–18,000 Dutch and Spanish soldiers, but just to siege Rocroi. The conquest of this place would clear the way to invest Charleville, a fortified town on either side of the Meuse River, on which Souches had already turned his attention. In exchange for this offer, William III expected that Souches would have crossed the Meuse with his cavalry in order to ensure the conjunction with the allied army. See in Nimwegen, *The Dutch Army*, p. 481.
122 See also in *Wars and Soldiers in the Early Reign of Louis XIV. The Army of the United Provinces of the Netherlands* (Solihull: Helion & Company, 2019), p. 144.
123 To Pomerania marched 4,000 Imperial troops under *Feldmarschall-Lieutenant* Georg Christian von Hessen-Homburg.
124 'L'armée est tout-à-fait misérable', in Kortzfleisch, *Der Oberelsässische Winterfeldzug 1674–75*, p.102.
125 A. Marr, 'Der Feldzug im Jahre 1675 in Deutschland …', p. 270.

infantry of the circles before Breisach to guard the French movements from there; while another corps of 4,000 foot under *Feldmarschall-Lieutenant* Adolph of Schleswig-Holstein was stationed in Upper Rhine before Trier, with the task of blockading the city and besieging it, together with the forces that Charles IV of Lorraine was gathering in Germany and Lorraine.

The main army was located between Ulm and the River Neckar, waiting for the arrival of new troops and recruits to fill the weakened regiments. In mid May, the Imperial army numbered 18,000 foot and 14,000 horse.[126] Considering this force balanced, on 16 May Montecuccoli marched with the vanguard to Oberkirch, before Strasbourg, and while waiting for the arrival of the incoming troops, established headquarters at Willstätt. Days later, the arrival of the Imperial cavalry at Kehl alarmed the French, who assembled troops near Sélestat, approximately 20,000 foot and 15,000 horse,[127] and marched to Strasbourg to impede the crossing of the Rhine. As Montecuccoli approached the east bank of the Rhine, Turenne advised the Strasbourg magistrates not to allow passage to the Imperial army. Cavalry reconnaissance spotted the French near Strasbourg and this persuaded Montecuccoli to operate a diversion on Philippsburg, in order to move Turenne from there and to cross the Rhine somewhere else.

On 1 June, the Imperialists crossed the Rhine near Speyer. Surely, both the two great generals would have shared Napoleon's claim that 'The best soldier is not the one who fights, but the one who marches.' Mindful of what happened in 1673, this time Turenne anticipated his enemy and gathered the troops from the winter quarters. With half of the army still to cross the river, Montecuccoli interrupted the march and turned back to the right bank. Turenne decided to follow and crossed the Rhine days later. The European gazettes proclaimed this action as an Imperial defeat.[128] The court of Versailles too exalted the event as a major victory:

> It is said that Montecuculi [*sic*] would have humbly passed the Rhine and that Monsieur de Turenne, for an excess of kindness, would have made him cross it again, and then pass it after him. The head must turn a lot to our poor enemies: the sight of Monsieur Turenne overturns them![129]

Now the two armies marched into Baden. Turenne made camp at Offenburg, but Montecuccoli did not yet consider it the right moment to engage in battle. At the end of June, the French army lacked forage, and also for the Imperialists the need for forage and food become urgent. For this reason,

---

126 Bérenger, *Turenne*, p. 411.
127 J. Lynn, *Wars of Louis XIV, 1667–1714* (New York NY: Routledge, 2013), p. 190.
128 On this campaign, as indeed for many other episodes of the Franco-Dutch War, there are many conflicting reports. Propaganda exercised considerable weight in formulating judgments and even when a battle ended with a tactical defeat, the commentators could overturn the outcome on the strategic plan. The campaign of 1675 between Montecuccoli and Turenne has been the subject of many recent studies, but even in this case there is a completely different reconstruction of the facts. Among the most relevant cases see Jean Bérenger's *Turenne*, and a classic such as John Lynn's *Wars of Louis XIV*.
129 Bérenger, *Turenne*, p. 412: letter of Madame Sevigne.

on 5 July, Montecuccoli moved south with the intention of throwing a pontoon bridge for re-supplying the army in Strasbourg. He left 5,000 men under Caprara to hold Offenburg. In response, Turenne immediately followed him while keeping a garrison in Willstätt, north of Strasbourg, with troops dispatched from Hagenau. On 6 July, Montecuccoli found the road blocked and immediately after that was warned of Turenne's arrival, which was about two kilometres from Willstätt. By this time desertion, disease and other accident had decreased each army to an approximate strength of 25,000 men.[130] Both sides suffered from supply problems and from the weather. Horses were reduced to eating leaves, and the troops suffered under continuous rain. While the armies marked time waiting for better weather, on 22 July the rain diminished and Turenne began a turning manoeuvre that sought to pin Montecuccoli against the Rhine. The French vanguard engaged the Imperials at Gamshurst but was driven off. Montecuccoli planned an attack of his own on 23, but this was hampered by fog. The day after, both the armies marched along the way between Offenburg and Rastatt. On 26 July the French found the Imperial army entrenching around the village of Salsbach, behind a stream of the same name, on a small plain at the foot of the mountains. The Imperial baggage train could be seen moving into the wood beyond the village. Montecuccoli took advantage of hedges and woods in protecting his troops, and placed musketeers in the village church and an old castle on his right flank. The Imperial commander had to hold this position because he was waiting for Caprara to join him. This officer was slow in arriving, however, because the presence of the French army had forced him to take a long march through the foothills.

27 July 1675 seems to be the day on which the campaign would be resolved with a great battle, the first between the two commanders after more than 30 years. Turenne was confident because he had fewer problems than his opponent, who was now nearly without supplies. The terrain, crossed by streams, woods and orchards, guaranteed a relative safety to the defenders, and on the contrary hindered the attackers. In the morning, the cavalry in the vanguards engaged in a fight in which the Imperialists prevailed, occupying the wood of Niederasbach. Charles V of Lorraine led the action, with cuirassier regiments *Montecuccoli* (IC-4), *Sporck* (IC-6), *Lothringen* (IC-7) and dragoon regiments *Chavaignac* (ID-9) and *Trautmannsdorf* (ID-7), 13 companies in all.[131] Imperial reports on the campaigns noticed a captain of the cuirassier regiment Heister (IC-9), who defeated an elite French cavalry unit. *General Wachtmeister* Dünewald assaulted an enemy outpost and dispersed it after killing 150 soldiers.[132] Now only a stream separated the two armies. At two o'clock in the afternoon Turenne, as usual, was together with his staff for reconnaissance. With eight other officers, he headed for a hill overlooking the valley. A cannon shot of 3 lb, fired from a few hundred metres, hit Turenne, killing him instantly. The same bullet removed the left

---

130 Lynn, *Wars of Louis XIV*, p. 140.
131 *Relations de ce qui s'est passé depuis quelque temps entre les deus Armées l'Impériale & Françoise, faite par un officier de l'Armée Impériale*, MDCLXXV, p. 8.
132 *Ibidem*.

The death of Henry de la Tour d'Auvergne, Vicomte de Turenne, occurred at Salsbach on 27 July 1675. The great French *maréchal* and Montecuccoli had been enemies since the Thirty Years' War. In the campaign of 1673, Montecuccoli outmanoeuvred his great rival on the Neckar and the Rhine, joined his army with the troops of the Prince of Orange on the lower Rhine, and captured Bonn. He retired in 1674, when the 'Great Elector' Friedrich Wilhelm of Brandenburg was appointed as commander-in-chief of the allied army on the Rhine. The brilliant successes of Turenne brought him back one year later. In the campaign of 1675, the two famous commanders manoeuvred for months against each other in the Rhine valley, but on the eve of a decisive battle Turenne was killed and the French army retreated. Engraving of Johann Ulrich Krauss (1655–1710) after a drawing of Johann Waldtmann (1672–1710). (Author's collection)

arm of his nephew, the Chevalier de Saint-Hilaire, *lieutenant-general* of the artillery.

For 48 hours the two armies faced each other without engaging in a fight. Then Montecuccoli learned from a deserter the news of Turenne's death: 'Today died a man who did honour to the whole of mankind', he said as an epitaph.[133] On the night between 29 and 30 July the French retreated. Montecuccoli decided to attack the retreating enemy columns. The enemy baggage train was stationed in the nearby village of Willstätt; hoping to capture it and re-establish direct communication with Strasbourg, a force of Imperial dragoons and cavalry unsuccessfully attacked on 29 July. After an initial confusion in the French command, Turenne's lieutenants Vaubrun and de Lorge compromised by agreeing to rotate command daily. The French army moved towards the pontoon bridge over the Rhine at Altenheim. Montecuccoli followed up, once more threatening to take Willstätt and the French supplies. Disputes between the French commanders caused delay, and this left the army divided when night came on 31 July, with Vaubrun's vanguard on the left side of the Rhine and the rest under de Lorges yet to cross. To reach the Rhine, de Lorges' troops had to first cross a small tributary called the Schutter. As they began to cross the river on 1 August, Montecuccoli attacked, while simultaneously cutting off their retreat by taking the bridge at Altenheim. Vaubrun, who held the command that day, counter-attacked and ejected the Imperialists from Altenheim, but he was killed in action.[134] The fighting ended in the evening, with both sides withdrawing. The French claimed about 3,000 casualties for their side against 4,500 Imperialists; on the contrary, these latter would have inflicted on the French more than 6,000 dead, wounded and prisoners; six standards too are mentioned as war trophies alongside 30,000 bread rations, against just 600 Imperial casualties.[135]

The death of Turenne had compromised the French campaign on the Rhine, forcing Louis XIV to replace the great *maréchal* with Condé from the Low Countries. The most important thing was that now the road to Kehl and Alsace was finally free for Montecuccoli, and with it the possibility of supplying his tired and hungry troops.

By the end of August, Montecuccoli deployed 18 infantry battalions with a force of 11,233 men, and 65 cavalry squadrons with 11,701 men.[136] Overall, the Imperial Rhine army numbered 22,934 men, but the need for garrisons in Swabia, Upper Rhine and Bonn decreased the available strength to 17,000 men.[137] Before the end of the month, further recruits increased the regiments' strength with 896 foot and 222 horse. A second objective under

---

133 The artilleryman who had fired, a certain Koch, asked the Emperor for a noble investiture. Marr, 'Der Feldzug im Jahre 1675…', p. 120.
134 The French rearguard included the English regiments. A French officer who participated in the battle described this action in his 'Memoirs' as one of the most glorious in the history of France. *Mémoires de M. le marquis de Feuquière* (Paris, 1765), p. 86.
135 *Relations*, p. 15.
136 The effective force of 11 infantry and 17 cavalry regiments. Marr, 'Der Feldzug 1675 in Deutschland…', p. 121.
137 *Ibidem.*

the care of Montecuccoli was the provision of food from the magazines of Strasbourg, which the Magistrate promised to deliver against payment by the Emperor.[138] Sadly, the treasury's coffers were nearly empty. Montecuccoli and the *Proviant* Director Count Capliers exhausted themselves in their reports, declaring the impossibility of planning any operation without money. In late August, Montecuccoli received just a part of the promised money with which he paid the troops and provided foodstuff to the magazines.

Despite this drawback, the campaign was turning in favour of the allies, who had achieved another important success in the battle of Konzer Brücke, fought on 11 August 1675. The Imperialists under Charles IV of Lorraine and Ottone Grana del Carretto, alongside troops from Germany and Lorraine, had repulsed the French corps led by *maréchal* François de Créquy, who attempted to relieve the besieged Trier.[139] The victory accelerated the conquest of the city, which surrendered in early September. Montecuccoli received letters from Vienna that insisted on the invasion of Alsace, and from the Dutch-Spaniards requesting a common plan against the French outposts on the Meuse and opening another front in the Moselle area.

Montecuccoli followed the Emperor's advice and moved through Strasbourg heading for Alsace. On 6 August the Imperial vanguard under Dünewald arrived at Kehl with 1,000 horses to catch up with news regarding the enemy. Here he heard that the French were located between Sélestat and Entzheim. He performed a reconnaissance, and near Molsheim dispersed a French 150-strong horse party. On 8 September the main army crossed the Rhine at Strasbourg, and after this Condé, who had established his headquarters at Entzheim, transferred the army to Bielefeld, avoiding the battle. Montecuccoli sent a cavalry corps under *General Wachtmeister* Gaspard de Chavagnac to Hagenau for the blockade of the fortress, but days later, after receiving news about the strong French garrison inside,[140] he turned his attention to another target. On 10 September the Imperialists laid siege to Saverne, but abandoned the action days later because of the unexpected defence of the garrison, and the French cavalry that menaced the supply line with continuous raids, which engaged the Imperialist cavalry in two violent fights on 12 and 15 September.

In early October Montecuccoli took winter quarters, displacing the troops on both banks of the Rhine, in Alsace and in Baden. For Montecuccoli this was the last campaign, as it was for Condé on the opposite side. The

---

138 *Ibidem*, p. 125. Half of the 100,000 *guilders* expected from the domains were still negotiated by the bankers in Württemberg at unfavourable rates. A further 10,000 *guilders* were demanded by the Swiss magistrates for refunding the expenditure after the recovering of the Imperial troops in Basel, whose preservation the Emperor had taken over.

139 The order of battle comprised: Imperialists: 26 Infantry and four dragoon companies under *General Wachtmeister* Grana del Carretto (2,500 men); Spaniards under Louvigny (2,000 men), Brunswick-Lüneburg, eight infantry and five cavalry regiments with 10 companies of dragoons, under Duke Georg Wilhelm of Brunswick-Lüneburg (13,000 men), Münster, five infantry battalions under General Granvilliers (3,000 men), Mainz, four regiments under the Count of Lippe (2,000 men), Trier, 2,000 men under the Baron of Leyen; Lorraine with the *Gardes*, four cavalry and two dragoon regiments under colonel Grondeur (3,500 men), overall 8,000 men. *Ibidem*, p. 123.

140 Quincy, *Histoire Militaire du regne de Louis le Grand Roy de France* (Paris, 1726), vol. i, p. 450.

health conditions of both commanders were much worse. The tone of the last letters written by Montecuccoli often alludes to the difficulty of maintaining command because of the strong pains that prevented him from marching on horseback. After proposing as his successor to the command the young and promising Charles V of Lorraine, Montecuccoli retired to his Austrian possession of Hohenegg. On 16 October 1680, after following the Imperial court to Lienz to escape the plague epidemic coming from Hungary, the *generalissimo* died. Condé would survive him by five years.[141]

For the campaign of 1676, Louis XIV assembled five armies. The largest army operated in the Spanish Low Countries under valiant commanders, but also another skilful general, the maréchal François Henri de Montmorency-Bouteville, Duke of Luxembourg, commanded the troops destined for Alsace. The allies' efforts were no less important. In the Low Countries, the Dutch-Spaniards aimed to assault Maastricht with 40,000 men, while the Imperialists assembled troops in Upper Rhine for besieging Philippsburg. Montecuccoli had already prepared the way to besiege the city, in possession of the French since 1644, by fortifying Lauterbourg and other outposts on the left bank of the Rhine. He had pursued this achievement after realising there was a lack of manpower for a successful defence on the Rhine. Thus, the Imperial general was compelled to develop new methods to hold the river line by enhancing the natural protection afforded by the terrain. By 1675, Montecuccoli had conscripted thousands of peasants to construct field fortifications to bar possible crossing points and block the Black Forest passes. These defences, called *Linien* (lines), were to become a major feature of Imperial defence also in the following conflicts. In their most sophisticated form, as perfected until the War of the Spanish Succession, they consisted of interconnected earth walls and ditches, redoubts and gun batteries, palisades and blockhouses that stretched for 90 kilometres or more.[142] The defensive preparations were accompanied by an intensified use of outposts. Small detachments were scattered along the lines, natural obstacles and fortified villages and towns formed a protective cordon to watch enemy movements and prevent contribution raids into the territory behind. Originally intended to screen winter quarters, these 'lines' became a permanent part of Imperial defence during the Franco-Dutch War.

Skirmish and cavalry encounters on both sides of the Rhine opened the campaign of 1676 in late May, but a major encounter occurred in June. After he left Strasbourg, the Duke of Lorraine entered Alsace anticipating the enemy, but Luxembourg, having learned about the forthcoming arrival of reinforcements from Flanders, did not oppose the crossing of the Rhine and awaited for an encounter. The news concerning the reinforcements

---

141 Another important Imperial commander died in 1675: Duke Charles IV of Lorraine, depriving the army of a valiant chief. His death opened the way to his nephew, Prince Charles, later Duke Charles V, as heir to Lorraine's throne.
142 Wilson, *German Armies*, p. 55. 'The impact on the local community and physical environment was considerable. No less than 1.6 million m3 of earth had to be moved during the construction of the 86 km. long Eppingen Lines in 1695–7. Traces of the ditches and banks survived into the twentieth century. Swaths of forest were cut down for use in construction or to create entanglements of sharpened branches up to 100 m across.'

General Wachtmeister Johann Rudolph Wertmüller (1614–1677). The aged Swiss officer directed the artillery during the siege of Philippsburg. Wertmüller was a veteran who had previously served in the French and Venetian armies before entering Imperial service in 1673. He wears an old-fashioned coat with plain cuffs and pockets placed unusually high; the ribbon on the right shoulder is the only decorative accessory. Unlike their German or foreign colleagues, Swiss officers often had a beard. (Author's collection)

arrived also with Lorraine, who sent a cavalry corps under *General Wachtmeister* Dünewald to know the enemy position and to seize the roads to Saverne in order to intercept the reinforcements. Imperial reconnaissance sighted the French encamped near Saverne. Luxembourg realised that the arrival of the reinforcements was under threat, and the enemy's strength was greater than his army.[143] On the night of 8/9 June the French commander decided to leave the encampment and head north, after deploying a detachment of infantry and dragoons to cover the march. Immediately, Lorraine marched to follow him. In the morning, the Imperial cavalry assaulted the French troops guarding the passage south to Saverne and forced them to retreat. Luxembourg sent his cavalry squadrons to engage and arrest the advancing enemy. Soon, the initial skirmish turned in a violent fight and both sides suffered heavy casualties. Among the losses, the French claimed the death of Colonel George Hamilton, commander of the English regiment in French service, while the Imperialists lost two companies of the regiment *Dünewald* (IC-26), taken prisoners.[144]

The French continued the march to join the reinforcements coming from Kockelsberg, while Lorraine's army moved to Strasbourg, which continued to favour the allied cause, and where the Imperial commissars were assembling all the necessaries for besieging Philippsburg.

On 22 June 1676, at the end of a week of manoeuvres to conceal their real objective, the Imperial vanguard under *General Wachtmeister* Prince Ludwig of Baden blocked the roads around Philippsburg. The fortress had a garrison of about 2,800 men under governor Dufay,[145] while the Imperialists numbered 32–33,000 men. Charles V of Lorraine divided the troops into two corps.[146] He left direction of the siege to Baden, assisted by the expert *General Wachtmeister* Rudolph Wertmüller, and with the rest of the army prepared to cover the besiegers. The approach trenches were opened in the night between 24 and 25 June, the Duke of Lorraine prepared a strong defence with an extensive entrenched countervallation. This measure was revealed to be very effective when on 6 August Luxembourg arrested the march of the relief corps four kilometres from the Imperial positions, but declined to assault it. The

---

143 Quincy, *Histoire Militaire*, vol. I, p. 490.
144 Wrede, *Geschichte der K. und K. Wehrmacht*, vol. III, part one, p. 165.
145 2,298 foot and 466 horse with 100 guns, *Hollandse Mercurius*, April 1676, p. 67.
146 *Ibidem*, 18,000 foot, 14,000 horse (including cavalry of Lorraine) and artillery.

THE IMPERIAL ARMY ON CAMPAIGN

Charles V of Lorraine (1643–1690) In 1683, on the eve of the siege of Vienna, the man who was preparing to led the Imperial army in the crucial campaign was aged 40. According to the judgment of many contemporaries, the appearance of the Duke was that of an insignificant man with poor health, not completely recovered from the wounds received in war. Jan Sobieski described the Duke when he met him in 1683: 'He has an aquiline nose, almost like the one of a parrot; he is pockmarked and his back is bent. He wears unadorned grey clothes (except for some new golden buttons adorned with brocade). His hat is without feathers, and boots that have not been polished for months, with cork heels. His wig (a rotten one!) is fair in colour. His horse is not bad and he rides with an old saddle and trappings of worn and poor quality leather. It is obvious that the Duke is not very interested in his appearance, but he has the bearing not like a merchant or an Italian, but of a quality person […] who deserves better luck.'

Surely, his appearance hid his devotion to the task and his attitude of making difficult decisions. Montecuccoli's legacy could represent a disvantage for him. The Italian general had been a savant, a war hero, and possessed of a steely temperament. Dead, he had no obvious replacement. Lorraine, whom the old general had respected, was not the natural substitute but the best available. He also possessed a quality that his old patron had lacked: charm and diplomacy. Lorraine was no great military thinker like Montecuccoli, and, despite his status as a royal prince and being connected to the Habsburgs by marriage, he was a most unlikely courtier. However, he elicited respect as an honest and courageous man, both calm and decisive. (Author's collection)

Company standard, regiment *Lothringen Cuirassieren* (IC-7), 1676. According to the biography of Duke Charles V of Lorraine, when he was appointed commander-in-chief of the Imperial army on the Rhine, he issued to his regiment green standards with silver embroideries and the motto 'Now or Never'. (Author's illustration)

siege progressed, notwithstanding a fierce defence. Baden and Wertmüller advanced with the approaches from east and west. On 8 September, a wide breach was opened in the bastion of Anguin, on the east side of the curtain. The day after, pressed by the shortage of ammunition and with just 1,500 soldiers available, Dufay opened talks for an honourable surrender.

The conquest of Philippsburg was widely celebrated in Austria and considered decisive to the outcome of the war, despite the fact that Luxembourg, unopposed, had collected contributions in Baden and Lorraine. The celebration was also useful to hide the failures in Hungary against the rebels. In winter 1676–77 concerns and growing military expense convinced the Imperial diplomacy to open talks for a general peace with France. As a result, the economic resources for the army on the Rhine considerably diminished, leaving the regiments under strength. Now Lorraine had approximately 35,000 Imperial troops, including the *Reichstruppen*, barely enough to maintain the garrisons in Philippsburg, Trier, Bonn, and the outposts along the Rhine from the Breisgau to Cologne.

However, the start of negotiations did not slow down operations. After reinforcing the garrison of Philippsburg, the Duke of Lorraine headed toward Strasbourg threatening an invasion into Alsace. Luxembourg, who had dispatched a corps under François de Créquy in Lorraine, moved the army behind the Vosges, realising that his forces were unable to hold the line of the Rhine. In mid April 1677, the Imperial field army entered Alsace with about 26,000 men. After leaving 4,000 men to secure the road to Strasbourg under *Feldmarschall-Lieutenant* Johann Georg of Saxe-Eisenach, Lorraine marched north for the Moselle. In May, Créquy, who had replaced Luxembourg as commander in Alsace-Lorraine, gathered 15,000 men and left Nancy, moving against the advancing Imperialists. He and Lorraine met on 15 May and engaged in a long duel with a series of manoeuvres, but always avoiding the battle. Realising that his move did not obtain the hoped result, on 15 June the Duke of Lorraine crossed the Seille at Nomeny and marched on Pont-à-Mousson. The French settled on the heights bordering the Moselle and the Seille, while the Imperial troops were marching in the valley at Morville. An artillery duel began the day after, but the French took advantage of their dominant position. Lorraine did not dare to attack the enemy positions and withdrew at night to return to Baden. The Imperial commander was far from joining the Dutch-Spaniards for the common objective of besieging Charleroi. By mid July most of the Imperial army was spread out between the villages of Gengenbach and Lahr, with a forward outpost at Denzlingen. In August the campaign seemed destined to fail, and Lorraine, distressed by the lack of troops, was unable to prevent his opponent from joining part of his forces with those in Alsace to attack Saxe-Eisenach on 7 September. Outnumbered by the French, the Imperialists retired from Strasbourg pursued by their enemies. Créquy advanced and occupied Offenburg. On 21 September, before the arrival of Charles of Lorraine, Saxe-Eisenach was surprised by the French and defeated near Gengenbach. Then, Créquy again crossed the Rhine to repair to Alsace, eluding Lorraine, who could only engage the enemy rearguard with the cavalry, at Klockersberg on 7 October. In late October, the Imperialists were preparing winter quarters behind Strasbourg and did not prevent the French advance into Breisgau, leaving a free hand to Créquy for an assault on Freiburg, which surrendered on 16 November.

The last year of the war saw the fiercest campaigns of the conflict. Although the main duel still took place in the Spanish Low Countries, a fierce struggle

THE IMPERIAL ARMY ON CAMPAIGN

began on the Rhine theatre to take over strategically important places in anticipation of the peace negotiations that were closing in Nijmegen. Notwithstanding the chronic shortage of supply and funds and with the regiments far from being completed, Lorraine began the operation earlier than usual. The plan agreed with the allies provided that the Imperialists would operate a diversion in Lorraine, for besieging Thionville or other forts in French hands, to threaten the enemy in the Low Countries from the south. The offensive also served to divert French attention on Charleroi, an objective that the Dutch-Spaniards wanted to achieve as soon as possible.[147] Surely, the occasion of challenging his opponents in the country from which his family had been driven by the hated French king represented an important incentive for the Imperial commander. On 13 April 1678 about 20,000 Imperialists crossed the Rhine at Strasbourg and occupied Bitche and Saarbrucken. Here the Imperial troops destroyed the French supply facilities, causing the firing of the city. Immediately Créquy moved on the Seille (a tributary of the Moselle) to block the way with the main army. Lorraine headed east in an attempt to attire the opponents, but Créquy planned for an assault in Baden with part of his army. In early May, after crossing the Rhine, the French commander dispatched some troops on the road to Rheinfelden to reduce the remaining Imperial strongpoints, and as a retaliation for Saarbrucken, ordered the destruction of Bad Säckingen. Then he returned to Bad Krozingen, 15 kilometres south-west of Freiburg.

In early June, Lorraine assembled the field army at Offenburg, now increased to about 24,000 men, behind the Kinzig River, a tributary of the Rhine providing a natural defence barrier. Then, he divided the army in three corps, which marching on different roads headed south. The main objective was the reconquest of Freiburg and this was certainly guessed by Créquy, who had prepared counter-measures. The Imperial commander tried to find a weak point in the French defences around the city, until a delay in supply and the lack of forage forced him to fall back on Offenburg. Créquy had received reinforcements from Flanders and in the middle of June he moved south towards Rheinfelden and to the border with Switzerland. Lorraine chased him with the main army and dispatched a 'flying corps' of 5,000 men under

On 1st August 1675, Montecuccoli engaged the French army at Altenheim and notwithstanding the indecisive outcome of the battle, invaded Alsace, where he faced another famous French commander, Louis II de Bourbon, best known as the Grand Condé. (Author's collection)

---

147 Nimwegen, *The Dutch Army*, p. 498.

The Siege of Philippsburg, in a contemporary print with the deployment of the besieging Imperial army. The French resistance lasted 76 days (*Theatrum Europeaum*, vol. XI, Frankfurt 1682).

General Wachtmeister Maximilian Lorenz von Starhemberg, who arrived in Rheinfelden on 6 July anticipating the enemy. The French were in numbers too superior to the Imperialists, who were forced to retreat with losses. The plan of Lorraine, who wanted to attack Créquy from two sides, had therefore failed due to the lack of troops. On 23 July the French attempted to cross the Kinzig but were prevented by the Imperial cavalry who defeated the French vanguard at Ortenbach. However, Lorraine refused to commit his forces to a general engagement and retreated to Oberkirch. This move was a fatal error, because it cut off his army from the Rhine, leaving Créquy free to seize Kehl on 27 July after two days of siege. Before leaving Kehl, Créquy destroyed the strategic bridge and the fortifications and finally threatened Strasbourg's magistrates. Then on 8 August he crossed the Rhine at Altenheim on pontoons and turned to Strasbourg to complete the destruction of the bridge on the western side.

For the Imperial side, the war was entering its fifth year. The costs and devastation caused by the passage of the armies had been enormous, pushing the most exposed states of the Empire to enlarge the party that demanded the immediate cessation of hostilities. The Imperial army, which had little money, turned to the states close to the war theatre to collect resources and billets, with serious consequences for the local population. By summer

1678, the situation was unsustainable. The Empire's collective defence now existed only on paper, reducing the Imperial army to the Emperor's own contingent and the auxiliaries supplied under bilateral arrangement. Lorraine, large parts of the Rhine Electoral, and half the Upper Rhine circles were occupied by the French, Swabia and Franconia refused to cooperate, while Bavaria's participation remained restricted to Salzburg. Any further support could come from other German states, mostly favourable to an agreement with Louis XIV. Lower Saxony was almost exclusively controlled by the three Brunswick duchies, with Westphalia and Upper Saxony split between Münster and Brandenburg, and Brandenburg and Electoral Saxony respectively.

The Dutch Republic signed the peace with France on 10 August 1678. Spain followed on 19 September, but Emperor Leopold continued to delay the peace in the hope of gaining some places. By this time, attrition and disease had reduced the army to an approximate strength of 20,000 men. Lorraine crossed back to the left bank of the Rhine at Philippsburg but found Créquy once again blocking his advance. In late September, the Imperial commander admitted the impossibility of continuing the campaign and withdrew to Upper Rhine. The war between France and the House of Austria was over and hostilities were suspended. The peace between France and the Holy Roman-Germanic Empire was signed on 26 January 1679, and Emperor Leopold I signed the treaty of Nijmegen on 2 February.

Prelude to Vienna, 1682–83

In the nine-month period between September 1681 and June 1682, the Viennese court had received three lots of bad news. The Sun King had occupied Strasbourg, then in northern Italy a French garrison had entered Casale in Monferrato, putting the Spanish possessions in Lombardy into a state of apprehension; and finally the Hungarian malcontents had resumed their struggle, frustrating the hopes arisen after the new truce convened at Szoboszló. The Papal party, however, marked a success and with it the German one, because the orientation of Rome was to find a solution in the Rhine area that would put an end to or at least suspend the disputes between the Christian states, although for Vienna it meant to bow to the French demands. The Hungarian question had to be resolved by force: as in Strasbourg the French occupation had strengthened the Catholic presence in the area, and even in Hungary the Habsburg offensive would have wiped away the hated Lutherans and Calvinists from the country. The epilogue went in the direction desired by the French diplomacy, because at that point the Hungarian rebels would have asked for the protection of the Porte. The Grand Vizier who succeeded Köprülü Ahmed appeared even less willing to negotiate. Merzifonlu Kara Mustafa, as resolute and despotic as his cousin Ahmed, embodied the archetype of the Ottoman ruling man, equally ruthless with enemies as, if necessary, with friends. The truce signed in Vasvár was still in force, because the 20 years of non-belligerence would have expired in 1684, but the formal reason to break the armistice was offered by Leopold's old enemy, Imre Thököly. The Grand Vizier threatened to intervene to support the right of the Hungarian prince, leader of the *Kuruc* league. On 7 July 1682 the Hungarian rebels seized the fortress of Kassa, taking prisoner the Imperial garrison and *General Wachtmeister* Ferdinand von Herberstein. This action reopened the crisis in Hungary and the events that followed provided Constantinople with the pretext to declare war against Austria on 6 August. Kara Mustafa had set the war in motion, and Leopold I would have been obliged to respond. The Porte and the House of Austria were now linked in a series of events from which there was no certain outcome.

The Habsburgs believed that they possessed a battle-hardened army, which, despite Montecuccoli's death in 1680, was still led by men who had learned their trade under his command. The Emperor and his councillors reassured themselves with comfortable memories of the victory at Szentgotthárd, proclaiming full confidence in the newly appointed *General-Lieutenant*, the Emperor's brother-in-law, Charles V of Lorraine. The new commander-in-chief was aged 40, but he seemed older because of poor health aggravated by wounds received in battle. In 1682 he was in semi-retirement, as the governor of Tyrol, in Innsbruck. Asked about the possible campaign in Hungary against the Ottomans, the Duke had expressed his belief in engaging the enemies on the field, facing them at the right time, as Montecuccoli did in 1664. Unfortunately, in 1682, many in Vienna were convinced that the Ottomans, although capable of gathering impressive forces, would not be able to launch an offensive capable of prevailing over the network of fortresses on the border. Moreover, the court relied too heavily on the militia of the Hungarian magnates loyal to Vienna and continued to believe in exaggerated estimates of the numerical strength of these contingents.

Furthermore, the Duke had to act in a context unfavourable to him, due to the hostility of many at court and of his fellow generals. The greatest difficulties lay in the scarce understanding he had with the Aulic War Council. There was a profound and irreducible rivalry between Hermann von Baden and Lorraine. After the death of Montecuccoli the presidency of the Aulic War Council had passed to the Margrave, who also expected to become commander-in-chief of the army, while the the younger Duke of Lorraine had assumed that position. This outcome was deplored by Baden, who openly opposed all the commander's advice. Like the Duke, Baden had been a field-general in the 1664 campaign under Montecuccoli and presumably knew the strategic scenario well, which appeared to him substantially unchanged. He was aware that a strong defence behind the line of strongpoints along the border would have held the enemy far from Vienna. His vision was supported by the fact that compared to 19 years ago the Imperial army could display more troops and stronger defences. Unwisely, the presidency of the Aulic War Council underestimated the threat coming from Transylvania and Upper Hungary, while continuing to support the negotiations with Thököly in order to find a reasonable agreement. Apart from the difference between official and effective strength, presumably Baden did not take into account in his calculations the forces available on the eastern border, where the fortress with the largest number of men, 1,700, was Szatmár and with perhaps another

3,000 represented the total available in the region.¹⁴⁸ The whole sector was under threat not only from the Ottomans, but also from Thököly, who could stop reinforcements and supplies from the west at any time.

Despite the eastern border continuing to be a concern for the Aulic War Council, Baden and the other councillors were distracted by the events in Germany and did not realise in time that the arrival of a large enemy army in Hungary would have completely changed the strategic scenario. No garrison, even defended by modern fortresses, could have arrested a preponderant force like the one that was being prepared in Constantinople. At first, in order to control the frontier sector closest to Vienna, Baden estimated the need for a corps of 10,000 men under the *Feldmaschall-Lieutenant* Johann Valentin von Schültz, with the task of controlling the roads from the Váh River to Leopoldstadt. On his right, guarding the routes from Győr to Körmend, the Hungarian militia under Eszterházy and Batthyány could be deployed. Another 1,600 cavalry and 3,000 infantry would have controlled the next area behind the Mur River, and from there to the Adriatic the defence could be entrusted to the Croatian *banus* and to the Inner Austrian militia. However, this plan was totally inadequate. A little at a time, both the Emperor and the Aulic War Council were persuaded that the existing line of fortresses required the support of a strong field army. A further important step was the reasoning that if the Imperial field army had been assembled before the arrival of the enemy, it would have been possible to take the initiative and force the Ottomans to modify their initial plan. The establishment of new regiments and the negotiations with the German princes to obtain auxiliary forces intensified in January 1683, but the disparity of forces remained high. Already in late 1682, the intelligence and the reports from neutral countries focused on the formation of a very large Ottoman army, whose strength never was esteemed under 100,000 men.¹⁴⁹

International politics was like the green gaming table in which the cards constantly changed. Now the source for military support could be found in Poland. The *Rzeczpospolita* had long played an ambiguous role in relation to the Habsburg policy in Hungary, but after the war against the Porte of 1672–76 the balances had changed, especially regarding the declining influence of French diplomacy. In late 1682, Leopold was clearly determined to buy in Poland what Sobieski could be induced to sell him. In early 1683, the Polish king promised to gather 40,000 soldiers to be directed into Hungary in order to join the Habsburg forces. The final figure was less than expected, because on 12 September during the battle of Kahlemberg, just 20–25,000 Poles were on the battlefield.¹⁵⁰

Meanwhile, Vienna made further attempts to defuse the threat dividing the enemy front. Undoubtedly, some of the Emperor's councillors still believed that Thököly would accept a new truce and that he might even change sides. Otherwise, the majority of the court began to be convinced that to repel an invasion it was necessary to join their forces with those of another country. In that way one could reasonably hope for a victory since, as shown by modern warfare, the interaction between fortresses and relief armies was

---

148 Stoye, *The Siege of Vienna*, p. 87.
149 Reports from Alberto Caprara, February 1683, in Cardini, *Il Turco a Vienna*, p. 235.
150 Thanks to Michał Paradowski for this notice.

the key to achieving victory. This consideration was right, but in early 1683, only a few people believed that the threatened fortress was indeed Vienna.

The game of bluff and double bluff played by the Ottomans with Thököly, and by Thököly with both the Ottomans and the Habsburgs, makes it difficult to be sure of anyone's motives or intentions. Neither man could trust the other. Thököly was secretly negotiating for an even better deal with Vienna, while Kara Mustafa was notorious for ruthlessly ridding himself of anyone who had opposed his person, but for the time being each suited the other's purposes. On 14 June, the construction of the bridges for crossing the Danube was completed at Eszék. The Grand Vizier and his ally led the Ottoman army across the bridge of boats, to the first settlement in Hungary. This was the true start of the war.

The preparations for the defence involved the population of all the Habsburgs' domains, but there were difficulties in finding material, especially wood for construction.[151] This was necessary in Vienna, where the works to strengthen the defences began in late May. The vital improvements to the defences were directed by the renowned military engineer Georg Rimpler (1636–83), one of the best fortress engineers in Europe. He had been employed at an enormous salary to improve the protection of the Habsburg domains, and above all Vienna, against an attack from the east. He had first advised strengthening the outer line of fortresses, especially Györ, and then turned his critical eye on Vienna itself. Rimpler had been present at the Ottoman siege of the Venetian fortress of Candia, and in 1671 and 1674 he had published two important studies on the use of artillery and on fortification. The two treatises revealed how deeply that experience in Candia had affected him. He brought with him to Vienna a team of experienced engineers, two of whom, a fellow Saxon, Daniel Suttinger, and an Italian, Leandro Anguissola, later produced detailed studies of the siege. Together they looked systematically at the flaws in the defences and what could be done to remedy them.

In the few days that he had available before the Ottomans arrived, the main task was to repair the first line of defence, the palisade. Then he worked ceaselessly, designing new strongpoints closer to the city walls. He ordered new entrenchments and new firing points on top of the bastions and the ravelins; he designed simple obstructions, dug trenches and erected temporary strongpoints that would shelter musketeers and gunners protecting the floor of the dry ditch. Held with determination, they could seriously delay the enemy's advance. The raw materials Rimpler needed were to hand: stout baulks of timber or even tree trunks, sharpened at both ends, ready to be hammered into the earth. Roped together, or strengthened with wooden cross-members, buttressed with more timbers behind, they could be used to make an open wooden wall. A thin man could turn sideways and slip between the staves, but an attacking mass of men would be brought to a halt. Rimpler's ingenious improvised defences were all designed to wear down the enemy, to negate his vast numerical advantage. And, if all else failed, he had

---

151 Stoye, *The Siege of Vienna*, p. 165.

planned to stretch heavy iron chains across the streets and then to turn every house into a little citadel.

As the defences' improvement proceeded, also the military forces were marching to the border. About 7,500 men left their quarters in Upper Rhine and moved east, to assemble in Kitsee, near Bratislava. A further 5,000 men of the newly raised regiment should have been available before the summer. Soon these calculations turned out to be wrong. The troops marching from Germany took longer than expected to reach their destination. In practice, the first companies arrived in Kitsee on 6 May, instead of 21 April as planned. The same day, the first war council met in Innsbruck. Charles V of Lorraine discussed the situation and disposition of the forces for the oncoming campaign. The council agreed to concentrate the troops for the main army in Komárom. The council proposed to leave Schultz in command of an independent corps north of the Váh River, to secure the lower Mur valley and the communication with Croatia. The Hungarian militia would assume the task of guarding the gaps between the two main forces.

In early May, the Duke personally inspected the border fortresses along with his staff, leaving to Jacob Leslie the task of coordinating the troop assembly between Kitsee and Bratislava. Here, the rain and the wind damaged the pontoon bridges that allowed the crossing of the Danube to enter the city. The Imperial officers realised with regret the lack of fodder and the poor condition of the troops, due to the spring being colder than expected. They also had the opportunity to comment on the uncertain news arriving about the entry of the Ottoman army into Hungary and the ongoing negotiations between the Emperor and the king of Poland. In Vienna, Leopold I prepared to leave for Bratislava and with him, councillors, courtiers and foreign ambassadors were expected for the troop review. Meanwhile, Lorraine always received worse news. During his visit, the Imperial commander realised that instead of the 6,000 men promised by the Hungarian magnates, less than 1,000 were actually mobilised.[152] The Duke came back to Bratislava to meet the Emperor on 6 May. In the camp of Kittsee, the troops totalled 21,000 infantry and 10,800 cavalry, 72 guns and 15 mortars, paraded regiment by regiment by Leopold I in person.

As the Ottomans advanced from Eszék, the Habsburg command still had no clear strategy and no sense of the enemy's intentions. They had no knowledge day by day how far the Ottoman army had moved forward, or even the direction in which they were heading. When Kara Mustafa arrived at Székesfehérvár, they were still no wiser. Almost every senior Habsburg officer had his own opinion, each trying to enforce his own strategic view, often in opposition to Lorraine. The Duke had to face a jumble of contradictory objectives and a clamour of advice. In Vienna, the Emperor and his inner circle believed that he should take the offensive, to demonstrate the battle readiness of the Imperial army, and perhaps lay siege to Esztergom, a weakly defended Ottoman fortress far to the east, or alternatively, he could attack the Ottoman stronghold of Érsekújvár. Hermann von Baden parroted this

---

152 In the following weeks, their number increased to 2,000 men. Stoye, *The Siege of Vienna*, p. 109.

view, because the offensive might encourage the Poles to come more rapidly to the support of their ally. Nevertheless, they also made it clear that none of these enterprises should be allowed to weaken the defence of Vienna or of Styria, so some troops would need to be detached so that they could guard the southern frontier along the Rába River. Lorraine reluctantly set out for Esztergom at the end of May, only to be summoned back by the Emperor, who had changed the objective to Érsekújvár.

While the men could march back and forth, the siege artillery could not be turned around so easily. By the end of the first week in June, siege artillery and mortars were stuck in the mud, some north, some south of the Danube. On 12 June, Lorraine arrived at his objective, but after 10 days of desultory investment, the army headed south again. All the time, the Ottoman columns were moving forward. Four days later the Duke of Lorraine crossed the Danube again and encamped at Berg, a few days' march away from Vienna. The Imperial army occupied the point opposite Bratislava, where a line of hills on the southern bank of the river matched the hills on the northern side. Ironically, the camp was not far from Kittsee, where he had gathered the army for the great parade two months before. This was the last position before Vienna at which the Imperial army could make a stand and still hope to stop the Ottomans in their advance, because beyond this high ground, at the village of Berg, the terrain became easier with the road open to the capital. As the Imperial commander had ridden out to review the position early in the morning, an officer galloped up from the east to tell him that the Ottomans had reached the town of Moson, where the Leitha River, which marks the boundary between Hungary and Austria, flowed into the Danube. As the Duke looked to the east, he could see a reddish cloud of dust rising into the air in the distance. Messengers noticed that there were numerous columns of smoke behind him, between the army and Vienna, indicating that the enemy's vanguard was already between him and the capital. On 7 July, the strategic situation deteriorated further for the Imperialists. Not far from Berg, there is the ford of Fishamend, that allowed crossing of a tributary of the Danube halfway between Berg and Vienna. Charles of Lorraine had divided the army into three columns, the vanguard led by *General Wachtmeister* Mercy and Gondola, another corps at its orders and a rearguard under *Feldmarschall-Lieutenant* Rabatta and *General Wachtmeister* Taaffe. Immediately behind the first column, the baggage with the supply waggons proceeded. The vanguard arrived at the ford in the afternoon, and suddenly, the train was attacked by Tatars who emerged from the forest. Mercy and Gondola tried to organise a defence and kept the train heading north for fear that other bands of Tatars would block the ford. The Duke of Lorraine was half an hour from the ford and at that time he was moving on relatively high ground when he learned that another enemy contingent, coming from Ungarish-Altenburg, had assaulted the rearguard. The column quickly turned around and marched to the aid of the rearguard. The battle took place near the Roman site of Carnuntum and took the name of the Battle of Petronell. The land, flanked by the Danube, was undulating and full of woods that favoured the action of the attackers. The Imperial cavalry of the rearguard valiantly gave support but, after suffering heavy losses, the

Montecuccoli Cuirassieren (IC-4) and the *Savoyen Dragoner* (ID-13) ceded and retreated in disorder. Charles of Lorraine sent more cavalry to restore the situation and revive the resistance. The reports of the encounter related that the Imperial commander tried to rally the fugitives by beating them with the handle of his pistol.[153] The battle ended with a counter-attack by the Imperialists who put the assailants to flight. The enemy casualties were minimal, but those suffered by the Imperial rearguard were 200 dead and wounded, included one colonel.[154] Apart from this damage, the army was still intact and without suffering other assaults, the columns continued their march to Schwechat, about 10 kilometres from Vienna. The following day the Duke of Lorraine learned that the Ottomans had set up a camp with 12,000 men in front of Győr, while the rest of the army proceeded north. Now it was evident that the enemy goal was Vienna. He also learned that all the Estates of Western Hungary had recognised Thököly's sovereignty, and that the *Kuruc* leader himself marched to Bratislava with his troops.

Meanwhile in Vienna, on Saturday 7 July, the Emperor heard mass in the early morning as normal, and proceeded impassively with his usual routine. The only sign he gave of any crisis was an instruction that the ancient crown of St Stephen should be brought to Vienna from the church in Bratislava where it was always kept for the installation of the Kings of Hungary. But from about midday, a stream of messengers brought worsening reports from the Hungarian border. The news was catastrophic. The huge Ottoman army was on the move, spreading like a tidal wave. The Tatars were across the marshes, moving fast, burning villages and setting fire to woodland and cornfields. Kara Mustafa and the field army were also on the march, moving very fast towards Vienna, creating a huge dust storm made by thousands of horses and marching men.

The Imperial command had consistently underestimated the capabilities of the Ottoman army. Many had assumed that it had become torpid and ineffective, that it would never even reach the frontier. Such intelligence as they had received appeared to confirm that judgement. Informers had suggested that the Grand Vizier was weak, undermined by rivalry and dissension among his commanders, and the host had relatively few good soldiers and a huge baggage train. Now Lorraine saw the enemy could outflank and overwhelm him. He knew that now he had only a couple of tasks. Firstly, to regroup his troops, strung out in positions on both sides of the Danube, keeping the army intact; and to recognise that with the weak forces at his disposal he could do nothing to prevent the siege and possible capture of Vienna. Lorraine and Starhemberg, in charge of the defence of Vienna, agreed to transfer into the city as many soldiers as possible, while the field army marched further north. Supply and ammunition were also sent into the city, enlarging an arsenal that comprised a varied collection of

---

153 As he tried to rally his troops, the Duke would have exclaimed: 'Gentlemen, do you dishonor the arms of the Empire? Are you perhaps afraid?' in Stoye, *The Siege of Vienna*, p. 120.
154 Giulio di Savoia-Carignano, brother of Eugene. This latter served as volunteer and adjutant under the cousin Ludwig of Baden.

weapons, including 824 wall muskets, 12,209 muskets, 456 cavalry carbines, 56 flintlock muskets.[155]

In the capital, the scenario of imminent catastrophe played out a few hours later in the Emperor's rooms in the *Hofburg*. There was a swelling chorus of rumours. Count Auersperg, sent by Lorraine, reported that the Ottomans had broken out from Győr; then came *General der Cavallerie* Caprara, who brought news that the enemies were across the Leitha; within the hour, Colonel Leonardo Filippo Montecuccoli (son of Raimondo) arrived to say that the Tatars were harrying Lorraine's retreating troops and (wrongly) that they had already seized the bridge across the River Fischa, the last natural barrier before the capital itself. The Emperor listened to this growing tumult of alarm and gave orders that his family and the War Council should prepare to leave immediately for the supposed safety of Lienz, 135 miles away, far up the Danube. It was said that almost 60,000 people fled from the city in the days following the Emperor's departure, with their places taken by refugees from the countryside seeking the protection of its walls. There was one week between the flight from the city to the arrival of the Turks and the beginning of an epic siege. In that time, the city had to be made ready for a fight to the end.[156]

---

155 *Hollandse Mercurius*, 1683.
156 The events of the siege were recorded by Johann Peter von Vaelckeren. The lawyer wrote a short book that was published in 1684 in Brussels both in French and Latin editions; in Linz in a German edition; in Vienna, Venice and Naples in Italian; in Cracow in Polish; and in London in English. Some other books simply plagiarised the published texts and produced the same stories under different names. Therefore the main account depends on Vaelckeren's books. There are also two less known accounts written by two eyewitnesses of the siege, which contain interesting details on the 1683 campaign. The first source is the diary by the *Hauptmann* Michele d'Aste, *Diarii degl'Assedii di Vienna del 1683* (edited by Ernesto Piacentini). D'Aste served in the Infantry regiment *Scherffenberg* (II-7) and left several accounts of the fighting. The second is the diary of Odorico Frangipane *Avventure e Memorie Estere di O. F.* (edited by Zanetti, Vigevani and Frangipane). He arrived in Vienna to enlist as volunteer in the city's militia, but due to his family ties with the Croatian Fran Krsto Frankopan, sentenced to death in 1671, he was considered unreliable and was not involved in the defence. Despite this, Frangipane left an accurate accounts on the different phase of the siege.

6

Uniforms, Equipment and Ensigns

Most of the works dealing with Imperial uniforms state that until the end of the 17th century, the *Obrist Inhaber* (colonel proprietors) maintained a monopoly on soldiers' uniforms.[1] They took advantage of these distributions to exercise a considerable part of earnings, reselling the uniform at an almost always increased price. Theoretically the colonels could choose at their will the colour and other details of the soldier's clothing, since the first actual regulations concerning the uniform appeared in Austria in 1700.[2] The autonomy enjoyed by the colonels in the matter of uniforms is one of the fundamental reasons why our knowledge about colours and other important details is still fragmentary. The purchase of the fabrics was dealt with by the colonel proprietor through his collaborators and rarely the documentation relating to these trades was transmitted to the Aulic War Council in Vienna. Probably the private archives of the families who in the 17th century included among their members a colonel, preserve some information on the first uniforms of the House of Austria's army, but it is a difficult task even for the most skilled archaeologists, and when such a document comes to light it almost always happens out of luck. However, there are indirect traces that allow us to form a fairly exhaustive scenario about the uniforms thanks to the notes on the reports attached to inspections and musters, especially those performed after 1682. It is only in this period, with the rapid numerical growth of the regiments following the war against the Porte, that the matter relating to uniforms began to be treated with greater care, thanks to the requests of Duke Charles V of Lorraine, who reiterated some of the proposals advanced by Montecuccoli before him.

The development of standing armies and the improvement of manufacturing technology coincided in the mid 17th century in increased uniformity of the troops. This trend appeared, more or less at the same time

---

1 Hummelsberger, 'Zur Bewaffnung und Ausrüstung sowie Verpflegung und Versorgung der Kaiserlichen um 1686' in *Blätter für Österreichische Heereskunde* (Vienna: Heeresgeschichtliches Museum, 1987), p. 67.
2 Hochedlinger, 'Austria's War of Emergency', p. 129.

throughout Europe. On this matter, the Imperial army followed the path traced in France, as well as in the Netherlands and Sweden.

The first document mentioning the adoption of identical dress for all soldiers of an Imperial regiment dates back to 1645. The reference appears in a letter attached to a contract signed by Count Matteo Galasso, concerning the supply of coats and breeches for his infantry regiment. The document is preserved in Vienna in the *Alte Feldakten* of the Austrian War Archives.[3] For greater manufacturing precision, the count also included a sample of light grey fabric (*blassgrau*: pale grey, in the original German text) to be used in the manufacturing of the uniforms. In addition, he sent samples of powder flasks and ammunition bandoliers to local suppliers who were charged with producing 600 pieces of each type. It is extremely unusual that the colour of the fabric is explicitly mentioned. In fact, these documents are often just administrative receipts reporting the amount of items or the total expense, while they were usually silent about the style, cut, materials, trimmings, or other specific relevant information for the contemporary military historian. Even when original material and braid samples have been attached, they have not always survived intact, or have radically changed in colour due to fading or deterioration of the fabric in question. In other circumstances, the information contained in the original documents does not allow us to readily understand which colours they really are. For instance, when a uniform is of 'red' cloth, could it be vermillion, scarlet, madder, wine red or crimson?

In other sources it is possible to find, with some luck, other references to the material chosen in the production of military uniforms. In his diary of the Thirty Years' War, published in 1651, the Zurich-born infantry captain Hans Conrad Lavater advised his fellow officers to dress their soldiers with practical clothing: sturdy shoes with nailed soles; woollen breeches, knitted socks; at least two shirts in a heavy winter; a leather buff coat; a double-cloth cloak of wool to protect them from wind and rain and a large felt hat. The clothes, writes Lavater, had to be cut very wide for warmth, but without quilting and with as few seams as possible to prevent a fertile ground for the breeding of parasites. This description is very useful, but even in this case, it is very difficult to determine types, styles and accessories used.

Portrait of Michele d'Aste, the Italian baron who served in the Imperial army during the siege of Vienna and in the Hungarian campaign until 1686, when he was killed in action at the siege of Buda. D'Aste left a very interesting account concerning military facts and other information that were less known until the discovery of his diaries in the 1680s. (Author's collection)

The scarcity of sources increases when we move back through the years, only partly offset by illustrations and prints. In any case, illustrations and depictions of Imperial soldiers in the years between 1655–1665 are extremely rare. Of all the existing illustrations about one of the armies with the richest traditions in the world, those of

---

3 Cited in Geoffrey Parker, *The Thirty Years' War* (New York NY: Routledge, second edition, 1998) p. 170.

UNIFORMS, EQUIPMENT AND ENSIGNS

the Imperial Army around the 1660s and 1670s came from to two or three sources at most.[4] Sadly, these representations of common soldiers are often reproduced in black and white. Portraits of officers are more numerous. However, they are conventionally depicted in equestrian full armour. On the other hand, there are a great number of paintings of infantry and cavalry skirmishes, a genre that flourished in the second half of the 17th century. Unfortunately, these works are almost never historically reliable, because the painters were rarely eyewitnesses to the campaigns and often they relied on generic models or standard references. Only when the client was an officer who had participated in a campaign against the Ottomans or the French, it is reasonably possible to hope to get some useful information regarding accurate dress and equipment.

Two paintings made on the recommendation of eyewitnesses participating in the battle of Szentgotthárd have come down to us; one is preserved in Vienna and one in Bavaria, but in both cases it is the cavalry that dominates the image. A third interesting and most valuable iconographic source dating 1664 is preserved in the Czech Republic. It is the fresco in the castle of Lisà representing the battle of Szentgotthárd. The fresco was commissioned by count Johann von Sporck a few years after the battle, and notwithstanding some parts are now deteriorated, it is the best source of documentation regarding the Austrian army of this age. The artwork depicts also troops of the Imperial circles and the French, and the arrangement of the troops coincides with the battle order issued by Montecuccoli before the assault that decided the day, an element that allows us to identify with reasonable security the

The Battle of Szentgotthárd depicted in the fresco at the Castle of Lysá, is an inestimable iconographic source for the Imperial army in the mid 1660s. Unfortunately the state of conservation of the fresco is not perfect and some parts are now compromised. It depicts the decisive allied attack that led to the final victory, on the afternoon of 1st August 1664, and shows the adoption of uniformed dress for all the units. The Imperial and allied troops are mostly portrayed from the back, but some details may be reconstructed from other figures.

---

4   The thirteen engravings by Bartholomeus Kilian for the *Kriegs Lexikon*, printed in Prague in 1663; the illustrations after the *Kriegsbuchliches Waffenhandlung*, printed in Nuremberg in 1660 and some of the last drawings of Stefano Della Bella.

The *Gutschenich Croaten* crossing the Rába River, depicted in the fresco of the Lysá Castle. (Author's photograph)

UNIFORMS, EQUIPMENT AND ENSIGNS

Detail from the fresco of Lysa Castle, depicting musketeers and pikemen in red cassocks with ensign in red-blue and a black double-headed eagle. According to the deployment established by Montecuccoli at Szentgotthárd, these troops could belong to the Westphalian circle regiment *Uffeln* (WI-1). The fresco shows the adoption of uniformed dress for all the units and they are consistently depicted according to the different specialties. Originally, the fresco showed a summary legend that today is partly illegible, however, it is possible to identify most of the units by comparing their position on the fresco with the place occupied in the battle order prepared by Montecuccoli. The castle of Lysa is located on the north-eastern outskirts of Prague and until 1677 it belonged to Count Johann von Sporck, who is depicted in the portrait in the hall on the left wall. Certainly, it was the Count who gave the painter directions. Sporck, in fact, participated in the battle as commander of the left wing of the Imperial cavalry. Around the fresco are depicted conventional battle scenes of Western European cavalry. (Author's photograph)

various contingents and also the single regiments. Other important episodes, such as the siege of Philippsburg, the battle of Vienna, or the conquest of Buda have been depicted in paintings and prints, and in some cases, we are faced with excellent sources for coherently reconstructing the first Imperial uniforms.

Other valuable iconography comes from contemporary paintings, especially those of artists active in Germany and Austria, who have left us very accurate images of officers and soldiers of the period. It is not always certain, however, that the soldiers depicted belong to the Imperial army. Although hardly numerous, some original artefacts of the campaign such as equipment or weapons also exist, preserved in museums and private collections in reasonably good order.[5]

There are also several drawings depicting Austrian soldiers produced many years after the event, mainly from the late 19th century, when regimental histories began to be published. In the works dedicated to the oldest regiments there appears images of soldiers with the first regimental uniforms issued or summary textual descriptions. The iconographic apparatus contributes to increase our knowledge of the uniforms in this period but there are few significant cases, often limited to a restricted number of regiments. Moreover, the accuracy of certain reconstructions leaves many questions open and cannot be relied on for authentication. Periodically, especially in connection with anniversaries of the battles, illustrated articles were published, depicting soldiers who participated in the campaigns against France or the Porte. These sources are not numerous and several reconstructions are not completely reliable.[6] Furthermore, several modern authors confuse the term uniform, and many of the reconstructions carried out at the end of the 19th century follow the canons of classical uniformology. In the last century, the first uniforms of the army of the House of Austria were the object of research for a small but hardened group of scholars. The most important and prolific was Karl Alexander Wilke (1879–1954). He published most of his research in the magazines *Die Muskete* and *Die Mölkerbastei*, and on this latter appeared many of his works related to the Imperial Army in the 17th century. Wilke was above all a skilled artist who left valuable reconstructions of Imperial soldiers from the Thirty Years' War and the period immediately following. Unfortunately, he almost never specifies the sources that inspired his artworks and in some cases, he commits several arbitrary reconstructions regarding weaponry. Despite this, Wilke's investigation on the transitional phases that led to the adoption of a modern uniform represents a praiseworthy deed, because he identified the specific 'Austrian' characteristics of military clothing between 1660 and 1680.

---

5   Austrian state preserves valuable collections in Vienna, such as the *Waffensammlung des Kunsthistorischen Museums*, and the *Heeresgeschichtliches Museum*, and in Graz, *Landeszeughaus*.
6   The most famous are the illustrations from F. Lallemand, *Die k.k. österreich. Armee im Laufe zweyer Jahrhunderte* (Vienna, 1840) and F. Gerash, *Das österreich. Heer von Ferdinand II., Römisch-Deutschen Kaiser, bis Franz Joseph I., Kaiser von Österreich*, (Vienna 1855).

UNIFORMS, EQUIPMENT AND ENSIGNS

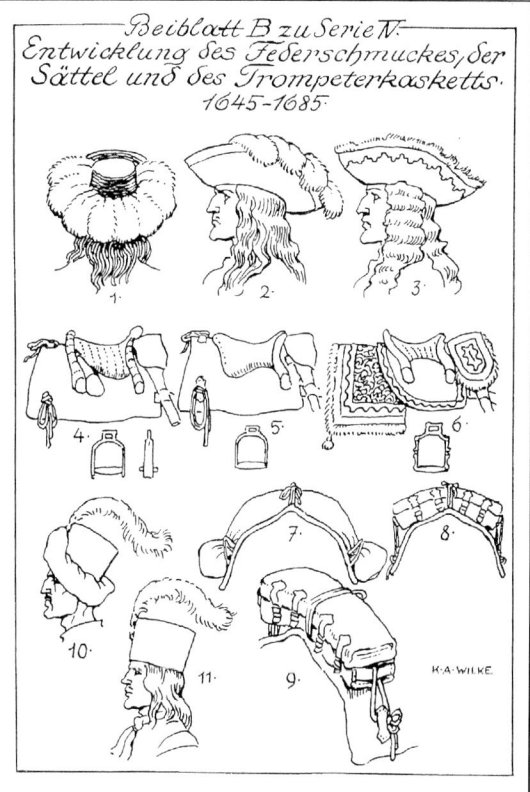

Drawings of Karl Alexander Wilke for the Austrian magazine *1683, die Mölkerbastei*, published in the 1970s. Wilke was an able illustrator and a skilled costume designer for the theatre and among the first to approach the early period uniforms of the Imperial army. Notwithstanding some arbitrary reconstruction, he left several interesting studies on dress and equipment. (Author's collection)

The Austrian magazines of militaria published numerous articles, some of which were based on archival research conducted with an appropriate methodological approach. The most important author was undoubtedly Eduard Czegka, who in 1933 published his investigation on the Imperial infantry uniforms starting from the late 17th century.[7] The researcher provided an exhaustive picture of the uniforms of most infantry regiments after examining the regimental histories and other documentation preserved in the library of the Viennese *Kriegsarchiv*. However, only in a few cases was Czegka able to provide information prior to 1716 and only once cited uniforms of the late 17th century.[8] The results therefore remained modest as far as the most ancient uniforms are concerned, however Czegka had opened the way to archival research and confirmed that the subject of 'military

---

7 E. Czegka, *Uniformen der kaiserlichen Infanterie unter Prinz Eugen*, in 'Zeitschrift für Heereskunde' Nr. 49, 50, 51; January-February-March 1933.
8 *Ibidem*, infantry regiment *Öttingen-Baldern* in 1691.

uniforms' apparently began to be examined more carefully by the Imperial military administration only in the 18th century.

In the 1950s, the research in this direction was taken up by Rudolph Donath, who published several articles in the magazines such the aforementioned *Die Mölkerbastei*, and the successors *Die Neue-Mölkerbastei* and *La Sabretache*. The most consistent part of his research, collected in the manuscript entitled *Die Kaiserliche und Kaiserlich und Königliche Österreichische Armee 1618–1918*,[9] includes infantry, cavalry and artillery uniforms from the years 1689–91 and in some cases provides general indications on military clothing for the period 1675–85. Although the manuscript does not contain the sources from which he reconstructed the uniforms, the reputation of Donath's research about the Austrian military matter suggests that they come from official documents from the Austrian war archive, of which he was an assiduous visitor. Though Donath did not declare the sources, most of the researchers who study the Imperial army have always turned to his manuscript.

All the major classical studies tend to confirm that throughout the period prior to the 1680s, regimental uniforms would have remained an exclusive matter for the colonels. The prevalence of German-language sources has restricted the field of investigation to mostly German or Austrian scholars, who rarely turned their attention to documentation from other countries. Especially, although partly available in 19th century translations, the remarkable documentary archive of Montecuccoli, preserved in the Vienna's *Kriegsachiv*, was very often ignored. Although the great Italian general has left very little testimonies regarding the uniforms of the Imperial soldiers, some of his notes bring an interesting light about the distribution of these items and their economic impact. In his writing entitled *Mal Governo della Camera Aulica* (Misgovernment of the Aulic Chamber) dated 17 July 1673,[10] Montecuccoli gives a very interesting detail about the uniforms issued to the soldiers in the 1660s. At point two, he writes that for years the Aulic Chamber distributed to soldiers 'bad clothes with short arms and at high price.'[11] The assertion seems to completely contradict the statement regarding the uniforms being distributed exclusively by the colonel proprietors, and in part it is true. Usually the uniforms, limited to headgear, coat and breeches, were issued every four years in garrison, and every two years (or more) in campaign.[12] In the first case, it was simple for the colonel to provide his

---

9   Private publishing, Simbach-Inn, 1971. In times closer to us, this subject has been taken up by some German self-produced publications, whose documentary value remains, unfortunately, inconsistent.
10 Testa, 'Le Opere di Raimondo Montecuccoli' p. 225.
11 Incidentally, Montecuccoli gives further information about the distribution of uniforms to the troops in campaign also in the *Aforismi Riflessi alle Pratiche delle Guerre prossime addietro dell'Ungheria*, in Luraghi 'Opere di Raimondo Montecuccoli' vol. II, p.395. The *generalissimo* complained how in the winter 1661-62 the troops did not receive new clothing because the shortage of money and the poor state of the communication lines between Austria and Hungary.
12 For the infantry, shoes and stockings were issued every year, or more, in campaign and every two years in garrison, in K.u.K. Kriegsarchiv, 'Feldzüge des Prinzen Eugen', vol. I, p. 389.

men with new uniforms, while on campaign this task obviously became much more complicated. This kind of problem already existed during the Thirty Years' War, but the need for a uniformed dress was less pressing and could be solved with several devices. Montecuccoli then explains how, already in the previous decade, the troops on campaign, as well as the ones headquartered in Hungary and Croatia, were supplied with uniforms directly from the Imperial Treasury, which was reimbursed by the colonels, and moreover at improved prices. This is important information, because the state's control over supplies for the army is one of the prerequisites in the establishment of modern armies and, above all, it marks the birth of the modern concept of military uniform. Although the quality of the clothing was poor, nonetheless uniformity was guaranteed and direct proof is the adoption of pearl grey coat for infantry and leather *Koller* for cuirassiers as a standard item of the Imperial troops since the 1660s. This does not mean that the Imperial infantry and cuirassier regiments wore the same uniform, but for practical reasons the establishment of a uniform dress took place also for merely organisational and economic reasons.

This partly also explains why the appearance of the Imperial troops left much to be desired. Many reports agree in describing negatively the clothing of the soldiers, especially the infantry. An anonymous Italian volunteer who in 1684 joined the Imperial Army in Hungary noted that the troops from Bavaria and Saxony as well dressed and equipped, while the Imperial soldiers appeared in 'a miserable state' and only the weaponry could be described as being in good order.[13] Years later, in the regulation written for his infantry regiment, Count Georg Oliver Wallis declared that it was not important if the soldier's dress had stains, as long as it was free of rips and tears so as to conveniently protect the soldier from cold and rain.[14] Once again, uniform is really a subjective concept in the 17th century.

Infantry

Karl Alexander Wilke relates that the adoption of pearl grey by the Imperial infantry would have occurred as early as 1639. He argues the choice of this colour was to distinguish the Imperial troops from the Swedish ones, who were dressed in dark blue, and from the Ottomans, who were mostly in green.[15] Another explanation was economic motives, considering that dyed cloth was much more expensive. However it does not seem entirely convincing. Even in the Swedish army grey was a very common colour for infantry, and at least until the 1680s the dark blue fabric was not the only cloth used for infantry uniforms. In addition, some Imperial infantry regiments continued

---

13 A. Bosco, L. Serravalle, P. Zotti (editors), *1684, un maremmano all'assedio di Buda* (Arcidosso: Effigi, 2012), p. 66.
14 *Exercitium, des General Graf Wallisschen Regiments zu Fuss sambt dessen Kriegs-Gebräuchen* (Salò, 1705).
15 A. Wilke, 'Das kaiserliche Heer unter Grafen Raimund von Montecuccoli' in *Die Mölkerbastei* 10/1950, p. 16.

to wear red, dark blue and even green uniforms until the early years of the following century. On the other hand, it is certainly true that grey clothes represented considerable economic savings, as indeed happened in almost all the permanent armies of this age. Often in the documents of the Aulic Chamber and in those of the Aulic Council of War the colonels are explicitly invited to use, for reasons of 'good economy', the cloth produced in Iglau (today Jihlava, in Czech Republic), namely to a national product, capable of satisfying all needs.[16] In the late 17th century, grey in several nuances was adopted also by the infantry of the Imperial circles, prevalently in the circles of Swabia, Franconia, and later Bavaria. Even the infantry of the electors of Trier and Mainz in the Westphalian or in the Rhine-Prince-electoral circles had had grey coats since the end of the 17th century. In the circles of the Upper Rhine and Lower Saxony, the infantry were instead dressed in blue, grey or red, traditional colours also for the infantry of the Palatinate, Brunswick-Wolfenbüttel, and Lüneburg-Celle and Hanover.

Austrian partisan for an infantry officer, copy of the drawing published in 2003 in the Ukrainian magazine *бібліотека*. This weapon was discovered in 2001, in an abandoned house in Dykanka village, Poltava region (Ukraine). Most likely this partisan belonged to an Imperial officer who served in the campaign against the Swedes in Poland. However, there are several queries concerning this discovery and its presence so far from the war theatre. The blade's length is 37.8 cm, the width is 5 cm. (Author's illustration)

Infantry partisan and halberd, *c.* 1670–80, collection of Český Šternberk castle, Czech Republic. Some late 17th century partisans for senior officers show gilded metal in the low section and natural steel on the top. (Author's photograph)

16 K.u.K. Kriegsarchiv, 'Feldzüge des Prinzen Eugen' vol. I, p. 365.

UNIFORMS, EQUIPMENT AND ENSIGNS

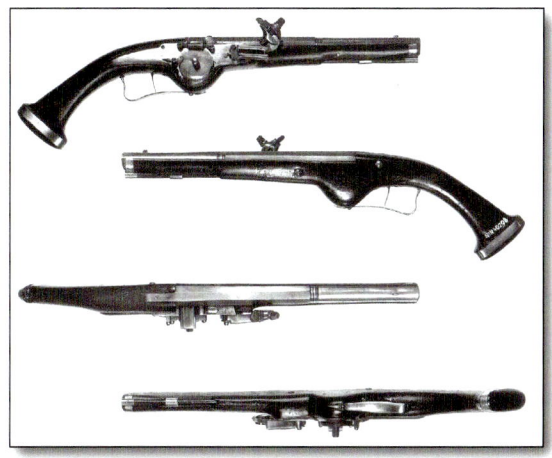

Cavalry *Radschlosspistole* (wheellock pistol); Austrian manufacture, 1650–60. overall length 49.5 cm. (Author's collection)

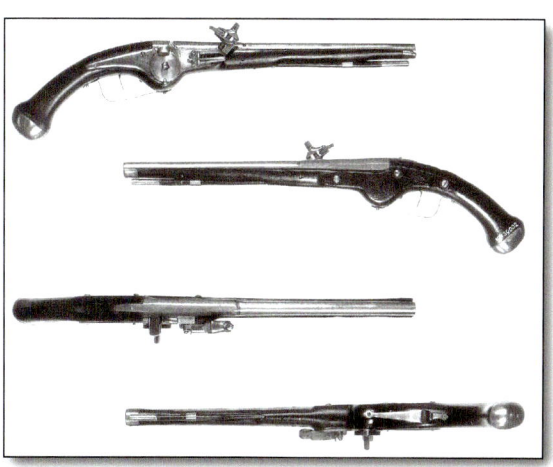

Cavalry *Radschlosspistole*; Austrian manufacture, 1660–70. overall length 55.5 cm. (Author's collection)

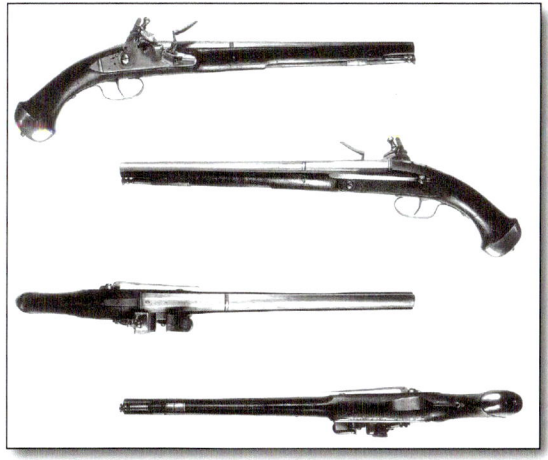

Cavalry *Steinschlosspistole* (flintlock pistol); Austrian manufacture, 1675–80. overall length 52.6 cm. (Author's collection)

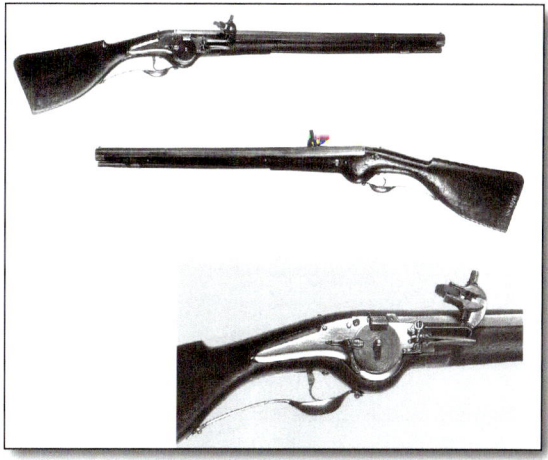

Cavalry *Radschlosskarabiner*, Austrian manufacture, 1670; overall length 93.5 cm. (Author's collection)

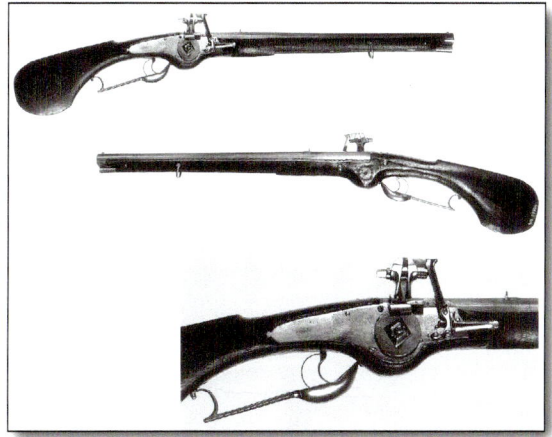

Cavalry *Radschlosskarabiner* (wheellock carbine), Austrian manufacture, 1655; overall length 96.5 cm. (Author's collection)

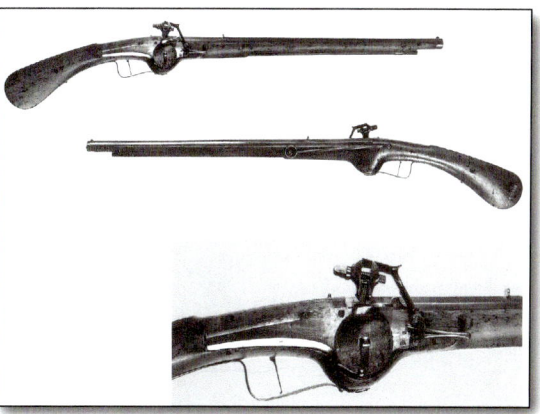

Cavalry *Radschlosskarabiner*, Austrian manufacture, 1660; overall length 103.4 cm. (Author's collection)

Grey become the predominant colour of Imperial infantry from the 1660s, as widely confirmed by the foot soldiers depicted in the fresco of the battle of Szentgotthárd in Lysà castle. It would also appear that in 1664 the main dress of the infantry was the long coat for both musketeers and pikemen. Indeed, contemporary iconography always shows Imperial infantry with more or less long coats with a few exceptions, while doublets are worn by officers and sometimes by NCOs. The diversity of clothing between the common soldiers and the officers is clearly visible in the prints relating to the war campaigns of 1657–60. Here the infantry officers do not dress very differently from contemporary civilians and appear substantially in line with the fashion of the period, including the unusually high 'Puritan' broad-brimmed hats. New kinds of coats and waistcoats replaced the short panelled doublet, and the officer's coat seems to have appeared in Germany and Austria in the 1660s, derived from the leather *Koller*, especially in the fashionable dress of the aristocracy. There are two fine examples of this in the portraits of the *Hauptmann* Jobst Joseph Moscon, dated 1660 and the one of the *General Wachtmeister* Johann Josef von Herberstein, painted 10 years later. This clothing differed slightly with the *justaucorps* introduced in France and in the Dutch Republic, except in the cut of the skirt, which adhered less to the figure and had no pleats. The coat-*Koller* become very popular in Austria and in Germany, remaining a classic dress for officers both of infantry and cavalry until the early 1680s, tailored in butternut, medium brown, grey or also red cloth. In this age, the Austrian aristocracy was much less permeable to external influences in matter of fashion, and remained more conservative, maintaining for their dress the 'Spanish etiquette'.

From this composite set of sources, we can observe a wide variety of clothing, confirming that in Austria

European officers did not follow the concept of uniform until the beginning of the 18th century and their dress had no effect on binding officers more closely to their men. In this print dated 1683, the newly appointed *Feldzeugmeister* Ernst Rüdiger von Starhemberg wears a fashionable *justaucorps* with large flap cuffs, fastened to the arms with a double series of buttons: an early example of 'Brandenburg' cuffs. (Author's collection)

Detail from the painting *Belagerung von Ofen 1686*, by Frans Geffels (1625–1694), preserved in the Szépművészeti Múzeum, Budapest. Note the mounted officer on the right wearing a *justaucorps* with Brandenburg cuffs. (Author's collection)

UNIFORMS, EQUIPMENT AND ENSIGNS

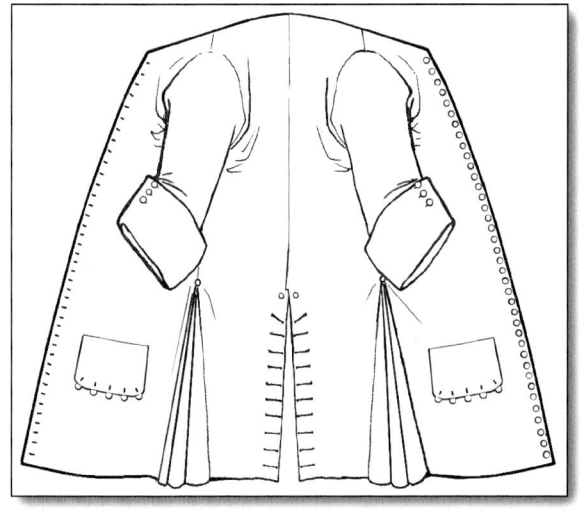

Author's reconstruction after the painting of Frans Geffel.

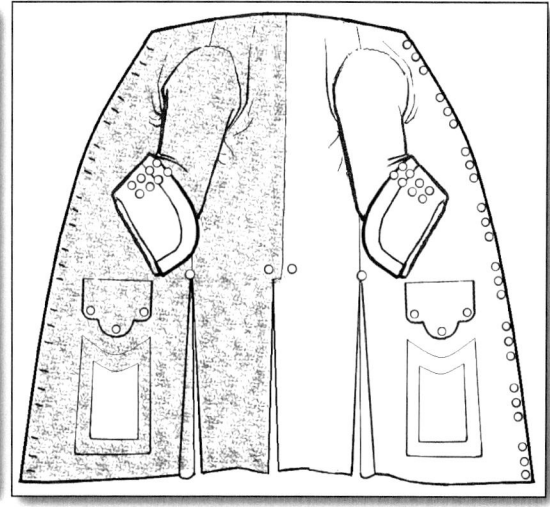

Justaucorps reconstruction after the 1683 print depicting Ernst Rüdiger von Starhemberg. (Author's reconstruction)

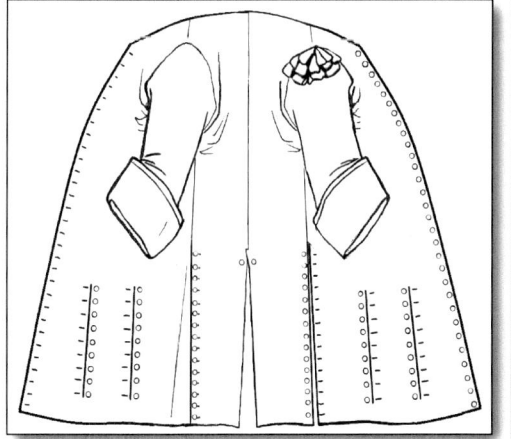

Justaucorps reconstruction after the 1677 print of the duel between Corbelli and Reich. (Author's reconstruction)

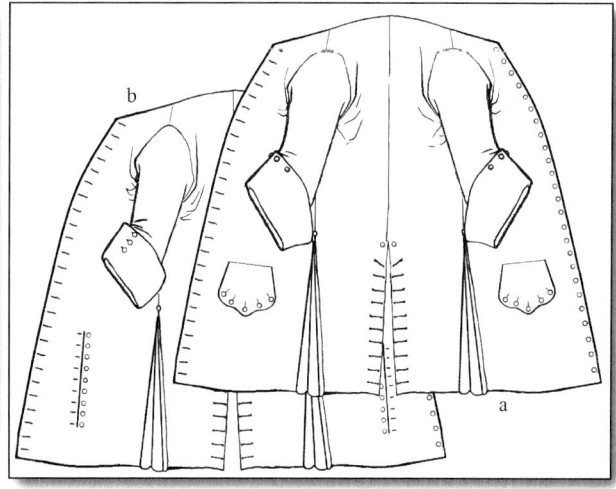

Rock (*justaucorps* coat), 1685–1687. (Author's reconstruction)

as well as in the rest of Europe, military dress was in a transitional period. However, on the basis of the original iconographic sources, infantry coats remain very simple in cut and for a long time do not adopt the flap cuffs as occurred in the Netherlands, France and Spain.[17] It was not until the late 1670s that the French style *juste-au-corps* (*der Rock* in Germany and Austria), would be adopted in the Imperial army, also conveyed by the growing number of foreign officers, especially Italians and Lorraines, or coming from the influence of the other German armies.

---

17 See the illustration in V. von Neuwirth, *Geschichte des k. und k. Infanterie-Regimentes Alt-Starhemberg Nr. 54* (Olmütz, 1894).

WARS AND SOLDIERS IN THE EARLY REIGN OF LOUIS XIV – VOLUME 2

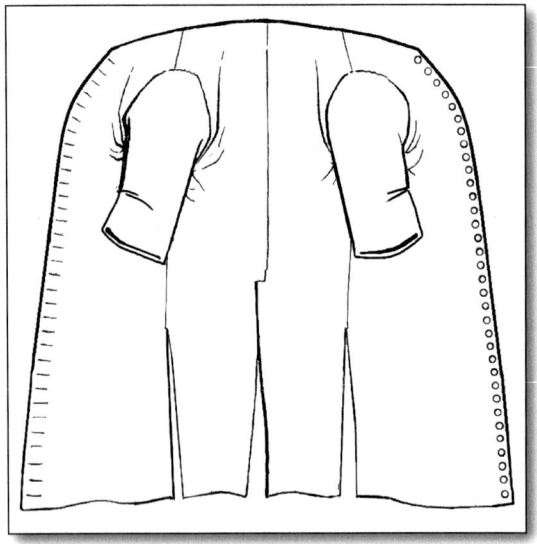

Rock coat, 1663. (Author's reconstruction)

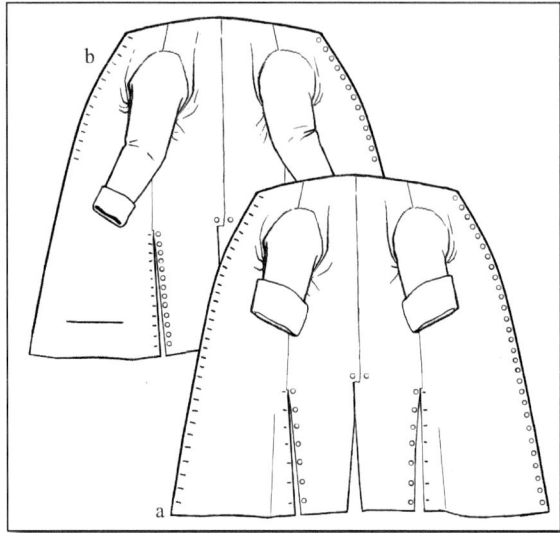

Rock coats: a) 1671; b) 1676–78. (Author's reconstruction)

Apart from the length of the coat, which reflected the biggest stylistic change in soldier's dress, in the second half of the 17th century the other significant difference related to the shape of the neck collar. In the mid 17th century, also in Austria, the falling band began to be worn, fastened with neck strings, replacing the traditional triangular flaps collar. As the century unfolded, this evolved into a cravat, trimmed with lace edging for officers, or the fully embroidered *rabat* collar. This latter was typical of the officers' dress, while common soldiers worn the simple cravat in white or, less common, in black. Donath suggests in the 1680s the adoption of red cravats by the Imperial infantry, but he remarks that exceptions were frequent.

Breeches, tight or wide, became less voluminous as the century progressed but they ended always under the knee, and were often enriched with colourful ribbons. In Austria leather breeches became common in the 1680s, especially among the private soldiers, which continued to be worn until the early years of the 18th century. A wide range of stockings, knitted, woollen, cotton and silk were being worn, sometimes with one pair worn over the other. The universally favoured headgear, prevalent throughout all ranks in the army, was the broad felt hat; in Austria the most common styles were round topped with a slightly lower crown, but also the aforementioned high 'Puritan' black headgear – typical of Northern Europe – appeared frequently in the early 1660s. Wilke stated that in the 1670s, the Imperial infantry seems to have adopted the black hat as distinctive headgear, and this is confirmed by Rudolph Donath for the following decade,[18] when the edge is completed with piping, usually in white, without relation to the coat's buttons. In the 1660s, pikeman are portrayed with morion helms in natural steel or black polished metal, usually worn with breast armour and back

---

18 R. Donath *Die Kaiserliche und Königlich Österreichische Armee, 1618–1918* (Simbach/Inn: private publishing, 1965-71).

UNIFORMS, EQUIPMENT AND ENSIGNS

Imperial *Regiment Portia zu Fuss* (II-42), 1660. Thanks to a 19th century copy of a 1660 lost watercolour, is possible to know the dress and equipment of an Imperial pikemen in the mid 17th century. In 1665 the regiment *Portia* marched to Southern Italy to aid Spain, and very probably Imperial pikeman in the 1660s wore similar clothing. Since the armour offered little protection against musketry, it gradually lost some parts, such as the tassets. Colour: carmine red short jacket, breeches and socks; helmet and all metal items in polished black; yellow-blue plumes; brown footwear and leather belts with brass accessories; pole of the pike painted in yellow-blue spirals. (Author's illustration)

Pikes of the Imperial army measured from 4 to 4.5 metres. The tip was normally fixed to the pole with a double screwed iron clamp to reinforce the final section of the weapon. In some iconography the poles appear painted with the colonel's livery. (Landeszeughaus Museum, Graz)

plate. Progressively, these items disappeared and already in the 1670s the pikeman differed little from the musketeer, equipment apart.[19] According to Wilke, in late 1650s and early 1660s, pikemen wore coats in leather or cloth lined with fulled fabric to improve resistance. Possibly this type of coat was issued to some regiments by their colonels, while in other cases pikeman are portrayed wearing an obviously cloth coat, like the regiment *Alfonso Portia* (II-42) in 1661–64.[20] However, in the following years further evidences show pikemen dressed like their musketeer counterparts.[21]

The fortunate discovery of a document dated October 1675 allows us to know important details about the uniforms of the Imperial army. It is a letter containing a report entitled *Stato delle Truppe di Sua Maestà Cesarea in Germania* (State of His Imperial Majesty's troops in Germany) compiled by an anonymous Italian officer, an eyewitness in the army that had fought the French in the Rhineland.[22] Together with the regiment's strength for

---

19 The diminution of the waggons for the transport of infantry equipment was certainly one of the reasons why the Imperial pikemen renounced to metal protections. (author's note)
20 Copy of a 1660 watercolour, preserved in the Kupferstichkabinett, Vienna.
21 See also in the aforementioned fresco of the Lysá castle.
22 Archivio di Stato di Napoli: 'Museo' vol. 994146 (Antonio Carafa di Stigliano), c. 13, *Stato delle Truppe Cesaree in Germania, il mese di Ottobre, l'anno 1675*. The document is in Italian, but the handwriting did not belong to general Antonio Carafa., and possibly was written by an officers of his regiment. The colours of the uniforms are registered using terms today unusual: if the *focato* fabric referred to is probably meant to be red, it could be vermilion, scarlet, madder or

Private musketeer, regiment *Starhemberg zu Fuss* (II-41), 1675–1680, published in Victor von Neuwirth's *Geschichte des k. und k. Infanterie-Regimentes Alt-Starhemberg Nr.54*. Some Austrian regimental histories are a useful source of knowledge on the first uniforms issued to the Imperial troops. (Author's collection)

the incoming campaign expressed in battalions and squadrons, the officer summarily registered the colours of each infantry regiment, referring to *giubba* and *calzette* (coat and stockings). Most of the infantry wore coats of *grigio oscuro* (dark grey) cloth with stockings of a different colour for each regiment.[23] No further information is recorded, however the fact that the distinctive colour is represented by the stockings, would seem to allude to the absence of flap cuffs, or – alternatively – these were of the same colour as the *Rock*. Even the description of the colour of the cloth – dark grey – suggests that the traditional 'pearl grey' was originally darker than thought until today. Several eyewitness of the early 1680s confirm the poor state of the Imperial infantry and outline the general rough appearance of the dress.[24] Probably, the need for actual regimental facings was less urgent considering the recurrent amalgamating of the infantry for tactical reasons as well as the formation of new regiments. The result was that for both economic and practical reasons, the Imperial soldiers maintained for a long time an obsolete and outmoded appearance.

Details of Imperial Austrian *Rock* pattern in the 1680s are rare in the available contemporary sources, and even the regimental history adds very little information concerning the style of dress. In its general pattern lines the *Rock* was single breasted and broad enough to be closed with buttons in variable number all along. Some accessories such as cuffs, pockets and collar, their shape and position might change but the general appearance of the coat remained unchanged until the end of the century. Some later sources report that the coat was manufactured with a double layer of cloth to make it more waterproof and that the outer cloth had to be tailored diagonally to increase its resistance to the rain. The inner lining could be of a different colour and in the 1680s usually coincided with the cuffs.

In general, many of the approximate recent contributions concerning the first uniforms of the Imperial army hastily dismiss the official and NCOs argument referring to the fact that they wore coats of reverse colour to those worn by troops. This statement is almost right for the NCOs of the early 18th century, while the evidence for the period 1660–80 shows no sergeant or corporal dressed by the facing colour of the regiment. Certainly, the number of sources is little but some significant contemporary iconography would confirm that the Imperial infantry NCOs wore the same coats as the troops.

---

carmine. Further doubts persist also regarding the right identification of the *marengo* (brown?), while the *saloniccho* [sic] could be turquoise-green.

23 Of 16 Imperial regiments registered, twelve wore grey coat, three had blue and one red. The document included also a summary description of the uniform worn by troops of the Franconian and Swabian circle.

24 M. D'Aste (edited by Ernesto Piacentini): *Diario dell'Assedio di Buda del 1686, in Diarii degl'Assedii di Vienna del 1683, e di Buda del 1686, distesi e scritti dal Baron Michele D'Aste che vi si trovò presente in tutte le sue Azzioni* (Rome-Budapest: Bulzoni-Corvina, 1991) and Anonymous (edited by Anna Bosco, Luca Serravalle and Piergiorgio Zotti): *1684, un maremmano all'assedio di Buda* (Arcidosso, GR: Effigi, 2012).

UNIFORMS, EQUIPMENT AND ENSIGNS

In the aforementioned fresco in the Lysà castle there are no identifiable NCOs wearing clothing of a different colour, except for some figures wearing armless leather coats. A more recent painting depicts Imperial infantry at the battle of Vienna of 1683. There are several paintings celebrating this episode, but the one preserved in the *Heeresgeschichtliches Museum* of Vienna is particularly interesting, because shows a great quantity of details. The author is unknown, but surely he was well informed about the battle when depicting Polish, Bavarian, Saxon and Imperial troops with their ensigns and dress. The Imperialists appear twice, an unidentified regiment of dragoons in yellow coats, and another of infantry in red. This latter has been identified with the regiment *Württemberg-Stuttgart zu Fuss* (II-90).[25] Private soldiers and NCOs are dressed in full red and only the officers wear a coat of a different colour: yellow with black flap cuffs for the leading officer and azure-blue for the ensign.

After 1683, simultaneously with the unfolding of campaigns in Hungary against the Ottomans, further important innovations in military clothing were introduced. First of all the adoption of the waistcoat, which proved to be useful in solving the problem of the damp climate of the Hungarian plain, but above all to save the coat from wear. The soldier preferably wore the waistcoat in garrison if not engaged on active service and even on the march in a hot climate, the coat could be rolled up and secured. All were measures dictated by previous experiences and the need to save money, and favoured by practical and clever commanders such as Duke Charles V of Lorraine and the Margrave Ludwig of Baden. Furthermore, as experienced by other contemporary armies, the waistcoat restricted the use of arbitrary informal clothing, which often made it difficult to identify deserters. Firstly waistcoats, known in Austria as *Kamisol*, are always slightly shorter than the coat and usually have sleeves but not cuff flaps. The waistcoat could be made of cloth or even natural leather, and in this case they were usually without pockets. Notwithstanding the absence of iconographic evidence, Imperial infantrymen resorted to a cloak in rainy winters or in the cold season, especially during the winter campaign in Poland, Jutland and Pomerania in

Imperial private musketeer, 1683–84, regiment *Pfalzgraf-Neuburg zu Fuss* (II-76), pearl grey coat, blue cuffs, buff waistcoat, white-azure striped stockings, tin buttons, red cravat. Except for officers, elites and specialist units, grey was the basic colour of uniform issued to common foot soldiers, the infantry being the cheapest, most numerous and least glamorous element of all armies. (Author's illustration)

---

25 The colonel of the regiment, the duke Georg Friedrich of Württemberg-Stuttgart, was allowed to open the sortie which took place simultaneously with arrival of the relief army. Captain Michele d'Aste confirms the episode in his memories.

Regiment *Württemberg-Stuttgart zu Fuss* (II-90), depicted during the sortie from Vienna on 12 September 1683. (Author's collection)

Left: Imperial musketeer with fur-trimmed *Tornister* (haversack) and *Schweinsfeder*; somewhere in Hungary, 1686–89. Another characteristic tool of the Imperial infantry in this period was the *Springstock*, a walking pole used by some regiments. Its function was analogous to the jumping stick of the Tyrolean alpine guides. The infantry used this tool when marching in the mountains. It was a wooden pole of 180 200 cm long, with a metal tip at one end and a wooden knob on the other. The *Springstock* was still used at the end of the 17th century even by officers. Their tool had the pole painted in black and the metal parts were of brass, and instead of the wooden knob there was one in gilded metal, with an embossed Imperial eagle, or a shield in the shape of a heart with the Imperial weapons. (Marsigli's collection, Bologna National Library)

Right: Imperial grenadier, with *Tornister* and early *Pelzmütze*, 1686–89. (Marsigli's collection, Bologna National Library)

UNIFORMS, EQUIPMENT AND ENSIGNS

1657–1660. Cloaks are never registered among the items issued to the infantry and probably they were purchased privately.

Also the equipment shows significant changes in the second half of the 1680s. After 1683, the baldric began to disappear replaced by the waist belt carrying sword and bayonet. In the same period the first knapsacks – *Tornister* – also began to appear, carried on the right shoulder and usually trimmed with fur. A bandolier for ammunition was carried always on the left shoulder, but the cartridges were now preserved in the *Patronentasche* (ammunition bag), usually closed with a black leather cover. It is likely that some metal badges were fixed on the bags' cover, more often on the ones issued to the grenadiers.

One of the first images of a grenadier cap is dated 1685. Before this date, probably also the Imperial infantry followed the example of other European armies, which equipped their grenadiers with floppy cloth hats, but unfortunately, there are no sources that prove it. Moreover, one of the first images depicting an Imperial grenadier dating to the mid 1670s shows him with the broad-brimmed hat.[26] In 1685, however, the grenadier's headgear shows the classic elements of the future *Pelzmütze* (bearskin cap) with the cloth bag, although it looks more like a Bohemian or Hungarian-Croatian fur-trimmed hat.[27]

Imperial infantry NCO 1664, after the fresco of Lysá castle. Black headgear with red feather, leather coat without sleeves, dark grey doublet and breeches, dark red stockings, black cravat. The *Feldwebel*, *Führer* and *Corporal* carried the halberd as a typical field sign of their rank, which according to some late 17th century regimental regulations distinguished them when the battalion was deployed in battle or in review. The corporal held the weapon on the left side, while the NCOs had it on the right. When marching, one of the *Führer* usually carried the ensign. (Author's reconstruction)

Detail from the anonymous engraving, *Belagerung von Neuhäusel*, 1685. Note the grenadier with early style *Pelzmütze*. (Author's collection)

---

26 In Lallemand, 'Die k.k. österreich. Armee im Laufe zweyer Jahrhunderte', plate 4.
27 Engraving by anonymous, Belagerung von Neuheusel, 1685'.

Imperial grenadier, 1677–78, after Franz Gerash. Illustrations of Imperial soldiers of late 17th century show a quite plain grey unlined coat with few embellishments or lace. The grenadier, though more colourful than the musketeer, is dressed very simply. Some contemporary descriptions relate the use of breast armour for the grenadiers when engaged in the siege. (Author's reconstruction)

The weaponry of the Imperial infantry changed little from the first half of the 17th century, with the heavy matchlock musket still being used in many regiments. Though the musket rest was rapidly going out of fashion, some weapons were modified, turning it into a spear, or *Schweinsfeder*, forming a useful *chevaux-de-frise* when combined with others. This defence became the norm against enemies like the Ottomans, whose army had always relied heavily on a high percentage of cavalry.

A characteristic tool of the Imperial infantry was the *Springstock*, used by some regiments when marching in the mountains. In fact, its function was analogous to the jumping stick of the Tyrolean alpine guides. The *Springstock* was composed of a wooden pole 180–200 cm long, with a metal tip at one end and a wooden knob on the other.

The bayonet was introduced in the late 1670s for grenadiers only, and it was the common plug model which remained unchanged until the next decade, when progressively all the musketeers were equipped with it.

The matchlock muskets had an average length of 160–165 cm, with calibres ranging from 18.8 to 18.2 mm. and fired balls with a weight ranging from 30 to 35 grams depending on the model. The total weight of the musket ranged between 5 and 6 kg and its useful range was 70–90 metres in absence of wind. The flintlock musket was shorter than 8–5 cm and weighed between 200 and 400 grams less than the matchlock, so as to allow better handling when armed with the bayonet. The calibre of the flintlock was more uniform, being between 17 and 17.5 mm; the ball weighed about 25 grams and the useful range reached almost 300 metres, although above 100 metres it proved to be of low precision. The stock and the box were made of wood, made dark by applying a coat of paint; the wooden ramrod iron tip was housed under the barrel in all models. From late 1680s, in each company four iron rods, consisting of several pieces to be assembled, were also delivered to each *Gefreite*. This rod was used to extract jammed balls from the barrel.

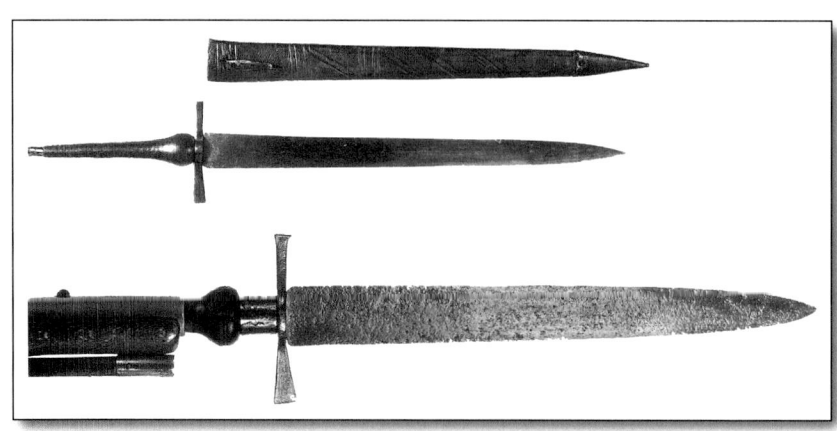

Plug bayonet, circa 1680. Blade length 465 mm; complete length 670 mm. (Heeresgeschichtliches Museum, Vienna)

UNIFORMS, EQUIPMENT AND ENSIGNS

Tyrolean militiamen, from an early 18th century print. Possibly this is the most ancient image representing the militia of Tyrol, where it formed the only permanent defence force throughout the 17th century. (Author's collection)

Imperial *Musketier Gemeiner* (private musketeer) 1658–60. The 1660s was a period of transition in military as well as in the civilian dress. Some elements and accessories from the past coexisted with the new clothing coming from France and Northern Europe. Since the late 1650s, the Imperial soldiers wore coats of a Swedish or Dutch pattern, usually shorter compared to the late models. (Author's reconstruction after contemporary prints)

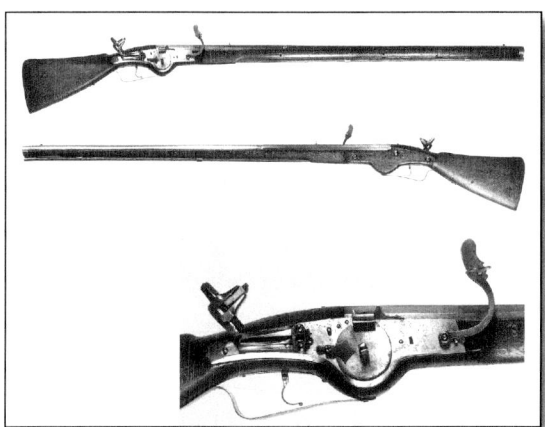
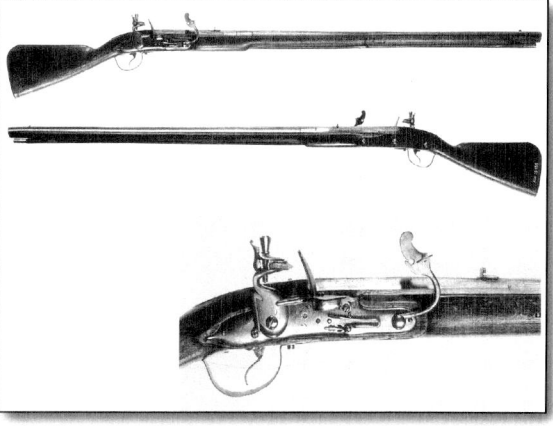

Modified muskets consisted of a serpentine and hammer. The addition of the wheel shot system is less common. The double system always guaranteed the function of the weapon, since above all the wheel mechanisms spoiled very easily and the stone was quickly consumed. The improved flintlock systems were produced in the Viennese arsenals of Seilerstätte starting from 1684, known as *Montecuccoli Muskete*. (Heeresgeschichtliches Museum, Vienna)

221

Most of the muskets were produced in the Viennese arsenal of Seilerstätte, which had also a laboratory for producing upgraded weapons and new prototypes. Montecuccoli was a great promoter of experiments to improve infantry weaponry, especially the firing mechanisms. In the late 1670s matchlock muskets began to be modified with flintlock 'batteries'. Because the first examples of flintlock had several technological limits and the arsenal did not produce flintlocks in sufficient numbers, several muskets were developed with double-firing systems, including wheel lock mechanisms. These weapons remained in use for several years, known as *Montecuccoli Muskete*, and during the War of the Spanish Succession they continued to be used by some Imperial regiments until 1704.

Cavalry

Cuirassiers were a well-established speciality of the Habsburg cavalry. Their appearance had not changed since the mid 17th century and black, leather-lined, polished metal armour and lobster helms appeared as well-established features destined to become iconic in the Imperial army of this age. Numerous examples of these protective items are preserved in the museums of the countries that were part of the Habsburgs' domains. The items show an almost unchanged style and only those manufactured for officers show variations dictated by the current fashion. Moreover, there are detailed descriptions about the characteristics of these defensive weapons. In the early 18th century, the Aulic War Council established the preferred resistance of armour, following the guidelines already introduced in the previous century for manufacturing these items. Cuirassier armour had to resist the shot of a ball of two *loth* (35 grams), and usually on the armour the sign of the shot remained visible as proof of the test.

A consolidated feature of the Imperial heavy cavalry was the typical colour of the metal, obtained by painting the plate in black and then finishing the metal with a protective varnish to restore its natural shine.[28] Although there is no certain evidence, in the 1670s cuirasses of painted leather were probably introduced into some regiments. Leather armour appeared in the German area especially in Württemberg, and, probably, these items provided a model imitated by some regiments of the Swabian circle. One of the rare iconographic sources in which this specific defensive armament appears,

---

28 Several armours and helms dating back to the 17th century are simply painted in black or dark brown. The true and authentic 'burnishing' was in fact a polishing process which consisted in passing an instrument on the metal surface – the 'brunitoio' – fitted with a hard stone (often an agate) which gave the metal a compact lustre and a much warmer tone, from which 'burnish'. The method of burnishing was very tiring and required skill and patience. The artisan slid the stone of the instrument by pressing it on the metal; furthermore the surface had to be constantly greased (for example with glycerine) so that the stone slipped well. The burnishing was used on the metal surfaces already worked and for the plates, whose shape did not allow an easy work the normal brush was used. It is therefore easy to understand why the authentic burnished-polished armour was the prerogative of a few wealthy aristocrats, while the common cuirassiers reserved metal protection simply painted (Author's note).

UNIFORMS, EQUIPMENT AND ENSIGNS

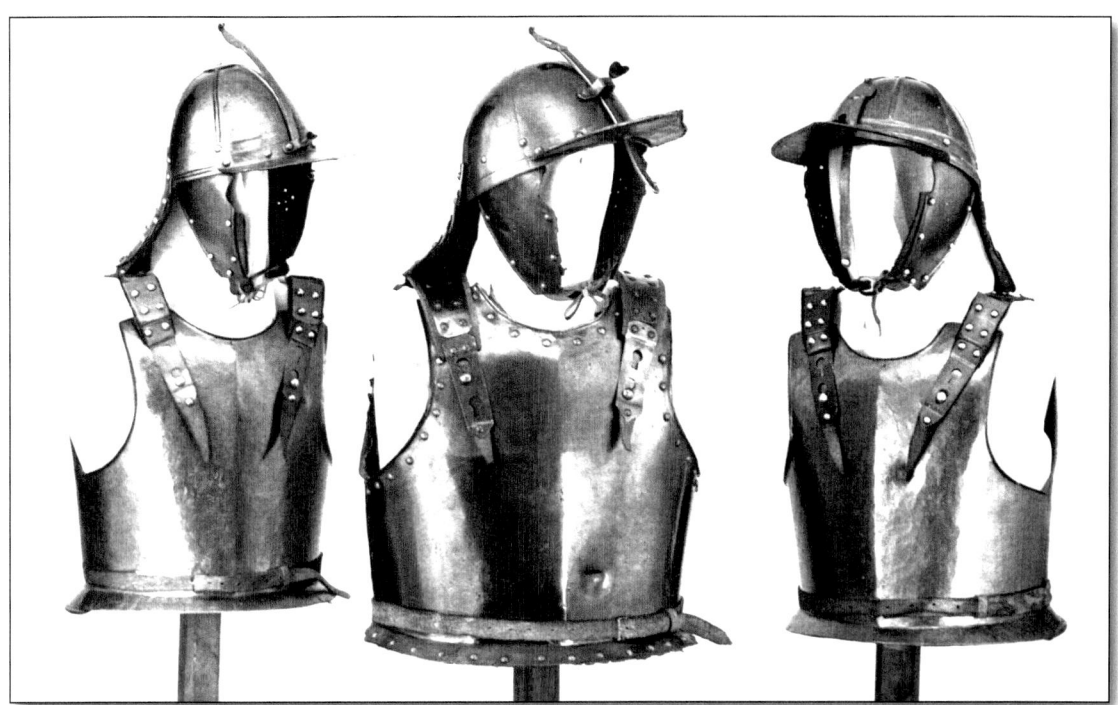

Late 17th century breast armour and *Zischägge* helms, now preserved in the Landzeughaus Museum of Graz. These weapons were mostly produced in Vienna. The Austrian commissar valued the characteristics of resistance and other details to be respected in the manufacture. The armour had to withstand balls of 2 *Loth* (35 grams).

comes from the illustrations of the early 20th century, relating to the history of an Imperial-German cavalry regiment.[29] Here is depicted a 1683 cuirassier of the Swabian circle regiment *Hönstett* (SC-5), wearing a dark brown leather cuirass. It is difficult to establish the documentary reliability of this source, however in the 19th century, the original findings were much more numerous than today and it is not unlikely that the figure was based on models dating back to the 1680s. Black remained the primary colour of the Imperial heavy cavalry's armour, but after 1670, with the entry into the Imperial Army of numerous Lorraine officers, began the tradition that allowed them to use natural metal armour as a distinctive feature.

The lobster helmet – *Zischägge* – continued to be the principal headdress for cuirassiers, at least in action, but they wore also the more comfortable broad-brimmed hats. Margrave Ludwig of Baden recommended a lobster helm against the Ottomans and other 'light enemies', but in several contemporary pictures broad-brimmed hats appear also when the cuirassiers are engaged in fighting.

Another characteristic of the clothing of the Imperial cuirassiers was the leather coat. Due to its characteristic elasticity and resistance, leather, properly tanned, effectively protected soldiers from sword cuts and could, therefore, replace armour. In the mid 17th century, the protective features offered by a leather coat took shape in the form of a specific item of military clothing known as the *Koller* in the Austro-German area.

---

29 New York Public Library, The Vinkhuijzen collection of military uniforms, Germany-Württemberg 1625–1735, *Schwäb. Kreis-Regiment zu Pferd v. Hönstett, 1683, jetz Ulanen-Regiment 'König Karl' (1. Württembergisches) Nr. 19.*

WARS AND SOLDIERS IN THE EARLY REIGN OF LOUIS XIV – VOLUME 2

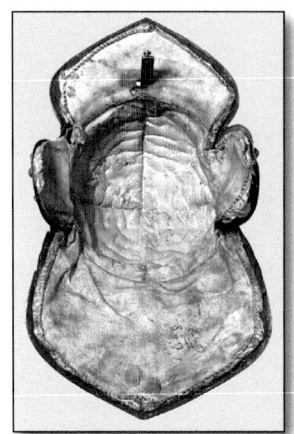 

Zischägge (lobster helm) made in Germany or Austria, mid 17th century, complete with the original quilting. Note the burnished metal that suggests it was intended for an officer. (Author's collection)

Koller and coat-*Koller* in four portraits. From the left: Count Ferdinand Bonaventura von Harrach zu Rohrau (1637–1706), wearing a *Koller* with open sleeves over Rhingraeve-style breeches, 1660 (Národní Muzeum, Prague); *Obrist-Lieutenant* Jobst Joseph Moscon, portrayed before 1668, while serving as an infantry officer for the Archduke of Habsburg Tyrol, wears a fashionable coat-*Koller* with red ribbons, note the sash in white and red (private collection, Austria); unidentified Imperial officer, dated 1678, wearing a *Koller* with embroidered sleeves and flap cuffs (Stibbert Museum, Florence); Count Josef of Herberstein (1633–1689), undated, in leather coat-*Koller* datable to 1685–89 with flap cuffs and pockets. Note the cuirass with the Maltese cross and the sash in red and silver. (Ptuj Regional Museum, Slovenia)

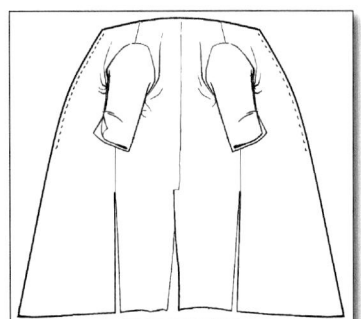 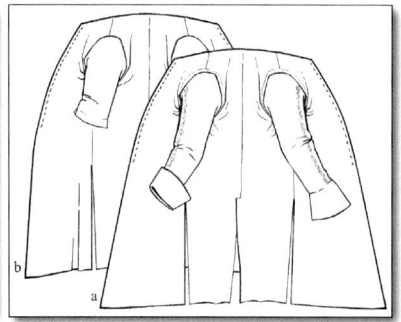 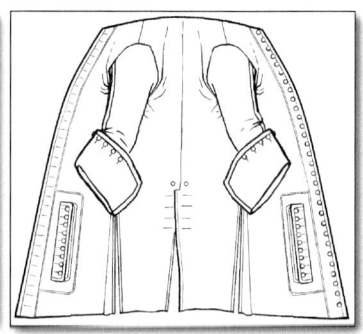

1660s *Koller* after the portrait of Count Ferdinand Bonaventura von Harrach. (Author's reconstruction)

1670s *Koller*, a) after the portrait of Ernst Rüdiger von Starhemberg (1680) and b) unidentified Imperial officer (1678). (Author's reconstruction)

1680s coat-*Koller*, after the portrait of count Joseph von Herberstein (1685–89). (Author's reconstruction)

UNIFORMS, EQUIPMENT AND ENSIGNS

Swabian cuirassier, early 1680s, Wehrgeschichtliches Museum, Rastatt. (Author's photograph)

Imperial cuirassier officer, c. 1683; Heeresgeschichtliches Museum, Vienna. (Author's photograph)

The *Koller* of this period can be traced back to a few models and even in this case it varied only for the garments produced for the officers. Unlike their leather coats made with deerskin or elk, and provided with quilting of amber powder and fragrant herbs, those of simple cuirassiers were made of cow or sheep leather, composed of seven parts for the body, the breast and back normally of double thickness. Simple laces closed the coat on the front up to the waist, but these remained covered when the horseman wore his armour. For the cuirassiers, who made up the bulk of the Imperial cavalry, it was therefore easier to retain uniformity and rationalisation of the equipment. Despite this, the peculiarities of the proprietary colonels also survived in the regiments of cuirassiers, but were limited to the clothing of musicians, dressed with the colonel's livery.

The iconographic evidence of the 1660s and 1670s usually shows the cuirassier *Koller* devoid of flap cuffs. The identification of the regiments was therefore entrusted to the colour of the saddle covers and ensigns. During the Thirty Years' War some regiments of Imperial cuirassiers were also distinguished by the colour of the horses, for which there were units with exclusively black or grey horses, and probably this device remained in use for many more years. The introduction of cloth flap cuffs for the *Koller* occurred very late in the Austrian area and the first iconographic sources showing these

The battle of Párkany, 7–10 October 1683, in a contemporary Austrian print. In the foreground, a cuirassier officer is riding a horse. He wears a *Koller* with flap cuffs and broad-brimmed hat and close to him, another man is in armour and a *Zischägge* helm. Note on the left, the marching infantry with bandoliers and baldrics. (Author's collection)

items date back to 1683.[30] Unfortunately, this source is a monochrome print which could mean their leather coat had leather cuff flaps. In fact, very few leather *Koller* with cloth cuffs are preserved in the Austrian collections, and one item dated as early 1680 – but with leather cuff flaps – has survived until now and is exhibited in the *Wehrgeschichtliches Museum* of Rastatt. Certainly, the greater resistance of leather compared to cloth has contributed to this result, but it is likely that the cuffs were removable and attached to the *Koller* with simple buttons. Another *Koller* surviving from the late 17th century is preserved in the *Heeresgeschichtliches Museum* in Vienna. This item has a pair of red, cloth, turned-back cuffs lined with yellow silk, because it belonged to an officer, as qualified by the carmine red sash with golden fringe. The buff *Koller* is devoid of pockets and buttons, it had been restored several times and probably the flap cuffs are not original.

A considerable part of the period iconography represents cuirassiers in full armour, including protection for the shoulders and forearms, especially the most ancient depictions. In the fresco of Lisà, the cuirassiers are depicted with leather coat, lobster helm and breast armour; some officers wear supplementary protection, but the figures are not enough detailed to identify further elements. One of the first coloured iconographic sources depicting cuirassiers wearing leather coats complete with cuff flaps, is a painting representing the siege of Buda in 1686. A group of cuirassiers is advancing through the main street of Buda's citadel, with an officer in a blue coat in front of them. The scene is well detailed, but the certainty that they are actual Imperial cuirassiers is questioned by the presence of some Bavarian infantrymen nearby. Furthermore, the dating of the painting could be 10 or more years later than the depicted episode, at least judging by the style

---

30 Print of the encounter of Párkany, 9 October 1683; anonymous engraver and artist, in Bánlaky J. *A Magyar Nemzet Hadtörténelme*, (Budapest, 1928–1942). vol. XVII.

UNIFORMS, EQUIPMENT AND ENSIGNS

The plundering of Buda, after the surrender of the city, occurred on 2 September 1686. The painting was probably commissioned by an eyewitness, and indeed it appears to be very accurate, although the figures appear dressed in a more modern style compared to the year of the event. In the centre, behind the mounted officer and the Ottoman prisoners, a group of cuirassiers is advancing dressed with *Koller*, black polished armour and *Zischägge* helms. Note the waist belts which have replaced the baldrics. (Private collection)

Cuirassier's *Koller*, 1700; after Ottenfeld-Teuber. The manufacture of this item required a large quantity of cattle or sheep leather, since the breast part was normally in double-layer. The *Koller* were usually made without pockets, but some models had flaps applied only for decorative purposes, while *Koller* with actual pockets were usually produced only for NCOs and officers.

of the dress, and in that case the artist would not have used contemporary models. The aforementioned document of the anonymous Italian officer dated 1676 increases the mystery on this matter, because when he described the uniforms of the cuirassier regiments, he recorded the *coietto* (leather coat) and separately the *mostre* (facings). Unfortunately, this term could be referred to cuffs as well as to saddle and pistol holders covers, leaving scholars with an uncertainty difficult to solve.

Another well-detailed representation of *Koller* with cuff is depicted in Teuber-Ottenfeld's famous study of the Imperial army.[31] Though this work deals with the uniforms starting from 1700, the Austrian artist reproduced an early leather coat with red cloth cuffs. The details and other particulars of the drawing suggest that Ottenfeld had used an original item as a model, as confirmed also in the drawings of the other uniforms: ancient clothing that in the previous century was still in a condition to be examined.

Before the 1680s, certain information about breeches and waistcoat is equally rare, also because *Koller* and *Rock* hid these items. Presumably, the waistcoat was introduced in the early 1680s as for the infantry.

According to Donath, in the 1680s saddle and pistol holster covers contributed to identify the regiments with large piping around the edge. Most examples were limited to yellow piping, but in other cases elaborate

---

31 R. von Ottenfeld and O. Teuber, *Die Österreichische Armee von 1700 bis 1867* (Vienna, 1867), plate *Kavallerie Röcke*,

WARS AND SOLDIERS IN THE EARLY REIGN OF LOUIS XIV – VOLUME 2

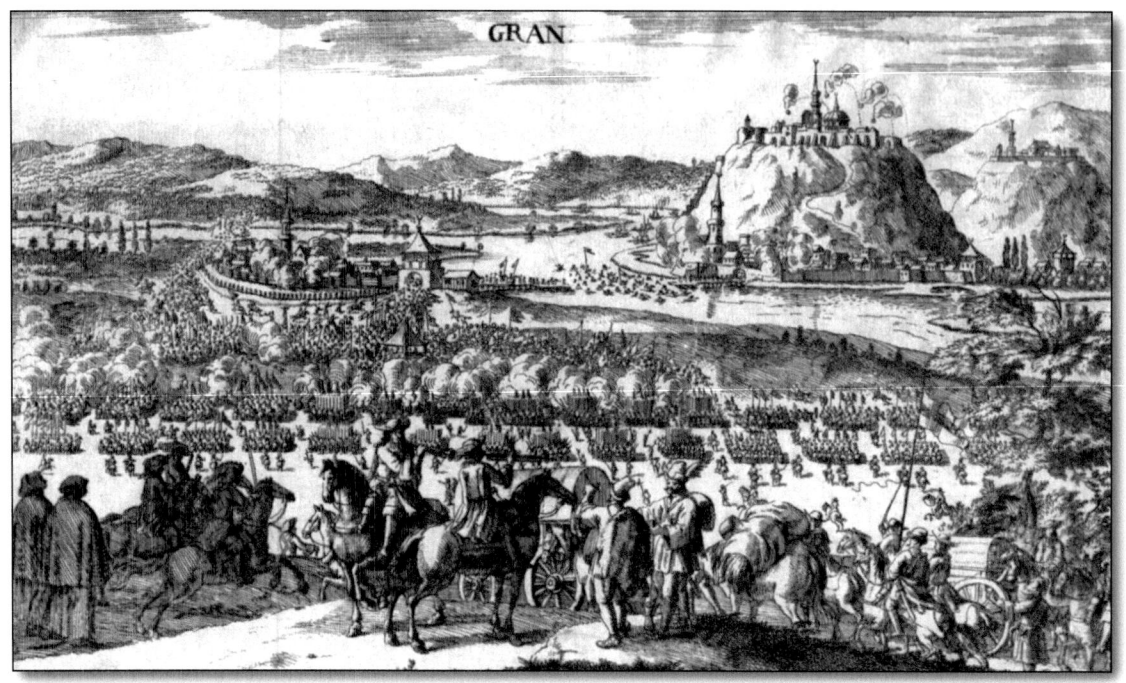

The Imperial army crosses the Danube at Esztergom in 1684, engraving by Nypoor. This kind of image, very numerous after 1683, is our major source of knowledge concerning the uniform and equipment of the Imperial army. Although sometimes they reproduce conventional scenes and often are not coloured, these images show several details on the actual appearance of the soldiers on campaign. Note, in the foreground, the trumpeters coated with *justaucorps* with false sleeves and broad-brimmed cap, certainly more practical than the Turkish *Mütze* exhibited in parade. Note the Hungarian *Grenzer* footmen wearing cloaks. (Author's collection)

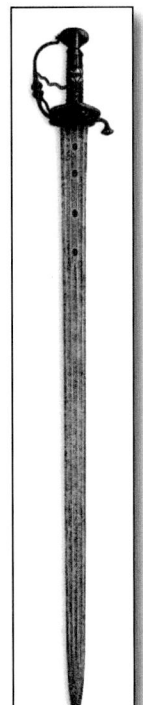

Early *Pallash* for heavy cavalry, Austria circa 1685. (Private collection)

German or Austrian small sword for officer with iron hilt, third quarter of the 17th century; overall length 71.2 cm. (Private collection)

Austrian dragoon or infantry sword; 1660–70; overall length 84.7 cm. (Private collection)

UNIFORMS, EQUIPMENT AND ENSIGNS

stripes of livery are described, similar to those introduced in the following century under the Empress Maria Theresa. However, both the iconographic evidence and the original items are absent, and it is difficult to think that such elaborate and expensive objects were exposed to the risks of a war campaign, and probably, if they really existed, were used only in peacetime service or in quarters.

On the contrary, cuirassier equipment and weaponry has survived until today in the major collections. Imperial cuirassiers continued to use the strong cavalry sword of the Thirty Years' War – known as the *Pappenheimer* – alongside the Walloon-type sword, which was not widespread in the Imperial cavalry before 1670.[32] The substitution of the old cavalry sword with a new type began in the early 1680s with the introduction of the heavy *Pallash* sword. This weapon derived from the analogous Turkish-Hungarian sword and compared to the previous one allowed the bearer to strike more effectively by slashing and thrusting. For this purpose, the grip had a slight curvature that allowed easier control. Until the 1670s, sword and musket – usually a short, wheel lock musket – were carried with bandolier and baldric crossed on the shoulders, but in the early 1680s, iconography shows the cavalry sword hanging from the waist belt, for cuirassiers as well as dragoons. The uniform of these latter was generally the same as that worn by the infantry. The iconographic source portraying one of the first uniformed dragoons is a print of Bartholomäus Kilian, dated 1663, representing military scenes of the Hungarian–Transylvanian campaign. Despite the low detail, the dragoon appears dressed with the long infantry coat, the ubiquitous broad-brimmed hat and leather boots. This kind of dress is confirmed in the aforementioned fresco in Lysá Castle. Kilian's print seems to have inspired two famous 19th century Austrian military illustrators, Fritz Lallemand and Franz Gerasch. Both artists represented early dragoons, dating them to approximately 1650–70 and 1680 with a simple light grey coat without flap cuffs and pockets, white neckcloth, black broad-brimmed hat and cavalry boots. Gerash adds a ribbon to the hat of his dragoon, the only concession to coloured accessories. The coat in the reconstruction of Lallemand has a pair of tight sleeves without flap cuffs – or hidden by the gloves – which would date the dragoons to the late 1670s or the early 1680s; Gerasch dates back his dragoon to 1650, and here the coat has the open sleeves, typical of the 1650s. In Lallemand's picture, bandolier and baldric are presumably of yellow leather, while Gerash depicts the same equipment in black, and the bandolier carries cartridges like those issued to the infantry. Apart from these differences, both authors represent correctly this early dragoon: an event that, for once, would confirm the reliability of the 19th century reconstructions. Richard Knötel turned to Lallemand for his *Handbuch der Uniformkunde*, when he depicted the dragoon for 1683.[33] Knötel included another pair of figures representing

---

32 The continuation of use of the Pappenheimer is confirmed in many portraits of the 1650s and 1660s. Moreover, the scarce number of swords with Walloon hilts preserved in the Austrian collections would confirm the poor fortune of this weapon in the Imperial cavalry before the 1670s (Author's note).
33 R. Knötel, *Handbuch der Uniformkunde* (Rathenow, 1896), p. 233.

Dragoon *Tambour*, 1683–85; author's reconstruction after K.A. Wilke. As mounted footmen, the dragoons had the same instruments as the infantry, except the regiment *Schulz* (ID-1), which captured a pair of Swedish cavalry kettledrums during the 1676 campaign in Jutland and received permission to use them for the *Leib-Compagnie*.

Dragoons of regiment *Savoyen* (Giulio ID-13) and *Savoyen* (Eugenio, ID-10), after Richard Knötel.

Imperial dragoons in late 17th century in the *Grosse Uniformenkunde*. The plate is in colour and depicts a private dragoon of the regiment *Savoyen* (Giulio, ID-13) in 1682 and a dragoon officer of regiment *Savoyen* (Eugenio, ID-10) in 1690.[34] The private wears a fashioned *Rock* (*justaucorps*) with red aiguillette on the right shoulder, flap cuffs and flap pockets. The coat is dark blue lined red and the saddle cover and pistol holster had an elaborate edge piping of white and azure with the Savoy coat of arms embroidered in red, azure and white. As for the elaborate cuirassier saddle cover, probably this item appeared only in quarters and on parade.

In the following decades, dragoon uniform followed the transformation of the infantry dress, while the equipment remained similar to that issued to cuirassiers. In appearance, the boots were the same as worn by the cuirassiers, but they were actually made of more supple leather for ease of service when dismounted.

---

34 R. Knötel, *Grosse Uniformenkunde* (Rathenow, 1890) vol. X, plate 29.

UNIFORMS, EQUIPMENT AND ENSIGNS

Imperial cuirassiers musicians, ensign and private dragoon, 1680–83, published in the 1970s in the Austrian magazine *1683, die Mölkerbastei*. (Author's collection)

Cloaks were issued as supplementary items for rainy weather, both for cuirassiers and dragoons. The late 17th century iconography represents the classic cloak with a supplementary layer of cloth on the shoulder and a high collar. Grey or light grey was the usual colour, but some authors speak of cloaks in dark brown, and even red or dark blue. Starting in the late 1680s, the cloak's collar repeated the facing colour of the uniforms.

Cavalry cloaks, 1670–80. (Author's reconstruction)

Imperial cuirassiers and dragoons, after Stefano Della Bella, 1660–64. (Author's collection)

Imperial dragoon, 1678–83, after Lallemand, *Die k. k. österreichische Armee im Laufe zweyer Jahrhunderte*, (Vienna, 1840)

UNIFORMS, EQUIPMENT AND ENSIGNS

In the same period in which the style of the uniform for cuirassiers and dragoons began to stabilise, even the hussars standardised some of the typical characteristics of their clothing, which – as is known – derived from the Hungarian and Croatian dress. Although some authors gave information on the adoption of uniform and regular clothing for the hussar regiments at the end of the 17th century, the situation remained precarious for a long time and full uniformity appeared very late, at least according to the statements of eyewitnesses and the iconographic evidence. However, the fresco in Lysá Castle clearly shows the Croat regiment *Gutschenich* (IHc-1) in 1664 wearing azure coat and red slouch hat trimmed with fur.

Hungarian cavalrymen receive the surrender of an Ottoman garrison in 1690. Note the officers with metal *Zischägge* helms and on left the one with leopard fur, while private hussars wear an *Attila* jacket and cloak. The absence of the fur jacket-*mentö* is not an illustrator's oversight, but reflects the simple clothing of private hussars who, against cold or rain, used more frequently cloaks of grey-white *halina* wool. Although some 19th century sources attribute uniforms for the early regiments of hussars, full regularity was achieved only after 1700. (Author's collection)

Hungarian hussar officer, detail from a popular print dated 1680. Red *mentö* (pelisse) with black cords and fur-trimmed slouch hat, dark yellow *Attila* (jacket) azure trousers, red leather boots. (Author's collection)

Artillery

Imperial artillerymen, early 1670s, after Lallemand. Grey coat with short red flap cuffs, *Die k. k. österreichische Armee im Laufe zweyer Jahrhunderte*, (Vienna, 1840)

In the Austro-German area, normal civilian clothing was worn by artillery crew with just some items making it possible to recognise a man as an artilleryman. Only the style of baldric or artillery accoutrements, like the powder flask and other technical instruments qualified the artillerymen as military personnel. According to Donath, since the 1650s the Imperial artillerymen dressed in blue with red facings and this scheme remained unchanged until the 1690s, when a grey *Rock* with red cuffs replaced the old uniform in the first years of the new century. Possibly, in the early 1660s, the first artillery uniform could have included blue doublets and breeches, but other sources relate grey and red already in the 1670s. Possibly Donath confused the grey of some ancient iconographic source for the blue, as in the drawings of Franz Gerash's series, where the *Constabler* wears a grey-azure coat with short sleeves and red cuffs. Pearl grey, which is quite similar to pale blue, could be altered to azure through oxidation of the print, considering that Gerash depicted this figure in 1855. The same subject was reproduced also by Lallemand 15 years before, but this time the artilleryman wears a pearl grey coat and breeches.

However, evidence on the blue coat of the Imperial artillerymen can be found in the painting of Frans Geffels relating to the siege of Buda. The artist depicted a battery with its servants. There are some artillerymen wearing red waistcoats and breeches and some in blue coats with red cuffs. Unfortunately, the artist leaves the matter unresolved, because other figures are dressed in grey. The artillerymen dressed in blue could be a musician or officer and possibly this hypothesis would solve the mystery.

Although there were no rules appertaining to dress and equipment for the men, strict regulations were observed for the guns, with specific prescriptions regarding the colour of the carriages, the finish of the accessories and barrel decorations. All artillery pieces cast in Austria were embossed with the emblem of the eagle and the motto CONSILIO ET INDUSTRIA on the barrel,

Imperial artillery, detail after the *Belagerung von Ofen* by Frans Geffels, 1686. Some servants wear red waistcoats, while other figures appear dressed in blue or grey coats with red facings. (Author's photograph)

UNIFORMS, EQUIPMENT AND ENSIGNS

while a name or an allegorical figure identifying the piece. As a tradition of the Imperial army, the coat of arms of the *General Feldzeugmeister* was added to the barrel. It was quite common to accompany both with slogans or some auspicious text. On a 2 lb culverin cast at the end of the 17th century there was a spiral engraved on the barrel with the inscription: *will niemand singen; sing aber ich über Berg und Thal, hört man mich!* (nobody wants to sing; but I sing through mountains and valleys, and you may hear me!)[35] Even the carriages were decorated to identify them as Imperial. All the wooden parts were painted in black, whilst the straps and metal accessories were in red lead. Only the wheels generally remained in their natural colour. However, large guns could have painted wheels to match the carriages.

Ensigns

Every company of infantry or cavalry had its own ensign which, with the exception of *Leibfahne* and *Leibstandarte* (Life Colour) carried by the first company, usually had an identical pattern for the whole regiment. The dimensions of the infantry flags were remarkable: over two metres per side in the 1660s and 1670s, though they became smaller in next decade. Cavalry standards measured between 65x65 cm and 76x76 cm including the fringed edge. There were no rules regarding colours or design, except for the black double-headed eagle depicted on one side. After 1650, the eagle became the main Imperial symbol and replaced the other heraldic figures used by the House of Austria, such as the Burgundy cross. Unfortunately, almost no infantry flags have been preserved intact to this day and the information comes mainly from the books illustrated by the Austrians' French adversaries, such as *Les triomphes du Roy Louis XIV*, in which are reproduced the flags captured during the wars of the late 17th centuries. Another significant group of ensigns, mostly standards and guidons, are preserved in the collection of the *Heeresgeschichtliches* Museum of Vienna. Some of these items are still in good condition, and this suggests that perhaps they never saw a battlefield.

Despite the lack of rules, and uncertainty regarding the meaning of certain symbols, it is possible to identify some characteristic elements that help us to position chronologically the ensign with reasonable precision. Every time an officer was appointed as colonel proprietor he assigned new colours to the regiment. The main colours were usually that of the colonel's livery or coat of arms. Usually the black two-headed eagle had a golden rostrum and claws and a red tongue, and was surmounted by an imperial gold crown; sometimes both heads could be crowned. Behind these elements there was the golden aureole, sometimes only with the highlighted edge. In some flags, as well as cavalry

Austrian linstock, mid 17th century. Note the iron head formed of six shaped flanges; length 51.5 cm. (Private collection).

Standard of the Swabian Cuirassier regiment *Gronsfeld* (SC-4), late 17th century. Yellow background with white oval and golden lions; white cross on black; green laurel and red ribbon; yellow-black fringes, 86x53 cm. (Copy of the original preserved in the Landesmuseum Württemberg, Stuttgart)

---

35 K.u.K. Kriegsarchiv, 'Feldzüge des Prinzen Eugen', vol. XVI, pp. 285–287.

Company standard, regiment *Caprara Cuirassieren* (IC-3). Azure with silver embroideries and golden fringes; silver and gold figures holding the shield: above, golden lion, below azure with golden eight pointed stars. (Author's illustration)

Company standards, possibly regiment *Saint-Croix* (IC-47), 1685. Red with silver embroideries and golden fringes; silver leaves on golden branches; black-golden eagle; silver armoured arm with brown spear. (Author's illustration)

standards, the eagle's chest carried the reigning Emperor's monogram: L-I for Leopold I. Exceptionally, the cipher was enclosed in a shield. The legs held either to the right or the left, the sceptre, the sword or the globe; all these elements were always in gold.

On the *Kompanie-Fahne* (company colour) the eagle could be on the obverse or reverse, but rarely on both sides. Unfortunately, almost all the drawings relating captured infantry flags depict only one side of the flag, the one with the eagle, and do not allow sight of other figures depicted on the other side. According to the regimental histories, the side opposite to the one with the double-headed eagle usually carried the image of a saint. The verse of the *Leibfahne* usually carried the image of the Virgin. Regarding the adoption of this image there are several tales and legends. According to some chroniclers, Leopold I renewed a vow made by his father to the Virgin of Mariazell. In 1676, during a pilgrimage, Leopold would have attributed to Maria the title of 'supreme general' of all the Imperial armies in time of war and Imperial 'plenipotentiary' in peacetimes. In this period the image of the Virgin of Mariazell, crowned and with her son in her arms, the little Jesus (*Jesus Kindelein*) would have been adopted on the Imperial war ensigns. The Marian cult would have favoured the introduction of another image of the

UNIFORMS, EQUIPMENT AND ENSIGNS

Imperial ensign, 1660–64. 1 – Cuirassier company standard, possibly regiment *Pfalz-Sulzbach* (IC-14): carmine red background; black eagle, gold shield, crown, fringe and inscriptions. 2 – company standard, possibly regiment Lothringen Cuirassieren (IC-7), 1664: yellow background, black eagle with Habsburg coat of arms red-white-red; silver fringes (reconstruction after the fresco of the Lysá castle). 3 – Standard of Hungarian *Grenzer* cavalry, c. 1660: red background with gold fringe, flames and lays; Mary's image in red waist and azure mantle on silver half moon (after Somogyi Győző's Magyar Hadizászlók; Budapest, 2011). 4 – Flag of an unidentified Hungarian foot militia unit: red and white stripes, gold shield with Hungarian arms (fresco of Rudolf Müller, 1653; castle of Sarvár, Hungary).

Virgin, through the preaching of the Franciscans in Austria, including the influential Father Marco d'Aviano. After 1683, the most common image of the Virgin on the Imperial *Leib* ensigns would become the Assumption, in which Maria appears surrounded by the rays of the sun, without her son, on a cloud and a crescent at her feet.[36]

Compared to the company flags, the *Leibfahne* always had both fields of white colour. The edge of the drapes had some decorative elements and among the most common, flames appeared frequently on the Imperial infantry flags of the late 17th century.

The classic texts concerning the Imperial ensigns provide only a few details regarding the period between the 1660s and the 1680s. Alfred Mell

---

36 Cardini, *Il Turco a Vienna*, p. 255.

WARS AND SOLDIERS IN THE EARLY REIGN OF LOUIS XIV – VOLUME 2

According to the Austrian magazine *Die Mölkerbastei*, in 1672 the regiment *Strein zu Fuss* (II-78) had a company flag in crimson red with a white lion with golden crown and monogram of Leopold I, green laurel and white-red chequered edge. The regiment was formed with recruits from Tyrol and Carinthia and completed with Swiss infantrymen who served under Archduke Sigismund Franz of Habsburg-Tyrol. There is no information as to whether the verso of the flags carried the black double headed eagle. (Author's collection)

Encampment flag, regiment *Alt-Starhemberg zu Fuss* (II-41); c. 1685. Red background; black eagle with yellow legs, flames and flint; white aureole, yellow-blue-black edge. (after the original preserved in Austria), approximate size 100x170 cm. (Author's illustration)

UNIFORMS, EQUIPMENT AND ENSIGNS

Company standard, probably regiment *Harrant Cuirassieren* (IC-31), after the original preserved in the *Waffensammlung* of Vienna. Red with golden fringes, flames and letters; black eagle with gold crown and legs; shield outlined in yellow, of azure with wall and towers in natural, white lion on black with red inner edge and white scroll. (Author's illustration)

discusses the ensigns captured by the Swedes in 1657, preserved in the Armémuseum of Stockholm, but he gives only vague information about the colours and the provenance.[37] Mell describes the more common allegorical figures depicted on the ensigns, such as the pelican, Fortune, the armed right arm, the laurel or the oak leaves.

Before this author, Heinrich Metzger collected memories and relations about Imperial ensigns since 1661.[38] He adds little detail on the infantry and cavalry colours of this age, except for some interesting descriptions regarding the figures carried on the ensigns and the circumstances of their choice as symbols. Metzger confirmed the tradition that obliged the freshly appointed colonel proprietors to order new flags for their regiments and, obviously, this event occurred also when a new emperor was elected.[39] However, the replacement of the flags could not take place instantaneously and therefore companies continued to carry the same ensigns for some time after. This is exactly what happened to the regiments that marched to Poland in 1657, on whose flags and standards there was still the monogram of Ferdinand III.

---

37 A. Mell, *Die Fahnen des österreichischen Soldaten im Wandel der Zeiten* (Vienna: Bergland Verlag, 1962), p. 32.
38 H. Metzger, *Fahnen-Historik der K. und K. Österr.-Ungar. Infanterie der Letzen 300 Jahre* (Wiener-Neustadt, 1898), pp. 30–35.
39 In 1661, the Sparr infantry regiment, just entered the Emperor's service, received nine new flags. Evidently, the first was the *Leibfahne*, paid 14 *Gulden*, while the others, coloured, cost 20 *Gulden*. Unfortunately, any indication has been recorded regarding the colours and eventual figures or symbols. *Ibidem*, p. 30.

Appendix I

Reichsmatricel of 1663 (in simplum)

State/Prince:	Cavalry:	Infantry:	or monthly:
Österreichischer Kreis (Austrian Circle)			
Habsburg-Österreich	120	554	3,656 fl.
Habsburg-Tyrol	48	184 2/3	1,218 fl. 40 kr.
Trent	14	91 1/3	532 fl.
Brixen	with Habsburg-Tyrol		
Kirchberg	1	4	28 fl.
Constance (Town)	3	50	236 fl.
	186	834	
Burgundischer Kreis (Burgundian Circle)			
Habsburg-Spain for Low Countries, Luxembourg and Franche-Comté	120	554	3,656 fl.
	120	564	
Kur-Reinischer Kreis (Electoral-Rhenish Circle)			
Kur-Mainz (Bishopric Electorate of Mainz)	60	277	1,828 fl.
Kur-Trier (Bishopric Electorate of Trier)	40	184	1,216 fl.
Kur-Köln (Bishopric Electorate of Cologne)	60	277	1,828 fl.
Coblenz	4	20	128 fl.
Nassau-Beylstein	1	2	24 fl.
Arenberg	2	6	48 fl.
Rheinegg	1	-	12 fl.
Nieder-Eisenburg	2	8	56 fl.
	170	774	
Fränkischer Kreis (Franconian Circle)			
Würzburg	45	208	1,372 fl.
Bamberg	30	182	1,088 fl.

APPENDIX I

State/Prince:	Cavalry:	Infantry:	or monthly:
Aichstätt	20	132	768 fl.
Teutsch Orden (Teutonic Order)	19	55	448 fl.
Brandenburg-Kulmbach	17	78	516 fl.
Ansbach-Bayreuth	17	78	516 fl.
Henneberg	15	44	356 fl.
Castell	1	4	28 fl.
Wertheim	4	25	160 fl.
Reineck (Kur-Mainz)	2	10	64 fl.
Hohenlohe	8	40	256 fl.
Reichelsperg (Würzburg)	1	4	28 fl.
Erbach	2	8	56 fl.
Limpurg-Semperfreyen	2	7	52 fl.
Limpurg-Gaildorfer	2	10	64 fl.
Schwartzenberg	1	3	24 fl.
Seinsheim	1	4	28 fl.
Nürnberg	40	250	1,480 fl.
Rothenburg	10	65	380 fl.
Windsheim	4	30	168 fl.
Schweinfurt	4	25	148 fl.
Weissenburg	3	16	100 fl.
	248	1,278	

Schwäbischer Keis (Swabian Circle)
Geistliche (Ecclesial)

	Cavalry:	Infantry:	or monthly:
Constance (Bishopric)	7	30	204 fl.
Reichenau	2	4	40 fl
Augsburg (Bishopric)	21	100	652 fl.
Kempten	6	20	152 fl.
Ellwangen	5	18	132 fl.
Lindau	-	5	20 fl.
Buchau	2	6	48 fl.
Salmonsweil	4	67	316 fl.
Weingarten	4	18	120 fl.
Ochsenhausen	4	20	128 fl.
Gengenbach	1	3	24 fl.
Elchingen	3	13	88 fl.
Yrsin	-	14	56 fl.
Auersperg	-	10	40 fl.
Rockenburg	2	10	64 fl.
Münchrot	1	8	44 fl.
Schussenried	2	14	80 fl.
Weissenau	2	14	80 fl.
Marchtal	2	5	44 fl.
Peterhausen	-	6	24 fl.
Wettenhausen	1	3	24 fl.
Baindt	-	3	12 fl.

State/Prince:	Cavalry:	Infantry:	or monthly:
Heppach	-	5	20 fl.
Guttenzell	-	5	20 fl.
Rottenmünster	1	4	28 fl.
Weltliche (Secular)			
Württemberg	60	227	1,828 fl.
Baden-Durlach	38	103	264 fl.
Hochberg-Röteln and Sausenberg (Baden-Durlach)			188 fl.
Baden-Baden			248 fl.
Hohenzollern-Hechingen	6	20	152 fl.
Hohenzollern-Sigmaringen	4	22 1/2	152 fl.
Alschausen	3	31	160 fl.
Montrfort	3	20	116 fl.
Tetnant-Argen (Montfort)	2	11	68 fl.
Rothenfels (Königsegg)	1	7	40 fl.
Wasserburg (Fugger)	-	2	8 fl.
Barr and Küntzgerthals (Fürstenberg)	6	30	129 fl.
Heiligenberg, Jungenau and Trochtelfingen (Fürstenberg)	4	22 ½	138 fl.
Gundelfingen, Haingen (Fürstenberg)	2	2	32 fl.
Oettingen-Oettingen	8	45	138 fl.
Oettingen-Wallerstein			138 fl.
Wisensteig	2	-	24 fl.
Zimmern	2	9	60 fl.
Lupfen	4	8	120 fl.
Mindelheim (Kur-Bayern)	3	10	76 fl.
Sultz	2	9	108 fl.
Blumenegg-Schellenberg	1	6	
Thüngen	1	-	
Weingarten-Hohenembs	10	45	312 fl.
Königsegg-Heulendorf	1	3	44 fl.
Königs-Eckerberg	-	5	
Grafenegg	1	2	20 fl.
Eberstein	-	4	16 fl.
Fugger	4	15	108 fl.
Justingen	-	5	20 fl.
Geroltzegg (Geroldseck)	1	2	20 fl.
Augsburg (Town)	25	150	900 fl.
Ulm	25	150	900 fl.
Esslingen	5	40	220 fl.
Reutlingen	3	38	188 fl.
Nordlingen	5	50	260 fl.
Hall	-	-	293 fl.
Überlingen	6	60	312 fl.
Rotweil	3	61	280 fl.
Heilbronn	4	40	208 fl.
Gmünd	-	-	176 fl.

APPENDIX I

State/Prince:	Cavalry:	Infantry:	or monthly:
Memmingen	4	50	248 fl.
Lindau (Town)	3	40	196 fl.
Dünckelsbühel	4	40	208 fl.
Biberach	3	40	196 fl.
Ravensburg	3	40	196 fl.
Kempten	3	30	156 fl.
Kaufbeuren	2	34	160 fl.
Weil	1	12	60 fl.
Wangen	2	14	80 fl.
Isny	2	14	80 fl.
Leutkirch	-	10	40 fl.
Wimpfen	2	14	80 fl.
Giengen	1	12	60 fl.
Pfulendorff	2	20	104 fl.
Aalen	1	12	60 fl.
Bopfingen	-	6	24 fl.
Bucahu	-	2	8 fl.
Buchorn	-	5	20 fl.
Offenburg	-	30	120 fl.
Gengenbach	-	15	60 fl.
Zell am Hamersbach	-	10	40 fl.
	348	1,721	

Ober-Rheinischer Kreis (Upper-Rhenish Circle)

State/Prince:	Cavalry:	Infantry:	or monthly:
Worms (Bishopric)	2	13	76 fl.
Speyer (Bishopric)	18	60	456 fl.
Strassburg (Bishopric)	18	100	616 fl.
Basel (Bishop)	2	15	84 fl.
Weissenburg	2	14	80 fl.
Odenheim	1	7	40 fl.
Johanniter Orden (Knights of Malta)	10	30	240 fl.
Fulda	17	50	404 fl.
Hirschfeld	2	9	60 fl.
Murbach	6	19	148 fl.
St. Gregorien (Münster)	1	4	28 fl.
Prumen (Kur-Trier)	1	13	64 fl.
Pfalz-Simmern (Palatinate)	3	10	40 fl.
Sponheim (Palatinate)			76 fl.
Pfalz-Lautern (Palatinate)		-	-
Pfalz-Zweybrücken	10	30	240 fl.
Pfalz-Lautereck	2	4	40 fl.
Hessen-Kassel	50	260	1,093 fl. 20 kr.
Hessen-Darmstadt			546 fl.
Nassau-Saarbücken	6	30	192 fl.
Nassau-Weilburg	6	30	192 fl.
Nassau-Wiesbaden	2	10	64 fl.

State/Prince:	Cavalry:	Infantry:	or monthly:
Wald und Rheingraf	4	12	96 fl.
Reipoltskirchen	1	4	28 fl.
Kriechingen	2	4	40 fl.
Salm	1	2	20 fl.
Hanau-Lichtenberg	6	22	160 fl.
Hanau-Münzenberg	10	30	240 fl.
Leiningen-Hartenberg	3	9	72 fl.
Leiningen-Westerburg	2	4	40 fl.
Falkenstein	2	4	40 fl.
Königstein	-	-	20 fl.
Ober Eisenburg (Hessen-Darmstadt)	6	24	168 fl.
Solms-Laubach	4	24	144 fl.
Solms-Braunfels	4	18	120 fl.
Witgenstein	1	4	28 fl.
Waldeck	4	18	120 fl.
Pless (Hessen-Cassel)	1	-	12 fl.
Fleckenstein	1	1	16 fl.
Kaysersberg	2	15	84 fl.
Türckheim	-	5	20 fl.
Ober-Ehenheim	2	14	80 fl.
Colmar	4	30	168 fl.
Strassburg (Town)	25	150	900 fl.
Rossheim	1	3	24 fl.
Schlettstatt	4	24	144 fl.
Hagenau	6	30	192 fl.
Weissenburg	2	22	112 fl.
Landau	2	18	96 fl.
Speyer (Town)	3	60	276 fl.
Worms (Town)	-	-	276 fl.
Frankfurt	20	140	800 fl.
Friedberg	-	12	48 fl.
Wetzlar	-	8	32 fl.
	282	1,419	

Westphälischer Kreis (Westphalian Circle)

State/Prince:	Cavalry:	Infantry:	or monthly:
Paderborn (Bishopric)	18	34	352 fl.
Münster (Bishopric)	30	118	832 fl.
Osnabrück (Bishopric)	6	36	216 fl.
Verden (to Sweden)	5	15	120 fl.
Minden (Bishopric and Town)	10	16	184 fl.
Werden	2	6	48 fl.
Stabel	2	22	112 fl.
St. Cornelij (Münster)	-	12	48 fl.
Corbey	3	9	60 fl.
Herforden (Herford, Abbey)	-	6	24 fl.
Essen	2	13	76 fl.

APPENDIX I

State/Prince:	Cavalry:	Infantry:	or monthly:
Cleve-Berg (Pfalz-Neuburg and Kur-Brandenburg)	70	323	2,132 fl.
Öst-Friesland	6	30	192 fl.
Nassau-Dillenburg	10	45	300 fl.
Holtzapfel	-	-	133 fl
Sayn	4	16	122 fl.
Bentheim	6	20	152 fl.
Tecklenburg	3	10	76 fl.
Ritberg	6	-	72 fl.
Pyrmont (Waldeck)	1	4	28 fl.
Oldenburg	10	44	296 fl.
Hoya	2	8	56 fl.
Diffolt	1	4	28 fl.
Schaumburg	6	26	176 fl.
Lippe	4	18	120 fl.
Cologne (Town)	25	200	1,100 fl.
Aachen	7	30	204 fl.
Dortmund	7	30	304 fl.
Herforden (Herford, Town)	1	15	75 fl.
	247	1,110	

Bayerischer Kreis (Bavarian Circle)

State/Prince:	Cavalry:	Infantry:	or monthly:
Kur-Bayern (Electorate of Bavaria)	60	277	1,828 fl.
Salzburg	60	277	1,828 fl.
Passau	18	78	528 fl.
Freising	12	80	464 fl.
Regensburg (Bishopric)	8	30	216 fl.
Regensburg (Town)	10	50	320 fl.
Waldsachsen	4	18	120 fl.
Kaysersheim	4	60	288 fl.
Berchtolsgaden	2	20	104 fl.
St. Haimaran	2	18	96 fl.
Nidermünster	1	3	24 fl.
Obermünster	1	3	24 fl.
Neuburg-Sulzbach	10	100	640 fl.
Leuchtenberg	6	14	128 fl.
Haag	4	10	88 fl.
Ortenburg	2	-	34 fl.
Ehrenfels	3	-	51 fl.
Wolfstein	2	4	40 fl.
Meichselrain	1	2	20 fl.
	210	1,044	

Nieder-Sächsischer Kreis (Lower Saxon Circle)

State/Prince:	Cavalry:	Infantry:	or monthly:
Magdeburg	43	196	1,500 fl.
Ertz (Bremen)	-	-	688 fl.
Halberstadt (Kur-Brandenburg)	14	66	432 fl.

State/Prince:	Cavalry:	Infantry:	or monthly:
Hildesheim (Bishopric and Town)	18	80	536 fl.
Schwerin (Mecklenburg)	3	5	56 fl.
Ratzenburg (Mecklenburg)	-	-	24 fl.
Braunschweig (Brunswick, Town)	-	-	686 fl.
Lüneburg (Town)	-	-	720 fl.
Grubenhagisch and Einbeck (Braunschweig- Lüneburg)	6	-	60 fl.
Brunswick-Calenberg (Hannover)	45	208	1,375 fl.
Brunswick-Lüneburg	20	120	720 fl.
Brunswick-Wolfenbüttel	45	208	1,375 fl
Mecklenburg-Schwerin	40	67	748 fl.
Holstein (Denmark)	40	80	800 fl.
Sachsen-Lauenburg (Kur-Sachsen)	8	30	216 fl.
Lübeck	2	177	960 fl.
Bremen	16	32	320 fl.
Hamburg	20	120	720 fl.
Gosslar	-	30	120 fl.
Mühlhausen	-	40	160 fl.
Nordhausen	-	20	80 fl.
	320	1,479	

Ober-Sächsischer Kreis (Upper Saxon Circle)

State/Prince:	Cavalry:	Infantry:	or monthly:
Kur-Sachsen (Electorate of Saxony)	65	301	1,984 fl.
Kur-Brandenburg (Electorate of Brandenburg)	60	277	1,828 fl.
Sachsen-Altenburg	15	49	772 fl.
Sachsen-Weimar			
Sachsen-Gotha	-	-	
Sachsen-Coburg	10	49	
Sachsen-Eisenach			
Meissen (Kur-Brandenburg)	6	6	96 fl.
Merseburg (Kur-Brandenburg)	6	6	96 fl.
Naumburg-Zeitz (Kur-Brandenburg)	6	6	96 fl.
Kamin	6	28	184 fl.
Walkenried (Brunswick-Wolfenbüttel)	2	6	48 fl.
Quedlinburg	1	10	52 fl.
Geringerode	1	6	36 fl.
Pommmern (Swedish Pomerania and Brandenburg-Pomerania)	34	200	1,208 fl.
Anhalt-Bernburg	9	20	188 fl.
Anhalt –Dessau			
Anhalt-Köthen			
Anhalt-Zerbst			
Reuss-Plauen	2	12	72 fl.
Reuss-Grätz	1	3	24 fl.
Schwartzenburg	7	29	200 fl.
Mannsfeld	10	45	300 fl.

APPENDIX I

State/Prince:	Cavalry:	Infantry:	or monthly:
Stollberg	3	12	84 fl.
Hohenstein	2	8	56 fl.
Beuchlingen	2	-	24 fl.
Mülingen	1	2	20 fl.
Leissnick (Kur-Sachsen)	1	2	20 fl.
Solms-Wildenfels	1	2	20 fl.
Schönburg	2	4	40 fl.
Tautenberg	1	2	20 fl.
Saalfeld	2	13	76 fl.
Altenburg	3	13	88 fl.
Brandenstein	1	4	28 fl.
	266	1,139	

Appendix II

Order of Battle and Army Lists

1) Campaign of Poland, June 1657

Infantry:
    Mers (II 3)   {
    George (II 18)   { 3,000
    Hatzfeld (II 12)   {

Souches (II 4)	1,100
La Corona (II 8)	800
Hunoldstein (II 9)	1,000
Baden-Baden (II 7)	1,000
Nicola (II 11)	1,200
Kaiserstein (II 15)	800
Kielmansegg (II 1)	800

Cavalry:

Hatzfeld Leibguardie (ic i)	150
Piccolomini Cuirassieren (IC 5)	1,000
Montecuccoli Cuirassieren (IC 4)	800
Sporck Cuirassieren (IC 6)	800
Caprara Cuirassieren (IC 3)	800
Heister Cuirassieren (IC 9)	800
Gonzaga Cuirassieren (IC 1)	800
Götz Cuirassieren (IC 8)	800
Schneidau Cuirassieren (IC 10)	300
Buschiere Dragoner (ID 1)	600

Sources: *Theatrum Europaeum*, vol. VIII, *Friedens- und Kriegs-Beschreibung, Von Anfang des 1657sten, biß an das 1661* (Frankfurt am Main, 1693), pp. 110–111.

2) The Military Border: *Kroatische und Meergrenze*, 1657:

General-Obrist with 4 *Musterschreiber* and *Feldschere*;
100 men of the *Arquebusieren Compagnie*, 4 horsemen in Bihać;
100 *Husaren*;
254 footmen of the *Karlstädter Deutsches Fähnlein* with staff, 13 Artillerymen;
200 *Sluiner* footmen; 134 footmen in Thurn; 221 *Oguliner* footmen, 84 footmen in Barilović and Skrad; 81 footmen in Tuin; 21 footmen in Ostarja; 28 footmen in Kamensko; 252 footmen in Zengg, 287 footmen in Otočac

Source: F. Vanicek: *Specialgeschichte der Militärgrenze aus Originalquellen und Quellenwerken geschöpft* (Vienna, 1875), vol. I, pp. 102–103.

3) Imperial Order of Battle at Léva, 9 July 1664:

Feldmarschall Louis Raduit de Souches

– Left Wing, *General Wachtmeister* Jobst Hilmar Knigge:
Batthyány Husaren (IHc-4) 1 sqn, *Koháry Husaren* (IHc-5) 1 sqn, *Caprara Cuirassieren* (IC-3) 3 sqn, *Knigge Cuirassieren* (IC-13) 3 sqn, *Holstein Cuirassieren* (IC-24) 5 sqn.

– Centre, *General Major* August von Holstein-Plön (Brandenburg):
Brandenburg Infantry 3 bat, Saxon Infantry 2 bat, *Montevergues* (II-3) 1 bat, *Souches* (II-4) 1 bat.

– Right Wing, *Feldmarschall-Lieutenant* Gottfried von Heister:
Heister Cuirassieren (IC-9) 4 sqn, *Pfalz-Sulzbach* (IC-5) 2 sqn, *Zeiss Cuirassieren* (IC-2) 5 sqn,
(unidentified) *Husaren* 2 sqn.

– Reserve:
Garnier Cuirassieren (IC-26) 3 sqn, Brandenburg cuirassiers 3 sqn, Brandenburg dragoons 2 sqn,
(unidentified) *Husaren* 1 sqn.

Source: Hessisches Staatsarchiv Marburg, *Bataille der Keyserl. Armée, womit die Türcken sambt denen conjungirten Wallachern und Moldauern geschlagen und die Vestung Leventz in Hungarn von der harten Belägerung befreyet den 9. July 1664*.

4) Szentgotthárd, 1st August 1664

Allied Order of Battle

Left Wing (Imperialist):	Centre (*Reichsarmee* and *Deutsche Allianz*):	Right Wing (French):
General Feldmarschall Raimondo Montecuccoli.	*Feldmarschall* Ludwig Wilhelm von Baden-Baden.	*General Lieutenant* Jean de Coligny-Saligny.
General der Cavallerie Johann von Sporck	*Generalleutnant* Franz *Graf* von Fugger	*General Lieutenant* Louis de la Feuillade
Montecuccoli Cuirassieren (IC-4) 3 sqn.	(Schwäbisches) Fugger zu Fuss (SI-2) 1 bat.	Grancey-Espagny infanterie 1 bat.
Sporck Cuirassieren (IC-6) 3 sqn.	(Bayerisches) Puech zu Fuss (BI-1) 1 bat.	Morvas-la Ferté infanterie 2 bat.
Lothringen Cuirassieren (IC-7) 3 sqn.	(Fränkisches) Pleitner zu Fuss (FI-1) 1 bat.	Touraine infanterie 2 bat.
Rappach Cuirassieren (IC-8) 3 sqn.	(N.Sächsisches) Ende zu Fuss (NsI-2) 1 bat.	Piemont infanterie 2 bat.
Schneidau Cuirassieren (IC-10) 3 sqn.	(Westphälisches) Uffeln zu Fuss (WI-1) 1 bat.	
Schmidt Cuirassieren (IC-28) 3 sqn.	(Schwäbisches) Pfalzgraf zu Fuss (SI-1) 1 bat.	*Brigadier General* de Gassion
Gutschenich Kroaten (IHc-1) 3 sqn.		*Brigade de cavallerie* Beauvisé 3 sqn.
Görtzky Dragoner (ID-5) 2 sqn.	*Generalleutnant* Georg Friedrich von Waldeck	*Brigade de cavallerie* Fourneaux 3 sqn.
Gerard Dragoner (ID-1) 2 sqn.	(Bayerisches) Hönig Cavallerie (BC-1) 1 sqn.	*Brigade de cavallerie* de Gassion 4 sqn.
De La Frette *cavallerie* (French) 1 sqn.	(N.Sächsisches) Schach Reitern (NsC-2) 2 sqn.	
Leibgarde zu Pferd Trauttmansdorff (ic-ii) 1 cmp.	(Westphälisches) Post Reitern (WC-1) 3 sqn.	
	(Fränkisches) Zobel Reitern (FC-1) 3 sqn.	
Feldmarschall-Lieutenant Wladislaw von Sparr		
Savoyen zu Fuss (II-6) 2 bat.	*Generalleutnant* Wilhelm Johann von Hohenlohe	
Spieck zu Fuss (II-11) 2 bat.	(*Deutsche Allianz*) Leyen zu Fuss 1 bat.	
Nassau zu Fuss (II-48) 1 bat.	(*Deutsche Allianz*) Waldeck zu Fuss 1 bat.	
Kielmannsegg zu Fuss (II-53) 1 bat.		
Tasso zu Fuss (II-12) 2 bat.	(*Deutsche Allianz*) Neuburg.-Lüneburg.-Münsterisches Reitern 1 sqn.	
Sparr zu Fuss (II-41) 1 bat.	(*Deutsche Allianz*) Lüneburgisches Reitern 1 sqn.	
La Corona zu Fuss (II-8) 1 bat.	(*Deutsche Allianz*) Schwedisches Reitern 1 sqn.	
	(*Deutsche Allianz*) Mainz-Württembergisches Reitern 1 sqn.	
Artillery: 10 field guns (8 and 12 lb)	Artillery: 14 field guns (3 and 6 lb)	

Imperialists: 5,000 Infantry (10 bat); 5,900 Cavalry (27 sqn and 1 comp.) with 10 field guns; *Reichsarmee*: 6,200 Infantry (6 bat); 1,200 Cavalry (9 sqn) with 14 field guns; *Deutsche Allianz*: 600 Infantry (2 bat); 300 Cavalry (4 sqn); French: 3,500 Infantry (7 bat) 1,900 Cavalry (10 sqn).

Total: 15,300 Infantry (25 bat), 9,300 Cavalry (50 sqn and 1 cp.); 400 artillerymen (24 field guns).

Source: Kurt Peball, 'Die Schlacht bei St. Gotthard-Mogersdorf 1664', in *Militärhistorische Schriftenreihe*, III-1964.

APPENDIX II

5) Contingent of the Imperial Circles for the Hungarian Campaign of 1664

Kreise (circles):	*Theoretical:*	*Effective:*
Fränkischer Kreis (Franconia)	2,255	2,450
Schwäbischer Kreis (Swabia)	3,500	3,512
Bäyerischer Krais (Bavaria)	2,461	1,060
Kur-rheinischer Kreis (Rhine-Electoral)	505	476
Ober-rheinischer Kreis (Upper Rhine)	1,500	1,873
Westphälischer Kreis (Westphalia)	2,450	2,422
Nieder-sächsischer Kreis (Low Saxony)	2,350	2,350
Ober-sächsischer Kreis (Upper Saxony)	3,950	1,024
Burgundischer Kreis (Bourgogne)	2,022	1,200
TOTAL	20,933	16,367

Source: Wilson, *German Armies*, p. 42; Tessin, 'Reicharmee und Allianzkorps in Turkenfeldzug 1663–64', in *Zeitschrift für Heereskunder* 308/309, 1983; pp. 133–137.

6) Field army, Campaigns of 1673:

Cavalry:	*Montecuccoli* (IC-4)	900
	Sporck (IC-6)	900
	Lothringen (IC-7)	900
	Heister (IC-9)	900
	Schneidau (IC-10)	900
	Caprara (IC-3)	900
	Alt Holstein (IC-5)	450
	Jung Holstein (IC-24)	900
	Dünnewald (IC-26)	900
	Rabatta (IC-13)	900
	Zeiss (IC-2)	900
	Harrant (IC-22)	900
	Görtzky (ID-7)	900
	Pálffy (IHc-8)	900
	Collalto (IHc-9)	900
Infantry:	*Souches* (II-4)	2,500
	Savoyen (II-6)	2,500
	Baden (II-70)	2,500
	Leslie (II-44)	2,500
	Portia (II-42)	2,500
	Alt Starhemberg (II-41)	2,500
	Alt Grana (II-12)	250
	Kayserstein (II-8)	250
	Knigge (II-3)	250
	Strein (II-68)	1,000
	Serény (II-66)	2,000

Source: *Theatrum Europaeum*, vol. XI (Frankfurt am Main, 1682), pp. 358–359.

7) Troops undet *Feldmarschall* Louis Raduit de Souches, Bamberg, 7 May 1674:

Cavalry:	*Schmidt* (IC-8)	5 sqn.
	Carafa (IC-30)	5 sqn.
	Sporck (IC-6)	5 sqn.
	Montecuccoli (IC-4)	5 sqn.
	Alt-Holstein (IC-5)	5 sqn.
	Metternich (IC-29)	5 sqn.
	Reiffenberg (ID-9)	5 sqn.
	Wopping (ID-6)	5 sqn.
	Pálffy (IHc-8)	5 sqn.
	Collalto (IHc-9)	5 sqn.
Infantry:	*Baden* (II-70)	2 bat.
	Savoyen (II-6)	2 bat.
	Grana (II-12)	2 bat.
	Herberstein (II-52)	2 bat.
	Starhemberg (II-41)	2 bat.
	Leslie (II-44)	2 bat.
	Reichstruppen	4 bat.

Source: *Hollandse Mercurius*, June 1674, p. 43.

8) Field Troops on the Rhine, Mustered in Winter Quarters – 1 February 1675

Infantry:		
	Kaiserstein (II-8)	421
	Strein (II-68)	404
	Serény (II-66)	321
	Reuss (II-71)	299
Cavalry:		
	Bournonville (IC-2)	772
	Lothringen (IC-7)	336
	Caprara (IC-3)	745
	Bayreuth (IC-33)	287
	Dünnewald (IC-26)	347
	Holstein (IC-5)	312
	Gondola (IC-10)	825
	Lodron (ID-8)	735
	Dragoons (6 companies)	340
Artillery:		120

Source: A. Marr, *Der Feldzug 1675 in Deutschland*, 1839, vol. I, p. 141.

APPENDIX II

9) Troops in the Medium Rhine, Mustered on 1 June 1675

In Bonn:
Deutsche Allianz Infantry:

Alt Grana (II-12)	10 comp.	1,500
Savoyen (II-6)	4 comp.	489
Starhemberg (II-1)	3 comp.	390
Wallis (II-79)	3 comp.	341

– Dragoons:

Chavaignac (ID-9)	4 comp.	283 (275 horses)

In Bernkastel:
– Infantry:

Kaiserstein (II-8)	4 comp.	600

Source: Marr, *Der Feldzug 1675 in Deutschland*, 1842, vol. II, p.141.

10) 'State of the Emperor's Field Army in Germany, October 1675'

In Alsace and Upper Rhine:

Infantry:	*Souches* (II-4)	2 bat.
	Baden (II-70)	1 bat.
	Reuss-Plauen (II-71)	1 bat.
	Kaiserstein (II-8)	2 bat.
	Alt-Grana (II-12)	2 bat.
	Starhemberg (II-41)	1 bat.
	Mannsfeld (II-44)	2 bat.
	Dietrichstein (II-58)	1 bat.
	Portia (II-42)	2 bat.
	Serény (II-66)	2 bat.
	Strein (II-68)	2 bat.
	Knigge (II-3)	1 bat.
	Jung-Grana (II-65)	1 bat.
Cuirassiers:	*Montecuccoli* (IC-4)	4 sqn.
	Bournonville (IC-2)	3 sqn.
	Alt Holstein (IC-5)	4 sqn.
	Lothringen (IC-7)	3 sqn.
	Heister (IC-9)	3 sqn.
	Caprara (IC-3)	3 sqn.
	Sporck (IC-6)	3 sqn.
	Carafa (IC-30)	3 sqn.
	Gondola (IC-10)	4 sqn.
	Rabatta (IC-13)	4 sqn.
	Dünewald (IC-26)	3 sqn.
	Jung-Holstein (IC-24)	4 sqn.
	Harrant (IC-31)	4 sqn.
	Gallas (IC-32)	2 sqn

Dragoons: *Trauttmansdorff* (ID-7) 3 sqn.
     Lodron (ID-8) 2 sqn.
     Chavaignac (ID-9) 3 sqn.

Trier, Bonn, Koblenz and Medium Rhine:
Infantry: *Wolfenbüttel* (II-69) 2 bat.
    Savoyen (II-6) Trier 2 bat.
    Waldeck (II-74) 2 bat.
    Avila (FC-2) 2 bat.
    (unidentified) 2 bat.
Cuirassiers: *Metternich* (IC-29) 4 sqn.
    Bayreuth (IC-33) 3 sqn.

In Anterior Austria and Swabia:
Infantry: *Thüngen* (FI-3) 2 bat.
    Durlach (SI-3) 2 bat.
Cavalry: *Bayreuth* (FC-2) 3 sqn.
    Fürstenberg (SC-2) 3 sqn.
    Württemberg (SC-3) 2 sqn.
    (unidentified) 1 sqn.

Source: Archivio di Stato di Napoli: 'Museo' vol. 994146 (Antonio Carafa di Stigliano), c. 13: *Stato delle Truppe Cesaree in Germania, il mese di Ottobre, l'anno 1675*.

11) Imperial Field Army, Campaigns of 1676

Cuirassiers:
Montecuccoli (IC-4), *Lothringen* (IC-7), *Sachsen* (IC-39), *Bayreuth* (IC-33), *Caprara* (IC-3), *Heister* (IC-9), *Dünewald* (IC-26), *Jung-Holstein* (IC-24), *Rabatta* (IC-13), *Schmidt* (IC-8), *Harrant* (IC-31), *Gallas* (IC-32), *Öttingen* (IC-5), *Gondola* (IC-10), *Metternich* (IC-29), *Carafa* (IC-30), *Kaunitz* (IC-38), *Württemberg* (SC-3), 40 *Frey Compagnien* (?) (12,500 troopers)

Dragoons:
Chavaignac (ID-9), *Trauttmannsdorf* (ID-7), *Schulz* (ID-1) and one auxiliary regiment (2,600 troopers)

Croats and Hussars:
Barkóczy (IHc-10), *Lodron* (ID-8), *Collalto* (IHc-09), 40 *Frey Compagnien* (3,600 troopers)

Infantry:
Souches (II-4), *Baden* (II-70), *Alt-Grana* (II-65), *Starhemberg* (II-41), *Strassoldo* (II-40), *Portia* (II-42), *Herberstein* (II-52), *Mannsfeld* (II-44), *Jung-Grana* (II-12), *Martini (Mussimi*?) (II-67), *Seréeny* (II-66) *Knigge* (II-3) *Waldeck* (II-74), *Sachsen-Weimar* (OsI-4?), *Savoyen* (II-6) and two auxiliary regiments (22,500 infantrymen).

Source: *Theatrum Europaeum*, vol. XI, pp. 1025–1026.

12) Siege of Philippsburg, Order of Battle, 11 May 1676

Infantry: *Souches* (II-4) 10 comp. *Savoyen* (II-6) 10 comp. *Alt-Grana* (II-65) 10 comp. *Jung-Grana* (II-12) 10 comp. *Portia* (II-42) 10 comp. *Starhemberg* (II-41) 10 comp. *Serény* (II-66) 10 comp. *Reuss* (II-71) 10 comp. *Mannsfeld* (II-44) 10 comp. *Kaiserstein* (II-8) 5 comp. *Knigge* (II-3) 5 comp. *Avila* (FI-2) 2 bat. *Thüngen* (FI-3) 2 bat.

Cuirassiers: *Montecuccoli* (IC-4) 10 comp. *Bournonville* (IC-2) 10 comp. *Sporck* (IC-6) 10 comp. *Lothringen* (IC-7) 10 comp. *Heister* (IC-9) 10 comp. *Caprara* (IC-3) 10 comp. *Bayreuth* (IC-33) 10 comp. *Dünewald* (IC-6) 10 comp. *Harrant* (IC-31) 10 comp. *Rabatta* (IC-13) 10 comp. *Gondola* (IC-10) 10 comp. *Jung-Holstein* (IC-24) 10 comp. *Gallas* (IC-32) 10 comp. *Alt-Holstein* (IC-5) 5 comp. *Bayreuth* (FC-2) 8 comp.

Dragoons: *Trauttmansdorff* (ID-7) 10 comp. *Chavaignac* (ID-9) 10 comp. *Lodron* (ID-8) 10 comp

Lorraine troops: 5 regiments and 3 company of cavalry, 2 regiment of dragoons.

Source: *Hollandse Mercurius*, April 1676, p. 67; Hessisches Staatsarchiv Marburg: *Abbildung der Belagerung der Festung Philippsburg am Rhein durch die Kaiserlichen Truppen, Mai bis August 1676*.

13) *Reichsarmee*, 1673–1678

Circle:	1673	1674	1675	1676	1677	1678
Franconia	2,151	2,800	3,100	3,100	3,100	-
Swabia	-	2,556	2,600	2,600	2,600	-
Upper Rhine	-	1,700	2,100	2,100	2,100	2,100
Westphalia	-	1,200	1,200	1,200	1,200	1,200
Upper Saxony	-	1,000	1,000	1,000	1,000	1,000
Lower Saxony	-	700	-	-	-	-
Bavaria	-	600	600	600	600	600
Total:	2,151	10,556	10,600	11,600	11,600	4,900

Source: P. Wilson, *German Armies*; H. Weigel, 'Die Kriegsverfassung des alten deutschen Reiches von der Wormser Matrikel bis zur Auflösung'; A. Marr, 'Der Herbstfeldzug Montecuccolis gegen Condé, 1675 am Rheine und an der Mosel', in *Österreichische Militärische Zeitschrift*, vol. II –1842, and 'Der Feldzug 1676 in Deutschland mit Benützung österreichischer Originalquellen', in *Österreichische Militärische Zeitschrift*, vol. III – 1844.

14) Imperial Garrisons, February 1683

In Bohemia: *Kaiserstein zu Fuss* (II-8) (10 comp.), *Gondola Cuirassieren* (IC-43) (10 comp.), *Piccolomini Cuirassieren* (IC-31) (10 comp.) *Sachsen-Lauenburg Cuirassieren* (IC-42) (10 comp.), *Götz* (IC-45) (10 comp.), *Küfstein Dragoner* (ID-10) (10 comp.).

In Moravia: *Alt-Starhember zu Fuss* (II-41) (5 comp.), *Baden zu Fuss* (II-70) (5 comp.) *Salm zu Fuss* (II-89) (5 comp.), *Caprara Cuirassieren* (IC-3) (10 comp.), *Rabatta Cuirassieren* (IC-13) (10 comp.) *Styrum Dragoner* (ID-6) (10 comp.).

In Silesia: *Knigge zu Fuss* (II-3) (5 comp.), *Thimb zu Fuss* (II-88) (5 comp.), *Lothringen zu Fuss* (II-77) (3 comp.), *Dünewald Cuirassieren* (IC-26) (10 comp.), *Veterani Cuirassieren* (I-44) (10 comp.), *Metternich Cuirassieren* (IC-35) (5 comp.), *Taaffe Cuirassieren* (IC-7) (5 comp.), *Schulz Dragoner* (ID-1) (5 comp.).

In Inner Austria: *Strassoldo zu Fuss* (II-40) (8 comp.), *Wallis zu Fuss* (II-79) (5 comp.), *Aspremont zu Fuss* (II-85) (10 comp.), *Heister zu Fuss* (II-81) (5 comp.), *Metternich Cuirassieren* (IC-35) (5 comp.), *Saurau Dragoner* (ID-11) (10 comp.).

In Lower Austria: *Dieppenthal zu Fuss* (II-82) (4 comp.), *Scherffenberg zu Fuss* (II-7) (8 comp.), *Beck zu Fuss* (II-89) (2 comp.), *Carafa Cuirassieren* (IC-30) (10 comp.).

On the Váh River: *Knigge zu Fuss* (II-3) (5 comp.), *Salm zu Fuss* (II-) (3 comp.), *Dieppenthal zu Fuss* (II-82) (5 comp.), *Salm zu Fuss* (II-89) (3 comp.), *Wallis zu Fuss* (II-79) (3 comp.) *Schultz Dragoner* (ID-1) (5 comp.).

In the Schütt Island: *Grana zu Fuss* (II-12) (9 comp.), *Mercy Cuirassieren* (IC-41) (10 comp.), *Hallewil Cuirassieren* (IC-46) (10 comp.), *Savoyen Dragoner* (ID-13) (10 comp.).

In Croatia; *Lodron Dragoner* (ID-8) (10 comp.), *Kéry Croater* (IHc-11).

In Upper Hungary: *Strassoldo zu Fuss* (II-40) (2 comp.), *Salm zu Fuss* (II-89) (2 comp.), *Dieppenthal zu Fuss* (II-82) (1 comp.), *Scherffenberg zu Fuss* (II-7) (2 comp.), *Wallis zu Fuss* (II-79) (2 comp.), *Heister zu Fuss* (II-) (2 comp.), *Lothringen zu Fuss* (II-77) (2 comp.), *Serény zu Fuss* (II-66) (10 comp.), *Khery Husaren* (IHc-11) (5 comp.).

In the Empire (Upper Rhine and Baden): *Alt-Starhemberg zu Fuss* (II-41) (5 comp.) *Baden zu Fuss* (II-70) (5 comp.), *Jung-Starhemberg zu Fuss* (II-6) (10 comp.), *Mannsfeld zu Fuss* (II-44) (10 comp.), *Stadl zu Fuss* (II-7) (10 comp.), *Souches zu Fuss* (II-4), (10 comp.), *Pfalz-Neuburg zu Fuss* (II-76) (10 comp.) *Beck zu Fuss* (II-80) (5 comp.), *Nigrelli zu Fuss* (II-78) (10 comp.), *Lothringen zu Fuss* (II-77) (5 comp.), *Croy Fuss* (II-86) (10 comp.), *Montecuccoli Cuirassieren* (IC-4) (10 comp.), *Taaffe Cuirassieren* (IC-7) (5 comp.).

Source: 'Das Kriegsjahr 1683 nach Akten und andere authentischen Quellen', in *Mitteilungen des k.k. Kriegsarchivs* (Vienna, 1883).

15) Imperial Field Army, Kittsee, 6 May 1683

Feldmarschall-General Charles V of Lorraine. *General der Cavallerie*: Sachsen-Lauenburg, Caprara. *Feldzuegmeister*: Lessl, Starhemberg. *Feldmarschall-Lieutenant*: Rabatta, Baden, Schulz, Dünewald. *General Feldkriegs Commissar* Breuner. *General-Wachtmeister*: Caraffa, Pálffy, Gondola, Mercy. *General Quartiermeister* Sellinger. *General Proviant-Meister* Kriechbaum. *General Vicarius-Pater* Braun. *General Kriegs Zahlmeister* Labernat. *Ober Kriegs Commissar*: Schipko, Frey. *General Adjutant*: Hoffmann, Dolm, Hasslinger, Auersper.

Infantry:	*Alt Starhemberg* (II-41)	2,000
	Baden (II-70)	1,500
	Strassoldo (II-40)	1,000
	Grana (II-12)	1,800
	Mannsfeld (II-44)	2,000
	Souches (II-4)	2,000
	Scherffenberg (II-7)	2,000
	Wallis (7 comp.) (II-79)	1,400
	Beck (7 comp.) (II-80)	1,400
	Thimb (II-88)	1,000
	Heister (II-81)	1,000
	Neuburg (II-76)	1,000
	Württemberg (II-90)	1,000
	Dieppenthal (II-82)	2,000
Total:	21,600	
Cuirassiers:	*Caprara* (IC-3)	800
	Rabatta (IC-13)	800
	Dünewald (IC-26)	800
	Pálffy (IC-37)	800
	Gondola (IC-43)	800
	Carafa (IC-30)	800
	Götz (IC-45)	400
	Dupigny (IC-47)	600
	Taaffe (IC-7)	600
Dragoner:	*Styrum* (ID-6)	800
	Castell (ID-12)	800
	Herbeville (ID-14)	800
	Küfstein (ID-10)	500
	Lodron (ID-8)	500

Hussars/Croats:		*Kèery* (IHc-11)	600
	Ricciardi (IHc-12)		400
Total:	10,800		

Source: 'Das Kriegsjahr 1683 nach Akten und andere authentischen Quellen', in *Mitteilungen des k.k. Kriegsarchivs* (Vienna, 1883).

16) Garrison in Vienna, 15 July 1683

Feldzeugmeister Ernst Rüdiger von Starhemberg. *General Wachtmeister*: Daun, Serény, Souches, Scherffenberg.

Infantry:	*Souches* (II-4)	10 comp.
	Scherffenberg (II-7)	10 comp.
	Pfalz-Neuburg (II-76)	5 comp.
	Alt Starhemberg (II-41)	10 comp.
	Mannsfeld (II-44)	10 comp.
	Beck (II-80)	7 comp.
	Heister (II-81)	5 comp.
	Wurttenberg (II-90)	5 comp.
	Kaiserstein (II-8)	5 comp.
	Thimb (II-88)	3 comp.
Cuirassiers:	*Dupigny* (IC-47)	3 comp.

Artillerie: *Oberst* Borner, *Oberstlieutnant* Pöckstein, 262 guns (including 94 heavy guns, 20 of them were 48 lb). Further 50 guns were taken from the town arsenal.

Total of regular troops:	14,163 men.
Wiener Stadtguardia (City Guard)	8 comp. (1,000)
under *Obrist-Wachtmeister* Ferdinando Domenico degli Obizzi	
City Militia 1 comp.	(200)
Ambrosius Franck *Frey Compagnie*:	1 comp.
Freiwillige Schützen	(80)
University bataillon	(700)
Hofbediente Bataillon	(960)
Butchers' company	1 comp.
Bakers' company	1 comp.
Shoemakers' company	1 comp.

Source: 'Das Kriegsjahr 1683 nach Akten und andere authentischen Quellen', in *Mitteilungen des k.k. Kriegsarchivs* (Vienna, 1883); *Wien und seine Bewohner während der zweiten Türkenbelagerung – 1683*, in 'Berichte und Mittheilungen des Altertums-Vereines zu Wien' (Vienna, 1845), pp. 26–90.

APPENDIX II

17) Order of Battle at Kahlemberg, 12 September 1683.

Commander in Chief: Jan Sobieski, King of Poland

Left Wing: Duke Charles V of Lorraine;

lst line of Infantry, Imperialists and Saxons: Enea Silvio Caprara; 2nd line of Infantry, Imperialists and Saxons: Herman von Baden; Saxon Cavalry: elector Georg III of Saxony; Polish Cavalry: Stanislaw Herakliusz Lubomirski.

Centre: Prince Georg Friedrich von Waldeck:

Franconian and Swabian circles Infantry: Georg Friedrich von Waldeck; Bavarian Infantry: Christoph Martin von Degenfeld; Imperial and Bavarian Cavalry: Antonio Carafa.

Right Wing: Jablonowski

Polish Infantry: Kontzki; Polish Cavalry: Jablonowski; Royal Guard *Reiter* Corps: Polanowski; Imperial and Saxon Cavalry: Julius Franz von Sachsen-Lauenburg.

Imperialists and *Reichsarmee*
– Infantry:
Grana (II-12)	(2 bat. less one comp.)
Baden (II-70)	(2 bat.)
Leslie (II-91)	(1 bat.)
Croy (II-86)	(1 bat.)
Thimb (II-88)	(1 bat.)
Württemberg (II-90)	(1 bat.)
Pfalz-Neuburg (II-76)	(1 bat.)
Beck (II-80)	(1 bat.)

 (Attached to Bavarians during the battle)

– Cavalry:
Caprara Cuirassieren (IC-3)	(10 comp.)
Montecuccoli Cuirassieren (IC-4)	(10 comp.)
Taaffe Cuirassieren (IC-7)	(10 comp.)
Rabatta Cuirassieren (IC-13)	(10 comp.)
Dünewald Cuirassieren (IC-26)	(10 comp.)
Palffy Cuirassieren (IC-37)	(10 comp.)
Piccolomini Cuirassieren (IC-31)	(10 comp.)
Caraffa Cuirassieren (IC-30)	(10 comp.)
Mercy Cuirassieren (IC-41)	(10 comp.)
Veterani Cuirassieren (IC-44)	(10 comp.)
Hallewyl Cuirassieren (IC-46)	(10 comp.)
Sachsen-Lauenburg Cuirassieren (IC-42)	(10 comp.)
Gondola Cuirassieren (IC-43)	(10 comp.)

Götz Cuirassieren (IC-45) (10 comp.)
Schulz Dragoner (ID-1) (10 comp.)
Lymburg-Styrum Dragoner (ID-6) (10 comp.)
Kufstein Dragoner (ID-10) (10 comp.)
Castell Dragoner (ID-12) (10 comp.)
Kery Croater (IHc-11) (8 comp.)
Ricciardi Croater (IHc-12) (4 comp.)
Lubomirki's Dragoons (Poles) (?)
Lubomirski's Cavalry (Poles) (?)

Estimated Total: 8,100 foot (not included *Beck zu Fuss*) and 12,900 horse.

– Circles' Troops:
Bavarian Kreis: *Rummel* (BI-4) 1 bat. (Attached to the Bavarians under Degenfeld).

Franconian Kreis: *Andlau zu Fuss* (FI-4); *Röth zu Fuss* (FI-5); *Brandenburg-Bayreuth Cuirassieren* (FC-3).

Swabian Kreis: *Durlach zu Fuss* (SI-4); *Oettingen zu Fuss* (SI-5), *Gronsfeld Cuirassieren* (SC-4); *Hohnstett Cuirassieren* (SC-5).

– Imperial Troops in campaign, but not engaged in the battle (and not included in Imperial strength figures):

– Infantry:
Wallis (II-79) (2 bat.)
Salm (II-89) (2 bat.)
Lothringen (II-77) (2 bat.)
Dieppenthal (II-82) (1 bat.)
Heister (II-81) (1 bat.)

– Cavalry:
Herbeville Dragoner (ID-14) (10 comp.)
Teutin Dragoner (ID 16) (10 comp.)
Lubomirski Dragoner (ID-17) (10 comp.)
Lodron Dragoner (ID-8) (5 comp.)
Savoyen Dragoner (ID-13) (10 comp)

Source: 'Das Kriegsjahr 1683 nach Akten und andere authentischen Quelle' in *Mitteilungen des k.k. Kriegsarchivs* (Vienna, 1883); Alphons von Wrede: *Geschichte der K.u.K. Wehrmacht von 1618 bis zum Ende des XIX Jahrhunderts* (5 vols) (Vienna, 1898–1905).

APPENDIX II

18) Allied Field Army in Hungary, Campaign of 1686

Infantry:
Alt Starhemberg (II-41)	1,500
Leslie (II-91)	1,500
Kaiserstein (II-8)	1,900
Baden (II-70)	1,500
Mansfeld (II-44)	1,500
Jung Starhemberg (II-6)	2,000
Serény (II-66)	1,500
Croy (II-40)	1,500
Salm (II-89)	1,500
La Vergne (II-12)	1,500
Stadl (II-71)	2,000
Scherffenberg (II-7)	1,500
Souches (II-4)	1,500
Metternich (II-3)	1,500
Dieppenthal (II-82)	1,500
Thüngen (II-96)	1,500
Neuburg (II-76)	1,500
Wallis (II-79)	1,500
Beck (II-80)	1,500
Aspremont (II-85)	1,500
Nigrelli (II-78)	1,500
Thimb (II-88)	1,500
Heister (II-81)	1,500
Lodron (ID-8?)	1,100
Lothringen (II-77)	1,500
Houchin (II-94)	1,500
Fürstenberg (II-95)	1,500
Spinola (II-90)	1,500

Cuirassiers:
Sachsen-Lauenburg (IC-42)	–
Caprara (IC-3)	800
Dünewald (IC-26)	800
Pálffy (IC-37)	800
Carafa (IC-30)	800
Gondola (IC-43)	800
Taaffe (IC-7)	800
Mercy (IC-41)	800
Montecuccoli (IC-4)	800
Veterani (IC-44)	800
Piccolomini (IC-31)	800
Heussler (IC-46)	800
Neuburg (IC-35)	800
Götz (IC-45)	800
Hannover (IC-49)	800

Seldik (?)		800
Fürstenberg (IC-50)		800
Pace (IC-13)		800
Truchsess (IC-51)		800

Dragoons:
Schulz (ID-1)		800
Styrum (ID-6)		800
Castell (ID-12)		800
Serau (ID-11)		800
Herbeville (ID-14)		800
Savoyen (ID-10)		800
Tetuin (ID-15)		800
Magni (ID-13)		800

Auxiliary forces:
Electoral Saxony	5,000
Electoral Brandenburg	7,000
Electoral Bavaria	8,000
Circle of Swabia	4,000
Circle of Franconia	4,000
Circle of Upper Rhine	3,600

Source: *Theatrum Europaeum* vol. XII, p. 1002.

19) The Imperial Army Strength, 1657–1687

	Official Strength:	Effective Strength:*
1657	79,000	41,400
1661	58,000	53,000
1668	48,000	29,633
1673	65,000	59,700
1675	76,500	60,187
1677	77,000	52,500
1683	80,000	55,700
1684	90,000	76,086
1687	91,000	63,800

* Mustered in April–May.

Source: M. Hochedlinger, *Austria's War of Emergence*, p. 104; J. Bérenger, 'Finances et absolutisme autrichien dans la seconde moitié du XVIIe siècle', in *Travaux du Centre de recherches sur la civilisation de l'Europe moderne, XVII*, (Paris, 1978); Österreichisches Kriegsarchiv Vienna: 'Das Kriegsjahr 1683 nach Akten und andere authentischen Quellen', in *Mitteilungen des K.K. Kriegsarchivs* (Vienna, 1883); A. von Wrede, *Geschichte der K. und K. Wehrmacht von 1618 bis zum Ende des XIX Jahrhunderts* (5 vols) (Vienna, 1898–1905).

Appendix III

List of Regiments

	Raised	Obrist Inhaber (colonel owner)	Engagements – Campaigns:	Uniforms:	History:

Imperial Infantry and Cavalry Regiments from 1657 to 1687

Infantry

Deutsch Regiment zu Fuss (German Infantry Regiment):

	Raised	Obrist Inhaber (colonel owner)	Engagements – Campaigns:	Uniforms:	History:
II-1	1613	1657 Heinrich Ulrich von **Kielmansegg** 1658 Johann Christoph **Ranfft** von Wiesenthal 1660 Ferdinand Ernst von **Breuner**	Cracow (1657)	-	Disbanded in 1660
II-2	1618	1647 Hans Christoph von **Pucheimb** 1658 Wilhelm von **Lamboy** 1660 Adolph Ehrenreich von **Pucheimb**	Transylvania	-	Disbanded in 1661
II-3	1619	1636 Franz von **de Mers** 1660 Louis de **Montevergues** 1669 Alberto **Tasso**, Jobst Himar von **Knigge** 1683 Philipp Emmerich von **Metternich**-Winneburg	Cracow (1657) Torun (1658) Graudenz (1659) Niytra, Léva (1664) Bonn (1673) Entzheim (1674) Dachstein (1675) Phillipsburg (1676) Pont-au-Mousson (1677) Freiburg, Kehl (1678) Leopoldstadt, Komárom (1683) Vác, Buda (1684) Érsekújvár, Esztergom, Szolnok, Szeged (1685) Buda (1686) Eszék, Harsány (1687) Belgrad (1688) Nîs, Widdin (1689)	(1675)[1] Private: dark grey coat, white-red striped stockings. (1689)[2] Private: black headgear with white piping, pearl grey coat with red cuffs and lining, natural leather breeches, red stockings, tin buttons, red cravat.	Disbanded in 1918 as I.R. 11

---

1 Archivio di Stato di Napoli, 'Museo' vol. 994146 (Antonio Carafa di Stigliano), c. 13: *Stato delle Truppe Cesaree in Germania, il mese di Ottobre, l'anno 1675*.
2 Donath, *Die Kaiserliche und Kaiserlich und Königliche Österreichische Armee 1618–1918*.

	Raised	Obrist Inhaber (colonel owner)	Engagements – Campaigns:	Uniforms:	History:
II-4	1629	1645 Louis Raduit de **Souches** 1676 Charles Louis de **Souches**	Cracow (1657) Torun (1658) Szent-Benedek, Léva (1664) Entzheim (1674) Türkheim, Altenheim (1675) Philippsburg (1676) Rheinfelden (1678) Vienna, Párkány (1683) Vác, Buda (1684) Érsekújvár, Esztergom (1685) Buda (1686) Harsány, Eger (1687) Belgrade (1688) Nîs (1689)	(1675)[3] Private: dark grey coat, crimson stockings. (1683)[4] Private: pearl grey coat and cuffs, natural leather waistcoat, red stockings, brass buttons, white cravat. (1689)[5] Private: pearl grey coat and cuffs, natural leather breeches, red stockings, brass buttons, white cravat.	Disbanded in 1809
II-5	1639	1643 Innocenzo **Conti** di Guadagnola	Darss (1660)	-	Disbanded in 1660
II-6	1642	1647: Johann Reichard von **Starhemberg** 1662: Pio Eriberto di Savoia (**Savoyen**) 1676: Prospero **d'Arco** 1679: Maximilian Laurenz von **Starhemberg** (**Jung-Starhemberg**) 1689: Filippo **Chizzola**	Torun (1658) Kammin, Wollin, Demmin, Stettin (1659) Léva (1662) Esztergom, Érsekújvár (1663) Szentgotthárd (1664) Bonn (1673) Seneffe (1674) Willstätt, Altenheim, Konzer Brücke, Trier (1675) Philippsburg (1676) Rheinfelden (1678) Kahlemberg (1683) Buda (1684) Érsekújvár (1685) Buda (1686) Philippsburg (1688) Mainz (1689)	(1675)[6] Private: dark grey coat, red stockings (1689)[7] Private: black headgear with white piping, pearl grey coat, cuffs, waistcoat and stockings, brass buttons, red cravat. Officer: black headgear with white piping, dark blue coat and waistcoat, white stockings, golden lace, golden straps (*Tressen*) on the left shoulder.	Disbanded in 1918 as I.R. 8
II-7	1642	1651 Leopold Wilhelm von **Baden-Baden** 1671 Louis de **La Borde** 1681 Sigmund Friedrich von **Scherffenberg** 1688 Guidobald von **Starhemberg**	Cracow (1657) Triebsee, Als (1659) Györke (1671) Sárospatak (1672) Nyirbeltek (1673) Szatmár (1675) Böszörményi (1677) Dóssza (1679) Petronell, Vienna (1683) Buda (1684) Érsekújvár (1685) Buda, Sziklós (1686) Harsány (1687) Belgrade (1688) Nîs, Viddin (1689)	(1683)[8] Private: pearl grey coat, blue cuffs, buff waistcoat, pearl grey stockings, red cravat. (1686)[9] Private and NCO: black headgear with white piping, pearl grey coat, lining and waistcoat, blue-white stockings. Musician: blue coat lined yellow-azure. (1689)[10] Private: black headgear with white piping, pearl grey coat, dark blue cuffs and lining, natural leather waistcoat and breeches, pearl grey stockings, brass buttons, red cravat.	Disbanded in 1809

---

3 *Stato delle Truppe Cesaree in Germania, il mese di Ottobre, l'anno 1675.*
4 Thadden, 'Uniformen in Wien 1683' in *Zinnfiguren* 1974; pp. 181–182.
5 Donath, *Die Kaiserliche und Kaiserlich und Königliche Österreichische Armee 1618–1918.*
6 *Stato delle Truppe Cesaree in Germania, il mese di Ottobre, l'anno 1675.*
7 A. Gartner von Romansbrück, *Geschichte der k. und k. Infanterie Regiment Nr. 8* (Brünn-Brno, 1892).
8 Thadden, 'Uniformen in Wien 1683'.
9 M. D'Aste, *Diario dell'Assedio di Buda del 1686, in Diarii degl'Assedii di Vienna del 1683, e di Buda del 1686.*
10 Donath, *Die Kaiserliche und Kaiserlich und Königliche Österreichische Armee 1618–1918.*

APPENDIX III

	Raised	Obrist Inhaber (colonel owner)	Engagements – Campaigns:	Uniforms:	History:
II-8	1642	1653 Giovanni **La Corona** 1665 Wolf Friedrich **Cob** von Neuding 1671 Johann Paul von **Kaiserstein**	Cracow (1657) Torun (1658) Érsekújvár (1663) Szentgotthárd (1664) Mühlhausen (1674) Türkheim, Altenheim (1675) Vienna, Párkány (1683) Buda (1684) Esztergom, Szolnok (1685) Szeged (1686) Harsány (1687) Belgrade (1688)	(1675)[11] Private: blue coat, white-red striped stockings. (1689)[12] Private: black headgear with white piping, pearl grey coat and cuffs, natural leather waistcoat, red breeches, white-red striped stockings, red cravat.	Disbanded in 1748
II-9	1655	Vogt Wilhelm von **Hunoldstein**	Cracow (1657)	-	Disbanded in 1660
II-10	1655	Jakob **Gehrard**	Stettin (1659)	-	Disbanded in 1660
II-11	1655	1656 Christoph **Nicola** 1658 Lukas **Spieck** zu Uibergau-Langenau	Cracow (1657) Torun (1658)	-	Disbanded in 1659
II-12	1656	Melchior **Hatzfeld** von Gleichen 1658 Piero **Strozzi** 1664 Alberto**Tasso** 1669 Ottone Enrico Grana del Carretto (**Alt-Grana**) 1685 Ferdinand **de la Vergne** 1686 Johann Joachim von **Strasser** 1689 Bonaventura von **Welsperg**	Stettin (1659) Érsekújvár (1663) Kanisza, Zrínyivár, Szentgotthárd (1664) Bonn (1673) Senette (1674) Altenheim (1675) Kahlemberg (1683) Vác, Buda (1684) Érsekújvár, Eger (1685) Buda, Szeged (1686) Harsány (1687) Belgrade (1688) Nis (1689)	(1662)[13] Private: grey coat and breeches, yellow stockings. Officer: yellow coat. (1675)[14] Private: dark grey coat, vermillion stockings. (1684)[15] Private: pearl grey coat and cuffs, red waistcoat and stockings, natural leather breeches, red cravat, brass buttons.	Disbanded in 1690
II-13	1656	Piero **Strozzi** 1658 Ferdinand Wenzel von **Losenstein**	Alessandria (1657)	-	Disbanded in 1660
II-14	1656	Wolf Friedrich **Cob** von Neuding	Alessandria (1657)	-	Disbanded in 1660
II-15	1656	Johann Paul von **Kaiserstein**	Cracow (1657)	-	Disbanded in 1660
II-16	1656	Oliver von **Wallis**	Wollin (1659)	-	Disbanded in 1663
II-17	1656	Adrian von **Enckhevoert**	Milan	-	Disbanded in 1660
II-18	1657	Hans **George** 1660 Wolf Friedrich **Cob** von Neuding	Cracow (1657) Torun (1658) Stettin (1659) Székélyhid (1663) Szent Benedek (1664) Upper Hungary	-	Disbanded in 1679

---

11 Archivio di Stato di Napoli, 'Museo' vol. 994146 (Antonio Carafa di Stigliano), c. 13 *Stato delle Truppe Cesaree in Germania, il mese di Ottobre, l'anno 1675.*
12 Donath, *Die Kaiserliche und Kaiserlich und Königliche Österreichische Armee 1618–1918.*
13 Archivio di Stato di Firenze, *Fondo Carte Strozziane, lettere e altra corrispondenza di Piero Strozzi*, ff. 73–76.
14 *Stato delle Truppe Cesaree in Germania, il mese di Ottobre, l'anno 1675.*
15 Reconstruction after *Avventure e Memorie Estere di O. F.* (Vienna 1683).

WARS AND SOLDIERS IN THE EARLY REIGN OF LOUIS XIV – VOLUME 2

	Raised	Obrist Inhaber (colonel owner)	Engagements – Campaigns:	Uniforms:	History:
II-19	1657	Carl Ludwig von **Hofkirchen**	*Milan*	-	Disbanded in 1660
II-20	1657	Sigmund Ludwig **Speyer**	*Milan*	-	Disbanded in 1660
II-21	1657	Wilhelm **Beltin**	San Giorgio di Mantova (1658)	-	Disbanded in 1660
II-22	1657	**Locatelli** von Eulenburg 1658 Johann **Bredimus**	*Transylvania*	-	Disbanded in 1660
II-23	1657	Ferdinand von **Liechtenstein**	*Poland and Pomerania*	-	Disbanded in 1660
II-24	1657	Philipp Ludwig von Schleswig-**Holstein**	Cracow (1657)	-	Disbanded in 1660
II-25	1657	Ferdinand Friedrich von **Fürstenberg**	*Poland and Pomerania*	-	Disbanded in 1660
II-26	1657	Claudio **Collalto**	*Poland*	-	Disbanded in 1660
II-27	1657	Jakob **Schlebush**	*Poland and Pomerania*	-	Disbanded in 1669
II-28	1658	Louis de **Montevergues**	Wollin (1659)	-	Disbanded in 1660
II-29	1658	Georg von **Stallnacher**	Damb (1659)	-	Disbanded in 1660
II-30	1658	Giacomo **Priami** di Rovereto	*in Bohemia as garrison*	-	Disbanded in 1660
II-31	1658	Heinrich **Blire** zu Scharditz 1659 Lukas **Spieck** zu Uibergau-Langenau	*In Bohemia as garrison*	-	Disbanded in 1660
II-32	1659	Annibale **Gonzaga**	*Croatia and Hungary*	-	Disbanded in 1660
II-33	1659	Gerhard von der Nathen (**Nath**)	*Anterior Austria as garrison*	-	Disbanded in 1659
II-34	1659	Ernst von **Ilten**		-	Disbanded in 1659*
II-35	1659	Carl **Tewes**		-	Disbanded in 1659*
II-36	1659	Friedrich von **Hohenembs**		-	Disbanded in 1659*
II-37	1659	Alfonso Filippo **Hercolani**		-	Disbanded in 1659*
II-38	1659	Hermann **Schmidt**		-	Disbanded in 1659*
II-39	1659	Johann **Wolf**		-	Disbanded in 1659*
II-40	1660	Heinrich Moritz von **Wolframsdorf** 1661 Johann Paul von **Kaiserstein** 1665 Oliver von **Wallis** 1667 Carlo **Strassoldo** 1685 Carl Eugen von **Croy** 1689 Johann Heinrich von **Herberstein**	*Holstein and Funen* Philippsburg (1676) Rügen (1677) Buda, Eperies (1684) Érsekújvár , (1685) Buda (1686) Harsány (1687) Belgrade (1688) Nis (1689)	-	Disbanded in 1693

APPENDIX III

	Raised	Obrist Inhaber (colonel owner)	Engagements – Campaigns:	Uniforms:	History:
II-41	1661	Wladislaw von **Sparr** 1669 Ernst Rüdiger von **Starhemberg** (**Alt-Starhemberg**)	Érsekúivár (1663) Kanisza, Zrínyivár, Szentgotthárd (1664) Tokay (1670) Vasvár (1672) Bonn (1673) Seneffe, Oudenarde (1674) Altenheim (1675) Philippsburg (1676) Rheinfelden (1678) Vienna (1683) Buda, Eperies (1684) Esztergom (1685) Buda (1686)	(1664)[16] Private: black headgear, dark grey coat and breeches, dark red stockings. Officer: red coat. (1675)[17] Private: dark grey coat, dark red stockings (late 1670s)[18] Private: black, ochre/grey coat, carmine cuffs, breeches, ribbons and stockings, brass buttons, white cravat. (1683)[19] pearl grey coat, red cuffs and waistcoat, pearl grey stockings, tin buttons, red cravat, (1689)[20] Private: black headgear with white piping, pearl grey coat, red cuffs, natural leather waistcoat and breeches, white-red striped stockings, tin buttons, red cravat.	Disbanded in 1918 as I.R. 54
II-42	1661	Lukas **Spieck** zu Uibergau-Langenau 1662 **Alfonso Portia**	*Hungary* Szent Benedek (1664) Bonn (1673) Freiburg (1676) Rheinfelden (1678)	(1661)[21] Private (pikeman): red doublet and breeches, black polished armour, grey stockings. (1675)[22] Private: dark grey coat and stockings	Ceded to Spain in 1665. Returned in Imperial service in 1673; disbanded in 1679
II-43	1661	Wolframsdorf (**Jung-Wolframsdorf**)	*Transylvania*	-	Disbanded in 1662
II-44	1662	Lukas **Spieck** zu Uibergau-Langenau 1665 Jakob von **Leslie** 1675 Heinrich von **Mannsfeld**-Fondi	Pécs, Kanisza, Zrínyivár, Eszék (1664) Szentgotthárd (1664) Bonn (1673) Seneffe (1674) Altenheim (1675) Philippsburg (1676) Stollhofen (1678) Parkány, Vienna (1683) Vác, Buda (1684) Érsekújvár, Esztergom. Szolnok (1685) Buda (1686) Eszék, Harsány, Eger (1687)	(1675)[23] Private: dark grey coat, blue stockings. (1683)[24] Private: grey coat, blue cuffs, buff waistcoat, grey stockings, tin buttons, red cravat. (1689)[25] Private: black headgear with white piping, pearl grey coat, dark blue cuffs and lining, natural leather waistcoat and breeches, brass buttons, red cravat.	Disbanded in 1918 as I.R. 24
II-45	1662	Georg Carl von **Schöneich**		-	Ceded to Spain in 1663

---

16 Reconstruction after the fresco preserved in the Castle of Lysá, Czech Republic.
17 *Stato delle Truppe Cesaree in Germania, il mese di Ottobre, l'anno 1675.*
18 Neuwirth, *Geschichte des k. u. k. Infanterie-Regimentes Alt Starhemberg Nr. 54.*
19 Thadden, 'Uniformen in Wien 1683'.
20 Donath, *Die Kaiserliche und Kaiserlich und Königliche Österreichische Armee 1618–1918.*
21 Reconstruction after a copy of a 17th century watercolour, Kupferstichkabinett, Vienna.
22 *Stato delle Truppe Cesaree in Germania, il mese di Ottobre, l'anno 1675.*
23 *Ibidem.*
24 Thadden,'Uniformen in Wien 1683'.
25 *Ibidem.*

	Raised	Obrist Inhaber (colonel owner)	Engagements – Campaigns:	Uniforms:	History:
II-46	1662	Abraham Bernhard Steiner von **Zwilling**		-	Ceded to Spain in 1663
II-47	1662	Erdmann von **Promnitz** 1664 Johann Max von **Schönkirchen** 1665 Ferdinand von **Breuner**	Szent Benedek (1664)	-	Disbanded in 1665
II-48	1663	Gustav Adolph von **Nassau**-Saarbrücken 1664 Johann Franz **Jonghen**	Szentgotthárd (1664)	(1664)[26] Private: grey coat	Disbanded in 1665
II-49	1663	Anton **Montfort** zu Tettnag-Argen	*Hungary*	-	Disbanded in 1665
II-50	1663	Louis de **Montavergues**	*Hungary*	-	Disbanded in 1665
II-51	1663	Annibale **Gonzaga** (*Wiener Stadt-Guardia*)	*Hungary*	-	Licensed in 1664
II-52	1664	Georg Ludwig **Füch s**von Kandernberg 1664 Johann **Geymann** 1670 Johann Ferdinand von **Herberstein** 1671 Ferdinand Ernst von **Herberstein**	*Upper Hungary* Philippsburg (1676)	-	Disbanded in 1679
II-53	1664	Heinrich Ulrich von **Kielmansegg**	Szentgotthárd (1664)	(1664)[27] Private: grey coat	Disbanded in 1665
II-54	1664	Jakob **Maxvell** von Tinelli	*Upper Hungary*	-	Disbanded in 1665
II-55	1664	Paris von **Spankau**	*Upper Hungary*	-	Disbanded in 1665
II-56	1664	Oliver **Wallis**	Zrínyivár (1664)	-	Disbanded in 1665
II-57	1664	*Cäesar* (Papal)		-	Disbanded in 1664
II-58	1664	**Silvio Portia** 1669 Raimund von **Thurn** 1671 Johann Georg **Strein** von Schwarzenau 1672 Hans von **Dietrichstein** 1678 Paul Anton von **Houchin**	Brunstatt (1674) Altenheim (1675)	(1675)[28] Private: dark grey coat, red stockings.	Ceded to Spain in 1679
II-59	1665	Anton **Montfort** zu Tettnag-Argen		-	Ceded to Spain in 1665
II-60	1665	Franz **Jonghen**		-	Ceded to Spain in 1665
II-61	1668	Heinrich Ulrich von **Kielmansegg**	Candia (1668–69)	-	Disbanded in 1670
II-62	1668	Francesco **Strassoldo** 1669 Nicola **Strassoldo**	*Milan*	-	Ceded to Spain in 1668
II-63	1668	Maximilian Reinhard von **Starhemberg**	*Spanish Low Countries*	-	Disbanded in 1669*
II-64	1668	Ernst Rüdiger von **Starhemberg**	*Naples*	-	Disbanded in 1669

---

26 Reconstruction after the fresco preserved in the Castle of Lysá, Czech Republic.
27 *Ibidem.*
28 *Stato delle Truppe Cesaree in Germania, il mese di Ottobre, l'anno 1675.*

APPENDIX III

	Raised	Obrist Inhaber (colonel owner)	Engagements – Campaigns:	Uniforms:	History:
II-65	1671	Enrico Grana del Carretto (**Jung-Grana**)	Bonn (1673) Cologne (1674)	(1675)[29] Private: dark grey coat, yellow stockings	Disbanded in 1679
II-66	1672	Johann Carl von **Serény**	Bonn, Ochsenfurt (1673) Altenheim (1675) Philippsburg (1676) Pont-au-Mousson (1677) Buda (1686) Eszék, Harsány, Kolosvár (1687) Belgrad (1688) Mainz (1689)	(1675)[30] Private: dark grey coat, green stockings (1685)[31] Private: pearl grey coat, cuffs, waistcoat and breeches, white-azure striped stockings, azure cravat. (1689)[32] Private: black headgear with white piping, pearl grey coat, cuff and waistcoat, natural leather breeches, white-azure striped stockings, tin buttons, azure cravat.	Disbanded in 1918 as I.R. 25
II-67	1672	Alessandro **Massimi**		-	Disbanded in 1679
II-68	1672	Johann Georg **Strein** von Schwarzenau	Sinzheim (1674) Türkheim, Altenheim (1675) Philippsburg (1676)	(1675)[33] Private: dark grey coat, black stockings.	Disbanded in 1679
II-69	1672	Georg Friedrich von **Sparr** 1675 August Friedrich von **Braunschweig-Wolfenbüttel**	Philippsburg (1676)	(1675)[34] Private: blue coat, brown (?) stockings.	Disbanded in 1676
II-70	1672	Ferdinand Ludwig von **Wopping** 1673 Hermann von **Baden-Baden** 1676 Ludwig Wilhelm von **Baden-Baden**	Bonn (1673) Sinzheim (1674) Türkheim, Altenheim (1675) Philippsburg (1676) Torna (1679) Kahlemberg (1683) Vác, Buda (1684) Érsekújvár, Esztergom (1685) Buda (1686) Harsány, Eger (1687)	(1675)[35] Private: blue coat, dark yellow stockings. (1689)[36] Private: black headgear with white piping, medium blue coat and cuff, natural leather waistcoat and breeches, medium blue stockings, tin buttons, red cravat.	Disbanded in 1809
II-71	1674	Heinrich von **Reuss-Plauen** 1679 Ferdinand von **Stadl**	Entzheim, Türckheim (1674) Altenheim (1675) Philippsburg (1676)	(1675)[37] Private: dark grey coat, red stockings. (1680)[38] Private: black headgear with white piping, pearl grey coat, dark pink facing, natural yellow leather waistcoat and breeches, pearl grey stockings, tin buttons, red cravat. (1689)[39] Private: black headgear with white piping, pearl grey coat with dark pink cuffs, natural leather waistcoat and breeches, pearl grey stockings, tin buttons, red cravat.	Disbanded in 1918 as I.R. 17

---

29 *Ibidem.*
30 *Ibidem.*
31 E. Czegka, *Uniformen der kaiserlichen Infanterie unter Prinz Eugen*, in 'Zeitschrift für Heereskunde' Nr. 51; March 1933.
32 Donath, *Die Kaiserliche und Kaiserlich und Königliche Österreichische Armee 1618–1918*.
33 *Stato delle Truppe Cesaree in Germania, il mese di Ottobre, l'anno 1675.*
34 *Ibidem.*
35 *Ibidem.*
36 Donath, *Die Kaiserliche und Kaiserlich und Königliche Österreichische Armee 1618–1918*.
37 *Stato delle Truppe Cesaree in Germania, il mese di Ottobre, l'anno 1675.*
38 Donath, *Die Kaiserliche und Kaiserlich und Königliche Österreichische Armee 1618–1918*.
39 *Ibidem.*

	Raised	Obrist Inhaber (colonel owner)	Engagements – Campaigns:	Uniforms:	History:
II-72	1674	Johann Georg von **Sachsen-Weimar**	*Upper Rhine*	-	Disbanded in 1675
II-73	1674	Alexander von **Vehlen**	*In Silesia as garrison*	-	Disbanded in 1675
II-74	1674	Christian Ludwig von **Waldeck**	*Trier, Konzer Brücke (1675)*	(1675)[40] Private: red coat, grey stockings.	Disbanded in 1679
II-75	1678	Carl **Mias**	*Lower Rhine*	-	Disbanded in 1679
II-76	1681	Ludwig Anton von **Pfalzgraf-Neuburg**	Vienna, Parkány (1683) Vác, Buda (1684) Érsekújvár (1685) Buda (1686) Harsány (1687) Székesfehérvár (1688) Mainz (1689)	(1683)[41] Private: pearl grey coat, blue cuffs, buff waistcoat, white-azure striped stockings, tin buttons, red cravat. (1689)[42] Private: black headgear with white piping, pearl grey coat, medium blue cuffs, natural leather waistcoat and breeches, white-azure striped stockings, tin buttons, red cravat.	Disbanded in 1918 as I.R. 20
II-77	1682	Leopold de Lorraine-Bar (**Lothringen**)	Parkány (1683) Visegrad, Buda (1684) Érsekújvár (1685) Buda, Siklos, Pécs (1686) Eszék, Harsány (1687) Belgrad (1688) Mainz (1689)	(1689)[43] Private: black headgear with white piping, pearl grey coat and cuffs, pearl grey waistcoat and stockings, natural leather breeches, white-blue striped stockings, tin buttons, red cravat.	Disbanded in 1918 as I.R. 18
II-78	1682	Ottavio **Nigrelli**	Munkács (1686) Harsány (1687) Székesfehérvár (1688) Nis (1689)	(1690)[44] Private: medium blue coat and breeches, red cuffs and stockings, brass buttons, red cravat.	Disbanded in 1918 as I.R. 27
II-79	1682	Oliver **Wallis** 1689 Franz Ferdinand **Jörger** de Tollet	Parkány (1683) Eperies, Vác, Buda (1684) Buda (1686) Harsány (1687) Belgrade (1688)	(1683)[45] Private: pearl grey coat with blue facings, pearl grey stockings. (1689)[46] Private: black headgear with white piping, pearl grey coat and cuffs, azure waistcoat, breeches and stockings, brass buttons, red cravat.	Disbanded in 1918 as I.R. 47
II-80	1682	Leopold van der **Beck**	Vienna (1683) Vác, Buda (1684) Érsekújvár (1685) Buda (1686) Harsány (1687) Székesfehérvár (1688) Mainz (1689)	(1683)[47] Private: pearl grey coat, scarlet cuffs, pearl grey or buff waistcoat, scarlet stockings, tin buttons, white cravat.	Disbanded in 1918 as I.R. 59

---

40 *Stato delle Truppe Cesaree in Germania, il mese di Ottobre, l'anno 1675.*
41 Thidden, 'Uniformen in Wien 1683'.
42 Donath, *Die Kaiserliche und Kaiserlich und Königliche Österreichische Armee 1618–1918.*
43 *Ibidem.*
44 *Geschichte des k.k. Infanterie-Regiments Leopold II, König der Belgier Nr. 27 von dessen Errichtung 1682 bis 1882* (Vienna, 1882).
45 Donath, *Die Kaiserliche und Kaiserlich und Königliche Österreichische Armee 1618–1918.*
46 *Ibidem.*
47 Thidden, 'Uniformen in Wien 1683'.

APPENDIX III

	Raised	Obrist Inhaber (colonel owner)	Engagements – Campaigns:	Uniforms:	History:
II-81	1682	Siegbert von **Heister**	Vienna (1683) Eszék (1684) Buda (1686) Harsány (1687) Belgrade (1688)	(1683)[48] Private: grey coat, red cuffs, buff waistcoat, green stockings, tin buttons, white cravat. (1689)[49] Private: black headgear with white piping, dark green coat, red cuffs, natural leather and breeches, dark green stockings, tin buttons, white cravat. Officer: black headgear with white piping and plume, carmine red coat with silver lace, dark green cuffs, red stockings, tin buttons, white cravat.	Disbanded in 1747
II-82	1682	Johann von **Dieppenthal** 1688 Leopold von **Anhalt-Dessau**	Buda (1684) Buda (1686) Belgrade (1688) Kanisza (1689)	(1689)[50] black headgear with white piping, medium-blue coat and cuffs, natural leather waistcoat and breeches, medium-blue stockings, tin buttons, white cravat. Officer: black headgear with white piping and plume, scarlet red coat and cuffs with silver lace, medium blue waistcoat, breeches and stockings, tin buttons, white cravat.	Disbanded in 1748
II-83	1682	**Sitten**		-	Disbanded in 1682*
II-84	1682	**Variaux**		-	Disbanded in 1682*
II-85	1682	Ferdinand von **Aspremont**-Reckheim	Vác, Buda (1684) Érsekújvár (1685) Buda, Siklós, Pécs (1686) Harsány (1687) Belgrade (1690)	-	Disbanded in 1690
II-86	1682	Charles Eugène de **Croy**	Kahlemberg (1683) Buda (1684)	-	Disbanded in 1684
II-87	1682	Johann Jakob **Khissel**		-	Disbanded In 1682*
II-88	1682	Johann Georg von **Thimb** 1687 Franz Carl von **Auersperg**	Vienna (1683) Eperies, Vác, Buda (1684) Kaschau (1685) Szeged (1686) Harsány (1687) Belgrade (1688) Nis (1689)	-	Disbanded in 1699

---

48 *Ibidem.*
49 Donath, *Die Kaiserliche und Kaiserlich und Königliche Österreichische Armee 1618–1918.*
50 *Ibidem.*

	Raised	Obrist Inhaber (colonel owner)	Engagements – Campaigns:	Uniforms:	History:
II-89	1682	Joachim Sigmund von **Trauttmansdorff** 1682 Carl Theodor von **Salm** (*Rheingraf*)	Buda (1684) Érsekújvár, Esztergom (1685) Buda (1686) Harsány (1687)	(1682)[51] Private: black headgear, pearl grey coat, red cuffs, waistcoat, breeches and stockings, brass buttons, red cravat. (1689)[52] Private: black headgear with white piping, pearl grey coat, carmine red cuffs, waistcoat and breeches, pearl grey stockings, brass buttons, white cravat.	Disbanded in 1809
II-90	1683	Georg Friedrich von **Württemberg-Stuttgart** 1685 Giovanni Domenico **Spinola** 1686 Guidobald von **Starhemberg** 1688 Carlo Archinto di Trainate (**Trayna**)	Vienna (1683) Eperies, Kaschau (1685) Munkács, Buda (1686) Eszék, Harsány (1687) Belgrade (1688)	(1683)[53] Private: black headgear, scarlet coat and cuffs, grey stockings, white cravat. (1686)[54] Private: grey coat, vermillion cuffs, buff waistcoat, grey stockings, tin buttons, white cravat. (1689)[55] Private: black headgear with white piping, pearl grey coat, cuffs, waistcoat, breeches and stockings, tin buttons, red cravat.	Disbanded in 1918 as I.R. 35
II-91	1683	Jacob **Leslie**	Kahlemberg (1683) Virovitica, Breznica (1684) Eszék (1685) Siklós (1686) Harsány (1687) Belgrade, Dervent (1688) Batočina, Niš (1689)	(1683)[56] Private: dark grey coat with dark blue cuffs, natural leather breeches, pearl grey stockings, brass buttons, red cravat. (1689)[57] Private: black headgear with white piping, pearl grey coat with medium blue cuffs, natural leather waistcoat and breeches, pearl grey stockings, brass buttons, red cravat. Officer: black headgear with gold piping and white plume, medium blue coat and cuffs with gold lace, natural leather waistcoat and breeches, white stockings, gold buttons, white cravat.	Disbanded in 1918 as I.R. 36
II-92	1683	Friedrich Erich von **Rosen** 1683 Johann Paul von **Rosenberg** 1685 Hieronymus von **Lubomirski**	Buda (1684) Érsekújvár (1685)	-	Disbanded in 1685
II-93	1683	Wilhelm Anton von **Daun**	Vienna (1683) Eperies (1684)	-	Disbanded in 1685

---

51 Reconstruction after *Avventure e Memorie Estere di O. F.* (Vienna, 1683).
52 Donath, *Die Kaiserliche und Kaiserlich und Königliche Österreichische Armee 1618–1918*.
53 After the painting of unknown artist 'The Relief of Vienna, 1683'; Heeresgeschichtliches Museum, Vienna.
54 Thidden, 'Uniformen in Wien 1683'.
55 Donath, *Die Kaiserliche und Kaiserlich und Königliche Österreichische Armee 1618–1918*.
56 *Geschichte des k.k. 36. Linien-Inf.-Regiment* (Prague, 1875).
57 Donath, *Die Kaiserliche und Kaiserlich und Königliche Österreichische Armee 1618–1918*.

APPENDIX III

	Raised	Obrist Inhaber (colonel owner)	Engagements – Campaigns:	Uniforms:	History:
II-94	1684	Paul Anton von **Houchin**	Érsekújvár (1685) Munkács (1686)	(1689)[58] Private: black headgear with white piping, pearl grey coat and cuffs, natural leather waistcoat, red breeches, white-red striped stockings, brass buttons, red cravat.	Disbanded in 1918 as I.R. 56
II-95	1684	Emmanuel Egon von **Fürstenberg**-Heiligenkreuz 1688 Ferdinand von **Kaunitz**	Esztergom (1685) Buda (1686) Harsány (1687) Belgrade (1688) Mainz (1689)	-	Disbanded in 1725
II-96	1685	Johann Carl von **Thüngen**	Buda, Pécs (1686) Eszék (1687) Dervent (1688) Batočina, Niš (1689)	(1689)[59] Private: black headgear with white piping, dark blue coat and cuffs, natural leather waistcoat and breeches, grey stockings, tin buttons, red cravat.	Disbanded in 1918 as I.R. 42
II-97	1685	**D'Erbey**		-	Disbanded in 1685*
II-98	1685	François Guillaume de **Maigret**		-	Disbanded in 1685*
II-99	1688	Nikolaus von **Bielke**	Várad (1689)	-	Disbanded in 1692
II-100	1688	Melchior van der **Beckh**		-	Disbanded in 1690
II-101	1688	Heinrich von **Sachsen-Merseburg**		-	Disbanded in 1693
II-102	1689	Jacob **Wilson** (Irish Rregiment)	*Ungheria*	-	Disbanded in 1693
II-103	1689	Albrecht III von **Sachsen-Coburg**	Mainz (1689)	(1689)[60] Private: black headgear with white piping, pearl grey coat, black cuffs, pearl grey waistcoat and breeches, black stockings, brass buttons, white cravat.	Disbanded in 1918 as I.R. 57
II-104	1689	Friedrich Carl von **Württemberg-Stuttgart**			Disbanded in 1700

* Regiments not completed

Hayducken Regiment zu Fuss (Hayduk-Hungarian Infantry Regiment):

II-105	1688	Nikolaus **Pálffy**-Erdödy	*Hungary*		Disbanded in 1700

Cavalry

Cürassier Compagnie (Cuirassier Company)

ic-i	1657	*Hatzfeld Leibguardie*	Cracow (1657)		Disbanded in 1658
ic-ii	1664	Carl von **Trauttmansdorff**	Szentgotthárd (1664)		Disbanded in 1664

Cürassier Regiment (Cuirassier Regiment)

---

58 *Ibidem.*
59 *Ibidem.*
60 *Ibidem.*

WARS AND SOLDIERS IN THE EARLY REIGN OF LOUIS XIV – VOLUME 2

	Raised	Obrist Inhaber (colonel owner)	Engagements – Campaigns:	Uniforms:	History:
IC-1	1625	1632 Luigi **Gonzaga** 1658 Giuliano **Braida**	Cracow (1657) Stettin (1659)	-	Disbanded in 1660
IC-2	1629	1652 Johann Christoph **Schaff** von Havelsee 1661 Christoph **Zeiss** 1673 Adam Quintin von **Herberstein** 1674 Alexandre Hyppolite Balthazar de **Bournonville** 1682 Bernard Coneberg-**Dupigny** 1683 Jean de **Cahuviray** 1685 Adam Bernard **Saint-Croix**	Szent-Benedek, Léva (1664) Bonn (1673) Mulhouse (1674) Altenheim (1675) Philippsburg (1676) Petronell, Vienna (1683) Buda (1684) Szent-Benedek, Hermannstadt, Buda, Szeged (1686) Harsány (1687) Belgrade (1688) Zwornik, Batočina, Nîs (1689)	(1675)[61] Private: natural leather *Koller*, red facings. (1689–91)[62] Private: natural leather *Koller*, red cuffs, waistcoat and breeches, brass buttons, white cravat, red saddle cover with white trim.	Disbanded in 1918 as D.R. 8
IC-3	1629	1656 Luigi **Caprara** 1663 Enea Silvio **Caprara**	Niytra, Szent-Benedek, Léva, (1664) Entzheim, Mulhouse (1674) Türkheim, Altenheim (1675) Kahlemberg, Parkány (1683) Weitzen, Buda, Hanszabék (1684) Érsekújvár (1685) Buda (1686) Harsány (1687) Viddin (1688) Nîs (1689)	(1675)[63] Private: natural leather *Koller*, azure facings. (1689–91)[64] Private: natural buff *Koller*, azure cuffs, waistcoat and reaches, tin buttons, white cravat, red saddle cover	Disbanded in 1701
IC-4	1632	1645 Raimondo **Montecuccoli** 1680 Leonardo Filippo **Montecuccoli**	Cracow (1657) Wismar, Warnemünde (1660) Szentgotthárd (1664) Seneffe (1674) Altenheim (1675) Petronell, Kahlemberg, Parkány (1683) Vác, Buda (1684) Érsekújvár (1685) Harsány (1687) Belgrade (1688)	(1675)[65] Private: natural leather *Koller*, blue facings. (1689–91)[66] Private: natural leather *Koller*, dark blue cuffs, waistcoat and breeches, brass buttons, white cravat, dark blue saddle cover.	Disbanded in 1735
IC-5	1634	1654 Giovanni Maria Testa-**Piccolomini** 1664 Philipp von **Pfalz-Sulzbach** 1668 Johann Adolph von Schleswig-Holstein (**Jung-Holstein**, 1672 **Alt-Holstein**) 1676 Phlipp von **Öttingen**	Cracow (1657) Nyborg (1659) Eszék, Kanisza, Zrínyivár, Léva (1664) Sinsheim, Seneffe, Oudenarde (1674) Altenheim (1675)	(1675)[67] Private: natural leather *Koller*, crimson (?) facings.	Disbanded in 1679
IC-6	1634	1647 Johann von **Sporck**	Warnemünde (1660) Szentgotthárd (1664) Sinsheim, Seneffe, Oudenarde (1674) Altenheim (1675)	(1675)[68] Private: natural leather *Koller*, blue facings.	Disbanded in 1679

---

61 *Stato delle Truppe Cesaree in Germania, il mese di Ottobre, l'anno 1675.*
62 Donath, *Die Kaiserliche und Kaiserlich und Königliche Österreichische Armee 1618–1918.*
63 *Stato delle Truppe Cesaree in Germania, il mese di Ottobre, l'anno 1675.*
64 Donath, *Die Kaiserliche und Kaiserlich und Königliche Österreichische Armee 1618–1918.*
65 *Stato delle Truppe Cesaree in Germania, il mese di Ottobre, l'anno 1675.*
66 Donath, *Die Kaiserliche und Kaiserlich und Königliche Österreichische Armee 1618–1918.*
67 Stato *delle Truppe Cesaree in Germania, il mese di Ottobre, l'anno 1675.*
68 *Ibidem.*

APPENDIX III

	Raised	Obrist Inhaber (colonel owner)	Engagements – Campaigns:	Uniforms:	History:
IC-7	1636	Johann von **Walter** 1664 Charles V de Lorraine-Bar (***Lothringen***) 1677 Francis **Taaffe**-Carlingford	Cracow (1657) Szentgotthárd (1664) Murányi (1670) Seneffe (1674) Altenheim (1675) Saverne (1676) Petronell, Kahlemberg, Parkány (1683) Vác, Buda (1684) Érsekújvár, Esztergom (1685) Buda (1687) Belgrade (1688)	(1675)[69] Private: natural leather *Koller*, red facings. Musician:[70] green coat with silver lacings. (1689–91)[71] Private: natural leather *Koller*, red cuffs, waistcoat and breeches, brass buttons, white cravat, red saddle cover with white trim.	Disbanded in 1775
IC-8	1643	1645 Sigmund von **Götz** 1662 Ferdinand Carl von **Rappach** 1664 Johann **Schmidt**	Cracow (1657) Komárom (1663) Kanisza, Zrínyivár, Szentgotthárd (1664) Böszörmény (1674)	-	Disbanded in 1679
IC-9	1655	Gottfried von **Heister**	Cracow (1657) Torun (1658) Brodnica, Marienburg, Elbing (1659) Segesvár (1662) Léva (1664) Sinzheim, Seneffe, Oudenarde (1674) Altenheim (1675)	(1675)[72] Private: natural leather *Koller*, dark pink facings.	Disbanded in 1679
IC-10	1655	Franz von **Schneidau** 1674 Francesco **Gondola**	Cracow (1657) Stettin (1659) Zrínyivár, Szentgotthard (1664) Sinzheim, Seneffe, Entzheim, Mulhouse (1674) Altenheim (1675)	(1675)[73] Private: natural leather *Koller*, red facings.	Disbanded in 1679
IC-11	1656	Juan Batista de **Areyzaga**	*Milan*	-	Disbanded in 1660
IC-12	1656	Detlef von **Capell**	*Milan*	-	Disbanded in 1660
IC-13	1657	Jobst Hilmar von **Knigge** 1669 Rodolfo **Rabatta** 1685 Carlo Maria **Pace**	Segeszvár (1662) Léva (1664) Seneffe (1674) Altenheim (1675) Petronell, Kahlemberg, Parkány (1683) Vác, Buda (1684) Buda (1686) Harsány (1687) Orsova (1689)	(1675)[74] Private: natural leather *Koller*, dark red facings. (1689–91)[75] Private: natural leather *Koller*, dark red cuffs, waistcoat and breeches, brass buttons, white cravat, red saddle cover with yellow trim.	Disbanded in 1775
IC-14	1657	Ruprecht von **Pfalz-Sulzbach** 1662 Luigi **Carafa**	Stettin, Demmin, (1659)	-	Ceded to Spain in 1664
IC-15	1657	Jacob von **Salis** 1659 Pietro **Planta**	Stettin (1659)	-	Disbanded in 1660

---

69 *Ibidem*.
70 J. Vial, 'Étude des armoires, devise, livrée, etendarts de la Maison des Ducs de Lorraine', in *Nec Pluribus Impar* (web-magazine), part II, pp. 45–48.
71 Donath, *Die Kaiserliche und Kaiserlich und Königliche Österreichische Armee 1618–1918*.
72 *Stato delle Truppe Cesaree in Germania, il mese di Ottobre, l'anno 1675*.
73 *Ibidem*.
74 *Ibidem*.
75 Donath, *Die Kaiserliche und Kaiserlich und Königliche Österreichische Armee 1618–1918*.

	Raised	Obrist Inhaber (colonel owner)	Engagements – Campaigns:	Uniforms:	History:
IC-16	1657	Luigi **Mattei**	Nyborg (1659)	-	Disbanded in 1660
IC-17	1657	Adolph von Schleswig-**Holstein**	Anklam. Stettin (1659)	-	Disbanded in 1660
IC-18	1657	Boguslav Leszczinsky (**Lezno**) 1659 Carl Ferdinand von **Rappach**	Stralsund, (1659) Darss, Warnemünde (1660)	-	Disbanded in 1660
IC-19	1657	Gerhard von der **Nath**	Nyborg (1659)	-	Disbanded in 1660
IC-20	1657	Joachim von **Ratschin**	Torun (1658) Brodnica, Marienburg (1659)	-	Disbanded in 1660
IC-21	1658	Luigi **Carafa**	Fredriksodde, Nyborg (1659)	-	Disbanded in 1660
IC-22	1659	Christoph Wilhelm von **Harrant**	*Milan*	-	Disbanded in 1660
IC-23	1659	Leonardo **Fabbri**	*Westphalia and Austria*	-	Ceded to Spain in 1664
IC-24	1662	Philipp Ludwig von Schleswig-Holstein (**Alt-Holstein**) 1672 Friedrich von Schleswig-Holstein (**Jung Holstein**)	Léva (1664) Sinzheim, Seneffe, Oudenarde, Entzheim, Mulhouse (1674) Altenheim (1675)	(1675)[76] Private: natural leather *Koller*, red facings.	Disbanded in 1679
IC-25	1662	**Post**	*Transylvania*	-	Disbanded in 1662
IC-26	1663	Hans Heinrich von **Garnier** 1664 Johann Nicolaus **Nostsitz** von Kunewald 1670 Johann Heinrich von **Dünewald**	Szent-Benedek, Léva (1664) Bonn (1673) Sinsheim Entzheim, Mulhouse (1674) Türkheim, Altenheim, (1675) Saverne, Philippsburg (1676) Krems, Kahlemberg, Parkány, Szécsény (1683) Weitzen, Buda (1684) Esztergom (1685) Buda, Szolnok, Arad, Szeged (1686) Siklós, Harsány (1687) Belgrade (1688) Mainz (1689)	(1675)[77] Private: natural leather *Koller*, dark red facings. (1689–91)[78] Private: natural leather *Koller*, red cuffs, waistcoat and breeches, tin buttons, white cravat, red saddle cover with yellow trim.	Disbanded in 1918 as D.R. 7
IC-27	1663	Giuliano **Braida**		-	Disbanded in 1664
IC-28	1663	Johann **Schmidt**	Szentgotthárd (1664)	-	Disbanded in 1665
IC-29	1665	Ferdinand Casimir von **Metternich**	Philippsburg (1676)	(1675)[79] Private: natural leather *Koller*, red facings.	Disbanded in 1679

---

76 *Stato delle Truppe Cesaree in Germania, il mese di Ottobre, l'anno 1675.*
77 *Ibidem.*
78 Donath, *Die Kaiserliche und Kaiserlich und Königliche Österreichische Armee 1618–1918.*
79 *Stato delle Truppe Cesaree in Germania, il mese di Ottobre, l'anno 1675.*

APPENDIX III

	Raised	Obrist Inhaber (colonel owner)	Engagements – Campaigns:	Uniforms:	History:
IC-30	1672	Antonio **Carafa** di Stigliano	Seneffe, Oudenarde (1674) Altenheim (1675) Philippsburg (1676) Kahlemberg (1683) Buda (1684) Tokay, Érsekújvár (1685) Buda, Szeged, (1686) Eger (1687) Belgrade (1688) Mainz (1689)	(1675)[80] Private: natural leather *Koller*, brown (?) facings. (1689–91)[81] Private: natural leather *Koller*, red cuffs, waistcoat and breeches, tin buttons, white cravat, red saddle cover.	Disbanded in 1918 as D.R. 2
IC-31	1672	Christoph Wilhelm von **Harrant** 1682 Enea Silvio **Piccolomini**	Seneffe (1674) Salsbach, Altenheim, Konzer Brücke (1675) Saverne, Philippsburg (1676) Grünberg (1680) Kahlemberg, Parkány (1683) Buda, Vác (1684) Esztergom (1685) Hermannstadt, Buda (1686) Harsány (1687) Derbent (1688) Banjaluka, Tešin, Kačanik, Batočina, Niš (1689)	(1675)[82] Private: natural leather *Koller*, red facings. (1689–91)[83] Private: natural leather *Koller*, red cuffs, waistcoat and breeches, brass buttons, white cravat, red saddle cover with white trim.	Disbanded in 1918 as D.R. 4
IC-32	1672	Anton Pankras von **Gallas**	Entzheim, (1674) Türkheim, Altenheim (1675) Philippsburg (1676)	(1675)[84] Private: natural leather *Koller*, carmine facings.	Disbanded in 1679
IC-33	1674	Christian Ernst von Brandenburg-**Bayreuth**	Entzheim, Türkheim (1674) Altenheim (1675) Philippsburg (1676)	(1675)[85] Private: natural leather *Koller*, black facings.	Disbanded in 1679
IC-34	1674	Gaspard de **Chavaignac**		-	Disbanded in 1675
IC-35	1674	Philipp Casimir von **Metternich** 1683 Otto Ferdinand von **Dietrichstein** 1684 Carl Philipp von **Pfalz-Neuburg**	Wolgast (1676) Fürstenfeld (1683) Esztergom (1685) Buda (1686) Harsány (1687) Belgrade (1688)	(1689–91)[86] Private: natural leather *Koller*, red cuffs and breeches, natural leather waistcoat, tin buttons, white cravat, red saddle cover with blue trim piped white.	Disbanded in 1734
IC-36	1675	Johann Andreas **Poiger**	Nyalábvár (1677)	-	Disbanded in 1677
IC-37	1675	János Károly **Pálffy** de Erdödy	Szatmar (1672) Kalló (1676)	(1689–91)[87] Private: natural leather *Koller*, red cuffs with azure edge, red waistcoat and breeches, tin buttons, white cravat, red saddle cover with withe-red-white trim.	Disbanded in 1700
IC-38	1675	Franz Carl von **Kaunitz**	*Hungary*	-	Disbanded in 1679
IC-39	1676	Friedrich August von **Sachsen**	Philippsburg (1676)	-	Disbanded in 1682

---

80 *Ibidem.*
81 Donath, *Die Kaiserliche und Kaiserlich und Königliche Österreichische Armee 1618–1918.*
82 *Stato delle Truppe Cesaree in Germania, il mese di Ottobre, l'anno 1675.*
83 *Ibidem.*
84 *Stato delle Truppe Cesaree in Germania, il mese di Ottobre, l'anno 1675.*
85 *Ibidem.*
86 Donath, *Die Kaiserliche und Kaiserlich und Königliche Österreichische Armee 1618–1918.*
87 *Ibidem.*

	Raised	Obrist Inhaber (colonel owner)	Engagements – Campaigns:	Uniforms:	History:
IC-40	1677	Friedrich Carl von **Württemberg** 1678 Friedrich Ludwig von **Hallewyl**	*Upper Rhine*	-	Disbanded in 1679
IC-41	1679	Pierre Ernest **Mercy** de Billets 1686 Charles de Lorraine-**Commercy**	Petronell, Kahlemberg (1683) Vác, Buda (1684) Érsekújvár, Esztergom, Szolnok (1685) Buda (1686) Harsány (1687) Mainz (1689)	(1689–91)[88] Private: natural leather *Koller*, yellow cuffs, red waistcoat and breeches, tin buttons, white cravat, red saddle cover with yellow trim. Musician: dark red cap, yellow coat with red lace.	Disbanded in 1775
IC-42	1682	Julius Franz von **Sachsen-Lauenburg** 1689 Giovanni Battista **Doria**	Kahlemberg, Parkány (1683) Esztergom, Buda (1684) Érsekújvár (1685) Szent-Benedek, Hermannstadt, Buda, Szeged (1686) Eszék, Harsány (1687) Belgrade (1688) Batočina, Nis (1689)	(1683)[89] Private: buff *Koller* and cuffs, grey waistcoat, red breeches, white or red cravat, red saddle cover. Musician: red coat with blue facings. (1689–91)[90] Private: natural leather *Koller*, crimson cuffs with green edge, natural leather waistcoat, red breeches, tin buttons, red cravat, red saddle cover with yellow trim.	Disbanded in 1918 as D.R. 9
IC-43	1682	Francesco de **Gondola**	Petronell, Kahlemberg, Parkány (1683) Vác, Buda (1684) Esztergom, Szolnok (1685) Buda, Szeged (1696) Harsány (1687)	(1689–91)[91] Private: natural leather *Koller*, red cuffs, waistcoat and breeches, tin buttons, white or black cravat, red saddle cover with white-red-white trim. Musician: red coat with silver lace.	Disbanded in 1802
IC-44	1682	Federico **Veterani**	Petronell, Kahlemberg, Parkány (1683) Eperies (1685) Szent Benedek, Hermannstadt, Buda (1686) Harsány (1687)	(1689–91)[92] Private: natural leather *Koller*, red cuffs, waistcoat and breeches, tin buttons, white cravat, red saddle cover. Musician: dark brown cap with white-blue plumes, blue coat with golden lace.	Disbanded in 1802
IC-45	1682	Hermann Otto von Lymburg-**Styrum** 1683 Johann Carl von **Götz** 1687 Georg Christian von **Schleswig-Holstein**	Petronell, Kahlemberg, Parkány (1683) Vác, Hanszabék (1684) Buda (1686) Harsány (1687) Derbent (1688) Nis (1689)	(1689–91)[93] Private: natural leather *Koller*, red cuffs, waistcoat and breeches, tin buttons, red cravat, red saddle cover.	Disbanded in 1768

---

88 *Ibidem.*
89 Treuenfest, *Geschichte des k.u.k. Bukowina'schen Dragoner-Regimentes Nr. 9* (Vienna, 1892).
90 Donath, *Die Kaiserliche und Kaiserlich und Königliche Österreichische Armee 1618–1918.*
91 *Ibidem.*
92 *Ibidem.*
93 *Ibidem.*

APPENDIX III

	Raised	Obrist Inhaber (colonel owner)	Engagements – Campaigns:	Uniforms:	History:
IC-46	1682	Friedrich Ludwig von **Hallewyl** 1684 Donatus **Heissler** von Heitersheim	Kahlemberg, Parkány (1683) Višegrad, Vác, Buda (1684) Érsekújvár , Esztergom, Szolnok (1685) Szeged (1686) Harsány (1687) Belgrade (1688)	(1689–91)[94] Private: natural leather *Koller*, carmine cuffs, waistcoat and breeches, tin buttons, white cravat, red saddle cover with white trim. Musician: red coat with white lace.	Disbanded in 1775
IC-47	1683	Bernard de **Dupigny** 1683 Jean-François **Chauviray** 1685 Adam Bernard de **Saint-Croix**	Petronell, Vienna (1684) Buda (1684) Szent Benedek, Hermannstadt, Buda, Szeged (1686) Harsány (1687) Belgrade (1688) Batočina, Niš (1689)	(1689–91)[95] Private: natural leather *Koller*, crimson cuffs, and breeches, natural leather waistcoat, tin buttons, black cravat, crimson saddle cover with yellow trim. Musician: crimson coat with white lace, blue cuffs.	Disbanded in 1775
IC-48	1683	Hieronymus **Lubomirski**	-	-	Disbanded in 1685
IC-49	1684	Friedrich August von Braunschweig-Lüneburg Kalemberg (**Hanover**)	Esztergom, Érsekújvár (1685) Buda (1686) Harsány, Osijek (1687) Derbent (1688) Niš (1689)	(late 17th century)[96] Private: natural leather *Koller*, azure cuffs and waistcoat, red breeches, tin buttons, red cravat, red saddle cover with azure-yellow-azure trim. Musician: azure coat, cuffs with silver lace, azure waistcoat, red trumpet banner and kettledrums cover.	Disbanded in 1768
IC-50	1684	Emanuel Egon von **Fürstenberg**	Szolnok (1685) Buda (1686)	-	Disbanded in 1686
IC-51	1685	Johann Eytel **Truchsess** von Wetzhausen 1687 Franz Leopold von **Noirquermes**	Érsekújvár (1685) Buda (1686) Osijek (1687) Niš, Viddin (1689)	(late 17th century)[97] Private: natural leather *Koller*, black cuffs, tin buttons, white cravat, red saddle cover.	Disbanded in 1802
Dragoner Frei-Compagnien (**Dragoon Free-Companies**)					
id-i	1675	Ferdinand **Schleichhardt** von Wiesenthal	*Upper Hungary*	-	Disbanded in 1679
id-ii	1675	Johann Christoph **Hausknecht**	*Upper Hungary*	-	Disbanded in 1679
id-iii	1675	Georg Ernst von **Logau**	*Upper Hungary*	-	Disbanded in 1679
id-iv	1675	Johann Jacob **Ranfthofen**	*Upper Hungary*	-	Disbanded in 1680
id-v	1675	Carl Heinrich **Steinsdorf**	*Upper Hungary*	-	Disbanded in 1680
id-vi	1675	Jost Bernhard **Zeis**	*Upper Hungary*	-	Disbanded in 1680
id-vii	1675	**Qualdo**	*Upper Hungary*	-	Disbanded in 1679
id-viii	1679	**Simoni**	*Hungary*	-	Disbanded in 1679

---

94 *Ibidem*.
95 *Ibidem*.
96 J. Belaubre, *Les Triomphes de Louis XIV* (Paris: private publishing, 1970).
97 *Ibidem*.

	Raised	Obrist Inhaber (colonel owner)	Engagements – Campaigns:	Uniforms:	History:
id-ix	1679	**Mechl**	*Hungary*	-	Disbanded in 1679

Dragoner Regiment (Dragoon Regiment)

	Raised	Obrist Inhaber (colonel owner)	Engagements – Campaigns:	Uniforms:	History:
ID-1	1631	1658 Pierre de **Buschiere** 1661 Jacob de **Gérard** 1676 Johann Valentin von **Schulz** 1686 Johann Jakob **Kissel** 1689 Jean-Louis de Bussy-**Rabutin**	Cracow (1657) Torun (1658) Segesvár (1663) Szentgotthárd (1664) Demmin (1676) Rügen (1677) Eperies (1678) Kahlemberg, Parkány (1683) Buda (1684) Eperies, Kaschau (1685) Szent-Jobb, Buda (1686) Harsány (1687) Titel, Belgrade (1688) Batočina, Nîs, Viddin (1689)	(1664)[98] Private: black headgear, light grey coat. (1689–91)[99] Private: black headgear with white piping, medium blue coat, carmine cuffs, lining and aiguillettes, dark blue waistcoat, natural leather breeches, tin buttons, white cravat, red saddle cover Officer: red coat with medium blue cuffs, silver lace.	Disbanded in 1918 as D.R.10
ID-2	1657	Martin de **Paconchay**	Kanisza, Zrínyivár, (1664)	-	Disbanded in 1664
ID-3	1657	Johann **Flettinger** 1660 Jobst von **Rust**	Torun (1658) Brodnica, Marienburg, Elbing (1659)	-	Disbanded in 1660
ID-4	1657	Paris von **Spankau**	Torun (1658) Brodnica, Marienburg, Elbing (1659)	-	Disbanded in 1660
ID-5	1662	Franz Paul **Görtzky**	Zrínyivár, Szentgotthárd (1664)	(1664)[100] dark brown headgear, butternut coat.	Disbanded in 1664
ID-6	1672	Ferdinand Ludwig von **Wopping** 1678 Otto Hermann von Limburg-**Styrum**	*Hungary* Petronell, Kahlemberg, Parkány (1683) Vác, Buda (1684) Esztergom, Szolnok (1685) Buda, Szeged (1686) Harsány (1687) Belgrade, Derbent (1688) Grabovac (1689)	(1689–91)[101] Private: black headgear with white piping, red coat, light green cuffs and lining, yellow aiguillettes, natural leather breeches, brass buttons, white cravat, red saddle cover with yellow trim.	Disbanded in 1748
ID-7	1672	Franz Paul **Görtzky** 1673 Joachim Sigmund von **Trauttmansdorff**	Bonn (1673) Seneffe, Entzheim, Mulhouse (1674) Türkheim, Altenheim (1675)	(1675)[102] Private: red coat and facings.	Disbanded in 1679
ID-8	1674	Nikola **Lodron** 1689 Giovanni Aloisio **Cavriani**	Altenheim (1675) Philippsburg (1676) Parkány, Kahlemberg (1683) Buda, Szeged (1686) Harsány (1687) Belgrade (1688)	(1675)[103] Private: red coat with black facings	Disbanded in 1700
ID-9	1674	Friedrich Philipp von **Reiffenberg** 1675 Gaspard de **Chavaignac**	Entzheim, Mulhouse (1674) Türkheim, Altenheim, Konzer Brücke (1675) Rheinfelden (1678)	(1675)[104] Private: green coat with red facings.	Disbanded in 1679

---

98 Reconstruction after the fresco preserved in the Castle of Lysá, Czech Republic.
99 Donath, *Die Kaiserliche und Kaiserlich und Königliche Österreichische Armee 1618–1918*.
100 Reconstruction after the fresco preserved in the Castle of Lysá, Czech Republic.
101 Donath, *Die Kaiserliche und Kaiserlich und Königliche Österreichische Armee 1618–1918*.
102 *Stato delle Truppe Cesaree in Germania, il mese di Ottobre, l'anno 1675.*
103 *Ibidem.*
104 *Ibidem.*

APPENDIX III

	Raised	Obrist Inhaber (colonel owner)	Engagements – Campaigns:	Uniforms:	History:
ID-10	1682	Johann Heinrich von **Küfstein** 1683 Eugenio di Savoia-Soissons (**Savoyen**)	Kahlemberg (1683) Vác, Buda (1684) Buda, Pécs (1686) Harsány (1687) Belgrade (1688) Mainz (1689)	(1690)[105] Private: black headgear with yellow piping, red coat, black cuffs, natural leather waistcoat and breeches, tin buttons, white cravat, red saddle cover. Officer:[106] black headgear with yellow piping and white plume, red coat with black cuffs and golden lace, black waistcoat, golden buttons, white cravat. (1689–91)[107] Private: black headgear with yellow piping, red coat, black cuffs, aiguillettes and lining, red waistcoat, natural leather breeches, brass buttons, white cravat, red saddle cover. Musicians: black coat with red cuffs, white lace and cravat.	Disbanded in 1918 as D.R.13
ID-11	1682	Carl von Saurau (**Serau**)	Buda, (1686) Harsány (1687) Belgrade (1688) Batočina, Nís (1689)	(1682)[108] Private: black headgear with white piping, blue coat and cuffs, red lining and waistcoat, blue breeches, tin buttons, withe cravat, red saddle cover with yellow trim. (1689–91)[109] Private: black headgear with white piping, medium blue coat, red cuffs and aiguillettes, lining and waistcoat, medium blue breeches, tin buttons, white cravat, red saddle cover with yellow trim.	Disbanded in 1775
ID-12	1682	Friedrich Magnus von **Castell**	Kahlemberg, Parkány (1683) Parkány (1683) Eperies (1684) Esztergom, Szolnok (1685) Szent Benedek, Hermannstadt (1686) Harsány (1687) Derbent (1688)	(1689–91)[110] Private: black headgear with yellow piping, medium blue coat, carmine red cuffs, aiguillettes, lining and waistcoat, natural leather breeches; brass buttons, white cravat, red saddle cover with blue trim piped yellow on both side.	Disbanded in 1721
ID-13	1682	Luigi Giulio di Savoia-Soissons (**Savoyen**) 1684 Carlo Alessandro **Magni**	Petronell. Parkány (1683) Vác, Buda (1684) Esztergom (1685) Buda, Szeged (1686) Harsány (1687) Lippa (1689)	(1682)[111] Private; black headgear with white piping and red ribbon, dark blue coat, red cuff, aiguillettes and lining, cloth button (red and blue), white cravat, blue saddle cover with blue-white-blue trim.	Disbanded in 1691

---

105 Belaubre, 'Les Triomphes de Louis XIV'.
106 Knötel, *Die Grosse Uniformenkunde*, vol. X, plate 36.
107 Donath, *Die Kaiserliche und Kaiserlich und Königliche Österreichische Armee 1618–1918*.
108 Belaubre, 'Les Triomphes de Louis XIV'.
109 Donath, *Die Kaiserliche und Kaiserlich und Königliche Österreichische Armee 1618–1918*.
110 *Ibidem*.
111 Knötel, *Die Grosse Uniformenkunde*, vol. X, plate 36.

WARS AND SOLDIERS IN THE EARLY REIGN OF LOUIS XIV – VOLUME 2

	Raised	Obrist Inhaber (colonel owner)	Engagements – Campaigns:	Uniforms:	History:
ID-14	1683	Louis d'**Herbeville**	Kahlemberg, Parkány (1683) Buda (1684) Munkács (1686)	(1683))[112] Private: black headgear with yellow piping, medium blue coat, yellow cuffs and lining, red aiguillettes, medium blue waistcoat, natural leather breeches; brass buttons, white cravat, red saddle cover with yellow trim. (1689–91)[113] Private: black headgear with yellow piping, medium blue coat, yellow cuffs and lining, red aiguillettes, medium blue waistcoat, natural leather breeches, brass buttons, red cravat, red saddle cover with yellow trim.	
ID-15	1683	Casimir von **Königsegg**, Jan Casimir **Tetuin** 1688 Carl Philipp von **Braunschweig**-Lüneburg	Sillein, (1683) Szent Benedek, Buda (1686) Harsány (1687)		Disbanded in 1700
ID-16	1683	Jan Casimir **Tetuin** 1683 Hieronymus **Lubomirski**		-	Disbanded in 1684
ID-17	1684	Georg Christian von **Schleswig-Holstein**		-	Disbanded in 1685
ID-18	1688	Donatus **Heissler** von Heitersheim	*Transylvania*	(1689–91)[114] black headgear with white piping, medium blue coat, red cuffs and aiguillettes, tin buttons, red saddle cover with white trim piped black.	Disbanded in 1918 as D.R.13
ID-19	1688	Gustav Hannibal von **Löwenschild**	*Transylvania*	(1689–91)[115] Private: black headgear with yellow piping, green coat, red cuffs, lining, aiguillettes, waistcoat and breeches, brass buttons, white cravat, red saddle cover with yellow trim. Musician: red coat, green cuffs and lining, yellow aiguillettes, golden lace.	Disbanded in 1918 as U.R.11
ID-20	1688	Christian Ernst von Brandenburg-**Bayreuth**	Mainz (1689)	(1689–91)[116] Private: black headgear with white piping, medium blue coat, red cuffs, aiguillettes and breeches, tin buttons, white cravat, red saddle cover.	Disbanded in 1721

Husaren & Croatische Frei-Compagnie (Hussar or Croats Free-Company)

	Raised	Obrist Inhaber (colonel owner)	Engagements – Campaigns:	Uniforms:	History:
ihc-i	1675	Ferenc **Kéry** de Ipoly-Kér (*Croaten*)	*Hungary*		Disbanded in 1682
ihc-ii	1683	Adam **Czobor** (*Husaren*)	Érsekújvár (1685)		Disbanded in 1685

Husaren & Croaten Regiment (Hussar or Croats Regiment)

---

112 Bealupre-Goldberg.
113 Donath, *Die Kaiserliche und Kaiserlich und Königliche Österreichische Armee 1618–1918*.
114 *Ibidem*.
115 *Ibidem*.
116 *Ibidem*.

APPENDIX III

	Raised	Obrist Inhaber (colonel owner)	Engagements – Campaigns:	Uniforms:	History:
IHc-1	1657	**Gutschenich** (*Croaten*)	*Pomerania* *Szentgotthárd* (1664)	(1664)[117] Private: fur trimmed red slouch cap, azure-blue coat.	Disbanded in 1665
IHc-2	1657	**Lubetich** (*Croaten*)	*Pomerania*	-	Disbanded in 1660
IHc-3	1664	Ferenc **Nádasdy** (*Husaren*)*	*Kanisza* (1663) *Körmend* (1664)	-	Disbanded in 1664
IHc-4	1664	Pal **Batthyáni** (*Husaren*)*	*Léva* (1664)	-	Disbanded in 1664
IHc-5	1664	Isztvan **Koháry** (*Husaren*)*	*Szent-Benedek, Léva* (1664)	-	Disbanded in 1664
IHc-6	1664	Lajos **Bercsény** (*Husaren*)*	*Hungary*	-	Disbanded in 1664
IHc-7	1664	**Serény** (*Husaren*)*	*Hungary*	-	Disbanded in 1664
IHc-8	1672	János Károly **Pálffy** de Erdödy (*Croaten*)	*Szatmár* (1672) (*Bonn*) 1673	-	Reformed as Cuirassiers on 1675 (IC-37)
IHc-9	1673	Matthias **Collalto** (*Croaten*)	*Nagy-Károly* (1675) *Philippsburg* (1676)	-	Disbanded in 1679
IHc-10	1675	Isztván **Barkóczy** (*Husaren*) 1680 Ferenc **Barkóczy**	*Upper Rhine* (1676–78) *Hungary* (1683-86)	-	Disbanded in 1686
IHc-11	1675	Ferenc **Kéry** de Ipoly-Kér (*Croaten*)	*Hungary* *Kahlemberg* (1683)	-	Disbanded in 1685
IHc-12	1682	Pietro **Ricciardi** de Lika (*Croaten*)	*Kahlemberg* (1683)	-	Disbanded in 1685
IHc-13	1683	Lajos Imre **Gombos** de Gombosfalva (*Husaren*)	*Hungary*	-	Disbanded in 1692
IHc-14	1684	Isztván **Zichy** (*Husaren*)	*Hungary*	-	Disbanded in 1684
IHc-15	1685	David **Petneházy** (*Husaren*) 1686 Lajos **Csáky**	*Buda* (1686) *Belgrade* (1688) *Nis* (1689)	-	Disbanded in 1698
IHc-16	1685	János **Horváth** (*Husaren*)	*Buda* (1686)	-	Disbanded in 1696
IHc-17	1685	Ladiszlaus **Semsey** (*Husaren*)	*Hungary and Upper Rhine*	-	Disbanded in 1692
IHc-18	1685	Balás **Kis** (*Husaren*)	*Hungary and Upper Rhine*	-	Disbanded in 1692
IHc-19	1685	Ladiszlaus **Barkóczy** (*Husaren*) 1687 Szigiszmund **Csáky**	*Szeged* (1686)	-	Disbanded in 1688
IHc-20	1685	Isztván **Károly** (*Husaren*)	*Hungary*	-	Disbanded in 1686
IHc-21	1688	Janos **Pálffy**-Erdödy (*Husaren*)	*Batočina* (1689)	-	Disbanded in 1918 as H.R.9
IHc-22	1688	Adam **Czobor** (*Husaren*)	*Upper Rhine*	-	Disbanded in 1721
IHc-23	1689	Pál **Gyürki** (*Husaren*)	*Hungary*	-	Disbanded in 1692

* Regiments formed enlisting 4,000 Hungarian *Insurrectionis* militiamen.

---

117 Reconstruction after the fresco preserved in the Castle of Lysá, Czech Republic.

Raised	Obrist Inhaber (colonel owner)	Engagements – Campaigns:	Uniforms:	History:

Infantry and Cavalry Regiments of the *Reichsarmee* from 1664 to 1687

Fränkischer Kreis (Franconian Circle)

Kreis-Regiment zu Fuss (Infantry Kreis-Regiment):

	Raised	Obrist Inhaber	Engagements – Campaigns	Uniforms	History
FI-1	1663	Johann **Pleitner**	Szentgotthárd (1664)	(1664)[118] Private: black headgear, red coat.	Disbanded in 1664
FI-2	1672	Franz Jacob von **Avila**	Entzheim (1674) Trier (1675) Philippsburg (1676)	(1675)[119] Private: dark grey coat, blue stockings.	Disbanded in 1676
FI-3	1675	Johann Carl von **Thüngen**	Philippsburg (1676)	(1675)[120] Private: dark blue coat, grey stockings.	Disbanded in 1676
FI-4	1681	Johann Heinrich von **Andlau** 1684 Georg Eberhard von **Hedersdorff**	Kahlemberg (1683) Buda (1684) Esztergom (1685) Buda (1686)	(late 17th century)[121] Private: black headgear with white piping, grey coat, scarlet cuffs, lining and stockings, grey waistcoat and breeches, brass buttons, white cravat.	Disbanded in 1793
FI-5	1681	Franz Jacob von **Avila** 1682 Johann Wilhelm **Röth** von Wanscheid	Kahlemberg (1683) Buda (1684) Esztergom (1685) Buda (1686)	(late 17th century)[122] Private: black headgear with white piping, grey coat, azure cuffs and lining, grey waistcoat, breeches and stockings, grey buttons, white cravat.	Disbanded in 1793

Cürassier Kreis-Regiment (Cuirassier Kreis-Regiment):

	Raised	Obrist Inhaber	Engagements – Campaigns	Uniforms	History
FC-1	1663	Johann Wilhelm **Zobel** zu Giebelsted	Szentgotthárd (1664)	(1664)[123] Private: black headgear, natural leather *Koller*.	Disbanded in 1664
FC-2	1672	Friedrich von Brandenburg-**Bayreuth**	Entzheim (1674) Trier (1675) Philippsburg (1676)	(1675)[124] Private: natural leather *Koller*, black facings.	Disbanded in 1677
FC-3	1681	Christian Ernst von Brandenburg-**Bayreuth**	Kahlemberg (1683) Buda (1684) Esztergom (1685) Buda (1686)	(late 17th century)[125] Private: natural leather *Koller*, scarlet cuffs, natural leather breeches.	Disbanded in 1793

Dragoner Kreis-Regiment (Dragoon Kreis-Regiment):

	Raised	Obrist Inhaber	Engagements – Campaigns	Uniforms	History
FD-1	1675	Wolf Peter von **Oberndorf**	*Upper Rhine*	-	Disbanded in 1677

Schwäbischer Kreis (Swabian Circle)

Kreis-Regiment zu Fuss (Infantry Kreis-Regiment):

	Raised	Obrist Inhaber	Engagements – Campaigns	Uniforms	History
SI-1	1664	Christian von Pfalz-Birkenfeld-Bischweiler (**Pfalzgraf**)	Szentgotthárd (1664)	(1664)[126] Private: black headgear, light grey coat, breeches and stockings.-	Disbanded in 1664

---

118 Reconstruction after the fresco preserved in the Castle of Lysá, Czech Republic.
119 *Stato delle Truppe Cesaree in Germania, il mese di Ottobre, l'anno 1675.*
120 *Ibidem.*
121 Belaubre, 'Les Triomphes de Louis XIV'.
122 *Ibidem.*
123 Reconstruction after the fresco preserved in the Castle of Lysá, Czech Republic.
124 *Stato delle Truppe Cesaree in Germania, il mese di Ottobre, l'anno 1675.*
125 Belaubre, 'Les Triomphes de Louis XIV'.
126 Reconstruction after the fresco preserved in the Castle of Lysá, Czech Republic.

APPENDIX III

	Raised	Obrist Inhaber (colonel owner)	Engagements – Campaigns:	Uniforms:	History:
SI-2	1664	Franz von **Fugger**	Szentgotthárd (1664)	-	Disbanded in 1664
SI-3	1674	Carl Gustav von **Baden-Durlach**	Trier (1675) Philippsburg (1676)	(1675)[127] Private: dark grey coat, carmine stockings.	Disbanded in 1677
SI-4	1683	Carl Gustav von **Baden-Durlach** 1683 Carl Wilhelm von **Baden-Durlach**	Kahlemberg (1683) Buda (1684) Esztergom (1685) Buda (1686)	(1683)[128] Private: grey coat, yellow cuffs and stockings. (1687)[129] Officer: scarlet coat, green cuffs, yellow stockings, white cravat.	Disbanded in 1801
SI-5	1683	Notger Wilhelm zu **Öttingen**	Kahlemberg (1683) Buda (1684) Esztergom (1685) Buda (1686)	(1684)[130] Private: light grey coat with dark blue cuffs. (1687)[131] Private: dark blue coat with white cuffs.	Disbanded in 1801

Cürassier Kreis-Regiment (Cuirassier Kreis-Regiment):

	Raised	Obrist Inhaber (colonel owner)	Engagements – Campaigns:	Uniforms:	History:
SC-1	1664	Maximilian Franz von **Fürstenberg**	Szent Benedek (1664)	-	Disbanded in 1664
SC-2	1674	Maximilian Franz von **Fürstenberg**	*Upper Rhine*	(1675)[132] Private: natural leather *Koller*, blue facings.	Disbanded in 1677
SC-3	1674	Friedrich Carl von **Württemberg**	*Upper Rhine*	(1675)[133] Private: dark grey coat, red facings	Disbanded in 1677
SC-4	1683	Johann Franz von Bronckhorst zu **Gronsfeld**	Buda (1684) Esztergom (1685) Buda (1686)	(late 17th century)[134] Private: black headgear with white piping, natural leather *Koller*, red cuffs, black leather armour, red waistcoat and breeches, tin buttons, white cravat, red saddle cover with white trim.	Disbanded in 1801
SC-5	1683	Quirin von **Hönstett** 1687 Ludwig von **Württemberg**	Buda (1684) Esztergom (1685) Buda (1686)	(1683)[135] Private: black headgear with white piping, pearl grey coat and cuffs, white cravat, yellow saddle cover with black trim piped white. (late 17th century)[136] Private: black headgear with white piping, natural leather *Koller*, light blue cuffs, black leather armour, light blue waistcoat, tin buttons, white cravat, light blue saddle cover with white trim.	Disbanded in 1796

Oberrheinischer Kreis (Upper-Rhenish Circle)

Kreis-Regiment zu Fuss (Infantry Kreis-Regiment):

	Raised	Obrist Inhaber (colonel owner)	Engagements – Campaigns:	Uniforms:	History:
OrI-1	1664	Adolph von **Nassau-Idstein**	*Hungary*	-	Disbanded in 1664

---

127 *Stato delle Truppe Cesaree in Germania, il mese di Ottobre, l'anno 1675.*
128 Belaubre, 'Les Triomphes de Louis XIV'.
129 *Ibidem*.
130 *Ibidem*.
131 *Ibidem*.
132 *Stato delle Truppe Cesaree in Germania, il mese di Ottobre, l'anno 1675.*
133 *Ibidem*.
134 *Ibidem*.
135 New York Public Library, 'The Vinkhuijzen collection of military uniforms', Germany-Württemberg 1625–1735, *Schwäb. Kreis-Regiment zu Pferd v. Hönstett, 1683, jetz Ulanen-Regiment 'König Karl' (1. Württembergisches) Nr. 19.*
136 Belaubre, 'Les Triomphes de Louis XIV'.

	Raised	Obrist Inhaber (colonel owner)	Engagements – Campaigns:	Uniforms:	History:
OrI-2	1664	Philipp zu **Solms**	*Hungary*	-	Disbanded in 1664
OrI-3	1664	Nikolaus Friedrich von **Zobel**	*Hungary*	-	In the *Reichsarmee* until 1664
OrI-4	1673	Adolph von **Nassau-Idstein**	*Trier (1675)*	(1674)[137] Private: grey coat with blue facings and blue-yellow ribbon, grey stockings, tin buttons.	Disbanded in 1678
OrI-5	1673	Philipp zu **Solms**	*Türkheim, Trier (1675)*	-	Disbanded in 1678
OrI-6	1685	Johann Ludwig von **Nassau-Saarbrücken**	*Pécs, Siklós (1686) Harsány (1687) Dervent (1688)*	(1685)[138] Private: black headgear with white piping, blue coat, grey cuffs and lining, grey stockings, tin buttons.	Disbanded in 1688
OrI-7	1688	Ludwig Sittich von **Goertz**	*Mainz (1689)*	-	Disbanded in 1697
OrI-8	1689	**Wittgenstein**	*Upper Rhine*	-	Disbanded in 1697

Cavallerie Kreis-Regiment (Cavalry Kreis-Regiment):

	Raised	Obrist Inhaber	Engagements	Uniforms	History
OrC-1	1664	Walrad von **Nassau-Usingen**	*Hungary*	-	Disbanded in 1664
OrC-2	1673	*Oberrhein*	*Hungary*	-	Disbanded in 1679
OrC-3	1685	Otto Rudolph **Rau** zu Holzhausen Wilhelm von **Spiegel** 1686 Johann Ernst von **Nassau-Weilburg**	*Pécs, Siklós (1686) Harsány (1687) Dervent (1688) Mainz (1689)*	(late 17th century)[139] Private: black headgear with white piping, grey coat, dark pink cuffs, lining and waistcoat, natural leather breeches, tin buttons, white cravat.	Disbanded in 1740

Bayerischer Kreis (Bavarian Circle)

Kreis-Regiment zu Fuss (Infantry Kreis-Regiment):

	Raised	Obrist Inhaber	Engagements	Uniforms	History
BI-1	1664	Ferdinand von **Puech**	*Szentgotthárd (1664)*	(1680s) Private: green coat with yellow facings	With the *Reichsarmee* until in 1664
BI-2	1664	Johann von **Flettingen**	*Upper Hungary*	-	Disbanded in 1664
BI-3	1664	**Freysing**	*Upper Hungary*	-	Disbanded in 1664
BI-4	1683	**Rummel** 1684 **Spilberg**	*Kahlemberg (1683) Hungary*	-	Disbanded in 1688
BI-5	1689	**Spilberg**	*Upper Rhine*	-	Disbanded in 1698

Cavallerie Kreis-Regiment (Cavalry Kreis-Regiment):

	Raised	Obrist Inhaber	Engagements	Uniforms	History
BC-1	1664	Nikolaus **Höning**	*Szentgotthárd (1664)*	-	With the *Reichsarmee* until 1664

---

137 J. Belaubre-K. P. Goldberg, *Les Armées qui combattirent Louis XIV : Oberrhein* (Paris: private publishing, 1974).
138 *Ibidem*.
139 Belaubre-Goldberg, 'Les Armées qui combattirent Louis XIV: Oberrhein'.

APPENDIX III

	Raised	Obrist Inhaber (colonel owner)	Engagements – Campaigns:	Uniforms:	History:
BC-2	1689	**Walser**	Mainz (1689)	-	Disbanded in 1691

Westphälischer Kreis (Westphalian Circle)

Kreis-Regiment zu Fuss (Infantry Kreis-Regiment):

	Raised	Obrist Inhaber (colonel owner)	Engagements – Campaigns:	Uniforms:	History:
WI-1	1664	Johann Gottfried von **Uffeln**	Szentgotthárd (1664)		Disbanded in 1664
WI-2	1664	Gerhard Wilhelm von **Hochstätten** (Pfalz-Neuburg)	*Hungary*		In the *Reichsarmee* until 1664
WI-3	1664	**Toller** (Münster)	*Hungary*	(1664)[140] Private: straw yellow headgear, carmine cassock, dark grey doublet and breeches.	In the *Reichsarmee* until 1664
WI-3	1672	Johann Emanuel **Waldbot** von Bassenheim	Bonn (1673)	-	Disbanded in 1679

Cavallerie Kreis-Regiment (Cavalry Kreis-Regiment):

	Raised	Obrist Inhaber (colonel owner)	Engagements – Campaigns:	Uniforms:	History:
WC-1	1664	Lothar von **Post** zu Bosfeld	Szentgotthárd (1664)		In the *Reichsarmee* until 1664

Obersächsischer Kreis (Upper-Saxony Circle):

Kreis-Regiment zu Fuss (Infantry Kreis-Regiment):

	Raised	Obrist Inhaber (colonel owner)	Engagements – Campaigns:	Uniforms:	History:
OsI-1	1664	Casimir Ferdinand von **Sparr**	*Hungary*		In the *Reichsarmee* until 1664
OsI-2	1664	Brandt von **Lindau**	*Hungary*	Uniforms:	In the *Reichsarmee* until 1664
OsI-3	1664	Wolf Albrecht von **Weidenbach**	*Hungary*)	-	Disbanded in 1664
OsI-4	1674	**Prinz Christian**	*Upper Rhine*	-	Disbanded in 1680

Cavallerie Kreis-Regiment (Cavalry Kreis-Regiment):

	Raised	Obrist Inhaber (colonel owner)	Engagements – Campaigns:	Uniforms:	History:
OsC-1	1664	Caspar Heinrich **Stange**	*Hungary*		Disbanded in 1664
OsC-2	1664	Henning von **Koller**	*Hungary*	Uniforms:	In the *Reichsarmee* until 1664
OsC-3	1664	Georg Friedrich von **Wolfamsdorff**	*Hungary*	-	Disbanded in 1664
OsC-4	1674	**Herzog Moritz**	*Upper Rhine*	-	Disbanded in 1680

Dragoner Kreis-Regiment (Dragoon Kreis-Regiment):

	Raised	Obrist Inhaber (colonel owner)	Engagements – Campaigns:	Uniforms:	History:
OsD-1	1664	Wilhelm von **Block**	*Hungary*	-	In the *Reichsarmee* until 1664

---

140 Reconstruction after the fresco preserved in the Castle of Lysá, Czech Republic.

	Raised	Obrist Inhaber (colonel owner)	Engagements – Campaigns:	Uniforms:	History:
Niedersächsischer Kreis (Lower Saxony Circle)					
Kreis-Regiment zu Fuss (Infantry Kreis-Regiment):					
NsI-1	1663	Job Bernhard von **Mücheln**	Pécs, Kanisza (1664)	-	Disbanded in 1664
NsI-2	1664	Rudolph von **Ende**	Szentgotthárd (1664)	(1664)[141] Private: black headgear, red coat.	Disbanded in 1664
NsI-3	1674	**Rolshausen**	*Upper-Rhine*	-	In the *Reichsarmee* until 1675
Cavallerie Kreis-Regiment (Cavalry Kreis-Regiment):					
NsC-1	1663	Christoph von **Rauchhaupt**	Pécs, Kanisza (1664)	-	Disbanded in 1664
NsC-2	1664	Josias von **Schack**	Szentgotthárd (1664)	-	Disbanded in 1664
NsC-3	1674	**Vieregge**	*Upper Rhine*	-	Disbanded in 1675
Kurrheinischer Kreis (Electoral-Rhenish Circle)					
Kreis-Regiment zu Fuss (Infantry Regiment):					
KrI-1	1664	Kuno von der **Leyden**	*Hungary*	-	Disbanded in 1664
KrI-2	1664	**Orsberg**	*Hungary*	-	Disbanded in 1664
KrI-3	1664	Josias von **Waldeck**	*Hungary*	-	Disbanded in 1664
Burgundischer Kreis (Burgundian Circle)					
Kreis-Regiment zu Fuss (Infantry Regiment):					
BuI-1	1664	Jean **Geys**	*Hungary*	-	Disbanded in 1664
Cavallerie Kreis-Regiment (Cavalry Regiment):					
BuC-1	1664	Caspar Casimir von **Hardunck**	*Hungary*	-	Disbanded in 1664

---

141 Reconstruction after the fresco preserved in the Castle of Lysá, Czech Republic.

Colour Plate Commentaries

Plate A

1) Pikeman, unknown infantry regiment, 1657–60
Sources relating to Imperial pikemen of the mid 17th century show a dress with little difference from the one worn by foot soldiers of western European armies. Coat or doublet and breast armour, this latter usually painted in black, were common in Austria as well as in southern Germany. Usually the coat was of cloth or leather, with plain cuffs and no pockets, worn over classical wide breeches or knee-length trousers. Morion helms seemed to be the most widespread protection for the head in the Imperial infantry. The use of two pairs of stockings was the simplest method of protecting the feet from humidity, and saving the first pair as long as possible. Reconstruction after a drawing of Karl Alexander Wilke for the Austrian magazine *Die Mölkerbastei*, and engraving of Bartholemeus Kilian (1663), Czech National Library, Prague.

2) Musketeer, Regiment *Strozzi zu Fuss*; 1663–64

3) Junior Officer, regiment *Strozzi zu Fuss* (II-12), 1663–64
Thanks to a receipt dated 3 February 1663, concerning the purchase of clothing and equipment for the foot regiment of *Feldmarschall Lieutenant* Pietro Strozzi (II-12) it is possible to attempt a reconstruction of the 'uniform' issued to this regiment, which participated in the war in Hungary in 1663–64. The 'Iglau' fabric (today Jihlava in Czech Republic) cited in the document alludes not only to the characteristics of the textile but, very probably, to the typical pearl grey of the Moravian manufactures. Count Strozzi must not have minded spending money on his soldiers, because the yellow *traliccio* textile (in Italian in the original text) had arrived from Florence and this particular linen fabric was commonly used to produce socks.

Yellow must have been the favourite colour of the Italian colonel proprietor, if we assume the use of this colour-livery for his subordinate officers. The cloak remained a valuable part of military dress, employed especially by officers. Cloaks were worn over the doublet and retained the shape of the circular shoulder-cape, much in vogue throughout the second half of the century. Reconstruction after contemporary illustrations of Bartholemeus

Kilian, 1663, Czech National Library, Prague; Archivio di Stato di Firenze, 'Fondo Carte Strozziane', *lettere e corrispondenza di Piero Strozzi*, ff. 73–76; 1657 matchlock musket preserved in the Landeszeughaus Museum of Graz.

Plate B

1) *Feldwebel*, Regiment *Mannsfeld zu Fuss* (II-44), 1670–75

In the progressive approach to a standard of homogeneity in the clothing of the troops, the Imperial army remained rather late compared to the major European powers. The basic single-breasted coat, often without pockets, become common in the early 1670s, known in Germany and Austria as a *Rock*. In the early model, the sleeves of the coat seem longer compared to those in the 1670s, when flap cuffs begin to appear, however, large back flap cuffs remain rare before 1680. Reconstruction after the figures in the engraving of the Hungarian Magnates' execution in Vienna, 1671.

2) Musketeer, Regiment *Starhemberg zu Fuss* (II-41), 1675–80

This figure is a reconstruction after an illustration in Victor von Neuwirth's *Geschichte des k. u. k. Infanterie-Regimentes Alt Starhemberg Nr. 54*, published in 1894. Grey, in different nuances, was the most widespread colour of the Imperial infantry uniforms; however, according to contemporary accounts, the quality of dress issued to soldiers was poor and only rarely were attempts to add some improvement, the more common being ribbons and lining. The uniform for the troops was a matter managed by the colonel proprietors, but when the troops were on campaign, clothing was issued by the Imperial Treasury and this certainly contributed to make the Imperial uniforms as essential and minimal.

3) Artillery, *Constabler*, 1671

There is a large variety of uniforms for the Imperial artillery in this period. Coats in blue with red facings are proposed by some scholars, while other sources relate that the Imperial artillery was dressed in *Rocks* of pearl grey with red cuffs. This *Constabler* wears a coat with short sleeves typical for this age. Black headgear become typical of the Imperial troops in the 1670s. After F. Lallemand, *Die k. k. österreichische Armee im Laufe zweyer Jahrhunderte* (Vienna, 1840).

Plate C

1) *Hauptmann*, Regiment *Heister zu Fuss* (II-81), 1685

Imperial Officers had no restrictions concerning their dress, and according to some sources of the late 17th century, they could choose the dress they preferred: 'as long as it was allowed by the colonel, so that their clothing was not too excessive or extravagant'. In the 1670s and early 1680s, the preferred item of the Imperial officer seems to have been the *Koller* coat but as an alternative, the French-style *justaucorps* became usual, especially in reversed colours. A sash in red and gold or red and silver remained the distinctive field sign of the Imperial officers until 1700. Reconstruction after Johann Christoph Wagner, *Delineatio provinciarum Pannoniae et Imperii Turcici in Oriente: oder, Grundrichtigen Beschreibung dess ganzen Aufgangs, sonderlich aber dess hochlöblichen Königreichs Ungarn, und der ganzen Türckey* (Augsburg, 1685).

2) Pikeman, Regiment *Thüngen zu Fuss,* (II-96), 1685–88

Figures 2 and 3 are based upon an engraving depicting the Imperial troops in the Hungarian campaign of 1685, entitled *Belagerung von Neuhäusel*. This regiment belonged to the Bishop of Würzburg, who ceded it to the Emperor in 1685, and dark blue was common for Würzburg's soldiery dress since the beginning of the 17th century. A red cravat became a distinctive for the imperial infantry in the late 17th century. Pikemen had discarded their armour since the 1670s, mainly because it was heavy on the march and the waggons had been diminished to one per company. In 1688, all the pikemen in the Army of Hungary were converted into musketeers.

3) Grenadier, Regiment *Scherffenberg zu Fuss* (II-7), 1685

The *Rock*-coat proved adequate for normal service, but guard duty at night or in rainy weather required extra clothing. Later experience or prolonged campaigning led to the introduction of waistcoats in this period, sometimes tailored from old coats. During ordinary service and also on marches – and especially in the encampment – in some regiments the soldiers wore a headgear called *Holzkappe*. It was a cap of which there were several types, and was usually made with old headgear, but it could have come from the province where the regiment recruited its men. This 'fatigue cap' was the origin of the first grenadier's *Pelzmütze*, like the one here reproduced, similar to the contemporary headgear of the Bohemian folk dress.

Plate D

1) Cuirassier Officer, 1660–64; 2) Cuirassier Trooper, 1658–64; unknown regiment

On campaign, the Imperial cavalry often renounced metal forms of protection. In Hungary, this was one of the main solutions adopted by cuirassiers to counter the Ottoman cavalry on reconnaissance duties and other tasks. However, cuirasses and helms were always worn in preordained battle. In the following years, in the eastern theatre of war, the Imperial heavy cavalry usually fought with metal protection, whereas in western battlefields its use was declining. Apart from the relative homogeneity of the equipment, in the second half of the 17th century there were still no signs of identification of the cuirassier regiments. Some regiments identified their companies with feathers on the headgear; another option was recognising units by joining together within the companies – and in some cases whole regiments – the horses of the same colour. The colonel of the Imperial army usually held assignments in the *General Stab*, and left the direction of the regiment to the lieutenant-colonels, acting as field commander. Reconstruction after Stefano Della Bella (1610–1664) and contemporary portraits; cover saddle is speculative.

Plate E

1) Dragoon, Regiment *Gérard Dragoner* (ID-1), 1664
According to Montecuccoli, a dragoon was not a 'skirmisher' in modern terms and in the open field fought in formations, which manoeuvred in much the same way as infantry musketeers. This did not change until the 1680s, when the increasing need of cavalry, especially in Hungary, modified the tactical role of the dragoons. The existing iconography and contemporary reconstructions of the 1660s depict the Imperial dragoons mostly dressed in coats of red or grey. Reconstruction after an engraving of Bartholomeus Kilian (1663), Czech National Library, Prague, and from the fresco of the battle of Szentgotthárd in Lysá Castle, Czech Republic.

2) Dragoon NCO, Regiment *Trauttmansdorff Dragoner* (ID-7), 1672
The dress of this figure is taken from the illustrations of Karl Alexander Wilke for the Austrian magazine *Die Mölkerbastei*, integrated with some details from contemporary iconography. Imperial dragoons were dressed like the infantry, but NCOs carried the same weapons as the troops. According to a 1675 eyewitness, this regiment had a full red uniform. White-silver or yellow-gold lacing was the distinctive sign of the cavalry NCO in the second half of the 17th century.

Plate F

1) Dragoon Officer, unknown regiment, 1675–80
Though the *Koller*-leather coat, and armour, were the favourite clothing of the Imperial cavalry officers, in some portraits they are depicted French-style justaucorps worn over a leather waistcoat. This fashion became typical in Austria and Southern Germany in the late 1670s, a sort of 'meeting of styles' of military dress. Reconstruction after Rudolph Donath, *Die Kaiserliche und Königlich Österreichische Armee, 1618–1918* and illustrations of K.A. Wilke for the Austrian magazine *Die Mölkerbastei*.

2) Dragoon, Regiment *Savoyen Dragoner,* (ID-13), 1682
This regiment is dressed with the same colours adopted by the Duke of Savoy's *Guardie* regiment, and belonged to a member of a cadet branch of the ruling Italian family. Colonel Luigi Giulio of Savoie-Soissons was killed in action on 7 July 1683 at Petronell. Richard Knötel did not leave information about the source from which he reconstructed this figure, but all the details are accurate and reliable for this period. The saddle cover and pistol holsters show the piped edge characteristic of the Imperial cavalry as related by several authors.

COLOUR PLATE COMMENTARIES

Plate G

1) Miklós Zrínyi (1620–1664)
There are several portraits depicting the Croatian *banus* and poet, in which he preferably wears red. Some contemporary pictures represent Zrínyi with breast armour with protections for the arm, worn over the classic Hungarian *Attila* short coat. A mixture of traditional native dress and western accessories qualified in the 1660s the most important officers in Croatia and Hungary.

2) Croat, Regiment *Gutschenich Croater* (IHc-1), 1664
A single regiment of Croatian light cavalry participated in the campaign of 1664 under the *Obrist* Gutschenich. In the late 17th century, Croatian and Hungarian light cavalry were mostly organised as irregular forces, but in this period begins the tradition of the standing *Husaren* regiments in the Habsburg army. Reconstruction from the fresco of the battle of Szentgotthárd in Lysá Castle, Czech Republic.

3) Hungarian *Hayduk Grenzer*, late 17th century
17th century images of the military border troops in Hungary show the typical *hajdú* footman with cloth *gepernek* cloak or fur mantle over the short *Attila* jackets and breeches. Headgear in black or dark brown felt was common since the previous century, often with crow's feathers. The Hungarian infantrymen were usually equipped with musket, sabre and axe. This latter was employed in close combat according to a specific technique of fighting codified to face the Ottomans, who were also trained to engage the enemy with cold steel. Reconstruction after the *Neu-Eröffnete welt-Galleria*, Nurnberg, 1703.

Plate H

1) Musketeer, Regiment *Uffleln zu Fuss* (WI-1), Circle of Westphalia, 1664
In the fresco of the battle of Szentgotthárd in Lysá castle appear some figures dressed with carmine-red cassocks over dark grey doublets, and wearing light ochre-yellow broad-brimmed hats. They are probably infantrymen of the Westphalian circle's infantry regiment formed by the Bishop of Paderborn and other smaller states for the Hungarian campaign of 1664. At Szentgotthárd, the regiment remained involved in the Ottoman counterattack during the first phase of the battle, losing half of its original force. The unknown author of the fresco executed the work following the indications of the customer, *General der Cavallerie* Johan von Sporck. The position occupied by the troops seems to coincide with the deployment established by Montecuccoli, allowing the identification of several units. The cassock was a common military item in the Dutch Republic and it possibly influenced the Westphalian states close to the United Provinces, such as the Bishopric of Paderborn. However, in 1664, it is very likely that in the regiments of the *Reichsarmee* complete uniformity of clothing was still far from being achieved.

2) Cuirassier, Regiment *Hönstett Cuirassieren* (SC-5), Circle of Swabia, 1683
Leather armour appeared in Württemberg, and probably, this protection provided a model imitated by some regiments of the Swabian circle, which included Württemberg. Reconstruction after the illustration *Schwäb. Kreis-Regiment zuPferd v. Hönstett, 1683, jetzUlanen-Regiment 'König Karl' (1. Württembergisches) Nr. 19*. New York Public Library, The Vinkhuijzen collection of military uniforms, Germany-Württemberg, 1625–1735.

3) *Tambour*, regiment *Nassau-Idstein zu Fuss* (OrI-4), Circle of Upper-Rhine, 1674–78
Reconstruction after J. Belaubre-K.P. Goldberg, *Les Armées qui combattirent Louis XIV: Oberrhein*.

Plate I

1) Imperial and Reichsarmee Colours
Before 1657 the Austrian Habsburgs' field ensigns show a great variety of symbols and colours, such as the red Burgundian cross on various background patterns, and with or without double-headed eagle and decorated edge. Under Leopold I the infantry flags show a scheme more regular and with few exceptions. This flag appears in a 1664 engraving of *Theatrum Europaeum* by Matthäus Merian, is very probably a *Leibfahne*, if it is assumed the background is white, and belonged to an unknown infantry regiment. The reverse side, with the sacred images of Mary and Jesus, is speculative, but both these figures already appeared on the colonel's ensigns in the first half of the 17th century. Later, the image of the Annunciation of Mary would become typical of the Imperial colonel's ensigns.

2) Swabian circle, Regiment *Függer zu Fuss* (SI-2), 1664.

3) Cuirassier company standard, unknown regiment, 1670–80; Heeresgeschichtliches Museum.

4) Cuirassier *Leibstandarte* with the image of the Annunciation of Mary, 1670–80 (Heeresgeschichtliches Museum).

5) Company flag probably belonged to regiment *Uffeln zu Fuss* (WI-1), Westphalian circle, 1664, after the fresco in Lysá Castle.

6) Company flag, unknown Imperial infantry regiment, 1683.

COLOUR PLATE COMMENTARIES

Plate J

1) Imperial Colours
Houchin zu Fuss (II-94), 1684; a: *Leibfahne*, b: *Compagnie Fahne*. The image of St Paul appears as onomastic of the colonel proprietor Paul Anton von Houchin, as related by Heinrich Metzger in *Fahnen-Historik der K. und K. Österr.-Ungar. Infanterie der Letzen 300 Jahre*.

2) *Sachsen-Lauenburg Cuirassieren* (IC-42).
A: Leibstandarte, b *Compagnie Standarte*; 1682. The same author describes this couple of ensigns, embroidered by the empress Eleanor of Pfalz-Neuburg, with the Virgin with the son and the image of Saint Julius, onomastic of the colonel proprietor.

Plate K

1) Imperial and Reichsarmee Colours captured by the French at Friedlingen in 1702. From MSS 'Les Triomphes de Louis XIV dit le Grand, roy de France et de Navarre représentés par les Drapeaux, Guidons et Etendarts…' (Bibliothèque Nationale de France, Paris)

The French captured these standards at Friedlingen in 1702, which belonged to the Franconian cuirassier regiment *Bayreuth* (FC-3), formed in 1681. Twenty-one years later, the colonel proprietor was always Margrave Christian Ernst of Brandenburg-Bayreuth and the composition of the regiment remained the same. The differences of the standards reflect the provenance of the companies which formed the regiment: a) The white standard with the eagle opposing the sun is the life colour belonging to the company of the colonel proprietor, as suggested by the these figures, adopted also by the margrave of Brandenburg-Bayreuth in late 17th century; b) Five red standards figured among the trophies and belonged to the ordinary companies; c) and d) These standards belonged to the companies formed by Ansbach, Schwarzenberg and Sinsheim; e) Two standards with an azure and white background were carried by the companies of Würzburg, while standard f) is of uncertain attribution.

Plate L

Cuirassier and dragoon saddle covers, late 17th century. (Graphics by Bruno Mugnai)

Plate M

Imperial colours at the Siege of Vienna 1683

a) Ensign of the *Wiener Stadt-Guardia* regiment in 1683. The city militia comprised four companies, one for each quarter or *Viertel*. Each company wore its own uniform. The *Stuben-Viertel* wore a yellow coat with black facings, the *Kärnthner-Viertel* red-white, the *Widmer-Viertel* light grey-yellow and the *Schotten-Viertel* red-yellow.

b) *Compagnie-Fahne* of the regiment *Württemberg zu Fuss* (II-90), 1683; after the painting by an anonymous artist, preserved in the Heeresgeschichtliches Museum of Vienna. Illustration by Bruno Mugnai.

Plate N

Flags 1 and 2 are Imperial standards of a cuirassier regiment, lost in 1657 during the Polish campaign under Montecuccoli; possibly regiment *Heister Cuirassieren* (IC-9); cm. 57x58, overall height included the pole 258 cm. The standard still bears the monogram of Ferdinand III. The original background was probably azure.

Flags 3 and 4 are the two sides of an Imperial cornet that probably belonged to regiment *Spankau Dragoner* (ID-4), captured by the Swedes at Torun, in 1658. This regiment was the only dragoon unit engaged in the siege. On the reverse appears the inscription relating the year '1656', but the regiment was formed in 1657. Possibly this difference derives from the date of appointment of Colonel Paris von Spankau as *Obrist-Inhaber*, who received the Patent some months before the actual formation of the regiment. Dimension 61x92 cm; overall height including the pole 267 cm. Collection of the Armémuseum, Stockholm.

Plate O

The Imperial Circles.

Plate P

***General-Lieutenant* Raimondo Montecuccoli (1609-1680)**
The *generalissimo* wears the classic dress of the mid-17th century senior officer: three-quarter armour, leather coat-*Koller* and plumed broad-brimmed hat. Montecuccoli was considered an austere man less interested in fashion, however in his portraits he loved to be depicted in highly sumptuous clothing. Armour and clothing are taken from the portrait executed after 1664 by Elias Greissler (1632–1682), preserved in the Heeresgeschichtliches Museum of Vienna.

COLOUR PLATE COMMENTARIES

Back Cover

***Cuirassier Trompete*, unknown regiment, 1665–70**
Before private soldiers, regimental musicians adopted a specific uniform. In the 17th century, liveries evolved from the dress of pages and heralds of the Middle Ages and Renaissance, and flourished in the Baroque age. Although it is not certain, the adoption by the Imperial cuirassier musicians of the characteristic Ottoman headdress appears to have happened during the *Türkenkrieg* of 1663–64. The cap imitated the typical Turkish *kavuk* around which was rolled the turban fabric spirals. (After an illustration of K.A. Wilke, for the magazine 1683, *die Mölkerbastei*)

Select Bibliography

Archive Sources

Österreichisches Kriegsarchiv Vienna, 'Das Kriegsjahr 1683 nach Akten und andere authentischen Quellen' in *Mitteilungen des K.K. Kriegsarchivs* (Vienna, 1883).
Österreichisches Kriegsarchiv Vienna, *Alte Feldacten*, 1663–1664.
Archivio di Stato di Firenze: *Fondo Carte Strozziane, lettere e altra corrispondenza di Piero Strozzi*, ff. 73-76.
Archivio di Stato di Napoli: 'Museo' vol. 994146 (Antonio Carafa di Stigliano) , c. 13 *Stato delle Truppe Cesaree in Germania, il mese di Ottobre, l'anno 1675*.

Contemporary Printed Sources

Anonymous, *Relation de ce qui passé depuis quelque temps entre le deux Armée, l'Impériale & Françoise faite par un officier de l'Armée Impériale*, MDCLXXVI (n.d.)
Anonymous, *Nuova e Vera Relatione del sanguinoso Combattimento seguito tra gli Esserciti Imperiale e Ottomano al fiume Raab* (Bologna, 1664).
Anonymous (edited by Anna Bosco, Luca Serravalle and Piergiorgio Zotti): *1684, un maremmano all'assedio di Buda* (Arcidosso, GR: Effigi, 2012)
Theatrum Europeum, vol. VIII and XI (Frankfurt am Main, 1643–1738)
Gualdo-Priorato, Galeazzo: *Historia di Leopoldo Cesare, contenente le cose più memorabili successe in Europa dal 1656 al 1670* (Vienna, 1670), vols. I–III.
D'Aste, Michele (edited by Ernesto Piacentini): *Diario dell'Assedio di Buda del 1686, in Diarii degl'Assedii di Vienna del 1683, e di Buda del 1686, distesi e scritti dal Baron Michele D'Aste che vi si trovò presente in tutte le sue Azzioni* (Rome-Budapest: Bulzoni-Corvina, 1991)
Wagner, Johann Christoph: *Delineatio provinciarum Pannoniae et Imperii Turcici in Oriente oder Grundrichtige Beschreibung dess ganzen Aufgangs, sonderlich aber dess hochlöblichen Königreichs Ungarn, und der ganzen Türckey* (Augsburg, 1685).

General Documentary Sources

K.u.K. Kriegsarchiv, *Feldzüge des Prinzen Eugen von Savoyen. Nach den Feldacten und anderen authentischen Quellen hrsg. von der Abtheilung für Kriegsgeschichte des K.K. Kriegs-Archives*, (Vienna, 1876–92), vol. I
Bánlaky, József: *A magyar nemzet hadtörténelme*, vol. XVII (Budapest, 1928–1942)
Campori, Cesare, *Montecuccoli, la sua famiglia e i suoi tempi* (Modena: 1876)
Evans, Robert J.W., *The making of the Habsburg monarchy, 1550–1700* (Oxford: Oxford University Press, 1979)
Lendvai, Paul, *The Hungarians, a Thousand Years of Victory in Defeat* (Princeton NJ: Princeton University Press 2003)
Nolan, Cathal J. (ed.), *Wars of the Age of Louis XIV, 1650–1715. An Encyclopedia of Global Warfare and Civilization* (Westport CT: Grenwood Press, 2008)
Redlich, Fritz: *The German military enterpriser and his workforce: a study in European economic and social history* (2 vols) (Wiesbaden: Steiner Verlag, 1964–5)

Setton, Kenneth M., *Venice, Austria and the Turks in the seventeenth century* (Philadelphia: American Philosophical Society, 1991)
Sutter-Fichtner, Paula, *Terror and Toleration. The Habsburg Empire Confronts Islam, 1526–1850* (London: Reaktion Books, 2008)
Whaley, Joachim, *Germany and the Holy Roman Empire. From the Peace of Westphalia to the Dissolution of the Reich, 1648–1806* (Oxford: Oxford University Press, 2012)

The Imperial Army

Dolleczek, Anton: *Geschichte der Österreichischen Artillerie von der frühsten Zeiten bis zur Gegenwart* (Vienna, 1887 – Graz: Akademische Druck und Verlagsanstalt, 1975)
Donath, Rudolph: *Die Kaiserliche und Königlich Österreichische Armee, 1618–1918* (Simbach/Inn: private publishing, 1965–71)
Hochedlinger, Michael: *Austria's Wars of Emergence. War, State and Society in the Habsburg Monarchy, 1683–1797* (London and New York NY: Routledge, 2013)
Klaje, Hermann: *Der Feldzug der Kaiserlichen unter Souches nach Pommern im Jahre 1659* (Gotha: Perthes, 1906)
Komjathy, Antony T., *A Thousand Years of the Hungarian Art of War* (Toronto: Rakoczi Foundation, 1982)
Luraghi, Raimondo, *Le Opere di Raimondo Montecuccoli*, vols. I–II (Rome: USSME, 1988)
Meynert, Hermann: *Geschichte der K. K. Österreichischen Armee, ihrer Heranbildung und Organisation, so wie ihrer Schicksale, Thaten und Feldzüge, von der frühesten bis auf die jetzige Zeit* (Vienna: Gerold, 1854) Vol. III.
Müller, Franz: *Die Kaiserl. Königl Österreichische Armee, seit der Errichtung der stehenden Kriegsheere bis auf die neueste Zeit* (Prague: Verlag, Druck und Papier von Gottlieb Haase Söhne, 1845)
Opitz, Eckardt, *Österreich und Brandenburg im Schwedisch-Polnischen Krieg 1655–1660* (Boppard am Rhein: Harald Boldt, 1970)
Payer, Gustav, *Armati Hungarorum* (Munich: Körösi Csoma Sándor, 1990)
Rothenberg, Gunther E., *Die österreichische Militärgrenze in Kroatien* (Vienna: Herold, 1970)
Schreiber, Georg, *Des Kaisers Reiterei. Österreichische Kavallerie in 4 Jahrhunderte* (Vienna: Speidel, 1967)
Testa, Andrea, *Le Opere di Raimondo Montecuccoli*, vol. III (Rome: USSME, 2000)
Thürheim, Andreas von: *Die Reiterregimenter der k.k. österreichischen Armee*, vols I–III (Vienna: Geitler, 1866)
Vanicek, Franz: *Specialgeschichte der Militärgrenze aus Originalquellen und Quellenwerken geschöpft* (Vienna, 1875), vol. I
Wrede, Alphons von, *Geschichte der K.u.K. Wehrmacht von 1618 bis zum Ende des XIX Jahrhunderts* (5 vols.) (Vienna, 1898–1905)

The *Reichsarmee*

AA.VV, *Handbuch zur deutschen Militärgeschichte, 1648–1939* (11 vols.) (Freiburg: Militärgeschichtliches Forschungsamt, 1983)
Belaubre, Jean *Les Triomphes de Louis XIV*, vols I–II (Paris: Privately published, 1970)
Dotzauer, Winfried: *Die deutschen Reichskreise in der Verfassung des alten Reiches und ihr Eigenleben (1500–1806)* (Munich: Wissenschaftliche Buchgesellschaft, 1989)
Fester, Richard: *Die armirten Stände und die Reichskriegsverfassung, 1681–1697* (Frankfurt-am-Main: 1886)
Fester, Richard: *Die Augsburger Allianz von 1686* (Munich: M. Rieger, 1893)
Knüppel, Günter: *Das Heerwesen des Fürstentums Schleswig-Holstein-Gottorf, 1600–1715* (Neumünster: Wachholtz Verlag, 1972)
Goldberg, Claus-Peter and Belaubre, Jean, *Les Armées qui combattirent Louis 14 – Le cercle du Rhin supérieur* (Paris: Privately published, 1974)
Schempp, Adolph von, *Der Feldzug 1664 in Ungarn unter besonderer Berücksichtigung der herzoglich württembergischen allianz- und schwäbischen Kreistruppen. Ein militärisches Kulturbild. Auf Grund zum Teil unveröffentlichter Originalquellen* (Stuttgart: Kohlhammer, 1909)
Schnur, R., *Der Rheinbund von 1658 in der deutschen Verfassungsgeschichte* (Bonn: Rheinisches Archiv 1955)
Storm, Peter Christoph: *Der Schwäbische Kreis als Feldherr: Untersuchungen zur Wehrverfassung des Schwäbischen Reichskreises in der Zeit von 1648–1732* (Berlin: Duncker & Humblot, 1974)
Weigel, Hanns, *Die Kriegsverfassung des alten deutschen Reiches von der Wormser Matrikel bis zur Auflösung* (Bamberg: 1912)

Wilson, Peter: *German Armies, War and German Society – 1648–1806* (Routledge: New York NY, 1998)

Wunder, B, *Frankreich, Württemberg und der Schwäbischen Kreis während der Auseinundersetzung über die Reunionen (1679–97)* (Stuttgart: Kommission für geschichtliche Landeskunde in Baden-Württemberg, 1971)

Articles and Essays

Ackermann, Jürgen, 'Verschuldung, Reichsdebitverwaltung, Mediatisierung. Eine Studie zu den Finanzproblemen der mindermächtigen Stände im Alten Reich. Das Beispiel der Grafschaft Ysenburg-Büdingen 1687–1806', in *Schriften des Hessischen Landesamtes für Geschichtliche Landeskunde 40* (Marburg 2002)

Bérenger, Jean, Finances et absolutisme autrichien dans la seconde moitié du XVIIe siècle', in *Travaux du Centre de recherches sur la civilisation de l'Europe moderne, XVII* (Paris, 1978)

Forst, Hermann: 'Die Reichstruppen im Türkenkrieg' in *Mitteilungen der Instituts für österreichische Geschichtsforschung*, vol. IV-1901

Gueze, Raoul: 'La Liberazione dell'Ungheria dal Turco (1683–1699) nelle fonti conservate in alcuni fra i principali Archivi di Stato Italiani' in *OSZK – Rivista di Studi Ungheresi* (Rome-Budapest, 1986)

Hummelberger, Walter, 'Der 1. August 1664 bei St. Gotthard, die Entscheidungs-schlacht zwischen zwei grossen Kriege', in *Truppendienst, Zeitschrift für die Ausbildung im Bundesheer*, II-1964, n° 4.

Hummelberger, Walter, 'Zur Bewaffnung und Ausrüstung sowie Verpflegung und Versorgung der Kaiserlichen um 1686', in *Blätter für Österreichische Heereskunde* (Vienna: Heeresgeschichtliches Museum, 1987)

Jähna, Max, 'Zur Geschichte der Kriegsverfassung des deutschen Reiches', in *Preussische Jahrbücher Nr. 39* (1877)

Langer, Herbert & Dudás, Janos: 'Die Kämpfe in Ungarn 1684 bis 1686 und die Rückeroberung Budas im Spiegel des *Theatrum Europaeum*' in *Acta Historica Academiae Scientiarum Hungaricae*, Vol. 34, No. 1, (Budapest, 1988), pp. 17–25

Kotzflesisch, Gustav von, 'Der Oberelsässische Winterfeldzug 1674–75 und das Treffen bei Türckheim nach archivalischen Quellen bearbeitet', in *Beitrage Landes und Volkeskunde Elsass-Lothringen*, XXIX Heft (Strasbourg, 1904)

Kroener, Berhard, 'Kriegswesen, Herrschaft und Gesellschaft, 1300–1800', in *Enzyklopädie deutscher Geschichte* (Munich: Oldenbourg, 2013)

Marr, Anton, 'Der Feldzug im Jahre 1675 in Deutschland. Nach österreichischen Originalquellen' in *Österreichische Militärische Zeitschrift*, Vol. III-1839, pp. 267–293, and Vol. I-1840, pp. 137–170

Marr, Anton, 'Der Herbstfeldzug Montecuccolis gegen Condé, 1675 am Rheine und an der Mosel. Nach österreichischen Originalquellen' in *Österreichische Militärische Zeitschrift*, Vol. II (Vienna: 1842), pp.129–152

Marr, Anton, 'Der Feldzug 1676 in Deutschland mit Benützung österreichischer Originalquellen' in *Österreichische Militärische Zeitschrift*, Vol. III-1844, pp. 11–26

Ní Mheara, Róisín, 'The Wild Geese in Austria', in *Seanchas Ardmhacha: Journal of the Armagh Diocesan Historical Society*, Vol. 16, No. 1 (1994), pp. 76–92

Nottebohm, Wilhelm, 'Montecuccoli und die Legende von St. Gotthard (1664)', in *Wissenschaftliche Beilage zum Programm des Friedrich Werderschen Gymnasiums zu Berlin* (Berlin, 1887)

Peball, Kurt, 'Die Schlacht bei St. Gotthard-Mogersdorf 1664', in *Militärhistorische Schriftenreihe*, III-1964

Perjés, Géza: 'A "metodizmus" és a Zrínyi-Montecuccoli vita', in *A korai stratégiai gondolkodás, szerk*; Veszprémy László (Budapest, 2005)

Rineteln, Anton: 'Die Feldzüge Montecuccolis gegen die Türken von 1661 bis 1664 nach Montecuccolis Handschriften und anderen österreichischen Originalquellen' in *Österreichische Militärische Zeitschrift* (Vienna, 1828)

Schüler, Theo, 'Die Nassauer unter den Truppen des Oberrheinischen Kreises im Reichskrieg gegen Frankreich 1674–79' in *Alt-Nassau* (VII, 87) 1917

Tessin, Georg, 'Die Oberrheinische-Kreis und seine Kreistruppen', in *Zeitschrift für Heereskunde* I-1985

Tessin, Georg, Die Inhaber der Fränkischen und Schwäbischen Kreisregimenter', in *Zeitschrift für Heereskunde* II-1985

Tessin, Georg, 'Reichsarmee und Allianzkorps im Türkenfeldzug 1663/64', in *Zeitschrift für Heereskunde*, VII-1983

Thadden, Franz-Lorenz von, 'Uniformen in Wien 1683', in *Zinnfiguren* 1974, pp. 181–182

Wilson, Peter, 'The German "Soldier Trade" of the Seventeenth and Eighteenth Centuries. A Reassessment', in *The International History Review* Vol. 18, No. 4 (IX, 1996), pp. 757–792

Woringer, R.U., 'Beiträge zur Geschichte der Hanauer Militärs', in *Hanauisches Magazin Monatsblätter für Heimatkunde* Nr. 9, 8; Hanau, Jahrgang 1929

SELECT BIBLIOGRAPHY

Regimental Histories

Anon., *Geschichte des k.k. Infanterie-Regiments Leopold II, König der Belgier Nr. 27 von dessen Errichtung 1682 bis 1882* (Vienna, 1882)

Anon., *Geschichte des k.k. 36. Linien-Infanterie-Regiments* (Prag, 1875)

Anon., *Das K. u. k. Dragoner-Regiment Nikolaus I. Kaiser von Russland Nr. 5* (Marburg an der Drau, 1893)

Beck, Fritz: *Geschichte des 1. Großherzoglich Hessischen Infanterie-(Leibgarde-) Regiments Nr. 115. 1621–1899* (Berlin, 1899)

Beck, Fritz, *Geschichte des Großherzoglich Hessischen Feldartillerie-Regiments Nr. 25 und seiner Stämme 1460–1883* (Berlin, 1884)

Gartner, von Romansbrück, Anton: *Geschichte des k. und k. Infanterie-Regiments Erzherzog Carl Stephan Nr. 8* (Brünn-Brno, 1892)

Janota, Robert: *Geschichte des k. und k. Infanterie-Regiments Graf Daun Nr. 56* (Teschen, 1889)

Maciago, Josef: *Geschichte des k. und k. galizischen Infanterie-Regimentes Feldmarschall Friedrich Josias Prinz zu Sachsen-Coburg-Saalfeld Nr. 57* (Vienna, 1898).

Mandel, Friedrich, *Geschichte des k. u. k. Inf. Regimentes Guidobald Graf von Starhemberg Nr. 13* (Vienna, 1893)

Neuwirth, Victor von: *Geschichte des k. und k. Infanterie-Regimentes Alt-Starhemberg Nr. 54* (Olmütz, 1894)

Tomaschek, Eduard von, *Geschichte des K.K. Dragoner-Regiments Nr. 8 Generallieutenant und Feldmarschall Raimund Graf von Montecuccoli, Reichsfürst von Melfi von dessen Errichtung 1617 bis zum Jahre 1888* (Vienna, 1889)

Treuenfest, Gustav Ritter Amon von, *Geschichte des k.u.k.Bukowina'schen Dragoner-Regimentes Nr. 9* (Vienna, 1892)